THE WORKS OF
JOHN SMYTH
FELLOW OF CHRIST'S COLLEGE, 1594-8

IN TWO VOLUMES

VOLUME I

Men whose life, learning, faith, and pure intent,
Would have been held in high esteem with Paul,
Must now be named and printed heretics.

JOHN MILTON.

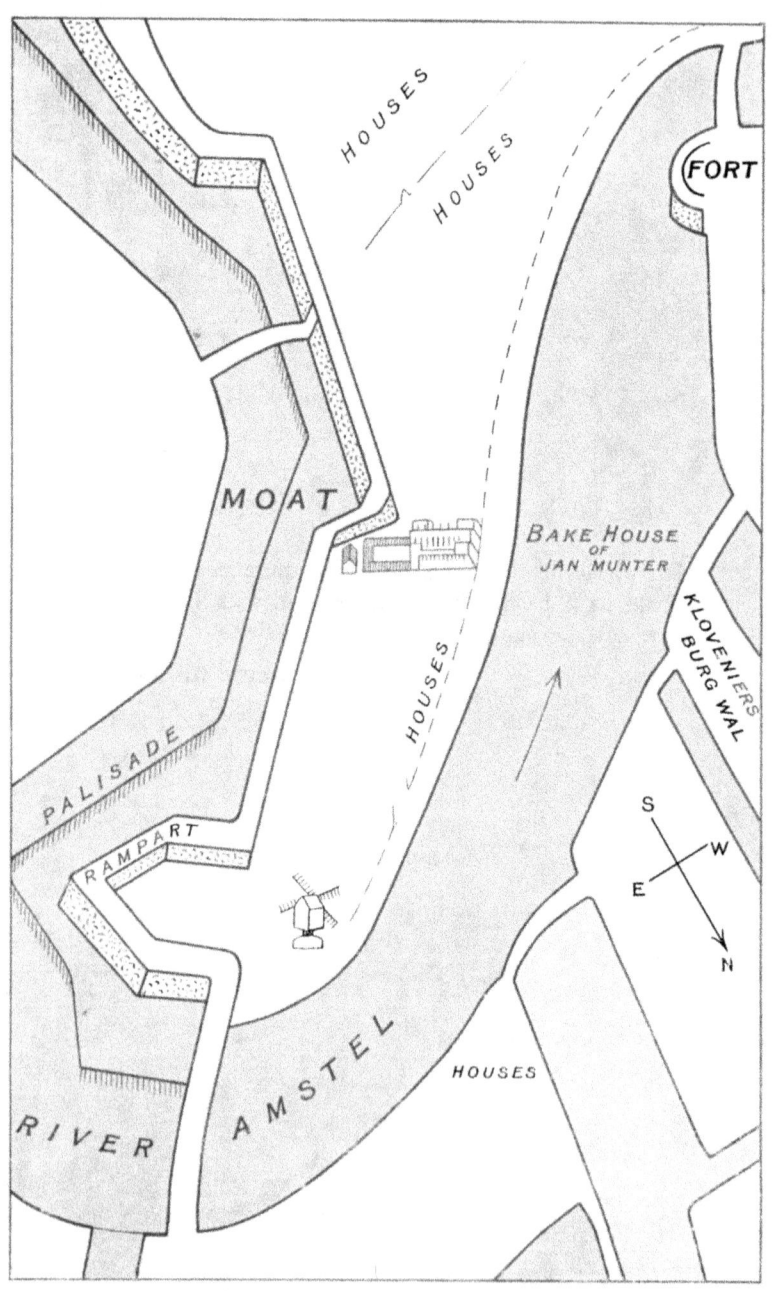

From a map in the Amsterdam archives

THE WORKS OF
JOHN SMYTH
FELLOW OF CHRIST'S COLLEGE, 1594-8

TERCENTENARY EDITION FOR THE
BAPTIST HISTORICAL SOCIETY
WITH NOTES AND BIOGRAPHY BY

W. T. WHITLEY
M.A., LL.D., F.R.Hist.S.
Sometime Exhibitioner of King's College

None of the English Separatists had a finer mind
or a more beautiful soul.
                                MANDELL CREIGHTON

Cambridge:
at the University Press
1915

he Baptist Standard Bearer, Inc.
NUMBER ONE IRON OAKS DRIVE • PARIS, ARKANSAS 72855

Thou hast given a *standard* to them that fear thee;
that it may be displayed because of the truth.
-- *Psalm 60:4*

Reprinted in 2009

by

THE BAPTIST STANDARD BEARER, INC.
No. 1 Iron Oaks Drive
Paris, Arkansas 72855
(479) 963-3831

THE WALDENSIAN EMBLEM
lux lucet in tenebris
"The Light Shineth in the Darkness"

ISBN-10: 1579782604
ISBN-13: 9781578782603

PREFACE

THIS edition of the works of John Smyth offers the opportunity for a pioneer to be studied at first hand. He had never been utterly forgotten, for when Americans who preferred to look to New England rather than to Virginia as the formative district of their nation, were telling its earliest story, they glanced casually at the friend of Brewster mentioned by Bradford; and when English Congregationalists were searching into their origins, they caught a glimpse of one who passed through their position. But in comparison with Browne and Robinson, Johnson and Ainsworth, or Jacob, Smyth has been but dimly known, chiefly by reflected light, even to Hanbury in 1839.

Fifty years ago, Benjamin Evans broke new ground and printed many documents long unknown to Englishmen, revealing Smyth's doings in Amsterdam. Further search by John Waddington, Robert Barclay and Henry Martyn Dexter was so far rewarded that a better background was afforded, and then the last named student earned thanks by recounting the *True Story* of Smyth "as told by himself and his contemporaries," and by exposing a stupid forgery which bade fair to confuse the tale. His posthumous work on the *England and Holland of the Pilgrims* reverted to the earlier treatment of Smyth as an appendage to those heroes, while John Brown and Edward Arber had naturally adopted the same standpoint.

The importance of Smyth's work had been discerned by Mandell Creighton, and when Henry W. Clark wrote the *History of English Nonconformity* to expound ideas rather than facts, a more sympathetic spirit was evinced. More errors were eliminated by J. H. Shakespeare in his study of *Baptist and Congregational Pioneers*, all too brief. When Walter H. Burgess prepared to publish on

Baptist Origins, he not only added to our knowledge of fact by his minute research; but placed Smyth in the forefront, both of the narrative and of the title. Next year, Champlin Burrage in his *Early English Dissenters* treated of him in true perspective with the attention to detail that is so conspicuous in all his work.

All students, however, who desired better acquaintance with Smyth, were seriously hindered by the difficulty of reading his works. Though seven books were published, only seventeen copies in all are known, and no town contains more than three works. At the very best, Cambridge, York, and Oxford must be visited; while Amsterdam must be added for manuscripts. Moreover, the typography of most of the books is trying in the extreme. So it has been far easier to read what Smyth's opponents said about him, or to copy some isolated sentence extracted for a purpose, than to consult the whole book and let Smyth speak for himself.

To rescue him from this predicament has long been the hope of the present editor, and means have been provided by the Hibbert Trustees (through the kind offices of Sir W. J. Collins), by Principal Gould and Sir George Macalpine, president and vice-president of the Baptist Historical Society, under whose auspices the edition appears. The librarian of Emmanuel College arranged for a transcript of the *Morning Starre*, a copy of the *Paterne* was lent by Dr Gould, Bodley's librarian permitted the *Paralleles* and the *Character* to be rotographed page by page, the editor copied the *Principles* and the *Retractations* at York Chapter library, the *Differences* at the Bodleian, and supplied a slight defect in the *Character* from the Museum. The manuscripts at Amsterdam were consulted by the courtesy of Professor S. Cramer, and in their study the editor was aided by Carel J. Ströer, who arranged for transcripts. The archivist of the city of Amsterdam cleared up a long-standing obscurity as to the last home of Smyth, and produced a contemporary map showing its site and appearance; from this the frontispiece has been copied.

In preparing for the press, it was felt best to offer a text such as Smyth sent to the printers, reproducing exactly except for obvious misprints; even these have been registered carefully, though it seemed needless to print all, and only a few are noted for the reader. Thus the vocabulary and orthography can be studied closely; those interested in the emergence of new words will find some not recorded in the Oxford Dictionary, and others at an earlier date than is there given; e.g. Pedobaptistry, Presbyterian; these he may have coined. For the accurate presentation of the text, in such typography as will no longer daunt the reader, the Cambridge University Press has spared no pains.

The editor has added notes on such points as seemed to need comment, and on such as had special interest for himself. He has also prefixed a study of the author's career. For this he has naturally used the works named, and the contemporary books that alluded to Smyth. He has accepted the assurances of the Registrary of Cambridge and the late Master of Christ's that nothing more is extant there than is here incorporated. He has sought at first hand, in both the municipal and the diocesan records at Lincoln, profiting by the aid of W. S. Linton and of the vicar of Welton, as well as of the official custodians. He has consulted the Mennonite and the civic archives at Amsterdam. Yet he does not claim to have added much to the facts known, and such trifles as he did discover or sent others to discover, have been communicated to and published by the late Master of Christ's and by J. H. Shakespeare. He does claim to have brought together every fact at present accessible, and to have ignored or to have explicitly labelled, many fictions often repeated. One incidental re-interpretation of known facts he hopes may provoke other students to renewed research.

For the story of the Pilgrim Fathers has inevitably come up for mention; but whereas Smyth has often been touched upon in telling their story, the proportions are here reversed, and two points can only be mentioned, not treated at the length they deserve. Their history is usually begun with Scrooby; but the data of Morton Dexter prove that no more than seventeen of them hailed from that district, the home of Bradford, as against thirty-two from Norfolk, the scene of Robinson's activity. It follows that all the wealth of learning accumulated by Brown, Arber, Dexter, etc., is really introductory not so much to Robinson's story as to Smyth's: had it not been for him the emigration from the north would not have taken place, and to him most of the emigrants adhered, those who passed over to Robinson being mostly relations and connections of the latter. It follows also that the main source of the Pilgrim Church has as yet been unrecognized and therefore neglected, that the career of Robinson in Norfolk—on which a little fresh light has recently been thrown—awaits treating with such loving care as has been already spent on the district around Austerfield. Further, in these pages is pointed out, what has escaped serious attention, the time, place, and circumstances when the Pilgrim Church was born. In the editor's opinion, the pre-natal and infant history of this church have been misconceived, and after due research will have to be re-written.

Apart from matters of fact, the editor hopes to have presented the subject afresh in three respects; the starting-point of Smyth's career, its consistency, and the permanent result of his work.

Scarcely ever has it been emphasized that Smyth was a Cambridge man. Like a greater alumnus of the same college, he was accustomed

> To walk the studious cloister's pale
> And love the high embowéd roof
> With antique pillars massy-proof
> And storied windows richly dight,
> Casting a dim religious light.

He is therefore not to be classed with the Legates and Muggletons, nor even with his saner followers Helwys and Murton. He ranks with Whitgift and Andrewes in his training; had they been cut off before the age of 45, as he was, their mark on their age would have been no deeper, and they would have left less of real permanence. Therefore some care has been given to show what actually was the training which they all received, to exhibit the foundations on which rested that which was peculiar to himself. It is as fitting as fortunate that so much of the material for this has been brought together by a Head of his own college, and it is a kindness that the present Head has read the proofs of that section.

What makes Smyth almost unique in his time, is that he had the scientific spirit so strongly developed. He announced that he would be, as Bacon put it, a "true pioner in the mine of truth"; he was persevering in following every clue, in declining to bow to mere custom or tradition, in recurring to first principles, in acting on what he discovered. He is exhibited here on his own line of development, which apart from one amusing excursus appears singularly straightforward.

For a few years after his death, it seemed as though he had spent his life almost in vain, and the chorus of opposition died away with words of pity for his failure. In the next generation only Paget's brother recollected that he had been one of the Grandees of the Separation. Not till 1738 was his name recalled to the memory of the churches that had arisen from his work; only when Adam Taylor, in 1818, published long extracts from the preface to the *Character*, did the nature of the man begin to emerge. When however, in 1908, European Baptists met in Berlin and a session was devoted to the Pioneers in Liberty of Conscience, by an American, a Frenchman, a Rumanian and a Bulgarian, it was pointed out that to the teaching of Smyth was due directly the founding of the earliest English Baptist churches, and this one man was thus placed in the vanguard of what is now literally an Œcumenical or Catholic communion.

W. T. W.

PRESTON,
November 1915

TABLE OF CONTENTS

VOLUME I

SIZAR AT CHRIST'S COLLEGE, CAMBRIDGE, 1586–1590.
Unknown origin—The college—Arts and theology—Domestic conditions—No holidays—The daily round—A sizar's lot—Serving and fagging—Chopping logic—The schools—Poetry and the drama—Sunday plays—College friends—Lecturers—Fellows—Francis Johnson—The Puritan ideals—Assemblies at Cambridge—Chaderton versus Whitgift
Pages xvii–xxvii

GRADUATE AND FELLOW, 1590–1598.
Johnson throws the gauntlet—Star Chamber fails—Conventicle Act—Smyth graduates and stays—Studies medicine—Hebrew and Greek—Bernard a sizar—Out-college friends—M.A. and regent—Fellow—Puritan—Opposition to Calvinism—Lambeth articles—Rise of a new party—Duties as fellow—Ordained at Buckden—Casual preaching—Pupils—Marriage—Parish minister or schoolmaster?—Inadequate endowments—Pluralism . . . . xxvii–xxxviii

LECTURER AT LINCOLN, 1600–1602.
Diocese and bishop—Christ's men near—Municipal patronage—Candidates and salary—Opportunities of the post—Roman Catholic influence—Magistracy—Intolerance—Propaganda—Separatist brethren—Anabaptist anarchy—Wray and Sheffield—"Factious preacher"—Discord on the council—Dismissed—Lawsuits—Guilty—Appeal . . xxxix–xlvii

OFFICIAL REFORM, 1603–1605.
Reconstruction of the Church of England—Two earnest wings—350 Puritan ministers—Proposal for parochial reform—Decisions of James—Acquiescence of the leaders?—Parliament restive—Canons codified—Conventiclers excommunicated—The Church not antichristian—Few petitions—Hundreds silenced—Most submit—Catholics tolerated—Is this satisfactory? . . . . xlvii–liii

MEDITATION AND DISCUSSION, 1605–1606.
Smyth's journeys—Gainsborough—The manor and its lord—Neighbours from Christ's—Thomas Helwys of Basford—Smyth as physician—An absentee vicar—Supplying his place—Presented again—Discussion as to

Table of Contents

possibilities—Clifton and Bernard—Conference with Hildersham—Advice sought from Suffolk—Self-governing churches of saints—Bernard's attack on the bishops—Study of the Bible for a pattern—Old Testament covenants—A church covenant—Provides for progress . . . . liii–lxii

PASTOR OF THE CHURCH AT GAINSBOROUGH, 1606–1608.

Opposition of A.S.—Imitation by Bernard—Gainsborough and Scrooby—Smyth ordained by the church—Bernard faltering—Queries to Helwys—Recantation—Smyth expostulates—Antichrist—Epithets returning to roost—Bernard prepares a book—Occupations and residences of the members—Robinson of Sturton—One church only?—Sources of information—Constitution—Worship—High Commission for the north—Snoden the pluralist—Arrests—Emigration?—Legal position—A midsummer exodus . . . . lxii–lxxiv

CHURCHES, CHURCH WORSHIP, CHURCH GOVERNMENT, 1608.

Amsterdam—Freedom of commerce and conscience—College life in a bake-house—Four religious groups—Arminians—English merchants—John Paget—The Bagijnhof—Real status of this congregation—The Ancient Church—No fusion with this—Sisterly intercourse—New organization under Robinson, departs to Leijden—Its nucleus a Norfolk group—Differences of worship—An authorized library—The human element in translation—Every Bible version fallible—Reading as a preparation for worship—The parallel discussion in Roman circles—Influence of Smyth's pleas in New England and among the old General Baptists—Singing and contributing—Pastors and deacons—Officers subordinate to the church—Acceptance in New England—Overton reproduces in army politics
lxxv–xc

BAPTISM OF BELIEVERS, 1609.

Separation completed—Transmission of baptism—The mark of the beast—Persons to be baptized—Previous English Anabaptists in the Netherlands—Their unimportance—Smyth's views adopted by most of his church—Communicated to Clifton—Discussion—Two printed books—Dissolution of the Church of Gainsborough—Baptism of believers—A new church—Smyth baptized himself—Baptism on the forehead out of a basin—"Anabaptists"—Obloquy of the continental Anabaptists—Absurdity of a second baptism—Criticisms—Hetherington—Effect of baptism—Joseph Hall—Self-baptism—Who may baptize?—Dutch Anabaptists—Literary activity—Different books for different topics, yet simultaneous—Succession—Occasional conformity . . . . xc–ci

NEGOTIATIONS WITH THE MENNONITES.

Praying circles of the fourteenth century—Organization in 1527—Imitation of Christ—Hofmann's theories—Persecuted by all—Disclaimed by "Protestants"—Münster—War disallowed—Bishop Menno—Rigid discipline—Eclipsed by Calvinists—Persecuted by Calvinists—Waterland subdivision—Polish influence—Confession of Ries and Gerritsz—Pre-Augustinian—Ries offers revised confession for comparison—Smyth's

church approves and offers its own—Anti-Calvinist—Alike though with different approach—Two points cause secessions—Incarnation—Succession —Application to Waterlanders—Apology for an independent beginning— Opposition by Helwys—Shelved—Five sets of English Anabaptists— Leonard Busher—Dipping—John Hancock—Further writings—Elaborate confession—Modified views—Death—Burial in the New Kirk—Return of Helwys to England—Posthumous publications—Renewed application to the Waterlanders—Acceptance—Gradual fusion—Mennonite tribute
ci–cxv

THE MAN AND HIS WORK.

Middle-class thinkers—University opportunities—Original lines of thought—Effective leader—Ready to accept correction—Inspired affection —Modern estimates—Separatism reinvigorated—Emigration—Fellowship independent of nationality—Liberty of conscience first asserted fully— Propagandist—Four existing churches in England due to him—Founder of one of the largest communions in the world . . . cxv–cxxii

	PAGE
THE BRIGHT MORNING STARRE (1603)	1
A PATERNE OF TRVE PRAYER (1605)	67
PRINCIPLES AND INFERENCES (1607)	249
THE DIFFERENCES OF THE CHURCHES (1608) . .	269

VOLUME II

CERTAYNE DEMAUNDES, ETC.	321
PARALLELES, CENSVRES, OBSERVATIONS (1609) . .	327
Lettre to Mr. Ric. Bernard (1607) . . .	331
Lettre written to Mr. A. S. (1606?) . . .	547
Lettre written to certaine brethren in S. (1606?) .	557
THE CHARACTER OF THE BEAST (1609)	563
NOMINA ANGLORUM (1610?)	681
CORDE CREDIMUS (1610?)	682
DEFENCE OF RIES' CONFESSION	685
ARGUMENTA CONTRA BAPTISMUM INFANTUM . . .	710
PROPOSITIONS AND CONCLUSIONS	733
RETRACTATIONS AND CONFIRMATIONS	751
APPENDIX	761
NOTES	763

LIST OF PLATES

The Last Home of John Smyth
   from a contemporary map in the Amsterdam archives.
   Frontispiece to Volume I.

The Lower Trent Valley
   showing places whence emigrants went to Amsterdam in 1608.
   Volume I, page lv.

Names of the English who applied in 1610 for union with the Waterlander church in Amsterdam. Holograph of John Smyth. *Frontispiece to Volume II.*

CHRONOLOGICAL TABLE

1586. John Smyth matriculates, sizar at Christ's.
1593. M.A. (First Conventicle Act.)
1594. Fellow. Ordained by Wickham of Lincoln.
1598. Vacates fellowship after Ladyday.
1600. Lecturer to the City of Lincoln.
1601 Preaches *The Bright Morning Starre*; page 1.
1602. Preaches *A Paterne of Trve Prayer*; page 67.
Inhibited, dismissed. Next two years spent in litigation and publishing.
1603. (Appeal of the Puritans to James for reform.)
1604. (Hampton Court Conference: new canons.)
1605. Practising as physician, lecturing at Gainsborough.
(Suspension of many clergy, ejectment, visitations.)
1606. Conference at Coventry with Puritan leaders.
Bernard: Against Episcopal Authority; unpublished.
Letter to S[uffolk] replying to K[newstubbs]; page 557.
Letter to A.S.; page 547.
Formation at Gainsborough of Separate Church.
1607. Bernard: Letter to Helwys; page 337.
Letter to Bernard; page 331.
Principles and Inferences; page 249.
1608. Bernard: Separatist's Schisme.
Emigration of the church to Amsterdam.
Hall: To Smyth and Robinson.
Helwys: Letter on the customs of the Ancient Church.
Differences of the Churches; page 269.
1609. Ainsworth: Defence of the Scriptures.
Certayne reasons propovnded to Mr. Rich. Clifton; page 574.
Clifton: Answer on 14 March; page 575.
Reply written by 24 March.
Church disbanded, baptism of all by Smyth.
Paralleles published, and in a few days the
Character of the Beast, the two incorporating all that led up to them.
Bromheads: Letter to Hamerton.
Conference with Hetherington; conversation with Mennonites.

Chronological Table

1610. Secession of Helwys and eight others.
XX Latin articles; page 682.
Ries: XXXVIII articles.
Helwys: Protest, XIX Latin articles, letter to Ries.
Approval of Ries' confession; see page 685.
Application for fusion; page 681.
Correspondence of Mennonites; no action taken.
Clifton: Plea for Infants.
Hetherington: Description of the Church of Christ.
Johnson: A brief treatise.
Bernard: Plaine Euidences.

1611. *Eighteen arguments against infant baptism* written? page 710.
Propositions and Conclusions drawn up; page 733.
Helwys: A declaration in XXVII articles; A short and plaine proof; Advertisement to the New Fryelers.

1612. Gerritsz. Dying wish for fusion.
Retractations and Confirmations, unfinished; page 751.
Helwys to Spitalfields: The Mistery of Iniquity.
Smyth buried on 1 September. Last two MSS. published by Pigott in time to be criticised by

1614. Robinson: Religious Communion.

1615. Fusion of Smyth's church with that of Ries.

JOHN SMYTH

SIZAR AT CHRIST'S COLLEGE, CAMBRIDGE, 1586–1590

In March 1586, a sizar of Christ's College matriculated, whose name was then spelt John Smythe. Before that time he has not been traced, no allusion to his family having been found in literature to give a clue. Even his county cannot be determined, though from his subsequent election as Fellow we know that he came from south of the Trent, outside London, Warwick, Stafford, Cheshire, Bedford and Northampton. His rank in life cannot have been high, for he was a sizar, and had not only to wait at meals in hall, but also to render personal services to the Master or a Fellow, such as cleaning boots, or dressing hair. He corresponded to the diligent class of poor students in America to-day, who work their way through college attending to the corridors and furnaces.

He was not even a Scholar, but an antiquary might yet examine the records of the eleven Lincolnshire towns which had grammar schools before this time. Alford, for example, a new foundation, was required to keep registers; but its special ties were with Magdalene and Jesus. Lincoln had lately fused two ancient foundations, of the cathedral and of the corporation. In some cases we know that the early registers have perished, as here and at Louth; but it is just conceivable that a clue might be discovered to the origin of John Smyth.

In after life his career crossed that of the Manners family, and it is noteworthy that the Earl of Rutland, its head, had many transactions with the corporation of Lincoln. On 22 September 1585, Edward, the third Earl, was asked to arbitrate on a case between the corporation and Robert Smith of the Black Monks, his decision being that Monks Leys should go to the city. Had Robert a young relation who attracted the Earl's notice?

Christ's College had absorbed God's House, founded in 1446 expressly to train masters for grammar schools. For this purpose special classes were still held on Fridays, since a school which could offer £10 yearly might claim a master from the university. The college however had a slightly wider outlook, being established for the study of arts and theology. Its founder was the Lady Margaret, descended from John of Gaunt, widow of the Earl of Richmond. Richmondshire was then not part of Yorkshire for all purposes, and her grandson, Henry VIII, severed it even ecclesiastically, transferring it to the new diocese of Chester. She therefore showed special care for it, and in her statutes of 1506 provided for at least six fellows and twenty-three scholars to be appointed from the counties north of the Trent; Richmond, Northumberland, Durham, Westmorland, Cumberland, York, Lancaster, Nottingham and Derby; not more than one fellow and three scholars from any county. As many more were to be appointed, and the statutes did not confine them to south of Trent, though in practice the far larger population ensured this. Edward VI had added a thirteenth fellow, with no restriction on residence.

When Smyth matriculated, the college master had for four years been Barwell, a weak nepotist, under whom it was rapidly declining from its position as the third most important. In Smyth's first year the college was officially visited by the Vice-Chancellor, who found things very lax. The statutes did expressly allow pensioners, boarders; but the master had added to his original quarters both the Foundress's rooms and the Fellows' common room, letting them off and appropriating the rent for himself. This letting was forbidden, though the common room was not restored; all bills were to be settled within six days, academic dress was to be worn, Latin was to be used in all conversation. After this visitation there would doubtless be greater efficiency for a year or two, to the profit of Smyth.

The domestic conditions can be pictured, thanks to Messrs Willis and Clark, and Mr Bass Mullinger. The college buildings formed one court, completely closed in, for Dr Caius had not in 1509 expounded how insanitary was such a plan. They comprised a library on the first floor to the right, a chapel on the far left for daily worship; opposite the gate was the master's lodge adjoining the chapel, then the hall for lectures and meals, with kitchens and butteries projecting on the right; most of the premises were for lodgings.

Any one standing in the court to-day can see it as it was in 1586, if he remembers that the ashler facing conceals the original alternate courses of red brick and clunch, a hard chalky material, and if he replaces in imagination the posts and rails round the edge. Outside there were elaborately carved posts, and Hobson's clear water did not yet flow.

A chamber till lately had had only shutters to open windows, with reeds and clay to face the walls and ceiling; but there had been recent plastering, panelling, flooring and glazing. The chamber next the chapel had two studies partitioned off, with desk and shelves in each; in the main room stood a bed for two Fellows, with a trundle-bed pulled out at night for the sizar, also a leaden cistern and trough, a table and two forms. Pensioners could, of course, bargain for their accommodation, and might have to pay as much as 23s. extra if they wanted a study. The community aimed at being self-contained, even the barber, porter, steward, cook, and the lad to whip dogs out of chapel being chosen from the sub-sizars. As pensioners were a source of profit, an annexe had been acquired almost opposite, and fitted with gates like the college proper; but even so, we wonder that the court and the inn could accommodate the 200 people whom we can calculate from the admissions and graduations.

There were university vacations, but they made little difference to residence in college, which was almost continuous till a higher degree was attained. The details of the daily life have been drawn by Dr Peile, the late Master.

A sizar would waken his tutor, valet him and tidy the chamber in time for chapel at five o'clock, when morning prayer was often followed by an address by a Fellow. Then he would get the bevers or morning-draught of ale for his tutor, with perhaps a manchet from the buttery.

As each Fellow had recently had his allowance for commons increased to three shillings a week, there would be more left for the sizar.

By six he was due in hall, where the Lector taught dialectic, logic, philosophy and poetry. Logic was the backbone of the traditional studies, and was still studied on the lines of Aristotle, with substance and accidents, quiddities, differences, and above all, syllogisms. Just at this time, indeed, the reforms of Ramus, a Huguenot slain on St Bartholomew's day, were much canvassed at Cambridge, especially in Christ's. Ramus attacked the artificial method of arguing, and urged that Cicero be studied, to see how men were really persuaded. But Smyth's works show that he was trained on the old-fashioned lines, all his thinking being cast in Aristotelian moulds.

For a sizar, the preparations for dinner would be important, to spread the high table, to fetch one of his tutor's two napkins, provided lest he be tempted to misuse the table-cloth, to hang the towel and fill the bowls for ablutions after the meal. The Fellows gathered on the Regent Walk, from the gate to the hall, marched in at ten o'clock for the chief repast of the day. When they had finished, and the sizars, like stewards on a liner to-day, had satisfied their appetites as far as the leavings permitted, the hall was cleared for more work. This time the seniors were set to oppositions in philosophy and theology, the juniors listening. Some afternoons were spent at more general sophisms, or discussions, or lectures on philosophy and logic.

Other afternoons however were free, and gave the opportunity of fetching out from Stangate Hole the stang or post on which late-comers to chapel were mounted and ridden round the court. While the scholars were enjoying football, a sizar would be due in the large area behind the court, to attend while his seniors were playing quoits, or to field in the brick tennis-court. He might be sent on errands into the town, and it would be strange if in summer he did not steal time for a dip in the Cam, even though he risked a public whipping in hall from the master. His tutor might occasionally want a walk in the country and might take along his sizar to carry the herbs and flowers he plucked; and so a native of fen-land would learn to scale the heights of the Gogmagog Hills. Perhaps in some fit of generosity he might be taken to see a rarity, such as a crocodile brought for exhibition. Such diversions are duly noted in the diary of Samuel Ward a few years later.

As evening drew on, chapel filled again, and the old organ led the praise. At five o'clock all assembled for the second meal, and when all was cleared away in hall, and the fire was replenished for the Fellows and Scholars, the sizar must withdraw to his cold chamber for study as prescribed by his tutor; unless he had made friends with the cook and could nestle in the warm kitchen. By nine in winter the curfew at Great St Mary's gave the signal for bed, though an hour's grace was allowed in summer.

Such is the round of training through which Smyth passed for three years. The college aimed only at Arts and Theology, both physics and law being quite without mention in its statutes. But with the fourth year his horizon would widen, for he would be taken by his tutor to the University Schools. Passing Great St Mary's, and the house where John Legate was now printing for the university, he would enter the court beneath Rotherham's Library, and be ushered into the Logic School opposite to listen to men of all colleges, each of whom was twice called upon to defend three propositions chosen by himself and approved by the proctor, and was in turn twice obliged to challenge some other champion hanging out his three shields for the tourney. He might even hear some such startling paradox as "Everything Aristotle taught is false," but too often the themes were well worn, and the proceedings were only of the same kind as in the hall of Christ's.

It would then open new possibilities to find that on the left-hand side of the Schools there were lectures given on the Civil and Canon Law, while in the great library above, Edward Lively and Andrew Downes with the other Regius professors lectured to all comers, often all too few; and that above the Logic School was that of Rhetoric. This apparently never received his attention, nor is there any appreciation of poetry evident in his works, though the Lector ought to have dealt with such matters.

This is the more to be regretted, as English poetry was at the dawn of a splendid day. Turberville had broken new ground with Epigrams, Songs and Sonnets, cultivated further by Wyat of John's. The standard old *Five Hundred Good Points of Husbandry* by Tusser of King's had found a new rival in the *Shepherd's Calendar* by Spenser of Pembroke. Lyly, incorporated from Oxford, celebrated the occasion by his *Euphues*, which made a deep if temporary mark. So obvious was it that a new era was blooming, that several books were written to analyze the styles: Gascoigne of Trinity led the way, Webbe of John's published in the year Smyth matriculated, Putenham before he graduated. But no one at Christ's seems to have been interested, and the lectures on poetry that Smyth heard were not only in Latin, but probably were on Latin poetry alone.

One special department of English literature would be brought to his attention less officially, the New Drama. Christ's had taken an honourable part in the creation of this species of English poetry. As early as 1544 a Latin play called *Pammachius* had been acted there, ventilating Lutheran ideas, and soon afterwards it had been rendered into English by Bale. More orthodox was the translation of Seneca begun by Heywood, the ten tragedies being now published in one volume. In 1560, Johnson of Christ's, a schoolmaster, wrote *Misogonus*, ten years later Preston of King's and Trinity put forth *Cambises*. These are certainly links with the past, but in 1566 Christ's opened a new vista by the performance of an English comedy, identified by Mr Boas with the famous *Gammer Gurton's Needle*, and attributed by him to Bridges of Pembroke, though it was published as by Mr S., Master of Arts.

The custom had grown up of relaxing by such an entertainment on the evening of Saturday or Sunday. College buildings offered two suitable places, so that both hall and chapel were employed. Three new plays at

Clare, Peterhouse and John's drew out the first opposition to the custom, in the year when Smyth matriculated. A namesake of his, himself of Christ's, inveighed at Great St Mary's against this use of Sunday. This was the beginning of what developed into the Sabbath question, so prominent with Puritans. In 1592, Still, the Vice-Chancellor, wrote to the Chancellor that English comedies were now stopped. Smyth was thus caught in the ebb-tide; in later years his writings show little sign of interest in these relaxations, his only allusion to the drama being to the virtue and vice of the medieval moralities; page 298.

Three years' drill in the college, and he must step out into the university arena for his four bouts; then further examinations by college and university would bring him to the rubicon, passing which he would emerge from the pupil status, and become a Bachelor of Arts. Thus until this stage he could hardly make friends outside the college walls, though he might admire some dexterous debater from another college at the Schools, and hear the more famous preachers at the various churches. We turn then to see some of the men under and alongside whom he received his moulding.

The lads who entered about his time were on the whole very mediocre; five of them became incumbents in Suffolk and Lincoln, counties with which Smyth afterwards was concerned. Very few deserve mention. At the high table sat James Montagu, one year Smyth's senior, joined there in 1588 by his brother Sydney: the latter went to the Middle Temple, the former laid the foundation stone of the new Sidney Sussex college in 1595 and became its master, winning the favour of the new king and climbing to a bishopric. Thomas Drax became vicar of Dovercourt, and in 1618 threw out the idea that the Separatists who would not return to the Church, should go to Virginia and convert the infidels: the suggestion was instantly adopted by Blackwell, and two years later by Brewster of Peterhouse, both then exiles in Holland. Samuel Ward helped Smyth in his tutorial work during 1596, and fortunately noted a few facts in his diary. Thomas Bywater fell under Smyth's influence more permanently, and will be met again.

Paul Baynes, who came up when Smyth was taking his degree, was destined to exercise much influence in the university as a preacher.

William Perkins at this time was Lecturer at Great St Andrew's, where he commanded great audiences. The system of Lectures was a great characteristic of the time. A clergyman could be inducted into a living at the will of the patron, and his duties were very mechanical. The printed services could be easily gone through by a man of very slight education. For preaching, he was provided with the official homilies, which he could read somewhat at his discretion. If he desired to preach his own sermons, he must be licensed by the bishop. Many parishioners resented this state of affairs, and the justices of Lincolnshire made careful enquiry in the very year Smyth went up, placing on record that whereas there were 590 livings, 154 were held by clergy who had other benefices and did not reside in the county, 301 did not attempt to preach, but simply read the homilies, while only 121 ever preached. There was a growing custom of obtaining other men to supply what they lacked, men who should preach or lecture. Manifestly Cambridge and the vicinity were in a splendid position for this, and Lecture-ships were established by subscription, or even endowed. Such a post was held at St Clement's by Laurence Chaderton, now master of the new Emmanuel College, but Fellow of Christ's till 1576; he and Perkins were the most prominent leaders of religion in the university.

Another Fellow was Richard Clerke, destined to be chosen in 1604 with Chaderton to revise the Old Testament. Another was Thomas Morton, fond of public disputations against the Papist recusants, and presently to climb the ladder of preferment to the sees of Chester, Lichfield, Durham; we can hardly fail to recognize in Smyth's early writings evidences of indebtedness to his polemic against Father Robert Persons, the Jesuit. Another was Robert Snoden, who also won ecclesiastical promotion, first as a member of the High Commission of the north, in which capacity his path crossed Smyth's in 1608, and then as Bishop of Carlisle.

If those three represent the men of affairs, who secured place and power, there were others of the stamp of Perkins, the men of thought and religion. Such a Fellow was Cuthbert Bainbridge from Durham, and of like type was Francis Johnson from Rotherham. It was to this man as tutor that Smyth was allotted, and we thus see what were the determining influences in his plastic years.

Though a sizar might not realize the currents that were flowing, the years 1586–1590 during which he was in his first stage, witnessed the culmination of the Puritan bid for reform. This was the chief domestic question in politics, and though Elizabeth had to temporize while the Spanish cloud lowered, yet as soon as the danger of the Armada passed, she struck hard and shattered the Puritan hopes. We must realize the issues.

As to doctrine, there was no question as yet. Calvinism was orthodoxy, the XXXIX Articles were really believed by all. But whereas Elizabeth had retained the general medieval scheme of ecclesiastical government, simply severing the bonds with the papacy as her father had done, there was now elaborated a very compact rival scheme, which was to be seen practised in France and Scotland. It had been worked out on paper for England in *The Book of Discipline*, and a meeting of leaders held at Cambridge about 1583 decided that attempts be made to start it universally. The proposed method of transition was rather ingenious, to persuade the archdeacons to conduct their visitations on the lines of mutual criticism, helpfulness and study, and so to convert them into something resembling a Scotch presbytery. Until such official sanction could be obtained, the plan was for parishes to group in dozens on a voluntary basis into a Classis, for a score of classes to group into a Synod, for delegates from the synods to come to a General Assembly. The minute book of the Dedham Classis for 1582–1589 has been published by the Royal Historical Society, and it illustrates how this system really was at work, 80 meetings being held of the ministers near Colchester. The whole movement centred in London and Cambridge, where the General Assembly met at the time when the Stourbridge Fair brought thither large numbers of people; Laurence Chaderton seems to have been the guiding spirit, now that Cartwright, deprived of his Lady Margaret professorship, had accepted the Mastership of Leicester's Hospital in Warwick with a promise to be quiet.

His great antagonist, Whitgift, was archbishop of Canterbury, bound to suppress this movement and maintain the whole apparatus of autocratic government. He found the greatest difficulty in East Anglia and Essex. The strength of the Puritans here was due largely to Lord Rich, grandson of a man employed to suppress the monasteries, who had acquired large numbers of advowsons, so that he filled the livings with religious men of his own stamp. No sooner did Whitgift hear the challenge of *The Book of Discipline*, than he took it up vigorously, and issued three Articles for the regulation of the clergy. Formidable lists are extant of men who were "not resolved to subscribe," and he proceeded to coerce them by the machinery of the bishops and the High Commission, suspending the recalcitrant from duty and from emoluments. In 1584 he was able to obtain a new High Commission for his province. It is very significant that whereas previous commissioners had been chiefly of laity, 47 out of 73 in the current body, these were now weeded out, and for the first time there were 24 clergy as against 20 laymen. This might seem to imply that after 20 years Elizabeth had at last trained some clergy to her ideas, and that the laity were still strongly Puritan; but Dr Usher has shown that the really active members of the commission were four civil lawyers and Richard Bancroft.

With his new machinery Whitgift set to work and presented his test Articles for subscription by the clergy. He soon scheduled 784 subscribers and 49 who refused; Ward of Christ's was suspended that year, and it is noteworthy that it did not prevent his attaining M.A. in the year Smyth matriculated. The Puritan answer to Whitgift was the foundation, by Sir Walter Mildmay of Christ's, now chancellor of the exchequer, of Emmanuel College with Chaderton at its head. The archbishop responded by securing control of the press, and passing new canons, which Elizabeth did not ratify. Petitions for the establishment of synods were organized. Bancroft was therefore set to investigate who was at the back of the movement, and how deep it was rooted, being rewarded with a canonry at Westminster.

Three Christ's men illustrate what went on in Smyth's undergraduate days. Arthur Hildersham, like Chaderton, had come up as a Catholic, and in the college atmosphere had become Puritan; he graduated 1586 and was appointed Lecturer at Ashby-de-la-Zouch, the patron settling on him the rectorial tithe, though the vicar collected the rest. Whitgift at once forbade him to lecture, both because he was not in orders, and because the lectures were not fit to be listened to. This was the beginning of a life-long contest, and Smyth was involved in it later on. Dent was presented by Lord Rich to the rectory of South Shoebury, and was in frequent trouble for not conforming to the ritual. Crane of Roehampton fared even worse, was thrown into Newgate, and died there 1588.

So great was the tension, that while this voluntary reform within the Establishment was spreading all over the eastern side of the kingdom, some few impatient spirits were breaking away and establishing separate churches; but this course, advocated by Browne, was opposed by Cartwright, and adopted by the merest handful, most of whom were soon lodged in jail.

Graduate and Fellow, 1590–1598

Smyth was one of about a hundred and eighty who became Bachelors of Arts in 1590, and emerged into wider life in the university. The year was marked by a crisis at Cambridge, with effects even on the national life; and Christ's was closely concerned. Johnson had preached at Great St Mary's early in 1588–9, on church government, when he openly advocated the Presbyterian system as agreeable to the New Testament, and preferable to the Episcopal. He was thrown into prison by the Heads of colleges, along with Bainbridge who was in some way implicated, and though bail was offered by prominent laymen like Knevett and Sir William Bowes, it was refused. Bainbridge made his peace quietly, Johnson petitioned Lord Burghley, Chancellor of the university, but refusing to make adequate recantation, was expelled the university in October. He appealed formally to Burghley, being supported on a point of order by the Vice-Chancellor and by 68 Masters of Arts, including such different men as Perkins and Morton. Yet he had to resign his Fellowship and go down. He found refuge first at Middelburg as chaplain to the English merchants of the Staple, with the splendid salary of £200 and the use of a Dutch church. For the London merchants were the financial mainstay of the Puritans, and Holland was a stronghold of the Reformed Religion.

Johnson's influence at Christ's remained strong for a few years, for the Vice-Chancellor wrote that he had been "complotting with his associates." But it would rapidly wane when the news came that he had thrown up his post, had joined an obscure band of Separatists in London, and by the end of 1592 was in the Clink prison for that reason. Next year his brother George, another Christ's man, was thrown into the Fleet on the same score.

Meantime there had been wholesale arrests of the Reformists; Udall of Christ's was indeed charged with being concerned in the Marprelate tracts, but Egerton, Cartwright, Jewel and others had simply aimed at developing the Presbyterian butterfly within the Episcopal cocoon. Perkins was brought before the High Commission in 1590, and with the help of many informers, a series of Star Chamber trials began. On the whole, they failed, and recourse was had to Parliament. All that could be secured was a Conventicle Act against Separatists, in 1593. This provided that people who denied the ecclesiastical jurisdiction and obstinately absented themselves from the parish services, must abjure the realm for life. Under this act, Johnson and his friends were soon driven out, and most assembled in Amsterdam. The Reformists were dealt with otherwise. Bancroft published a clear exposition of what had been going on, and what was aimed at; the result was to alienate public sympathy to a large extent. And in 1594 Hooker published his *Ecclesiastical Polity*, examining carefully the contention of the Puritans that their Classical system was the only one warranted by the word of God, and contending that the Episcopal was allowable. For the rest of the reign we hear no more of *The Book of Discipline* or of any meetings of the voluntary Classes. Two new points arose, both at Cambridge, which soon engaged general attention. And Smyth by this time had attained a rank which would oblige him to take a side.

For Smyth had stayed at Christ's. He might have gone on from the university to an Inn of Chancery or an Inn of Court, as Barrowe of Clare and Bacon of Trinity had gone to Gray's Inn, and as Richardson of Christ's had gone to Lincoln's Inn, thus beginning a career that led him to the King's Bench as Chief Justice. There was one other possibility, that he might have attached himself to the household of some great courtier, but except for the Montagues no such family was yet represented at the college.

The university indeed had been stereotyped by Whitgift on such lines that it offered little attraction to any in search of real education. Those who went there or to Oxford often quitted it speedily, as did Raleigh, who afterwards said that his training was that of a gentleman and soldier; or else they supplemented its meagre training by a course of foreign travel, as Milton did in the next generation. The Inns of Court at this time attracted all who sought a liberal education, even without the intention of a legal career; Sir Thomas Gresham, despairing of the universities, was founding his college in London. But these centres offered no assistance such as sizarships, and it may well be that Smyth's means would not support any such course.

Whatever his motive, he followed the line of least resistance and continued the prescribed course of study, now including astronomy, perspective and Greek, with the possibility of profiting by the lectures of the university professors. This course almost limited his natural future to a career either academic or clerical. He might indeed have turned his attention to law, as did his fellow-student

Snoden, but this was a rare course at Christ's. He certainly did attend a few physic lectures in the University Library, hearing of glass eyes, of the automatic action of the stomach in chilling, and of the liver in making blood; here he learned that the heart was enclosed in a bag, which under certain circumstances contained "water," and he afterwards reasoned on these facts and considered the death of our Lord in the fashion that Dr Stroud long afterwards elaborated by his treatise on the *Physical Cause of the Death of Christ*. Smyth's attainments in medicine were such that he did not hesitate in after life to practise the healing art, and to support his family by his labours as a doctor.

Once in the library, which had been thoroughly repaired in the year he came up, he could explore its treasures, such as they were. For want of chains to the books, they had been reduced to 180, but now were beginning to increase. Beza had presented the two tetraglot editions of the Hebrew Law printed at Constantinople by Soncino in 1546 and 1547; also a far older diglot manuscript of part of the New Testament, from the monastery of Irenaeus at Lyons. Smyth gives evidence that he had at least some smattering of the original languages of the scriptures.

Within the college he would now have a seat at meals, at the Bachelors' table, except when he took his turn at reading from the Latin Bible on the lectern during dinner. With increase of privilege went a widening of interest in public affairs. Ecclesiastical charges must come up for discussion, and while the non-Puritans might occasionally express a difference of opinion, there would be general satisfaction that Robert Browne of Corpus, who had broken away from the Church of England, now saw the error of his ways, was accepting the rectory of Achurch, and was duly ordained deacon and priest on 30 September 1591, by the Bishop of Peterborough. That same year an appeal was made to the Queen's Bench in Cawdry's case, and Coke reported on behalf of all the judges that the Ecclesiastical Commissions were quite legal, that the Common Law judges would recognize their sentences and permit them to be executed. This showed that unless

Parliament would alter the law, the Puritan ideals would be suppressed.

To the pensioners' table there came up two men in this time who deserve a word. John Hodgson was destined to make a pitiable failure when trying for his degree, and he at once obtained ordination at Lincoln; this is a good illustration of the way the ministry was recruited. From Epworth came up Richard Bernard, as sizar; in two years he would have to wait on Smyth, who would have a fellow-feeling for the poor lad.

A Bachelor had an easier time within his college, and Smyth would also be allowed now to go beyond its walls, no longer on errands, nor chaperoned by a master. He might be asked to look up a lad from Sturton-le-Steeple in Notts, John Robinson, who came up to Corpus in 1592. Hildersham might send word of a promising recruit from Ashby, Joseph Hall, entered at Emmanuel. And he might hear of a fine scholar of Caius, Henry Ainsworth, who had profited by the presence of Jews hard by, to become proficient in Hebrew. The great Hebraist however, Hugh Broughton of Christ's, returned to England just at this time, and Smyth certainly did devote himself to the language with such effect that not only did he employ commentaries, but he even felt able in after life to use the Hebrew Bible and offer an extempore translation as a regular habit; see pages 283–4, 297.

It was at this period that the college authorities began to lay out the ground behind, making a beginning in 1591–2 by erecting butts in the orchard, where archers might draw the long bow. As yet however there was no bowling green, nor had the authorities averted the temptation to bathe surreptitiously by providing a pool in the grounds. If however Smyth was now caught at a dip outside, as a Bachelor he only risked being set in the stocks and no longer being whipped.

Midsummer of 1593 saw Smyth commencing as Master of Arts his full university life. By seven in the morning the processions were marshalled to take their places in Great St Mary's, where Legge of Caius presided, finishing the year begun by Still of Trinity. One or two discussions in Divinity lasted till eleven, and the graduation of the inceptors took another hour. Then came the discussion in Philosophy and the graduation of the inceptors in Arts from King's. About three o'clock an adjournment was made to the Regent House on the north side of the schools opposite, where Smyth would be graduated. The candidates in Law, Physic and Music followed, and by five o'clock the ceremonial was ended.

Certain oaths and promises were exacted as the condition of the degree, two of which are important. He professed his faith in the scriptures, and in the Church as their rightful interpreter; this had been assailed by Johnson, and Smyth must already have been aware of the counter claim that the right of private judgment was inalienable. He swore to stay in Cambridge for two years, and take his share in the university life; by some this obligation was evaded, but by Smyth was well fulfilled. It was the more necessary, as the average number of undergraduates in residence was nearly 2000, and only about 650 graduates remained, to carry on all the teaching, moderating, governing and legislating.

The question of a future career would now become prominent. A fellowship might be aspired to, this involved taking holy orders, and so would open out three avenues; either he might settle down permanently to an academic life like Bainbridge; or like Knight he might seek the patronage of some Puritan noble and become a parish minister; or he might follow the example of Whitgift from Grimsby, who through four colleges and two chairs of divinity had won court favour and had been successively prebendary of Ely, dean of Lincoln, bishop of Worcester, and now was archbishop of Canterbury, still looking carefully at his university and ready to promote likely men.

When we scrutinize in Dr Peile's register the careers of the Fellows, we find that Thomas Graye vacated his fellowship at Midsummer, 1594. It was not long left vacant, and next Michaelmas Smyth appears on the bursar's books as drawing dividend.

Of his colleagues there is little that need be said; except for Perkins they were quite ordinary. But to their table came some fellow-commoners who brought a breath of a wider life. Three brothers Manners of the Rutland family, Fish from Southill, Pepper from Richmond, belonged to houses with some experience of public affairs. It would compel attention outside the schools when Elizabeth called on Christ's in 1595 to equip a horseman to help suppress the rebellion of Tyrone. But Smyth had now set his face away from these things, and they seem to have left him untouched.

One college storm in a tea-cup reveals his position. There was a contested election to a fellowship in 1596, and the division was on the line, Puritan or anti-Puritan. Whether or no Smyth had thought seriously on this question before, he now had to take sides; and he ranked himself with the Puritan majority. That the election was annulled on a point of order was doubtless important to the rejected candidate, but it committed Smyth openly. It was the more interesting, because at the same time there was a more serious disturbance, on a kindred issue, in the larger university world.

Perkins had touched off a train which led to the explosion. He had felt deeply the quashing of the Presbyterian Classes, and when publishing his *Armilla* in 1590, dated it "in the year of the last suffering of the saints." Since then he had been lecturing on the Creed, and in 1595 he published his *Exposition*, which was not only strongly Calvinistic, but glossed the sentence on the Descent into Hell. A young man called Barrett performing his exercise in Great St Mary's for the degree of B.D., criticised this book, and was promptly called upon to justify his criticism. The Divinity professors were the proper authorities, but it turned out that they did not see eye to eye. Whitaker of John's, the Regius professor, was a staunch Calvinist, but Baro of Trinity was laxer. Baro was a Huguenot, ordained by Calvin, introduced at Cambridge by Goad of King's, now Vice-Chancellor. He had at first been lecturer in Hebrew, but had been elected to the Lady Margaret chair in 1574 and re-elected at the end of each term of office. He had already figured in one celebrated case, summoning Laurence Chaderton before the consistory over two theological points; and now he did not seem eager to condemn the young candidate. Therefore the Vice-Chancellor and heads of colleges took the matter up, composed a recantation, and compelled Barrett to read it publicly. This he did with such an ill grace that he was threatened with expulsion. He complained to Whitgift, and the university to its Chancellor, raising a quarrel in London as to jurisdiction. Whitaker and the dean of Ely took Barrett to Whitgift, who condemned him, and drafted nine articles setting out the most strenuous Calvinism. These he sent down to all the colleges, meaning "not to suffer any man to impugn them openly or otherwise." Barrett disappeared, went to the continent and turned Roman Catholic. But Burghley objected to Whitgift's intervention, and there was talk of his having broken the law by drafting new articles and trying to get other bishops to approve, without leave from the crown, so that Whitgift wrote again to explain away his action. Baro was emboldened to criticise the new Lambeth Articles in Great St Mary's, and at once there was a sharp division. Even Goad sided against him, and though he was backed by Andrewes of Pembroke and Jegon of Corpus, and though Whitaker had died, it was evident that the opposition of Christ's and Emmanuel and all the Calvinists would prevent his re-election when his term expired. He retired therefore to London, happy in the favour of Burghley, and at his death in 1599 was shown honour by Bancroft.

The cross-currents in this conflict, which lasted eighteen months, revealed not only the jealousy of the civil and the ecclesiastical authorities in the nation, the jealousy of foreigners so easily aroused, the jealousy of college and college, but a new factor. Here for the first time was a reasoned dissent from Calvinism, within the Church of England; and though the flag was raised by a Frenchman in presbyterian orders, yet there rallied round it many Englishmen who were presently to regard themselves as *the* Church party, and in the next generation were to arrogate the title Orthodox, which they were at present so flatly denied by Whitgift. It was the beginning in England of Arminianism.

The matter was pondered over by Perkins. There had been no lack of controversial writers against

Catholicism, among whom Whitaker was prominent. But no one had tried an irenicon, and he occupied a new field when in 1597 he set forth in his *Reformed Catholike* how far it was possible to find common ground. He would probably have been much surprised if he had foreseen how this would fall in with the wishes of the administrators, and how in rallying most Englishmen to the established church, it would alloy the theology then current, by a revival of semi-Pelagianism. Meantime the victory lay clearly with the Calvinists. Another sign of their influence both in court and university circles, was that the lady Frances Sidney, countess dowager of Sussex, and related by marriage to the earls of Rutland, founded a new college which like Emmanuel was largely a daughter of Christ's. There was a miscalculation as to endowments, and even the Master was only to receive £15 yearly at first, so that there may not have been eager competition for a post there.

We do not know whether Smyth had the offer to go and help mould the new foundation, along with Montagu; certainly he remained at Christ's. Nor did he ever attain the post of Proctor, held in his time by his colleagues Bainbridge and Bolton, but would have to take his share in moderating over the wranglers in the schools. For his college career, Mr Burgess has rescued from the diary of Samuel Ward the catechist, a few references which show that not only was Smyth a popular teacher to whom more students wished to come than the four allowed, but that he gathered little meetings for prayer in his room. We trace also more advanced ideas of teaching astronomy than were contained in Ptolemy, by the use of a globe.

These references prove that Smyth remained in residence, and relieve us from the enquiry to what living he was appointed. It has been forgotten that Fellows were ordained as such, and that ordination did not imply settlement at a parish. Smyth incidentally lets us know that he had his orders on his fellowship, and therefore by Christmas, 1594, from Wickham, bishop of Lincoln; see page 493. This was in accordance with the statute that every fellow must take priest's orders within a year of his election, so that during 1595 we look on him as fully ordained. At first sight we wonder why he sought this prelate rather than his diocesan of Ely, or one of the many bishops sprung from Christ's, such as Rogers of Dover, Hughes of St Asaph, Watson of Chichester, Sterne of Colchester, Still of Bath, Bancroft of London. The explanation however is simple: the Lincoln diocese was now in two disconnected pieces, and the chief residence of the bishop was not at the cathedral city, but at the palace of Buckden, just beyond Huntingdon, and therefore quite accessible from Cambridge. The diocese was far the largest, and it might be an advantage to be brought to the notice of that bishop.

Meantime Smyth would have to take his turn at reading and preaching in chapel, and conducting the exercises there in philosophy and theology. More than that, the college revenues were partly derived from tithes, and it was necessary to provide for services in return. Manorbier in Pembrokeshire of course needed a resident vicar, and it had been agreed that vicarages should be endowed at Helpston in Northamptonshire and Navenby in Lincolnshire, taken over from the old God's House. Kegworth, Sutton Bonington, Clipston, were all so far away that they must be provided for; so that all these livings really might be looked forward to by a Fellow who preferred parish work. But Bourn and Fen Drayton were within reach, and Fellows paid Hobson a shilling for a horse to take them out and back, charging the same to the college fund. Even Moulton might occasionally be served in the same way.

Among his pupils at college might be not only Baynes and Bernard, but William Ames from Norfolk and the Manners brothers. Some of these younger men would doubtless enjoy the joke played on the mayor and the town generally, when the gownsmen invited them to witness a new play at Clare, which turned out to be a skit on the dignitaries of the borough, whose very clothes had been borrowed to deck out the actors. But this would be beneath the dignity of a Fellow to countenance.

In that year, 1598, Smyth drew his last dividend. We soon find him in company with a Mary Smyth, and it seems fair to infer that he married. But no one has explored the registers at Bourn or Cambridge to find an entry; and there are many Johns, Marys, Smiths, to bewilder the enquirer. It must have been a love match, for the next post we find him holding was not available for a beneficed man, and so for more than a year we have to imagine a plucky pair facing the world with no very substantial means of support. It was a similar domestic strait which prompted Lee of Christ's to attack the problem of knitting, with such success that in this very year he presented the queen with the first pair of knitted silk stockings.

From Lady Day, 1598, to September, 1600, Smyth's doings are uncertain. Bernard wrote in after years incidentally that "hee was instituted into a living," but the context implies that this was an inference, not a known fact. Smyth's successor at Lincoln as lecturer was also rector of a city church in Bernard's time, and probably Bernard assumed that such had been the case with Smyth; but it was not. Indeed the very condition of the appointment as lecturer in 1600 was that the candidate held no benefice.

This leaves open the possibility that Smyth was a parish minister for the two years, and to test that theory we examine the Composition Books. They show nine John Smiths instituted about this period, but only two who deserve even a minute's comparison. The incumbent of Hutton Cranswick in York vacated the benefice about 1600, but he had been there when Smyth was busy lecturing at Cambridge: the rector of Osmundeston in Norfolk was appointed in 1598, but in 1603 he stated he was no graduate, and he lived there till 1616, after Smyth had died at Amsterdam. We conclude that no case has yet been discovered of any living that he could have held. Evidence may yet be produced, but none is yet forthcoming, and we may therefore ponder probabilities, remembering that a ton of them will be outweighed by an ounce of fact when discovered.

Consider the value of a "living." In 1530 there had been enough tithe in kind or money to sustain a bachelor priest; but values had changed, and parish ministers were now allowed to marry. Whitgift showed that a thousand benefices were worth less than £2 gross, 1978 less than £5 gross, 1565 less than £10 gross, 3642 less than £26 gross, which was the least on which a pensioner could subsist at Cambridge; that only 600 parishes were adequately endowed. In another and careful report at the beginning of James' reign, he said that out of 9244 parishes, the tithes of 3888 were appropriate to colleges or ecclesiastical purposes, and of 3849 were impropriate to laymen; only in 1507 parishes were they payable to the rector. The consequence was, as Whitgift pointed out, that university men hesitated to accept the so-called "livings," and that only 3804 graduates were beneficed.

If a graduate had rich friends, he might hope for a chaplaincy. If he were in favour with well-to-do burghers, he might hope for a Lecture-ship. The really rich livings were too often conferred on friends of courtiers, who were allowed to absent themselves from the parishes, and often were pluralists. But a master of a grammar school, such as Christ's trained, could easily command £20, as at Louth; even the usher would have £10, more than many a vicar, and not needing to pay firstfruits, tenths, visitation fees, etc. There were also other posts, such as Cartwright held at Leicester, which were desired by Puritans because they seemed to evade some of the difficulties usually felt.

We may imagine Smyth supporting himself and bride, either by tutoring at Cambridge, or as chaplain, or curate, or more probably as master of a school. In 1599 the college living of Navenby in Lincolnshire fell vacant, and it was given to a junior man, Hamby, from Alford: presumably Smyth either had some more lucrative post, or at least saw one within reach. The register of licences granted in the diocese of Lincoln from 1598 to 1606 inclusive, for curates and schoolmasters, does not record any granted to him. The Rev. A. Hunt, present vicar of Welton, who has investigated every ramification of the relations of Richard Smith, 1533–1602, founder of Lincoln's Christ's Hospital, knows nothing of him.

Lecturer at Lincoln, 1600–1602

In September, 1600, Smyth was chosen Lecturer to the city of Lincoln. This most ancient city was then governed under a charter confirming and enlarging the customs dating from the reign of Rufus; it was endowed by Henry VIII with four advowsons, for there had been a very large suppression of religious houses in the county, including in or close to the city three priories of monks, five friaries and four hospitals. The mayor and aldermen therefore had some ecclesiastical patronage.

The cathedral is one of the glories of the city; but at this time the dean was no preacher, the dean and chapter appear to have been negligible.

The bishop now seldom came to the city, but when not in London, frequented chiefly the palace of Buckden in Huntingdon. It therefore seemed both to the corporation and to Smyth that he too was negligible, which proved a mistake. The bishop was now William Chaderton, not to be confounded with Laurence Chaderton whose whole life was bound up with Cambridge. William too had been a Christ's man, but had gone to Queens', and had been bishop of Chester, where he had had a hard task to curb the Papal recusants, and had had to encourage the Puritans as a counter-irritant. After that experience, it was now felt that he was taking things too easily in Lincoln, and was allowing the recusants to recover strength.

The diocese had been immense, and even after Ely, Oxford and Peterborough had been carved out of it, it was still the largest in England, with 1255 parishes. And it easily ranked first in the number of preachers licensed, having 920. This point is important and will claim attention.

The control of the pulpit was considered essential by the governing authorities. That the friars had received general rights of preaching, had made them disliked by such classes; and when they were disbanded in England, care was taken that all preachers in future should be individually licensed. As a general rule, the bishop issued the licence, but the king and the universities also exercised the right. Latimer had been licensed by the king despite the opposition of the university; Cambridge was now licensing chiefly Puritans, despite the opposition of many bishops.

Bernard of Christ's came down in 1598, was presented to the living of Epworth, and took a licence from the bishop enabling him to preach throughout the diocese. He was only one of 15 Christ's men, contemporaries of Smyth in college, now holding benefices in Lincolnshire, with eight more in Notts. Besides the parish clergy, there were lecturers in Alford, Grantham, Grimsby, Horncastle, Louth and Market Rasen. If therefore Smyth were seeking academic and clerical society, he would not lack material.

But he was now transported into a municipal atmosphere, which unfortunately was subject to fierce storms. The history of his office is recoverable from the City Records, courteously opened to inspection by the Town Clerk. In 1571 the city granted an annuity of £5 to a clerk for three sets of duties; to act as chaplain to the mayor, to preach at the parsonages appertaining to the city (so that the city could draw the tithes) and to preach within the city. Seven years later the terms were varied; 20 marks to a learned man appointed with the advice of the dean, to be reader in the Minster and to preach every Wednesday in some parish church. Five years later they had become more generous; £20 to a virtuous and learned preacher to teach and visit the sick: but in 1586 the dean got the post for himself. In 1590 they rose to £40, but fell to the old level next year.

In 1597 Thomas Luddington was appointed, at the rate of £30 and his diet at the mayor's table. He belonged to a county family, had won a Fellowship at Lincoln College, Oxford, and continued to hold it till he disappeared over Smyth's horizon. His divided interests evidently prevented him giving all the care to city affairs that the corporation desired, and on 3 May, 1600, it was decided that no minister or preacher be chosen who should have any benefice or charge out of the city, but only one who should live continually amongst the citizens. It was only too usual for holders of "livings" to hold two or three, and therefore to be absent; but if a decent salary was paid, it was intended to obtain the whole time of a competent man.

Edward Dynnys on 27 September proposed Smyth for the post, and he was elected by eight votes, seven being cast for Luddington. Considering the local connection of the latter, the probability is strong that Smyth also had local connections, though we cannot trace him in the family tree of Robert Smith of the city, proctor of the ecclesiastical court, or of Richard Smith the "City's Attorney General." It is probable that the Manners influence helped him: Roger the fifth earl, was only lately down from Cambridge, and his three brothers had actually sat at the high table of Christ's with Smyth; though the earl was not lord-lieutenant of Lincolnshire for three years yet, but only constable of Nottingham Castle, yet the family counted for much in the city.

The election over, the stipend was fixed next month at £40, with £3. 6s. 8d. for house rent, and leave to keep three kine on the commons. This was thrice as much as the rector of Saundby received, four times as much as the vicar of Sutton-cum-Lound, eight times as much as the vicar of Sturton-le-Steeple, ten times as much as went to Hugh Bromhead, vicar of North Wheatley.

It follows then that Smyth was now well to do in money matters, and held a post that might enable him to exert influence. In such a position Huldreich Zwingli had swayed the destinies of Zurich; from such a position at Geneva John Calvin had moulded the doctrines of half Europe. Granted that Lincoln was a free city only in name, with a real bishop in power, yet the example of Perkins showed what could be done in England at this time. If for a year or two a man could prove himself worthy, then friendship with the Manners, the Sidneys, the Riches, could open the path to much preferment; it was still possible for a cleric to sit at the council-table, and even to hold seals of office.

It is a pity that no burgess of Lincoln kept a diary at this time, such as Machyn had kept in London, Harvey had kept in Cambridge, Josselyn and Rous were to keep in Suffolk. Under these circumstances it is fortunate that we have two specimens of Smyth's preaching to show how his mind worked. The first impression left is that he was very conscious of the danger from Roman Catholics. It reminds us that the last Catholic bishop of Lincoln had died in prison only eighteen months before Smyth went up to Cambridge.

Dr Usher's study of the *Reconstruction of the English Church* enables us to see how Smyth would realize their strength as soon as he settled at Lincoln. The bishops reported three years later that there were 8630 papal recusants presented to them; the judges next year reported 6126 indicted at the assizes; Father Rivers wrote to Parsons that between 1597 and 1602 the number known to the government had increased 20,000. In these last years of the aged Elizabeth, when it was uncertain what the new reign would bring forth, the Catholics grew very bold. The law might declare that no Catholic should stir five miles from home, that if he contributed to any Catholic fund at home or abroad he forfeited property and liberty, that every priest was ex officio a traitor and liable to death; but the facts were that they sent their young men abroad to be trained as priests, these came back and were present to the number of 200 (they boasted indeed of 500), they had redivided England for their purposes and had a fairly complete organization in two provinces, for which they wanted new bishops, and had actually obtained an archpriest. In Lincolnshire their numbers ranged from 15 per cent. of the population near Boston to half near Grimsby, a phenomenon unknown at Cambridge. So serious did the situation seem to the government, and so evidently had fifty years of coercion failed, that Bancroft was laying his plans, and actually had a Catholic petition presented to the queen promising complete loyalty in everything temporal, asking for liberty of conscience and for the suppression of the Jesuit books. Though she declined, a scheme was being worked out which would give the Recusants what was denied to the Puritans.

In view of this, it is not surprising to find that Smyth when discussing justification, the eucharist, and forgiveness, turns aside for very explicit dealing with "subtle and crafty priests," or opposition to "doltish papist distinctions." And although his fellowship record shows that he had taken a Puritan stand, he now realized that there was need for some strong machinery of government. So breaking away from the Presbyterian position, he acknowledged that every king had authority to appoint ecclesiastical magistrates according to the word, to govern the Church, to exercise jurisdiction, to visit churches, to ordain ministers; which persons in England are called Bishops; page 158. And it is in view of the Catholic petition that we understand best his objection to a toleration of many religions, whereby the kingdom of God would be shouldered out of doors by the devil's kingdom. But even so, it is rather surprising to find that he agreed the magistrates should cause all men to worship the true God, or else punish them with imprisonment, confiscation of goods, or death, as the quality of the cause required; page 166. Perhaps that was not really preached in 1601, but was added after the panic of the Gunpowder Plot. In any case, he soon retracted it and pleaded vigorously for the opposite.

In one matter he was ahead of his age. Few Protestants were alive to the duty of labouring by all possible means to bring home the Jews and the Turks and all other barbarous nations with whom there was traffic, to the knowledge and love of the truth; page 65. Yet the Puritans who emigrated to Virginia in 1611, and some of his own friends who later on settled in New England, were conscious of their obligations to the natives. And before his death he would hear of a missionary seminary founded at Leijden.

For the rest, he seems a fair specimen of a moderate Puritan, accepting set forms of prayer, vocal and instrumental music in church, as he had heard for the last twelve years at college. He shared the prejudices of his age, believing in the reality of witches, along with Perkins and James VI of Scotland, who had lately combated Scott's *Discovery of Witchcraft* by his own *Daemonologie*; pages 37 and 95.

In the matter of church polity, he was hardly consistent. He accepted the Genevan ideal of five species of officers in a congregation; page 158; yet he admitted the need of bishops to govern. He regretted that a few people such as his tutor Johnson had separated from the Church, though he would not disown them as brethren; page 81.

Of religion outside England he knew nothing, and accepted without question the slanders current about the Anabaptists, as that they were anarchists; page 165. It was of course natural that he should not know the highly organized Communion of the Anabaptists in Moravia, with their Servants of the word, Servants of need, Council of elders, Bishop; for though it flourished all his lifetime, Moravia was far away. He might however have recollected that at Münster with an Anabaptist king duly crowned, it was absurd to talk about anarchy. And he could not foresee that in a few years he would be in close contact with the Anabaptists of Holland, where Menno Simons had been bishop of Gröningen, Dirk Philips bishop of Appingadam. For the present he thought of England only.

In the county town there would be frequent gatherings of the county gentry, at least to welcome the judges of assize. And among these the City Preacher would have opportunities of making friends. Two we can identify. To Glentworth, halfway from Lincoln to Gainsborough, had come the Wrays from Yorkshire. This family had lately provided a Speaker and a Chief Justice stern against Separatists; Sir Thomas of Glentworth was a great proprietor in Lincolnshire. Smyth found him to be also a principal professor and protector of religion in the district, a benefactor of many faithful ministers, a good friend and patron to himself; pages 1, 2. We get a glimpse also of his virtuous lady and children; one of these, Isabel, who took as her second husband Sir William Bowes, we shall meet again. Further down the Trent, amid a tangle of the waterways rose the Isle of Axholme, on which stood Butterwick. This was the seat of Edmund, Lord Sheffield, a great potentate, whose interests however lay across the border. For in those days the Trent was a most important boundary. Not only did it separate the ecclesiastical province of York from that of

Canterbury, so that Whitgift and the High Commission of which Londoners thought so much had no authority beyond it; but it was a civil boundary. Henry VIII had been appealed to to erect a separate jurisdiction for the north, somewhat like those in the counties palatine of Durham, Lancashire, Cheshire. He responded to this, almost alone of the demands in the Pilgrimage of Grace, and constituted a Council of the North to sit at York. As this was abolished in 1641, its existence has often been overlooked, and no one seems to have chosen it as a theme for investigation. Lord Sheffield had been appointed its Lord President in May, 1602, and Smyth came to see the advantage of being on good terms with this magnate, and presently to settle absolutely on the frontier, where ten minutes would take him from one jurisdiction to another. Meantime we note that he made Sheffield's acquaintance, and in Axholme found also humbler friends to be mentioned presently.

But there was a weakness about his position; for the tenure was only annual, and he had been put in by a party vote. Feeling was running high in the corporation, and alderman Leon Hollingworth conceived that a lecture of Smyth expounding the phrase "as a lion," was aimed at him; though Smyth quite denied the intention; pages 43–46. He certainly came to be regarded as a party man, and therefore shared in the obloquy that fell on his friends. Trouble may have begun as early as 27 January, 1601-2, when in St Peter at Gowts there was registered the baptism of a daughter to John Smith, Clerk; her name was not Mary, after her mother, but Mara, as if her parents felt that the Almighty was dealing bitterly with them.

Matters came to a crisis on 2 September, 1602, when Edward Dynnys, the mayor, who had originally proposed him, broke open the city chest, took out the seal, and affixed it to numerous grants, contrary to custom. One of these grants appointed Smyth for life, defining his duties. We cannot wonder that this high-handed proceeding recoiled on Dynnys and all his friends, and created a turmoil which lasted for years, each side in turn going down, law-suits being raised, arbitrators called in, leading men disaldered. We need not trace them in detail, but they do entitle us not to believe every word that the other party put on the minutes about Smyth; their epithets may be discredited when we see that it was Hollingworth who accused him of enormous doctrine, undue teaching of matters of religion, and personal preaching. Winnowing away such chaff, we retain the wheat of facts.

Smyth had never asked for a licence from the bishop to preach; he may have thoughtlessly continued acting in Lincoln as he had been accustomed to do for his college. The omission was noted, and as he was technically in the wrong, a definite inhibition was secured. Then the other party mustered on 13 October, led by John Beck and Leon Hollingworth, and when reversing nearly everything that Dynnys had done, not only cancelled the life-appointment of September, but on the ground that a man inhibited from preaching could not be the City Lecturer, annulled every order relating to Smyth. The party victory was marked by replacing Luddington.

Dynnys had foreseen trouble, and in his grant had provided that Smyth could have leave of absence for suits and troubles at law. The Cambridge wrangler justified his friend's opinion and took steps to uphold the deed, so that Beck, the new mayor, had to secure from his supporters a promise that his expenses should be met. He also countered by exhibiting articles before the bishop against Smyth, and attempted to secure from Dynnys and his friends a written retractation of all their deeds. This was never forthcoming, and it was seen that if city business was to go forward, there must be compromise. It began over the preachership; Luddington was dropped, as well as Smyth, and by July a neutral was appointed, in the person of Mr Dalby, who held it till he obtained a great living at Kirton in Lindsey and removed thither. On the many other issues Lord Sheffield was asked to arbitrate.

Here then was Smyth, plaintiff in the common law courts, defendant in the ecclesiastical court. He had nothing to hope from the Manners family, for the Earl and his brothers had joined the Earl of Essex in his rising, were all captured and liable for high treason; the Earl only escaped by a fine of £30,000, and had no leisure to give to a far-off preacher. The money claim was one of the details referred to Sheffield, and the dedication of 1605 shows that Smyth was satisfied with the award. But the proceedings in the bishop's court were fought out longer, and his records remain to show the wearisome proceedings: they have been examined by the courtesy of Canon Foster.

At Buckden on 9 December, 1602, a commission was issued to take evidence in the church of St Peter at Arches next month, and report. On 16 February and 10 March the case came up, and on Tuesday, 1 April, it was held that judgments were now sufficiently proved against the said Smyth. He promptly gave notice of appeal to competent judges, saying that if that appeal were not sufficient he would appeal in writing formally to be heard by his Lordship in person. Friends were not lacking, and a Mr Draw of Lincoln may be met again. On Tuesday, 10 May, 1603, he appeared in person with William Long, his proctor; but the record shows a series of adjournments in which it is hard to find the final issue. And indeed Smyth would scarcely improve his standing in the minds of the officials at Buckden, who presently had complaints about him from quite another quarter, and on new scores altogether.

Meantime he used the opportunity of being back near Cambridge to justify himself from the accusations of Hollingworth. The best answer to the charge of personalities in his preaching was to print the sermons. He was under no illusion as to any money profit, knowing well that it was jest-books and romances that sold; but objecting to see John Legate reduced to thus prostituting the University Press, he published his first work with a dedication to Sir William Wray, who had sought to help him in his litigation.

OFFICIAL REFORM, 1603–1605

The year of this publication was also the break up of a winter which had become bleak and cold. English life had been slowly freezing: beneath the ice were running strongly some new forces, but on the surface all was immobile. When on the last day of 1602–3 Elizabeth breathed her last, and the post galloped on 25 March, 1603, past Buckden towards Scrooby and Edinburgh to summon James VI as James I of England, the ice broke up, and as the floes crashed, the floods began to spread. England within the next two years was greatly transformed, and before the transformation was fairly complete, Smyth found that it no longer permitted him a home. His second book reflected conditions already past in 1605.

At the accession of James there were three religious parties in England. Three-quarters of the population were as indifferent as they are to-day, with no personal interest in religion. They may perhaps have attended worship better, for fear of fines, but it mattered little what was the type of worship: the squire and the minister, often his nominee, settled that, and they followed as a matter of course. A very careful estimate has been made by Dr Usher of the relative strength of those who cared, and it shows that in every ten people, seven were simply inert, attached to things as they were, though they were willing to see slight changes; two were devout Roman Catholics, one was an earnest Puritan. The question for the statesman was, which of these two wings it was worth trying to conciliate and attract; for of course the sheepish mass would acquiesce in anything. The constitution of the Church of England had been left undefined, in accordance with Elizabeth's inveterate habit of procrastination; in defining it, which party should be considered and angled for? Perhaps no one foresaw that the cleavage was permanent, and that three centuries later there would still be three camps, the census revealing 23,918 ministers in the Established Church, 11,981 in the Nonconformist, 3302 in the Roman Catholic; and that an exact record of attendance in London would show four out of five people either hostile to or careless about public worship.

The Puritans thought they had this in their favour, that James had been all his life under Puritan influence; and they had not grasped how intensely he detested this tutelage. They somewhat overrated their importance, for "so far as there was any party, it was mainly composed in 1603 of about 350 men, supported by the gentry and town corporations of their districts in the face of more or less apathetic congregations, having the adherence of perhaps 50,000 able-bodied men, pretty well distributed over the Eastern Counties, the Midlands, and the South. The strength of the laity seems to have been chiefly in the weaving districts," Usher i. 280. Their hope was to replace the remnants of ecclesiastical machinery retained from the Middle Ages, by the oligarchical system of government elaborated in France, Holland and Scotland. With a view to this, they promptly petitioned James on his southward journey, asking for reform; but they gained cold comfort. Bishop Chaderton preaching before him at Burley had tokens of favour that boded ill for them. So by June Henry Jacob began sending out circulars in the hope that a thousand adherents might be found to the "Millenary Petition," while Arthur Hildersham ably backed him. The petition dealt with many details, but its chief proposal was: One preacher resident in each parish, supported by restoring the tithes impropriated to bishoprics and colleges, and a seventh of those appropriated by laymen.

This roused at once the bishops, the universities, and the gentry enriched by the property of the monasteries, and an organized opposition developed. Before the year ended, James took the opinion of the judges what means he had of having the ecclesiastical laws obeyed; they assured him he could go as far as depriving of livings. In January the whole cause came to a hearing before James in the Privy Council, assembled at Hampton Court. At the final scene, 32 leading Puritan ministers were called in to hear his decisions, which he entrusted at once to committees to be worked out. A new catechism was ordered, and a new version of the Bible, with revision of the rubrics and lectionary; statistics of the clergy and parishes were to be gathered, with a view to rearrange plural livings, and even to augment the stipends from some unknown source; the high commissions for church government were to be reformed, and better control of the press to be arranged; the gospel was to be better propagated in Wales, Scotland and Ireland.

Then came an appeal of the greatest importance, which has only lately been noticed. James "further aduised the preachers to perswade their brethren in the Country to unity and conformity" according to Harleian MS. 828. Dr Usher, who has compared nine contemporary accounts, declares that they all agree that the ministers gave their unanimous assent. He prints five of them, not one of which contains this crucial statement; but it is possible that he found it somewhere. He emphasizes its importance, and if they really made the promise, it would indeed be noteworthy: that the leaders of the Puritans should accept the decision of James as a reasonable compromise, and should pledge themselves to try and win their brethren to accept it, would be a triumph for the king. And though it is singular that it was not commented on at the time, and that it has escaped notice ever since, we shall have occasion to observe two incidents which would seem to be attempts to fulfil such a pledge.

Anyhow, it was a surprise agreement, as at Nicæa, and on calmer thought, most Puritans were not inclined to ratify it. Therefore in April the contest was transferred to Parliament and the Southern Convocation. James tried to silence the debates in the Commons, where 48 Puritans held the balance of power, but he was told in reply that he had no right to alter religion or make laws concerning the same without its consent. For he had already authorized the changes in the Prayer-book by his sole authority, and thus had begun to weld the ecclesiastical and political opposition to bishops and kings. A petition to reconsider these changes was rejected by convocation, a warning was given to conform by 24 June, and Parliament was prorogued without any settlement.

Convocation had considered a code of canons drawn up by three Cambridge men, and passed them by special royal licence in June. On 6 September, James confirmed them, and ordered them to be observed as the law of the whole Church. He had overlooked that it was only the Convocation of Canterbury which had considered them, and though he wrote to the archbishop of York on 19 February, 1604–5, the northern convocation simply ignored them. Not until 10 March, 1605–6, did it "decree and ordain" them without any variation, to hold north of the Trent. The uncertainty as to the position in Nottingham meanwhile was of interest to Smyth.

As to the persons affected by them, it was then held that they bound everybody, clergy and laity alike, as Parliament assenting to Henry VIII's laws had delegated the right of such legislation; but a contrary opinion was soon broached, and after 1640 has commanded more assent, that they bind only the clergy, who by their representatives did agree. In this great code of law, gathered up in 141 canons, 47 defined the position as against Puritans, ten as against Catholics. Two of the former set soon came to bear on Smyth: "Whosoever shall hereafter affirm or maintain that there are within this realm other meetings, assemblies or congregations of the King's born subjects than such as by the laws of this land are held and allowed, which may rightly challenge to themselves the name of true and lawful churches, let him be excommunicated ipso facto," etc. "Whosoever shall hereafter affirm that the government of the Church of England under his Majesty by archbishops, bishops, deans, archdeacons and the rest that bear office in the same, is anti-christian or repugnant to the word of God, let him be excommunicated ipso facto," etc. Thus a man who in word or deed objected to the Church of England as formally constituted, thereby put himself outside its pale; a man could be an Englishman, but not a Churchman. Dissent was recognized as a fact. Of course it was recognized as an evil fact, and painful consequences might follow; but the old theory was implicitly discarded that Church and State were one.

Another proclamation of July extended the period of grace till November. The Puritans spent the time in considering what points of law to raise, and in promoting petitions. One such was presented by a few gentry of Lincolnshire, and another on 1 December by 32 ministers of the diocese. To find so few adherents is surprising, considering how much had been said; and to scan the names, at the British Museum in Additional MS. 8978, folio 116, is to show that not a single man except Hildersham emerged from obscurity. Not any of those whose names come into our story, signed it, not even Smyth himself, who indeed was not beneficed at the moment. A crisis came on 9 February, 1604–5, when a petition signed by 39 Northampton men was handed to James, who at once imprisoned the three gentlemen that brought it. Four days later, in a great assembly before the judges started on assizes, they publicly declared that the High Commission might deprive disobedient clergy, that they would not interfere with the Commission in that or in its ordinary work, and that promoting such petitions came very near to treason. Within a few weeks, nearly 300 ministers were silenced or suspended. When the blow fell, many shrank back, and within a few months, when Yelverton on behalf of the Commons was pleading for mercy, Bancroft was able to answer that the numbers had fallen to 60, so that the problem had almost vanished.

Then on the other side, the Gunpowder Plot of 1605 was the starting point for vigorous legislation against Catholics. But while Parliament passed the penal laws, the Government framed, in concert with the archpriest, an oath of allegiance, which he publicly took and avowed. At the annual February meeting of 1607–8, the judges were directed to tender the oath, and to execute none who would take it. Within a few years, the Catholics were split, and all who swore to be loyal found themselves really recognized and tolerated, with a bishop of their own before the reign ran out.

Thus the Church of England was organized, and its ministers drilled into conformity; while two small bodies of dissenters were recognized as inevitable. The Catholic dissenters seemed to be no menace whether in rebellion or in parliamentary action; so they were largely left alone when they took the oath. But the Puritan dissenters were strongly represented in Parliament, and therefore lest they should reverse the new settlement, attention was paid to them to enforce the laws.

Such was the situation for Smyth to consider about

the end of 1605, when he had seen his second book through the press, and realised the intention to overhaul the Church generally, by rendering the Visitations thoroughgoing enquiries to be followed up by action on the weaknesses disclosed.

MEDITATION AND DISCUSSION, 1605–1606

Smyth's movements have not been traced between 1603 when he was at Buckden and Cambridge, and 1606 when he was at Gainsborough. His book of March, 1604–5, was printed at London; it had "the privilege of the press," being no surreptitious issue, and was dedicated to the Lord President of the Council of the North. He was therefore still in good standing, and conceivably may have been in London and seen some of these stirring events. William Bradford of Austerfield dates the formation of the churches at Gainsborough and Scrooby, of which he was a member, "about a year" before the emigration to Holland "in the years 1607 and 1608." Nathaniel Morton writing in 1669 and naming 1602 as the date, is clearly wrong by about four years.

Smyth may not only have visited London, but also Suffolk, where were many of his contemporaries at Christ's, and some of the great Puritan gentry: we shall presently find correspondence which shows that they had sought his advice. But he returned to Lincolnshire, where the Earl of Rutland was now lord lieutenant, and settled at Gainsborough, the third town in the county, with a population of about 1500, a port with continental traffic, near gulfy Dun, on

> Trent, who, like some earth-born giant, spreads
> His thirty arms along the indented meads.

The manor had lately passed from the lords Burgh to the Hickmans, an Essex family enriched during the suppression of the monasteries. They had protected Knox, Foxe, Hooper and other advanced preachers had taken refuge in Mary's time at Antwerp in the very Merchant's House that had sheltered Tyndale. Returning on Elizabeth's accession, they settled here in the Old Hall, to whose timber-frame and stone they added a brick tower. While the staunch old lady lived, Smyth might feel assured of a welcome, though it is not clear whether her son William would uphold the family tradition.

Close by was Marton, where the rector was a Christ's man three years Smyth's junior. Down in Axholme, Langley of Christ's had just become curate of Belton, after serving Epworth. From that place Bernard had gone, in 1601, to Worksop, a large parish with five or six hundred communicants, page 462; at Markham, also in Notts., the rector was Francis Chapman, who had been sizar along with Smyth. If then Lincoln was no longer a convenient home, lest old troubles should break out anew, here was a good centre amid old friends. It was not certain whether he might still count among these Doctor Snoden, who took over the young Manners when he went down from Christ's, and was now on the Council of the North; or Thomas Bywater, who in the very month when he issued his *Paterne* was imprisoned for issuing a "seditious book, falsifying scripture."

New friends too would soon be discovered. Six miles down river was Laughton, where Robert Gifford was more intent on preaching than on conformity to ritual. Three miles up river on the other side was Sturton-le-Steeple, where lived a substantial yeoman, John Robinson, who had sent his son of the same name to Corpus, where he became a Fellow in the year that Smyth had quitted Christ's. Seven miles west lay Babworth, where Richard Clifton was rector, a man of about 50 years old. Only three miles from Gainsborough was North Wheatley, where Hugh Bromhead was in charge. To all these men Smyth soon became leader.

There was also one family dotted over both counties, whose pedigree has been carefully traced by Mr Burgess, and published in the *Transactions of the Baptist Historical Society*, iii. 18. A cadet, Gervase Helwys, son of John, a servant of the Earl of Rutland, now held estates at Worlaby and Gainsborough, and across the river at Askham and Saundby; he was soon to follow his uncle Geoffrey to London, to become Lieutenant of the Tower, and to make a tragic end for the murder of Sir Thomas Overbury. An aunt was married to Nicholas Hamerton,

apparently living near Burton-on-Stather by Axholme; he came from Horncastle where in 1572 John Hamerton had married Isabel Smyth; of this family we shall hear again. There was another uncle at Habblesthorpe, too often confounded with his namesake the head of the family. This was Thomas Helwys, residing at Broxtowe Hall in Basford near Nottingham. His father Edmund had been important enough to be summoned by the Earl of Rutland to show a horse and weapons, and had obtained a grant of coat-armour. Thomas was not sent to Cambridge, but after three years at Gray's Inn had married Joan Ashmore at the end of 1595, and now had several children. This Thomas Helwys, evidently about the same age as Smyth, soon became his closest friend.

Meantime Smyth had to earn something, and he turned to account his medical knowledge, practising as a physician. Such a transformation surprises us till we think that it is only one century since any course of education was enforced for doctors, and that still some ministers are amateur practitioners. But there was one restriction of which he could hardly be ignorant; he ought to have obtained a licence from the bishop. And that he did not, after his experience of what was entailed by neglect, shows that he was rapidly moving to open hostility.

More than that, the vicarage of Gainsborough had been held since 26 March by Jerome Phillips. But while he took the revenues, he did not discharge the duties, either in person or by deputy. How could a shepherd stand by and see a flock unfed, unwatched? Smyth stepped into the breach, and "did read the forme of prayers till he came to ye psalmes, and then he expounded the psalmes appointed for yt day, standinge in ye place where ye minister useth to reade and not having anie surplisse on, and the time being paste before he had ended his exposition, he so concluded with a praier for ye kinges majestie." How often this occurred is not clear, but it shows that there was some excuse for the blunder that he was Vicar of Gainsborough.

Early in 1606 Bancroft ordered a thorough visitation of his province, and it was when the archdeacon came here that all these irregularities came to light; the record has been published in the *Lincoln Diocesan Magazine* for 1891, vii. 139. Smyth did not deny the facts, but appeared in person and confessed as above. The result showed that his previous record told against him, and what might have been regarded as a praiseworthy attempt to supply another man's neglect, was actually accounted another mark of recalcitrancy. This of course would oblige him to consider his position, and the position of an organization which thus tripped up a well-meaning man on trivial points of order, instead of condoning technical irregularities and commending his real energy. For nine months he debated the question with himself and with friends in many directions. Three letters he wrote to make his position clear to others who sought his counsel. They were not printed for three years, and then only as embedded in or appended to a longer work, so that their relevance to this period has not always been recognized. Unhappily only one can be dated, to about October, 1607; the others we suppose to be rather earlier, as then the progress of thought is coherent. But they show a man free from doubts, and there are some allusions to the period of indecision which occupied part of 1606.

Richard Clifton was one with whom he discussed, and in after days even when differences had sprung up, he frankly acknowledged that Smyth had convinced him of the necessity of Separate Churches. Bernard was rather annoyed that Smyth did not talk more with him, fancying himself better able than Clifton to follow Smyth's arguments. The opportunity was given him by his patroness, Isabel Wray, who had married Sir William Bowes of Coventry, the man who had offered bail for Johnson at Cambridge, and was interested in church reform. She arranged a conference in her home for leading ministers to consider what they had better do in the position brought about by the new canons, the general visitation, the silencing and deprivations. The Nestor of the district was Barbon, prominent ever since he signed *The Book of Discipline* in 1584; Arthur Hildersham of Ashby-de-la-Zouch, vicar now, was invited; John Dod of Jesus College was another local leader, silenced once in the diocese of Oxford, and now at Canons Ashby in Northamptonshire, threatened anew.

To these Midland men, came Smyth, Bernard and Helwys. The situation seems to have been discussed from every angle, and yet Bernard at least did not thoroughly grasp Smyth's position, while each seems to have over-rated what he actually accomplished. Hildersham, it must not be forgotten, was one of the 32 who are said to have solemnly promised James to win over his brethren and secure conformity, and this would be his aim now. Smyth was quite clear-sighted enough to recognize that the years of winking and tolerance were over, and that it was needful either to conform or to separate. He took the bold line that the result of Hampton Court and the new canons was to refuse all reformation, that it revealed the Church of England as an institution corrupt, and contentedly corrupt, with ministers corrupt, worship corrupt; therefore that it behoved every man who would not himself be corrupted, to linger no longer but depart out of Babylon. All night long the debate proceeded, and it seems to have left the four leaders where they stood, Bernard in a state of woeful indecision, Helwys convinced of the soundness of Smyth's attitude. There was no quarrel, and when Smyth was asked to close with prayer, he thanked God for the peaceable and quiet conference. As he and his friends returned, they discussed further, and Smyth spent some time at Broxtowe, possibly determining what the next step should be. Lady Bowes continued sympathetic, protected Puritan clergy, and when her third marriage made her a peeress with a right to chaplains of her own, the diocese of York profited: among them was Beriah Dyke, father of Daniel Dike, one of Cromwell's Tryers, and at last assistant to Kiffin. Lady Bowes also won the respect of Helwys, who five years later dedicated a book to her.

If Northamptonshire was one Puritan stronghold, Suffolk was another; 64 ministers had been disciplined 20 years earlier by Whitgift, and Knewstubbs of Cockfield was one who survived and was at Hampton Court. After his promise to try and secure peace, he spoiled the effect by asking a further period of grace for Suffolk, and was refused with the remark that it was unreasonable to prefer the credits of a few private men to the general peace of the church. He therefore was now doing his best as Hildersham had done, and found 75 men who in the first instance refused to submit.

They might remember how when Mary came to the throne, eight bishops and hundreds of clergy were ejected; how when Elizabeth followed, even before her system was expressly denounced from Rome, some 1875 clergy gave up their livings; they might reasonably expect that the accession of a third monarch with a revised settlement would produce another wholesale exodus. But there were some slightly new elements; James and Bancroft were in practice permitting the Catholics to exist, though fined and disfranchised, and even to organize. It was conceivable that if a number of Puritans comparable in number and importance, should quit the Establishment, they might at the price of civil and economic liberty purchase a similar toleration. Knewstubbs was pledged to oppose any such secession, and indeed all the leaders of the past, Egerton, Wilcocks, Jacob, had similarly surrendered at Hampton Court, and had been adjured to work for conformity.

It was advisable then to seek counsel from new men, and in Suffolk there were many who knew Smyth. William Knight, lately fellow of Christ's, was now rector at Culford; Ralph Kenrick, sizar one year before him, was vicar of Great Finborough; Richard Hart, sizar one year after him, was vicar of Swilland.

Perhaps there were some who had already seen that they could no longer continue in communion with the Church of England, and had separated, but desired advice as to their positive action; for even in 1580 Browne had preached often at Bury St Edmunds. But it is more probable that they were not quite so advanced, and that it was the receipt of this letter which converted them into Brethren of the Separation, as they were when the letter was published in 1609.

So we interpret the events which led up to the brethren

in S. writing to Smyth, with the consent of Mr K., to obtain a statement of his views for discussion with Mr K. His reply, printed here at pages 557–562, shows a succinct statement of his position, in four propositions. Churches ought to consist of saints only. Each church ought to elect, approve, and ordain its own ministers. Worship should be spiritual and not limited by prescribed forms. Each church should be governed by a college of pastors.

As a primer, this was sufficient; it did not go on to elaborate any scheme for a federation of local churches, but it was clear, and it challenged not only the position of Bancroft, but that of Knewstubbs. *The Book of Discipline* was as cramping as the Book of Common Prayer; let a man be free to follow the promptings of the Spirit in the worship of God. The pentagonal Genevan fortress of Pastor—Teacher—Elder—Deacon—Widow was as unscriptural as the pyramidal Lambeth system of Archbishop—Bishop—Archdeacon—Rural Dean—Rector; each church shown in scripture had a college of pastors. Smyth did not examine the tacit postulates; that all churches in the apostolic days were uniformly organized; that any, or the, apostolic pattern was of permanent obligation. But even if two of his positions were open to criticism, he formulated a new programme with great lucidity, and his next three books simply expounded and defended it.

If Smyth was thus appealed to from distant counties, his influence in Nottingham was considerable. Bernard, Bromhead, Clifton, Gifford decided to resist the new disciplinary measures. Bernard, a man "able to dive into the depths of Smyth's arguments," wrote a pamphlet to prove that the authority of the bishops was antichristian, and lent it about among his friends. But there was weakness in his character, and when it was proposed to print it, he dared not affix his name, though he was willing that it should appear anonymously; page 336.

This reminds us that the control of the press was not perfect, any more than in the day of Martin Marprelate; Catholics not only imported from Douay, but managed to print secretly in England. Smyth when dedicating the *Paterne* emphasized that it had the privilege of the press, thereby implying that tracts could really be issued without it. And it would be with recollection of this fact that he began to set down principles and inferences concerning the visible church, supporting every point with an array of proof texts.

If Smyth thus was encouraging secession, he was bound to provide positive organization. If he had had leisure to enquire, he might have written to his old tutor Johnson at Amsterdam; he would probably refuse to call and see Robert Browne, who had conformed to some extent, and would refuse to read his books. Why should he ask at second hand? The Bible lay open to him as to them. So to the Bible he went, Old Testament and New alike, not stopping to ask if there was any Church before Jesus Christ, and not considering yet the bearing of his doctrine that the Old Testament institutions and ceremonies were typical and not to be reproduced.

That sacraments were seals, was a common-place. Pilkington had written "As it is not enough to write the conditions of a bargain in an indenture, except it be sealed; so God for our weakness thought it not sufficient to make us promise of His blessings in writing in His scripture; but He would seal it with His own blood, and institute His sacraments as seals of the same truth." Smyth now asked, What are the conditions which are sealed by baptism? for if the covenant is not published, the seal is set to a blank; page 278. He might have discovered from scripture that there was an Old Covenant prescribed at Sinai, a New Covenant ratified at Calvary. But his attention was caught by precedents when the people of Israel were reforming; Asa induced them to enter into a covenant to seek the Lord, the God of their fathers, with all their heart and with all their soul; Josiah followed Hezekiah's example and made a covenant to walk after the Lord and keep His commandments with all the heart; Nehemiah wrote a covenant to walk in God's law as read by Ezra, and the leaders sealed it.

These seemed to give the answer, and so whereas Bancroft was exacting subscription to Whitgift's articles, and a promise to obey the new canons, Smyth drew up a brief covenant, paraphrased by Bradford of Austerfield, who took it, in memorable words. "They shooke of this yoake of antichristian bondage, and as ye Lords free people, joyned them selves (by a covenant of the Lord) into a church estate, in ye fellowship of ye gospell, to walke in all his wayes, made known, or to be made known unto them, according to their best endeavours, whatsoever it should cost them, the Lord assisting them."

There had been covenants taken before, of which Smyth was fortunately ignorant. They were long and involved, mixing fundamentals and details. He took the essential point as he found it in scripture, to walk in all God's ways. He added four qualifications, of which one only is important. He and his friends were pioneering, it was improbable that they had yet grasped all that was involved; revelation was progressive, so that Paul had owned he was only pressing on to attain; the covenant therefore stereotyped nothing, but promised that they would conform to what should become known. It was this feature that most surprised and annoyed other people; within the next six years they saw Smyth move rapidly from one position to another; no sooner was one book in their hands than it was superseded by another with fresh points broached; things once advocated were dismissed as unimportant, or with Augustine's frankness were retracted as mistakes. How far Smyth was in advance of his age is to be seen not only in the need for frequent reminders of this point, but also in that one after another of the covenanters halted in the discovery, and settled down to some conventional position. And how far he was in advance of many in this age is to be seen in the modern defences of those who halted and even retraced their steps, as with John Robinson.

Pastor of the Church at Gainsborough, 1606–1608

This bold new departure excited criticism and imitation. An old university acquaintance intervened, apparently a pluralist able "to oppose against this truth in your pulpits," page 556. It is somewhat curious that he did not address Smyth, but wrote to Helwys some reasons proving his Church and Ministry true. Possibly the idea was to reclaim an inexpert layman being misled, possibly it was to cut the nerve of the new movement by detaching the member most able to suffer "losse of goods," possibly it was to deal with a neighbour at Broxtowe rather than with Smyth who had no fixed residence. The uncertainty of motive is the greater as we cannot be sure who Mr A. S. was; no Christ's man appears to fit the conditions, and it is but a conjecture that this was Alexander Southworth. Helwys did not reply, and lost the letter; A. S. wrote again, assuming that his case was unanswerable, wherefore Helwys passed on the letter to Smyth, who wrote temperately, explaining why he had separated, and asking for a careful consideration and private conference, lest he should commit himself prematurely by open opposition. He invited him also to communicate the reply to their common friend Bernard, evidently with the hope that both would take the same decisive step. But we know only Edward, Robert and Jane Southworth who did covenant, and they in after days chose different paths to walk in.

Meantime from the borderlands of Lincoln, Nottingham and Yorkshire, one after another took the covenant. Bernard grew jealous, and started a similar movement, which according to his own account afterwards, was intended only to keep people from Smyth; though we may hope that at the time there was a nobler motive. For this he sent out proctors or agents through a hundred parishes, and won many adherents.

When it came to a question of organization, the question of a place or places for worship would be very practical. Fixed places were usual, and since Smyth's recent experience at Gainsborough showed that the parish churches were not available, they had to consider what buildings could be borrowed. That town was eminently desirable as on the frontier, in case of constables being set to work; and so long as Rose Hickman lived, or Thomas Helwys could borrow his cousin's house, premises would not be lacking. But Worksop was too far away, and was on the edge of the district affected;

so when it was noticed that the postmaster at Scrooby, himself a Cambridge man, and an old retainer of the Bowes family, lived in the archbishop's manor-house close to another county border, and had joined the movement, this settled a second centre. If Bradford is to be trusted, writing in the next generation, twin churches were organized, as at Jarrow and Wearmouth in the days of Bede.

Smyth's position was accepted, that churches must choose and ordain their own ministers; he renounced his ordination by Bishop Wickham, was chosen and ordained by the church at Gainsborough. It is not clear whether any appointment was made by the group at Scrooby which contained Clifton; perhaps they waited for Bernard to follow Smyth's example.

He however was beginning to feel the awkwardness of his undecided position. He was vicar, and yet agent in gathering a knot of people out of many parishes; vicar, yet silenced in his own church; vicar, and not prepared to renounce his ordination and be ordained anew by a number of tradesmen; vicar, and yet likely to get no tithes. It was impossible to stay long like that. Was it impossible to do what Hildersham and Knewstubbs had done, to put up with a good deal that he disliked, and continue his ministry in peace? If Naaman deliberately bargained to bow down in the house of Rimmon, his heart being with Jehovah, and if Elisha heard the proposal without demur, could not he tolerate much that he disapproved, and retain his position of usefulness? Indeed, was it not incumbent on every faithful man to stand to his post when the visitations were revealing such neglect and inefficiency? One rector was practically a cattle-dealer, another a husbandman, another a gardener. The new policy was to encourage exchanges so that if the tithes of one parish were so scanty as to drive the rector to such means of livelihood, he could hold also, not some distant parish, but one close at hand, and could actually serve both. Might he not obtain Saundby, or perhaps Gainsborough itself? Could he not do more good in the well-known official position there, using the venerable parish church, than Smyth at the Hall, a fugitive like the hunted mass-priests?

Bernard therefore drew up a list of his doubts and objections to the course that Helwys was taking, and, as if he were a Surveyor of Income Tax, sent them on a sheet ruled in double column for replies to be annexed. Helwys was not accustomed to this kind of scholastic disputation, and forwarded the document to Smyth, who filled it in and added some counter questions, to which Bernard did not find it convenient to reply.

Meantime archbishop Matthew was making it plain that a bridge remained over which he might retreat, and that he would be welcome to resume his ministry; he recrossed his Hellespont, signed the articles tendered to him, dissolved his covenanted band, and was restored to the vicarage at Worksop. Apparently he had to eat some humble pie, for he had first to follow the archdeacon from court to court and pay many fees; then he actually went so far as to write a little pamphlet pleading for the official system, page 462.

Smyth felt this defection keenly, and took three days to write a letter of expostulation. It ranged over many details, of which two may deserve mention. One was the sort of argument Butler used with the Deists; you hold already certain doctrines, these lead logically to mine. Hall of Halstead employed this style soon to scare people back from Smyth, Canne of Amsterdam employed it later to lure Ames further. Smyth's illustration was from the assembly of people who gathered Sunday by Sunday in the parish church of Worksop. To these, Bernard was bound to minister the word and the sacraments, and even under the new canons he could not in practice repel from the Lord's table those who were unworthy. He had tried to evade the difficulty, a very ancient one, by gathering a select band of covenanted professors from the country around. But could a college Lector, unhappy in his official position, combine with it the private tutoring of men from all and sundry colleges? might the sheriff of Notts. be recruiting bands of personal retainers from Lincoln, York, Derby and Rutland? was not Bernard either neglecting his official duties or poaching on the preserves of others? Surely the logic of his position was to organize his covenanted people into a

Separated Church, and to resign his post, for no assemblage of people living in one area could be a Church, as scripture set forth a church.

If it were asked, What then is that body to which you deny the title of Church? the congregation at Worksop; or on the grand scale, What is the whole mass of congregations, knit together for centuries, and known by the venerated name of the Church of England? Smyth had a startling reply. He did not give the historic answer, Two provinces in revolt; he gave a theological answer, A masterpiece of Satan; or in his own stinging word: Antichrist.

Now that a pope, or the papacy, or the church at Rome, or the whole Roman communion, was Antichrist, was an axiom with the Elizabethan reformers, and Jewel had amassed testimonies of previous writers to the same effect. But they had broken with Rome, and since the days of Parker at least, had been free from all intercourse, nay, were actively opposing. Yet many Puritans had been uneasy as to whether all the poison were worked out of the system, and Smyth had been anticipated in his painful discovery. When Barrowe of Clare had been examined before the Council, he was so evidently hinting at this, that the Lord Chancellor asked him what was his view as to the office of the archbishop of Canterbury, sitting at his side. Whitgift had done a great deal to reform the Church, and was a staunch Calvinist; yet Barrowe could not get over the fact that he was not simply a minister of God's word, but also the head of a great system of ecclesiastical machinery, and the first peer of the realm, actually sitting there to judge. So he rashly blurted out that such a man was "a miserable compound...neither ecclesiastical nor civil, even that second beast spoken of in Revelation." The personal application had been forced by the chancellor, but Andrew Melville had volunteered the same thing quite recently in full council, when he strode up to Bancroft, and shook his lawn sleeves as "romish rags and a part of the Beast's mark." Smyth was writing, and was not tempted to such personalities, but his position was substantially the same. And just what scores of the

Elizabethan reformers had said and were saying about Rome, he said of the Church of England. Just as Sandys of York had quitted the Roman communion, so it behoved Bernard of Worksop to quit the Anglican.

Bernard however had taken his hand from the plough, declining to run such a solitary furrow. He sent no reply in writing, but began to prepare a book as an answer in print, taking six or seven months over it and finishing in June, 1608, just as Smyth was leaving the country. It was entitled *Christian Advertisements and Counsels of Peace. Also disswasions from the Separatists schisme*, etc. It called forth an elaborate response from Smyth in 1609, incorporating much of this correspondence in 1607.

Smyth was busy enlisting, organizing, and ministering to his select company. An analysis of more than 70 names found in various documents of the next few years, enables us to see the occupations of some adherents. Three were county gentry, three ministers or university graduates, one was a servant to a city magnate; a bricklayer's labourer, a house carpenter, a painter and a tinsmith represent one side of work; four bombazine workers, two damask workers, a fustian worker, an embroiderer and a furrier, represent another. It is possible that some of these trades were taken up for the first time after emigration, but some are named immediately on arrival. The places named extend from Epworth in the north to Market Overton on the south, Ingoldsby in the east to Dalton in the west, but on the whole formed a circle of 25 miles in diameter round Sutton-cum-Lound as centre. His activity was not limited even to this area, for some people lived as far away as Tunstall on the coast of the East Riding, and on another far-reaching tour he fell ill and had to be nursed at Broxtowe.

An important adherent was won in this anxious time. John Robinson of Sturton, whose career at Corpus had overlapped Smyth's at Christ's, had been chiefly in Norwich since, minister of a parish whose land-holders had the right of choosing their own vicar. Suspended from exercising his ministry, he seems to have returned to his native district and to have been attracted by the movement. For it was afterwards cast in his teeth that he had been among a company of the Separation and had renounced his ministry, after leaving Norwich, and before he went to Cambridge to consult with Baynes and Chaderton. But we must not overlook the possibility that he went no further than the brethren in Suffolk who consulted Smyth by letter. Whether it was south or north that he abandoned the Church of England, he did ultimately return here and throw in his lot with the Nottingham group, practically taking the place that might have been Bernard's, a worthy assistant to Smyth, ministering chiefly to the group centering at Scrooby.

We must not anticipate the later fame of Robinson, earned at Leijden; Joseph Hall even in 1610 wrote to Robinson contrasting him with Smyth in such phrases as: "Your partner, yea your guide; M. Smith and his shaddow, so I perceive he was; M. Smith whom you followed; Master Smith your oracle and generall." Such terms show clearly that the two men were associated, and that Smyth was the leader.

On the other hand, too much reliance has been placed on Bradford's account of these proceedings, in which he was certainly concerned as a lad of seventeen, but which he only narrated at some time between 1630 and 1646, when his memory for details is hardly trustworthy. He indeed says plainly enough that the people became two distinct bodies or churches, in one of which was Smyth who afterwards became pastor. The obvious reading of this is that they were two churches from a very early stage, before Smyth was pastor of the Gainsborough church. Now that they were two churches in Holland is certain, but there is no contemporary evidence that they were two churches in England, and many trifles suggest the contrary. Hall's language rather implies one body, under Smyth assisted by Robinson. Bradford admits that Robinson was only chosen pastor of the second church in the Low Countries, and he does not name Clifton as pastor before. If there were a second church in England, it would have met usually at Scrooby; but some of Smyth's adherents lived as far from Scrooby on the south and west as Gainsborough was on the east;

and so would have to pass Scrooby to attend worship at Gainsborough; Margaret Maurice and Gervase Nevile lived actually in Scrooby, yet belonged to Smyth's church.

Richard Clifton did not unite in this church, for he said in 1608 (page 575): "I and divers others had once purposed to have committed our soules" to Smyth. He does not seem to have formed a church at Babworth, nor is there any contemporary allusion to the "church at Scrooby." It is possible that the church at Gainsborough was the only organized body in the district, meeting at various places as proved convenient; and Scrooby would certainly be most convenient. It is barely possible that the one pastor presently expanded into a college of pastors, though there is no evidence of this, and the probabilities are against it. On the whole it would rather appear that there were many people who had definitely separated from the Church of England, and more who had practically ceased to attend the parish worship, who were habitually meeting together, but had taken no formal steps towards organization; and of these both Clifton and Robinson appear to be specimens.

The constitution of the church was set forth ideally by Smyth in his *Principles and Inferences concerning the visible church*, and when he discovered in Holland that the Ancient Church of 1592 did not conform in all respects to the pattern he had expounded, he published a long appendix expounding the Differences of the Churches of the Separation, and defending his own customs. From these sources we have a clear picture of the constitution and the worship of the church.

There was one pattern laid down in scripture, to which every church must conform, and no other religious society was tolerable. A church must consist only of saints, joined to God and one another by covenant. Some of these would be gifted to lead in worship, others only private members. In the whole body resided the full power of Christ, the church collectively was to administer the affairs of the church in obedience to the will of the Lord; the existence or presence of officers added nothing except order, they were the creatures of the church which could if need arose discipline or depose them. Mutual care, watchfulness, helpfulness was of the essence of church-life; sin was to be detected and admonished with a view to its abandonment. Officers were of two types, for the spiritual and the temporal affairs of the church. The former were called indifferently bishops or elders or presbyters or pastors or teachers or governors; in so far as the names were not interchangeable, they emphasized one aspect or another of the officer's duty. The latter were called deacons, or if women, widows, and their special care was to fill and wisely administer the treasury of the church.

These points were emphasized also by Helwys in a letter of 26 September, 1608, discovered at Lambeth by the diligence of Mr Champlin Burrage, and published in 1912. It indicates some details of worship, which however are known better by a long letter of Hugh and Anne Bromhead to their cousin William Hamerton in London. This letter, which is persistently referred to with a wrong pagination, but is really Harleian MS. 360, folios 70* and 71, is becoming yearly more illegible; several transcripts have been made, two by the present editor, and some have been printed. It contains long unacknowledged quotations from books, but also gives some original information. Here is the account of the worship of their church:

"We begynne wth a prayer, after reade some one or two chapters of the bible, gyve the sence therof, and cōferr vpon the same, that done wee lay aside oure bookes, and after a solemne prayer made by the .1. speaker, he propoundeth some text ov^t of the scripture and prophesieth ov^t of the same by the space of one hower, or the Quarters of an hower. After him standeth vp A .2. speaker and prophesieth ov^t of the same text the like tyme and place sometyme more sometyme lesse. After him the .3. the .4. the .5. &c as the tyme will geve leave. Then the .1. speaker cōcludeth wth wth prayer as he began wth prayer, wth an exhortation to cōtribution to the poore, wch collection being made is also cōcluded wth prayer. This morning exercise begynes at eight of the clock, and cōtinueth vnto twelve of the clocke, the like course and exercise is observed in the afternoone from .2. of the clock vnto .5. or .6. of the clocke. last of all the execution of the govermēt of the church is handled."

This sketch does not explain how the singing was handled; Helwys expressly says that no book was used for this, any more than for praying or preaching; it is difficult to divine whether words and tune were memorized, in which case there might be congregational singing, or whether they were extemporized, in which case it must surely have been solo—or chaos. At a later period singing was dropped altogether. The liturgical practices of Johnson's Ancient Church were different, and Smyth unfortunately was led to mention the resemblances, which were fundamental and numerous, in five lines, and to describe the differences in scores of pages, so as to emphasize trifles and caricature the whole. The letters of the Bromheads and Helwys are invaluable as showing the real practice and the due proportion. We can trace the dominant spirit of Smyth; there was room for any brother to pray, any one to read and expound and compare passages. But with the worship proper, he opens with prayer and an address of an hour, Clifton, Bromhead, Robinson, and others, may glean after him, but he closes as he began, though Bywater and Helwys and Nevile may take up the collection.

In the matter of government it will be noted that the church abandoned not only the medieval pattern and the Elizabethan modification, but the Genevan pattern also; a college of pastors, a college of deacons. The question never became important to Smyth how one church was related to another, so he never raised it, much less examined scripture to answer it. He neither affirmed nor denied Independency.

Such a movement could not be viewed lightly by the authorities, and since the spring of 1606 there was no doubt that the new canons held north of the Trent as well as south. A new High Commission was appointed, which sat at Auckland, Durham, Ripon, York, Bishopthorpe, Cawood and Southwell. One of its most active members was Doctor Snoden, who knew this county well. He came from Mansfield Woodhouse, became rector of Hickling before he gave up his fellowship at Christ's, and soon added the prebend of Southwell, both pieces of preferment apparently due to the Manners family, whom he had coached. He now figured as judge in the prosecutions set afoot around his centre of Southwell.

By July, 1607, Joan Helwys was arrested, and the oath ex officio was tendered to her, to answer every question put to her. Along with her were John Drewe and Thomas Jessop, so that there was no special aiming at one class more than another. The legality of proffering this oath had been much challenged, and though the common-law judges had declared it legal, public opinion was by no means unanimous. The three Separatists declined, and were remanded to York Castle. Several Scrooby men were next prosecuted, found guilty in their absence and fined by Snoden with his fellow commissioners sitting at Southwell, but the only other actually captured was Gervase Nevile, who also was lodged in York Castle, and ordered to be kept in solitude, till the end of March, 1607-8.

It was now clear that England was no home for the church, and it became necessary to consider the alternatives open. Emigration to an English colony was still rather too venturesome, though Leigh had written from Guiana in 1604 for some well-disposed preachers. A settlement in Virginia had come to grief, Henry May's shipwreck on the Bermudas was directing attention there; two companies had been chartered to colonize the mainland between 34° and 45° north latitude, and Jamestown was indeed built by August, 1607. Also in the mouth of the St Lawrence feeble attempts were being made to use the islands. But the Separatists had not time to inquire and negotiate, nor capital to equip an expedition. The France that had expelled or massacred the Huguenots was far too dangerous. The United Netherlands however had so far secured their independence that negotiations were proceeding with Spain for a peace or a truce, and they were so promising that in June, 1608, a treaty was concluded between them and England for a defensive alliance, conditional on the peace with Spain. As moreover the house of Orange had brought about a religious truce, so that all communions might exist and worship, Holland was clearly a place fitting on many scores. Even its physical configuration would attract the dwellers in and near the Isle of Axholme, soon to be reclaimed by Dutch engineers.

There was also one reason personal to Smyth, which should attract him to Amsterdam. His former tutor, Francis Johnson, was there, at the head of a Separatist church composed mostly of Londoners; and at the Coventry conference Smyth had expressed his intention of going to see him, though his motives were not clearly understood by Bernard. It was obviously fitting that two churches which had independently been driven to the pitch of separation, should become more closely acquainted.

There were some curious legal points which doubtless Helwys would consider. Magna Carta expressly allowed emigration, and the custom was for emigrants to obtain formal leave, in a written pass. The famous Conventicle Act of Elizabeth in 1593, provided that a man who obstinately refused to frequent his parish church, might be brought before a justice and compelled to abjure the realm, going straight to a port specified by the magistrate, and proceeding into permanent exile. It was under this law that Johnson had been transported to the Gulf of St Lawrence; it had been enacted afresh in 1604, and a curious book printed, apparently at Amsterdam, in 1611 with the title, *Mr Henry Barrowes Platform*, gives an anecdote of four people who after three months in prison for separatism, were fined, obliged to take the oath, and ordered to begone within a month. Now Helwys might well argue that he might claim to emigrate as a right, though doubtless it had been threatened as a penalty. And he certainly set himself to organize a general exodus. Among their members was a ship-master, Gainsborough was a sea-port, and the matter seemed to present no serious difficulty. No secret was made of the matter; Joseph Hall heard both at Middelburg and in England that a harbinger had been over to Zeeland planning for the removal to Amsterdam; the authorities therefore must have been as well informed.

But attempts to realize property and take coin out of the realm were in the teeth of all accepted doctrines of political economy. And it was felt in at least some quarters that the law was never meant to encourage such an emigration as this bid fair to be. The accepted methods of England and France were, to drive away the religious leaders of dissent, but retain the people and coerce or persuade them into uniformity. To let them go forth in triumph with their silver and gold, lusty young men, hardly one feeble person among their tribes, might ruin the country if it were allowed to pass, and might be taken as a precedent.

And so at the last, proceedings were hurried. Henry Cullandt had his banns of marriage with Margaret Grymsdiche published in the parish church of Sutton-cum-Lound, by Richard Clifton, deprived of his own living, and assisting James Brewster the vicar; but word came that they must all start at once, and the marriage must wait. Only in Amsterdam was the wedding carried out, on 5 July, 1608, and within a few weeks not only did Clifton follow, but other weddings of the emigrants were registered. The alarm once given, every difficulty was thrown in the way of those who had dallied and were not ready to pass over at once, and some of their adventures are told by William Bradford; but it is evident that one large company did arrive in a few weeks, and that Helwys was acknowledged as the promoter and capable organizer of the expedition. Smyth however seems to have been in charge of one band, for in his last book he distinguished between the company of Helwys and that company of English people that came over with himself; though his language may possibly refer to the state of affairs in 1611. Outward adventure never seemed important to Smyth, who was more intent on spiritual development. This proceeded apace in the new home, and it proved that most of the emigrants had, in fact if not in law, abjured the realm for life, and had entered on a new phase of the inner life.

Churches, Church Worship, Church Government, 1608

"In Amsterdam the people are like rooks, living on the tops of trees." So said Erasmus of Rotterdam, and it was true that buildings could only be reared when the peat had been consolidated by thousands of piles. When the New Church was contemplated in 1408, six years had to be spent in driving these down, before the building could commence. Thus the city had been laboriously created throughout 350 years since the dam held up the waters of the Amstel. Numerous islands had been reclaimed, and a gridiron of canals provided ample waterways and wharves for ocean-going ships, while foot-bridges linked the narrow streets that faced the water. Landwards there was a rampart, guarded again by a moat, and lest this itself should become a help to an assailant, a palisade along its midst formed a further protection.

Antwerp had been the commercial capital of the world, but the tyranny of Philip of Spain had produced a general revolt of the Netherlands, and a generation before Smyth's arrival at Amsterdam, Antwerp had been so ravaged that it lost its pre-eminence, to which Amsterdam rapidly succeeded. The long war left this almost untouched, and it became a centre of freedom. There was a civic revolution when all friars and leading Catholics were expelled, and henceforward the Calvinists were the dominant party in religion and politics alike.

In learning also it took the lead. By the writings of Coornhert, Dutch was attaining rank as a language; and a brilliant band of dramatists and authors was even now within the city walls. Smyth however did not live long enough to come into touch with them.

Nor did he ever come into close relations with the great merchants. In one way only did he profit by the naval activity of the city, acquiring a home. Ever since the opening out of the East by Spain, the Dutch had been great carriers. The war of independence had diverted their energies to new routes, and they had repeatedly sought a passage round the north of Europe and Asia to the riches of the East Indies. Baulked in this, they sent an armed expedition round the Cape, and forced themselves into the eastern archipelago with such success that a Dutch East Indies Company had lately been incorporated. The trade of victualling the ships for these long voyages was very important, and on the narrow strip of ground between the ramparts and the Amstel where this turns west, one of the characteristic windmills worked to produce flour. A few yards west of this, three gables facing the river marked the great Bakery where Jan Munter made this up into ships' biscuit; the central building was flanked by four minor houses, joined with still smaller rooms, in a way that might have suggested to Smyth the stately chapel of King's College with its four turrets and its many little chantries, were it not for the rows of chimneys that testified to the ovens within. Behind the Bakery proper, a courtyard reached to the ramparts, with outbuildings around.

This characteristic mass of buildings had in it great possibilities for a band of exiles, clinging together in a strange city. There was a central hall where they could all meet, for meals and worship, there were plenty of rooms where the families could settle; it would be college life over again for Smyth. And so, Helwys probably making all the business arrangements, the English band settled in to their strange lodgings.

Of all the outward details of life, Smyth is silent. His writings tell nothing of wife and children, of his homes in England, so it is not surprising if he is equally reticent now. It is from a devoted friend that we learn he continued to act as physician, so disinterested that fees were not sought, and the very cloak he wore was once given to a needy patient.

Smyth was but little interested in the details of outward life; he was a man of thought, and he had soon to take his bearings in the new city of thinkers among whom he lived. Amsterdam was no university, like Cambridge; Leijden and Gröningen were the chief centres of learning; but since it was the chief city in the United Netherlands, there was no lack of cultivated society for one who came with due passports. Though

Dutch was a strange tongue, yet Smyth with his command of Latin would be able to enter promptly into the intellectual life around.

There were four groups of very different character with which it was desirable or necessary to establish relations; the English Separatists including Johnson of Christ's, the English merchants, the local authorities, and their landlord. Each group had a distinct religious flavour, and the discovery of these with consequent readjustments occupied the rest of Smyth's life. Yet one of these may be mentioned only to be explained at once, and then dismissed. The local authorities of Amsterdam were just becoming involved in a great quarrel with the rest of the Netherlands, on grounds at once political and theological. Jacobus Arminius, educated at Leijden and then at Geneva and Basel at the expense of Amsterdam, had become a leading divine in the city, and organized its educational system so splendidly that most boys knew Latin, most girls French. Having been asked to oppose the theological views of Coornhert, akin to those of Baro, he came to adopt them, and the Cambridge controversy was repeated on a greater scale. Arminius was perfectly aware of the succession, and one of his early works was an examination of the lectures of Perkins. A great plague breaking out, and carrying off the famous Junius, professor at Leijden, he was appointed to succeed him, and as the other theological professor was a most extreme Calvinist, the controversy waxed hot, rapidly engrossing attention throughout the Netherlands. Arminius himself sought to restrain it, so his death in 1609 precipitated trouble, in which his disciples claimed full liberty of conscience, and were supported by the province of Holland against the six other provinces headed by Maurice, the great general who had just secured a truce with Spain. Now it might have been expected that Smyth would be drawn into this dispute, but there were other matters which claimed his attention first, and presently he himself originated a discussion practically new to Englishmen. We may therefore neglect the Arminian controversy altogether.

Nor need we attend much to the great colony of

English in the city. The population had rapidly swollen to 130,000 since the fall of Antwerp, and the English merchants had their establishment within which they might govern themselves. They were strongly Puritan, and the chaplains whom they chose were therefore Calvinistic in doctrine and in polity. This indeed was the case at nearly all these "factories" in foreign cities, for no bishop resident in England could have any effective control, and the chaplains could go their own way regardless of Acts of Uniformity and Canons. They were on excellent terms with the Dutch Calvinists, who usually assigned them some church for services in English, returning the compliment paid when the Austin Friary in London was made over for Dutch worship. In Amsterdam however events took a slightly different turn. On the outskirts of the city there had been for two centuries a settlement of nuns, living in a quiet court like the almshouses at Coventry. So numerous had they become that when they needed a chapel of their own, it had to be built diagonally within the court to secure room enough. The expulsion of all Catholic priests from the city, and the prohibition of Catholic worship, left this building available, and it was made over for the English.

This was the more necessary, as King James had given leave to the Dutch to recruit regiments in both of his kingdoms. Each regiment had a chaplain, James Douglas for the Scottish, John Paget for the English. Peace being now assured, these troops were naturally withdrawn from the front, and it was desirable to provide for their worship when in garrison. Paget had been minister at Nantwich, but had in 1598 found it advisable to leave, because of his nonconformity. In 1605 he accepted the Confession of Faith of the Dutch Reformed Church. That communion and the civic authorities soon constituted a new congregation, of that communion, whose worship should be in English. "In the yeare of our Lord and Saviour 1607, the third day of the moneth commonly called February about four of the clocke in the afternone is the Church in the Round Bagijnhof opened and in praesens of Mijnheer de Schout and D. Petrus Plancius, minister of the Reformed Dutch

Church in Amstelredamme is the praeching-stoel brought in that same Church and set up for the English-people dwelling at Amstelredamme in Holland." Thus if to-day the Huguenot from France can worship at Bloomsbury in French, according to the liturgy of the Church of England and under her laws, so the Englishman can turn from the crowded Kalverstraat, find massive Bibles of the seventeenth century to read in, and after English worship and sermon will be greeted in the vestry by a British minister and Dutch elders. He will find there among the disused service-books, those which show the many sources whence the worship has been fed; the liturgy of the Netherlands, the psalter of Tate and Brady, the hymns of Joseph Stennett and of Isaac Watts.

There are misconceptions about this congregation in the modern guides, one of which calls it Scotch Presbyterian, another the English Protestant; and even an American Congregationalist with some technical knowledge styles it the English (Episcopal). It is therefore advisable to define it more exactly, in terms approved by its present minister, the Rev. W. Thomson. The records of the church quoted above show that the building was formally opened by the Schout—say Mayor—and a Dutch minister. Thus the State and the Church concurred in constituting the congregation. It was, and is, a congregation in full communion with the Netherlands Reformed Church, accepting its standards, sending its minister and elders to the church courts, governed by its laws. That communion had taken shape in 1569 at Emden and in 1572 at Dort; a more famous Synod met at Dort in 1618 to settle the Arminian question, when the comity of the Churches of England and Scotland was evinced by James sending dignitaries of both, including Joseph Hall; but whatever definitions of doctrine have taken place, or variations of government, the congregation in the Bagijnhof was the creation of, and remains an inseparable part of, the Dutch Church. The first article in the General Regulations of that communion reads: De Nederlandsche Hervormde Kerk bestaat uit al de Hervormde Gemeenten in het Koninkrijk der Nederlanden,

Waalsche, Presbyteriaansh-Engelsche en Schotsche, soo wel als Nederduitsche.

In the State Papers, Domestic, of the reign of Charles I, vol. 310, document 103 is concerned with the status of the 17 English ministers in the Netherlands, and reports that Her Majesty Queen Elizabeth by an act under her hand and Seal yielded to the States, that her own subjects in this land should not use the forms and discipline of the Church [of England], but only conform themselves to the Dutch Church. And this is very true that such a Grant was made and is now to be seen. Some of the preachers desired a separate English Classis, and did obtain it in the year 1621. Of those opposed to the Classis some are of the Dutch, some of none. Paget [of Amsterdam and four others] are of the Dutch.

Thus it will be seen that this congregation is neither Scotch nor English, though it worships in the language common to both, and like the sister congregations at Middelburg, Flushing and Rotterdam, retains some British usages.

Had Smyth come over six years earlier, he would have been at home here, and his name might have headed the roll of ministers, instead of figuring on another wall half a mile away. But he had devoted much time to thinking out the nature of a church, and having decided to follow the New Testament alone, was no longer inclined to accept any system in which the exigencies of state had induced a compromise. Thus there is no trace of any intercourse between him and Paget, and it says something for the grace of both that they went quietly on their different paths without quarrel. Social meetings there may have been between the immigrants from Nottingham and Lincoln, and the English settlers from other quarters who centred here, but they have left no sign yet discovered.

Very different was the case with the Separatists who abounded in the city, and these we may attend to in more detail. One group of these had been ministered to by Henoch Clapham, ordained by Wickham, minister in Lancashire at first; he however had conformed again, and his adherents here had apparently joined a second group. This was chiefly of Londoners, originally under Barrowe and Greenwood; since their execution, most of the members had come to Amsterdam, where they had completed their elaborate organization on the five-fold pattern, with Francis Johnson of Christ's and Henry Ainsworth of Caius at their head. A third group came from the district of Bradford-on-Avon, Westbury, Warminster; and among them was Thomas White, another clergyman who after a time returned to conformity. A fourth group was connected with Norwich.

The arrival of the Nottingham-Lincoln immigrants produced some rearrangement. The "Ancient Church" of 1596 had subscribed and bought land, on which two brethren and a widow erected, in 1607, a composite building, part meeting-house, part rooms for lodging, used by some of the members. In these premises, this church formed the natural nucleus to which many would attach themselves when bereft of other leaders. And Clifton, with many others, gravitated to this community.

It has indeed been supposed that they all joined, Smyth included, and as the conjecture has been repeated from book to book, and has only been refuted once, by Dr Dexter, it is well to be explicit here. He had already arrived at conclusions as to the nature of a church which were not those reached and practised by Ainsworth and Johnson; it would be hard for one who had set forth his principles and inferences as to bishops and deacons as on pages 258, 259, to bow to the different system in vogue down the Brownists' Alley. He had queried whether the church might suffer her officers to be translated from herself to other churches upon any ground whatever, page 264; was it possible for him to lay down the office of pastor of the Church at Gainsborough, and become member or officer of the Ancient Church? He was charged with many changes, both of opinion and of church fellowship; but it was never asserted by any contemporary that he had changed his opinion as to the officers, and then had changed back again. Nor is there any statement that the two churches had fused into one. Ainsworth said in 1608 (*Counterpoyson*, 41) that Smyth never was an officer, much less a pillar, in the Ancient Church:

and no one has ever suggested that he was a mere member without office, after having been ordained pastor at Gainsborough, even when his later proceedings as to disbanding did receive close scrutiny. Therefore we conclude that what was formerly the Church at Gainsborough continued a separate body, known now as the Second English Church at Amsterdam. These two Churches of the Separation were not organized on exactly the same pattern, and their customs were different in many respects, for they had originated quite independently. But being now side by side in the same city, and being ignored as mere sects by the magistrates and ministers, even by the English congregation under Paget, junior to the Ancient Church, they naturally lived on sisterly terms. Clifton indeed passed into that church, and writing to Smyth in 1610 said (*Plea for Infants***): "To the Elders and brethren were you most welcome, and glad they were of you, so long as you walked in the fayth with them."

But while some of Smyth's friends did join the Ainsworth-Johnson or Ancient Church, and most continued their separate existence as the Second Church, a score or more joined a third church, and about February, 1609, applied to the burgomasters of Leijden for leave to come and settle. They were headed by John Robinson; but the precise time when this group organized, when Robinson was appointed pastor, and if he were ordained by them, seem not to have been discussed seriously even by those who have spent much time on the Pilgrim Fathers. Paget a few years later (*Arrow against the Separation*, 58) when arguing on a kindred point against Ainsworth, states as a fact that "Robinson and his companie... gathered a new Church apart from you in the same citie, you being here a Church before them." This statement was allowed to go by default, and thus we may put down the organization of the Pilgrim Church as distinct from Smyth's church, in the end of 1608 or the beginning of 1609. This is confirmed also by considerations connected with Joseph Hall of Emmanuel, just returning to England after three years as tutor and chaplain at Spa and Frankfort; he sent a letter "To Mr. Smyth and Mr Rob. ringleaders of the late separation at Amsterdam." This letter was written no less than a year and a half before Hall's *Common Apologie*. This was registered on 16 January, 1609–10, therefore the letter must have been written about July, 1608, when Smyth had been only a few weeks in Amsterdam. Hall did not write as if there were then two churches, one under Smyth and one under Robinson. And when the latter replied, he wondered whether Hall imagined they gathered churches by town-rows as in England; the precise point indeed is parochial boundaries, but if the emigrants had already divided, the paragraph would have better run differently.

There is another illusion that needs to be dispelled, as to the relation between Scrooby and Leijden. The diligence of Morton Dexter has analyzed the Leijden records, and his results cover 50 pages of *The England and Holland of the Pilgrims*. Out of 137 members whose counties can be traced, only 17 belong to the Gainsborough district, while 32 come from Norfolk and 59 from Essex, London and Kent. This shows that the idea of the Pilgrim Fathers and their Leijden friends being the descendant of the Scrooby circle is very wide of the mark; it was probably due to Bradford the historian himself belonging to that minor contingent. But dull arithmetic shows that most of the Yorkshire-Lincolnshire-Nottingham group remained with their leader, Smyth. Also that the nucleus of the new church was naturally a group from Norfolk where Robinson had ministered. What the Pilgrims derived from the north was their covenant; and its progressive character, the one thing that makes it memorable, is due to Smyth. The method of organizing this third church has been preserved to us by John Murton, who wrote in his *Description*, about Robinson: "Do we not know the beginnings of his Church? that there was first one stood vp and made a couenant, and then another, and these two ioyned together, and so a third, and these became a Church," etc.

Thus the third church was not constituted by any action of Smyth's church, still less of the Ancient Church;

it churched itself. This act of spontaneous generation was accepted as normal in Separatist circles, and the theory underlying it was soon applied more trenchantly, to the matter of baptism. There was however another topic which excited discussion about the same time, and fortunately the two debates were conducted separately. We attend first to the conduct of public worship.

The Church of England was tied down to uniformity in public worship, whereas before the Reformation there had been various diocesan Uses. A book of Common Prayer had been compiled in 1549, varied in 1552, augmented in 1559 and again in 1604: but from the current edition no departure was permitted. Books of Homilies had been put out under Edward and Elizabeth, and no minister might preach anything else without licence from the bishop, as Smyth had good reason to know. Articles of religion had been drawn up, varied, and imposed on all the clergy. While several versions of the scripture were available, the Authorized Version of Henry VIII was admittedly obsolete, the Bishops' Version was only authorized by the bishops of the southern convocation, and was not generally used: James was now intending to displace the popular Genevan Version by a new Authorized Version, and bestow a monopoly upon it, however good or bad it might turn out to be. For singing, the pioneer hymns of Coverdale had long been supplanted by the Metrical Psalms of Sternhold and Hopkins; and these with their tunes were usually bound with the Bible. But for public reading, a table of lessons had been drawn up, which deprived the minister of nearly all discretion, and bound him to a limited selection.

Against this authorized library and compulsory uniformity there were many protests. Robinson at this very time was replying to Hall (*Works*, 1851, Vol. III. pages 411, 412, 418): "What is the adoring of your truly human, though called 'Divine,' service-book, in and by which you worship God, as the Papists do by their images?... Might not the Lord now be also purely and perfectly worshipped, though this printed image, with the painted and carved images, were sent back to Rome; yea, or cast into hell, from whence both they and it came?... The Word of God is perfect, and admitteth of none addition. Cursed be he that addeth to the Word of the Lord.... The daily sacrifice of the service-book, which, instead of spiritual prayer sweet as incense, you offer up, morning and evening, smells so strong of the Pope's portuise [breviary] as it makes many hundreds, amongst yourselves, stop their noses at it."

Smyth went one step further in this direction. All his friends had long chafed at the limitation to these printed books, the Separatists had cast off their bondage generally. He now asked whether a printed English version of the whole Bible was any more infallible than a printed English metrical version of the Psalms, or a printed English prose version of the Psalms made earlier than the others; all three of which were used in the Church of England daily. In face of the fact that a new version was actually being made, from which all notes were to be kept out, unlike the Genevan, but like the Henrician Authorized Version, it was clear that even in Scripture, as popularly understood, there had been a very human element, to which objection had been taken from many sides. Smyth saw that this was inherent not only in notes, but in the translation itself. Even where there were no theological prepossessions to warp the translators, it was perfectly possible to render very differently. Thus Matthews' Bible rendered Isaiah xxi. 7: "He sawe two horsemen; the one ryding upon an asse, the other upon a camell. And the lyon cryed: Lorde I have stande wytynge all the whole daye, and have kept my watche all the nyght." The Bishops' Bible rendered: "And he sawe a charret which two horsemen sat upon, with the cariage of an asse, and the cariage of a camel: So he looked, and took diligent heede. And he cryed, a lion, my lorde, I stande continually uppon the watche towre in the day time, and am appoynted to keepe my watch every night." Now what would happen in passages which were debated between Geneva and Rome may be guessed; the Genevan version of 1560 and the Rheims of 1582, recently revised at Antwerp in 1600, are now little known as they lay before Smyth; but in notes and in text alike they were very human, and very different.

In the minute discussion that arose, it is curious for us, who know that the version ordered by James has attained a commanding position, to observe that Smyth was utterly unconscious anything particular was going on, although he must have known well eight or nine of the Revisers, including Chaderton, Clerke, Ward. There is not any allusion to a new version being actually in the press. Smyth was intent on one point only, the proper use to be made of any version.

Negatively, he objected to any book at all being used in the actual worship, and translations shared in the general ban. But he was quite willing that they should be used as a preparation for worship. King Henry had ordered that in every parish church there should be placed a large Bible, which people might read at any time of day. A familiar picture shows us a young man reading aloud in a cathedral from a Bible chained to a pillar, while people throng around to listen to the scriptures. How better could souls be attuned to praise God? Smyth therefore was quite willing they should be read, should be read publicly, should be read on Sunday immediately before public worship; but he declined to apply the term Worship to that reading. The point was fine, and it is no wonder that it was misunderstood, but the letter of the Bromheads quoted above is explicit as to the fact that they did read from printed Bibles but laid them aside before the sermon. Smyth said that the Worship technically began after the books were laid aside, but the Bromheads did not grasp his point, and instinctively included the reading in the worship.

Unfortunately this difference, little more than verbal, was magnified. Smyth actually put in writing a request to the Ancient Church: "We desired that [translations] might be refreined for our sakes, that we might keep communion." This was naturally refused, Smyth made it a grievance that the Ancient Church would not follow his practice and nomenclature, and broke off communion between the two churches. The pretext seems as trivial as those which severed the churches of Constantinople and Rome; but once the members of one church were excluded from the table of the Lord at the other, other

Biography

differences were found and invented, in the seventeenth century as in the ninth. The result was that Smyth published a pamphlet on the *Differences of the Churches*, to which Ainsworth replied with a *Defence of the Scriptures*. The point had been raised at the Council of Trent, where alarm had been taken at the appearance of many new versions of the scripture, some with the approbation of the Church, and more without. It had been decided to leave Hebrew and Greek to scholars, and to prepare one standard edition of the ancient Latin Vulgate, which should be accepted as authentic for all public readings, debates, preaching and exposition. This edition had assumed its final form in 1598, after episodes and discussions which showed afresh the very human element in any translation: a book had appeared in 1600 dwelling on this very point, and may have influenced Smyth.

Mr Burgess has pointed out that Smyth's pleas did bear fruit in two quarters, New England and the General Baptists. The Pilgrims from Leijden had read this book, and their customs influenced the Puritans who went direct to Massachusetts. The Bible was read and expounded, at home or at church; but bare reading in meeting-house without note or comment was eschewed. It has generally escaped notice that the old General Baptists, lineally descended from this Amsterdam congregation, acted on Smyth's opinion. Grantham, in 1678, published a folio ranging over their doctrine, discipline and customs. Sixteen chapters are devoted to the various acts of worship, and there is no mention of reading the scriptures. This is not because they were disused in other respects. The book opens with an introduction on their divine authority, and closes with an appeal to scripture, while citations abound. In a chapter on family devotion, masters of families are urged to cause the scriptures to be read in their families, and to talk of them at all convenient times. Yet as to reading publicly on Sunday, there is no word. And the Orthodox Confession of the same date in its article 37, Of the Sacred Scripture, insists on authority, and on the need to read in particular places and families, but is silent as to use at public worship. But the Puritan method of running exposition or interpolated comment during public reading, survived among Calvinists in England, and was popularized afresh by Spurgeon.

Whatever was valuable in Smyth's pleas on this point, is recognized in the liberty enjoyed in non-Episcopal churches, of using any version at public worship, and even of varying it from the margin or from the results of study.

But in the discussion, there emerged other differences. Smyth objected to sermons being read, and to psalms being sung from a book. Here his views were accepted more widely, and the habit of reading the first verse of a hymn still testifies to the former method, when a hymnbook was a rare possession, and each verse was dictated, and to the still earlier method when the minister wrote his own hymn and lined it out for singing. All these customs do not compare in importance with other points which were raised.

Smyth held that contributing to church expenses was an act of worship, not to be participated in by outsiders, and to be hallowed by prayer. In theory nearly all agree; and in practice the outcries about "tainted money" show that the principle is being extended even to philanthropic funds.

He raised objection to the staff of officers maintained in the Ancient Church, a staff recommended in the notes to the Genevan Bible, and generally regarded desirable in all Puritan circles. There was general agreement to ignore the archbishops and other officers taken over from the medieval system, and to go to the New Testament. This involved dismissing from mind all officers concerned solely with the relations between one congregation and another: the only point involved was what officers a single congregation ought to have. The editors of the Genevan Bible had written notes on Romans xii. 6, and 1 Timothy v. 17, which had been the point of departure for a pattern of church organization well represented at Amsterdam. The Ancient Church had a pastor, Francis Johnson, a teacher, Henry Ainsworth, ruling elders, a deacon, a deaconess. Smyth attacked the idea of three types of Elders, and said there should be but one. And although in Presbyterian communions there is still a distinction between two sorts of elders, both ordained, as well as between them and deacons, yet the simpler plan of two sets of officers, usually styled pastors and deacons, is generally adopted by Baptists and by Congregationalists, and regarded as most akin to Pauline practice.

Still more important was the question as to the relative powers of Church and officers. By the practice of centuries, the laity had no voice in church affairs. Against this, Robert Browne had raised his voice, and in Separatist circles it was admitted that all members might take part. The precise relation was discussed by Barrowe, with an oligarchic bias, and now in Amsterdam Johnson and Ainsworth were yielding to his arguments, in differing degrees, but with the natural instinct of officers to magnify their office. Smyth had spoken clearly enough before leaving England as to the power of the church, page 388; he now lifted the banner of democracy, and challenged the claims of officialdom, page 326: "Whether the Eldership hath a negative voice in the Church so that nothing can be concluded without them? Whether if most of the Church consent and the Elders dissent, the matter cannot pass against the Elders dissent? Whether, seeing the Church may depose and excommunicate the Eldership, they may not pass other sentences without or contrary to their liking? Whether may not a man propound his matter to the Church without acquainting the Elders with it in the first place?" Thus a clear lead was given, which has been generally followed in Baptist and Congregational churches.

In his positive teaching, page 315, three points deserve notice. His university training biassed him to assert that the elders were to "moderate" in all matters of government. The wrangling methods of the schools were assumed as normal in a church meeting: this idea has sometimes been adopted as thoughtlessly, with no advantage to the "causses of the Kingdom." Smyth further taught expressly that churches without officers, are yet fully competent to transact all business: this was not held by the remnant of the Ancient Church in

London, or by the portion of the Leijden church that migrated to New England; but it is in accordance with this principle that Smyth in another connection felt no hesitation in baptizing himself. A final corollary was destined to be applied by others, not in the sphere of church government, but in that of politics: the church has powers which the officers have not, can resume its full powers, can depose its officers for just cause. Here we have the enunciation of those theocratic ideas which Borgeaud has shown gave rise to the democratic ideas of New England; another interesting parallel would be the election by the New Model Army of Agents from all the regiments, and the constitution of the Army Council. Still more important is it to notice that the publication of constitutions asserting the supremacy of the people over their elected representative, sprang from a circle including Richard Overton, bred in this very church at Amsterdam.

Baptism of Believers, 1609

Smyth came into notoriety at this same time on a very different issue, which has proved of permanent interest. Worship may well vary in its forms from age to age, or as between nation and nation; government of churches will always be influenced not only by the scriptures, but by the methods current in civil life. But to raise the question of the qualification for membership in a church was to quit the temporary for the permanent, to deal with fundamental principles. Separatists agreed that every member must make personal application, and must fulfil certain conditions; Smyth declined to waive these conditions in favour of a member's children, and took a stand so logical, so radical, so scriptural, that he inaugurated a new era. His principles and his practice speedily won adherents, churches gathered on the lines he indicated, and the oldest existing Free Churches of Englishmen are those which are sprung from his teaching. Separatism is older, but the Ancient Church followed the example of his own church, and merged into a congregation at Amsterdam; the Pilgrim Church went to New

England, and while it leavened the Puritans who followed, it was content to subside into dependence on the State. Independency in England is younger, and its first church, founded in 1616, after Smyth's death, grew within a generation into seven, of which six had adopted his cardinal principle, and the other soon vanished. Smyth was the founder of the senior Free Church denomination, the Baptist.

The chain of argument was singular. Separatists agreed that the Church of England was antichrist, that a politico-ecclesiastical lord-bishop was the beast. At Gainsborough they had renounced fellowship with antichrist, their leader had renounced his ordination at the hands of the beast. Now they asked, What is the value of confirmation at his hands? What is the value of baptism at the hands of antichrist's servants?

The question had been asked half-a-century earlier, in connection with baptism at the hands of a Catholic priest. The point proved too knotty; Bradford and Bullinger agreed that though Rome was antichrist, yet true baptism had somehow been preserved. Whitgift urged that the character of the priest did not affect the validity of the act. The question was as old as Cyprian, and had been answered by adopting the Roman solution.

Then there was one point about the Beast that had never been cleared up. What was the mark imprinted on the foreheads of his followers? Some Reformers had explained it away as a figure of speech for obedience; Tyndale, Bale and Bradford had declared it to be the tonsure given to all priests, monks and friars. But this was for a limited class; surely there were others sharing in the same dedication. Surely it was the water applied to every child in baptism and the cross signed upon the forehead, that answered to the mark of the beast foretold. It followed not simply that baptism in the Church of England was worthless, but that it was absolutely a dedication to evil, and must be repudiated.

Yet there was one alleviation of this painful discovery. That baptism had not been wilfully or ignorantly sought by anyone, it had been imposed in infancy; it was no sin, only a misfortune. And so attention was drawn away from the minister of baptism to the subject of baptism. And reference to scripture showed no warrant for it to be administered to any except those who confessed their faith and their sins.

Smyth was by no means the first to suspect this. In the Ancient Church the point had arisen, and had called for public comment as early as 1590. Johnson himself testified in 1606 that a little while after 1593 when the church emigrated, "divers of them fell into the heresies of the Anabaptists (which are too common in these countreys) and so persisting were excommunicated by the rest." John Payne in 1597 mentioned the English Anabaptists bred in the Low Countries; and Henoch Clapham the same year had trouble with some in his Separatist Church in Amsterdam. Three years later, Clapham declared that he knew some who blew off their baptism; one baptized himself and then baptized others. The evidence for this has been published frequently and need not be repeated.

Smyth may have met some of these men, though in that case he might have considered consulting with them and accepting baptism at their hands. Once the question was started in his circle, and became a matter of discussion, it is almost impossible that he should not have heard of such a recent occurrence among people excommunicated from the Ancient Church. But whereas their doings and their names have escaped general attention, he was a man who did not hide his light under a bushel, or whom men could afford to ignore. His views were adopted apparently by all his church, and were promptly communicated to other of the English. Clifton was approached by Edward Southworth and Hugh Bromhead, two of the most prominent in Smyth's circle, and agreed at last to read a plain statement of the new position. Smyth promptly sent it, brief enough to be on a half sheet, and stating two propositions; That infants are not to be baptized; That Antichristians (i.e. conventional Christians baptized in infancy) converted are to be admitted into the true church by baptism. Clifton discussed the matter orally with Mrs Ursula Bywater, and on 14 March, 1608–9, returned a brief

Answer to two Anabaptistical Opinions. Before the year ran out on 24 March, Smyth completed a long reply to this and sent it to Clifton, who set to work on an elaborate confutation. Both published, and each pamphlet gathered up the previous stages, so that Smyth's *Character of the Beast* contains the Two Opinions, the Answer, the Reply, with preface; while Clifton's *Plea for Infants* is even more involved. If we find these pamphlets not exactly light reading, we are bound to admire the scrupulous fairness with which each debater cited the opinions of his adversary in the original words, before he proceeded to discuss them. The discussion down to the stage when Smyth published, some time in 1609, led him to one more conclusion of far reaching importance. Clifton's answer reminded him that even while Israel was apostate, circumcision was still held valid for all infants, was not renounced, nor repeated. Hereupon Smyth objected to any analogy from the Old Testament being admitted to combat, vary, or extend any explicit command of Christ and His apostles.

Smyth's logic was keen and rapid, nor did he ever recoil from appropriate action. He and his friends now esteemed themselves simply "Antichristians converted"; their covenanting at Gainsborough was null and void. All united in explicit acknowledgment; pastor and deacons laid down their office, the church disbanded or avowed itself no church, and all stood as private individuals, unbaptized. All being equal, Smyth proposed that Helwys their social leader should baptize them, but he deferred to his spiritual leader. Smyth therefore baptized himself, then baptized Helwys and the others. Thus, and not by the Old Testament ceremony of covenanting, they prepared for a New Testament church of people baptized on profession of their repentance and faith in Christ.

Here was material for fresh canvassing: two questions emerged at once: May a man baptize himself? May any one once baptized however imperfectly be baptized again? But it is necessary to diverge and notice two misconceptions as to fact, started by an English Baptist historian in 1738 and popularized by two others in 1811 and 1818. The one is simple: Did Smyth baptize himself? and the answer may be seen at page 660 of this edition in his own words. The manuscript in his own writing is yet at Amsterdam, with his signature "incoeperint seipsos baptisare"; and if there be a slight ambiguity, his last book discusses whether men "may, being as yet unbaptized, baptize themselves (as we did)." Clearly one of the group baptized himself, and within a year Clifton, Ainsworth, Robinson, I.H., and Gerritsz, all actually in Amsterdam and knowing Smyth, said that he was the man. That point caused a difference of treatment in his case as distinguished from all the others. It is beyond dispute that Smyth baptized himself.

But what did he do? What act did he perform? Here again obstinate incredulity has attempted to transfer the Baptist customs of England and America in the eighteenth century back to Holland in the seventeenth: and a most heated controversy raged in America for a generation before people would be guided by contemporary evidence. This is both clear and ample, and only a few representative statements need be adduced. Joseph Hall challenged Robinson next year: "If your partner M. Smyth should ever perswade you to rebaptize, your fittest gesture (or any other at full age) would be to receive that Sacramentall water, kneeling.... Shew you me where the Apostles baptized in a Basin... as your Anabaptists now doe." (*Common Apologie*, xxxvi, xxxvii).

In the Ancient Church, Johnson "took water and washed the faces of them that were baptized," according to Daniel Buck, one of the members (Strype, *Annals*, IV. 245). Smyth speaks of the "basen of water" used at baptism by Puritans generally, though it was technically illegal, in a way that implies he himself habitually used it; page 568. The very title-page of this publication quotes two texts as to the mark on the forehead, and repeated allusions throughout the book imply the application of water there. Within a short time the whole transaction was closely examined by the Dutch Waterlander church, who reported that they had enquired into the foundation and form of their baptism, and had not found that there was any difference, in the one or the other, between the English and the Dutch (als oock bevraecht t'fondament en de forme van haer doop, en hebben niet bevonden datter enich v[er]schil soe in t'een als int'ander tussche[n] haer e[nde] ons was). Now in 1535 the predecessors of these Waterlanders at Maastricht had been called upon to explain exactly what they did, and one man replied that the baptizer took water out of a small dish, another said that the baptizer baptized him with water upon his head, a third that while he was being baptized he was kneeling down upon his knees (Jos. Habets, *De Wederdoopers Te Maastricht.* Roermond, 1877, pages 136, 144, 152, translated by Whitsitt, *A Question in Baptist History,* Louisville, 1896, page 45). Menno, the reorganizer after 1537, refers to baptism as receiving a handful of water; and J. G. de Hoop Scheffer, professor at the Mennonite college, discussing the introduction of immersion into the Netherlands within a limited circle during 1620 by a Dutchman under Polish influence, makes it clear that the usual method before then was "een handvol water op 't hoofd" (*Doop bij Onderdompeling,* Amsterdam, 1883, page 145).

Thus the uniform custom of Smyth's former friends, the silence of his opponents on the spot as to any strange act, the express statement of the Waterlanders as to the similarity of form, make it clear that there was no innovation as to the act performed, but that water was applied to the forehead. We may now return to see what a commotion was actually caused at the time for two other reasons, Renouncing infant baptism and being baptized afresh, Smyth baptizing himself.

Clearly the whole group had become Anabaptists in the usual sense, people who had been baptized again, on the ground that their baptism in infancy was nothing. The Gainsborough church had already excited much criticism in England, page 271, and was being charged with inconstancy. But this latest advance was likely to forfeit all sympathy.

As to a second baptism, Smyth said that if you looked at the act rather than the intention of the act, then John the Baptist, Christ and the Apostles all baptized people who had been baptized repeatedly before; page 655. If you regarded the intention of the act, no one had been baptized on his own profession of faith in infancy, therefore his recent baptism was not Anabaptism. But the sting of the word Anabaptist lay in its recent associations.

Anabaptists had been notorious ever since the tragedy at Münster in 1535. No slander was too absurd to be believed about them, and in the general obloquy the custom whence they were named had shared fully. A second baptism ranked with the marriage of a married man or a priest, an act inherently wrong. So deep was the prejudice that the doctrine had found scarcely any English adherents. Continental Anabaptists had fled over for refuge, and had been vigorously rooted out by Catholics and Protestants alike. If here and there a stray Englishman had adopted the same view, and acted on it, nothing had been published to explain, no propaganda had attracted any notice. Smyth himself had quite recently written of Anabaptists with horror, and now had to defend his change of view, which he did very vigorously in his reply to Clifton. It was the first exposition by an Englishman, and it called forth general condemnation by his fellow-countrymen.

One of these was on the spot soon after, and talked over the whole matter with some of Smyth's friends, who invited him to write out his views. This he did, and published in 1610 a readable book, free from syllogisms and irritating personalities, under the title *A Description of the Church of Christ with her peculiar privileges*. He gave only his initials, I.H., and we are indebted to Mr Champlin Burrage for identifying him with John Hetherington or Etherington, who besides helping in a second pamphlet of 1623 with the name of Jessop, published in 1644 with the initials I.E. a third pamphlet against Anabaptists, and who was otherwise interested in prophetic and sectarian movements.

Hetherington could quite appreciate logic, and agreed with Smyth in many respects. Thus he told the Reformists who lingered in the Established Church that they simply talked while Smyth acted: "And therefore you must of necessity, either ioyne with them, or change your minds, or else hide your selues for shame." This trident had been evaded by Clapham with the thought that if baptism in the Church of England were useless, "we must be all unbaptised till some other John Baptist or Christ himself come down again to begin and lay the foundation anew, except it be lawful for every man to baptise and then I see not why others before us as well as now did not well enough baptise."

Underlying all such arguments was the idea lingering that baptism really effected something. The Catholic Church did teach, in harmony with the opinion of even the second century, that baptism is the essential means established for washing away the stain of original sin: the Church of England agreed, spoke of the baptized infant as regenerate, taught children that in their baptism they were made members of Christ, children of God, and inheritors of the kingdom of heaven. With such beliefs, it was of course important to be sure that a given ceremony was baptism, and that the person administering was duly qualified. For those who believed that baptism effected no change in the candidate, but was chiefly a public testimony by him to a change previously effected, such questions were of very little importance.

Smyth however did not raise such a radical point. His argument was essentially a parallel which Separatists like Clifton his immediate antagonist would appreciate. If ordination in the Church of England was a mere nothing because that Church was constituted on a false, nay Antichristian, basis; then baptism in the Church of England was equally nothing.

Joseph Hall thoroughly agreed with the force of the argument and used it to draw back any waverers into the official fold. To Robinson he addressed himself publicly next year: "Either you must go forward to Anabaptism, or come back to us. All your Rabbins cannot answer that charge of your re-baptized brother: if we be a true church you must return, if we be not (as a false church is no church of God) you must re-baptize. If our baptism is good then is our constitution good." These arguments have seldom been stated more clearly, or improved in any way for three centuries since.

But there was one point involved which drew even

more attention at the time; the fact that Smyth baptized himself. This was a part of the general question, What is the qualification to baptize? The Catholic Church had been driven, by its assertion that baptism was necessary to salvation, to widen beyond priests to laymen, beyond men to women, beyond Christians proper to heretics. A discussion between Whitgift and Cartwright showed that the Puritans strongly preferred drawing the line at ministers; and James at Hampton Court had agreed so far as to exclude women. But no one had seriously discussed the question whether an unbaptized person might baptize—and self-baptism was but a particular case of this. At the time, Smyth felt no compunction on the point. If he knew how Clapham had written, he might brush aside his difficulty with the thought that no new and special commission was needed, as the Familists thought, while there stood the general commission, Go and baptize all nations, accompanied by the promise, "Lo I am with you alway, vntill the end of the world." But in considering Clifton's paragraph as to a warrant for baptism, he thought the point unworthy of answer; page 658.

To Clifton's criticism of his self-baptism, he replied that it was as sensible for a man to baptize himself as to administer the Lord's Supper to himself, which was enjoined in the Prayer-Book in harmony with unbroken custom. He referred also to the Old Testament orders that a man who was unclean should wash himself, that a priest about to sacrifice washed himself, this being even mentioned as a type of baptism.

He found however that this self-baptism was challenged on many sides, and the remark that produced some effect was that of Hetherington: "It was wonder that you would not receive your baptisme first from some one of the Elders of the Dutch Anabaptists." The suggestion was obvious; the Waterlanders might be in error on many points, but at least enquiry might have been made, so as to avoid what was certainly a novelty. Hetherington probably pointed out this alternative in the oral discussion, months before he printed; certainly Smyth soon turned his serious attention to these Dutch dissenters. Hitherto he had naturally been in touch with his own countrymen, but henceforward he turned to cultivate his neighbours. Of them he knew as yet about as much as a modern chaplain in Amsterdam cares to know, or as a minister of the American church in Petrograd knows of some Raskolnik sect.

Yet his ministry to his fellow-citizens was in truth but begun. Clifton found that he must reply, because Smyth's book was sent over to England and was spread abroad into the hands of many. It is no surprise when a few years later there emerge to light not only two churches in London, offshoots of his in Amsterdam, but four churches which were based on the principles he expounded; one at Lincoln itself, one at Coventry, where he had already defended his views, two at Salisbury and Tiverton, which had sent emigrants to Amsterdam. The book is very rare to-day, but before it fell on sleep, it served its own generation.

The year 1609 was crowded with events for Smyth. Not the least onerous of his toils must have been the writing and printing of his two largest works. His correspondence of 1607 with Suffolk, with A.S., and with Bernard, was prepared for the press; and Bernard's printed reply was being considered paragraph by paragraph. Smyth's letter of 1607 was however chosen to determine the form, and his new work of 1609 was ranged as parallel to his earlier writing. The intricacy was complicated by the fact that Ainsworth of the Ancient Church had already replied to Bernard's book, and Smyth felt it courteous to acknowledge this, as well as necessary to indicate some few differences. Commenting on one of these, the ruling power of the Elders, Smyth invited Ainsworth to expound his view "for the satisfaction of the brethren of the Seperation"; page 440. Now these were almost negligible outside Amsterdam, and it seems to follow that Smyth's church had already ceased to be Separatist, and had become Anabaptist, when he corrected the proofs.

Further, the main reply to Bernard, at page 457, while not diverging to new points, specifies that "baptisme be administered simply as Christ teacheth without

Godfathers, the crosse, questions to infants"; and that "a baptized person, must baptize into the true Faith of Christ, a person capable of baptisme"; page 475. These passages, which do not read like insertions at a late stage, but as if part of the book when penned, show that the writing was done when Smyth was already convinced on three points, the nullity of infant baptism, the necessity of asking for baptism, the baptizer being himself baptized. Thus while this lengthy book keeps clear of all discussion on these points, it was prepared for press when Smyth already regretted that he had baptized himself. It is remarkable that on page 385 he left a sentence implying that Anabaptists were not Saints; apparently he was still not acquainted well with the Mennonites; for if he had taken the ground that as infant baptism was nothing, believers' baptism was not anabaptism, then it would be hard to say where any Anabaptists were to be found.

It is in the light of this situation that we see how the subject of Succession, discussed from page 396 to 416, was so interesting him. As the question had been put by Hetherington, Why did you not go to the Mennonites for baptism? he would have to attend closely to what would be involved in such a proceeding. And we note the incidental acknowledgment on page 356 that the new church was not constituted by covenant, as the church at Gainsborough had been.

Another point emerges, that Occasional Conformity was already discussed and practised; page 371. Church Papists there had long been, but now there were some who from the Puritan standpoint refused communion as a rule, yet felt free to listen to sermons, and even occasionally to communicate. Smyth testified against this half-way method, and repudiated fellowship with its votaries. Only seven years were to elapse before Henry Jacob, promoter of the Millenary Petition, consulted with other Reformists who stayed in the Establishment, and with their approval formed a church on a mediating basis; more than that, he persuaded Robinson to recede from Smyth's extreme position, and to write not only his letter of 1624 acknowledging Jacob's church, but a treatise on the lawfulness of hearing ministers of the Church of England.

The two books must have been passing through the press at the same time, for his opponents complained that they could not keep pace with him, the *Character* coming close on the heels of the *Paralleles*. Yet from page 570 we learn that another manuscript was already complete, on the covenants and circumcision; this would naturally expound his views on the true relation of the Old Covenant and the New. It is unfortunate that this has been lost, unless he gave it a new title and we are to recognize it at page 710.

NEGOTIATIONS WITH THE MENNONITES

The research of many historians has resulted in exploding many wild tales about the continental Anabaptists, and producing such sane accounts as Americans read in the pages of Newman, and Britons in those of Lindsay. The latter traces them back to communities of pious Christians who lived quiet God-fearing lives, and believed all the articles in the Apostles' Creed, but who were strongly anti-clerical. Before the end of the fourteenth century they were known to the Inquisitors; desiring service in the vernacular, they met in their own houses to read and comment on the scriptures; they were most practical in their charities, maintaining schools and leper-hospitals; in doctrine they repudiated baptismal regeneration. The invention of printing was a great boon, and they devoted themselves to promoting a catechism and versions of the Bible in French, German, Bohemian, and perhaps Italian, all of which were in wide circulation before Luther was born.

When in 1524 north Germany was convulsed by the Peasants' War, and Zwingli was consummating his reformation at Zurich, a conference of these Praying Circles met at Waldshut, resolved on overt separation from the Medieval Church, drew up a directory for living, and a confession of faith. In 1527 a General Synod met at Augsburg and completed the organization, which was subsequently imitated closely by Presbyterians, the only difference being that the Brethren retained bishops, elected by and from the pastors. Their fundamental idea was that they were called to reproduce the beliefs and practices of the earliest days: it followed for them all, that a State Church was absurd, that a real church was composed of believers only, that infant baptism was inconsistent with true Christianity.

The movement soon was obvious all over Central Europe, from Poland and Hungary, throughout modern Germany, Holland, Belgium, Switzerland, North Italy and Austria. On the lower Rhine, much influence was exerted by Hofmann, who discarded the dogma of passive resistance, and broached remarkable theories of millennialism and the body of Christ. Each must be briefly noted.

Persecution was early and fierce, at the hands of Catholics, Lutherans and Reformed. The death-penalty was accepted on all hands as appropriate for Anabaptists. To take a few early examples from the Netherlands. A widow of Monikendam was strangled and burned at the Hague in 1527, three Waterlanders were slowly roasted at Haarlem the same year; in 1530 nine men of Amsterdam were beheaded at the Hague, and their heads returned to be exposed on poles so as to be seen by all ships frequenting Amsterdam; two years later three men from Hazerswoude were roasted at the Hague, the wife of one was drowned at Haarlem, and another was beheaded at Leeuwarden.

Now in 1531 the Zwinglians did not hesitate to go to war with the Catholic cantons of Switzerland; but the great Protest two years earlier had expressly put Anabaptists beyond the pale of toleration. So when Hofmann's teaching that the kingdom of God was about to be established began to take shape, and after Strasburg and Amsterdam had been seen not to be the local centre, but Münster had been identified as the New Jerusalem, it was reckoned a scandal when the Anabaptists there became the majority and installed a Town Council of their way of thinking. Steps were taken to subdue them by force, and then it was esteemed a worse scandal that they followed the Zwinglian example and defended themselves. Distorted tales as to what went on in the besieged city were used to blacken all the brotherhood, and by the time it was reduced, with its last defenders massacred or tortured in cold blood, the name of Anabaptist had become a horror everywhere.

Another conference was therefore called at Buckholt in 1536, when the peace party, led by Obbe Phillips, impressed its views on the whole, and the doctrine of non-resistance became generally adopted. Next year Menno Simons accepted the office of bishop of the Brethren in Gröningen, and soon was the most prominent literary champion of the body. "As regards oaths, magistracy, warfare, and capital punishment, he was in agreement with the evangelical parties of the Middle Ages and with the great majority of the Antipedobaptists." But while vigorously opposing Hofmann's chiliasm and willingness to take the sword, he accepted that teacher's view of the incarnation: this was that the human nature of Christ was not derived through Mary, but was a direct divine creation; that even His body passed through her as water through a pipe. This doketic view he advocated as though it were of the first importance, and it rapidly created a new scandal among theologians: indeed in England the bishops usually tested immigrants and suspects by this tenet. Despite this aberration, it would seem that his success was great, and till 1553 the Mennonites were far the most numerous and influential of the evangelicals in the Netherlands.

Then two factors weakened them, the rigid discipline of Menno, and the rise of Calvin. Menno went to extraordinary lengths in excommunication, and a general European conference of the Anabaptists was called at Strasburg in 1555, which he did not attend. The conference declared that speculation on the incarnation had far outrun the scriptural data, and had become unprofitable; it also sent a deputation to urge on Menno a relaxation of his iron discipline. He responded by defining his position in the *Foundation Book*, his last important work before his death in 1559. Soon the Netherland Anabaptists had separated into four groups, of which the Flemings exaggerated Menno's discipline, the Frisians and Germans were intermediate, while the Waterland churches followed the decisions of Strasburg.

In external affairs, the Netherlanders by 1566 began self-defence against attack, like the Münster Anabaptists a generation earlier. Under great provocation, the Mennonites remained true to non-resistance, so despite their numerical preponderance, they clearly could not take the lead. Followers of Luther, Zwingli and Calvin were all to be found, and when an ecclesiastical conference was called at Emden in 1569, there was a curious compromise. The Mennonite organization was adopted, bishops however being dropped; the civil lines of polity were followed so that however many church-buildings existed, all the church-members in one city formed one church, all the ministers and elders formed one consistory; the supreme court in each province was the synod, and no provision was made for a regular Netherland Assembly. A confession of faith based by Guido de Brès on the French Confession, and the Heidelberg Catechism, were adopted as doctrinal standards. The establishment of universities at Leijden and Franecker consolidated the Calvinist position, and the usual Calvinist intolerance soon appeared. With the help of the Earl of Leicester, they tried to become recognized as the Established Church, with power to put down dissent; though their membership was then only about one tenth of the population. Early in the new century they translated and published a book by Beza justifying the execution of heretics. Newman sums up recent proceedings: "In 1603 a Reformed synod asked the government to restrain the Mennonite bishops from travelling from place to place, preaching and baptizing; in 1604 the government was asked to prohibit the ordaining of young ministers by the Mennonites; in 1605 it was petitioned not to allow them to build any more chapels."

Though thus harassed, they kept their footing, and in Amsterdam they were represented by two groups, one of the rigid Flemings, the other of the liberal Waterlanders. To the latter belonged the landlord of the Bake-House where Smyth's friends lived, and through Jan Munter it was easy to compare views. The Waterlanders had

Biography

been somewhat influenced by thinkers in Poland, where the Anabaptists were very strong, and had powerful protectors. In 1574 a preacher named Schomann put forth at Cracow a confession and catechism which were tinged with new views on the person of Christ, the topic which was so burning among all Mennonites. So in 1580 Hans de Ries and Lubbert Gerritsz, two Waterlander leaders, drew up XL articles of faith backed with an enormous array of proof texts. This was not adopted at any synod, but became known throughout the churches of their group. In the thirty years that had elapsed, the Polish Brethren had been deliberately moulded by Faustus Socinus, an Italian refugee; and his views on the person of Christ had become known in the Netherlands, decidedly leavening the Waterlanders. When however Smyth opened communication with them, and came into touch with Gerritsz and Ries, they naturally referred him to their own confession.

This statement of faith transported Smyth almost back into the Middle Ages. The Mennonites generally had inherited the old-evangelical views held then so widely, and in so far as the Polish influence had been felt, it had carried on the thought of Duns Scotus. They owed scarcely anything to Luther or Calvin, with their revival of Augustine's doctrines, and the persecution by the Calvinists disposed them absolutely to distrust any contribution from that quarter. Yet in thirty years, Ries had altered somewhat, and it is remarkable that he dropped a long article emphasizing that knowledge of Christ after the flesh was of no avail, and that He must be known after the spirit, being formed within: this omission is hardly balanced by a slight toning up of the article on faith, which had at first been defined as a knowledge about God. Then again there had been a very experimental article on Regeneration, which he now suppressed, leaving all the emphasis on Justification.

In church organization, Ries had once spoken of teachers, bishops, deacons; but the version that came to Smyth spoke of elders rather than bishops; in other details the Mennonite system would seem nearer scripture than the Calvinist. A point that was put very clearly was the seat of authority: So much as is needful for us to salvation we find written in the scriptures of the New Testament, to which we join whatever in the canonical books of the Old Testament is consonant with the doctrine of Christ and His apostles. Ries omitted one or two hits at Menno's extravagant discipline, and even in his 1580 edition had neglected chiliasm. On the sacraments Smyth would find general agreement.

The points which would at a glance surprise one bred in a Calvinist university would be few. The Fall of man was judged to be closely followed by his Restitution so that none of his posterity is born guilty of sin or blame; the ability to accept good when offered, remains in all his posterity. Since God is love, He is unable not to have willed that happiness and salvation should fall to His creatures; He neither predestinated any to be condemned, nor decreed that they should live in sin whereby they would be condemned.

Other points emerged on closer consideration, but while there was much novelty, Smyth gave a general approval, and saw no obvious difficulty in prosecuting enquiries with a view to union. So he and many of his friends signified to Ries and his church that they subscribed to the truth of the articles, desiring however further instruction. On the other hand he supplied to Ries XX articles of the faith held by himself and his friends (page 682). These are not dated, but can hardly be as late as April, 1610. They show an extraordinary departure from Calvin's views: God has ordained all men to life, no one being reprobated; God imposes no necessity of sinning on any one; There is no sin of origin, and therefore infants are sinless; The grace of God is to be offered to all, not in pretence but in good faith; Justification consists partly of inherent righteousness produced by the Spirit; Ministers are bishops and deacons.

This document has by various writers been styled a Personal confession, as though it were peculiar to John Smyth, who signs it. But it is prefaced in the plural: Corde credimus, et ore confitemur. It appears to be the earliest confession by any Baptist church, given to the Dutch in return for the confession drafted by Ries, in order that each party might understand the position of the other.

It deserves attention that the Mennonites and Smyth were approaching these subjects from different quarters. They were descendants of the medieval evangelicals, untouched by Augustinianism; and they might conceivably be affiliated to the Paulicians and other sects which indeed had worked out their theology independently of all councils in the Roman Empire. He had been nourished on the Institutes of Calvin, who came of a different lineage; and at Cambridge the teachings of Baro had been deliberate modifications of that Genevan standard. It was also true that a Netherland theologian, Arminius, had done parallel work, and in Amsterdam there was thus a third influence in the same direction. But there is no reason to think that either Smyth or the Mennonites were directly influenced by the Arminian teachings: they compared notes directly, and on the whole it was he who learned the more and advanced the more to a meeting.

For the articles of Smyth and of Ries were mutually acceptable, and correspondence continued. But just in so far as the way was open for fellowship here, it closed for fellowship with other Englishmen, bred in Calvin's theology and unable to keep pace with Smyth's thought. Indeed, not only did it end all relations with the other Separatists, but it caused a cleavage even in the faithful company who had been baptized at his hands.

The whole company moved along with him so far as to repudiate Calvin, as we have the writings of Helwys and Murton to show: a Latin confession of theirs in XIX articles is quite explicit in denying all original sin and in asserting God's desire for all men to be saved. But the idea of becoming friendly with the Mennonites caused a scrutiny of Hofmann's doctrine of the incarnation, and this raised qualms in some; Smyth ultimately rested in the Strasburg decision not to enquire more closely than was written, as appears in his final confession; but before that he had excited some mistrust. Then it seemed to Helwys that the negotiations with the Mennonites were imperilling another principle hitherto strenuously upheld, and were pandering to the old ideas of Succession. It proved on enquiry that the Mennonites attached great importance to the ordination of officers by elders, with the imposition of hands; where Smyth had insisted on the competence of each church to choose and ordain its own officers. Helwys therefore felt it his painful duty to oppose the movement towards the Mennonites in every way. He and three other men with four or five women quitted Smyth's church, and sent several letters to the Mennonites notifying them and warning them not to accept Smyth. About the same number dropped off also for other reasons, possibly connected with the Hofmann theory, leaving only thirty-two with Smyth. A consideration of these figures, easily verified by comparing the signatures to the extant documents, will show a certain presumption in Helwys styling his little group, Vera Christiana Ecclesia Anglicana, and in his writing again that Smyth and his thirty friends were "cast out from" us ten. We may take his word for it that he excommunicated Smyth, but to the ordinary man the transaction presents itself as a secession of a handful from a larger body, which without bitter words kept on its course.

This course was to apply for union with the Waterlander church under Ries, and a formal request was made, with an acknowledgment of a previous mistake. The precise point of this appears to have been missed: the exact words are, quod inceperint seipsos baptisare, contra ordinem a Christo constitutum. It has been taken for granted that they admitted they were wrong in their baptism; but this is not the case, for the Mennonites accepted it as sufficient, except in the case of Smyth himself, and it could not be said that baptism was contrary to Christ's order. The point was that they made a new beginning. This was what Hetherington had indicated, and this was what they acknowledged. While there was any church within reach where they could have obtained baptism, they ought not to have ignored it and acted independently.

Helwys and his friends sent a letter to Ries, opposing the application, and asking; "For the other question,

Biography cix

that Elders must ordeyne Elders, if this be a true perpetuall rule, then from whence is your Eldership come?" This letter is dated 12 March, 1609, and comparison with the cognate dates, which show not only Clifton and Smyth but some Waterlanders using the Old Style, shows that this is what may be called 12 March, 1609, Old Style, or 22 March, 1610, New Style.

The fusion of two churches is not an ordinary transaction; and when they are of different races and of different origins, there is reasonable cause for care. So Ries and Gerritsz consulted sister churches, saying that they themselves and their church were satisfied, and were ashamed at the long delay after repeated application and interviews. The Leeuwarden church in July strongly dissuaded, declining to accept responsibility, and the matter was allowed to drop.

Thus hostile critics laughed at five different sets of English Anabaptists in Amsterdam. There was a group including Pedder and Martin, once members of the Ancient Church; Smyth's group desiring fusion with the Mennonites; the smaller group with Helwys, desiring no union, and meditating a return to England to witness for their truths; a group with Leonard Busher, charged by Clifton with holding the error about the incarnation of Christ; and John Hancock who had a separation all to himself, to the amusement of Lawne.

Busher was not one of the Lincolnshire emigrants, though an English subject; so he styled himself in a book written during 1613 as an appeal to James and the Parliament. This was printed next year, but is only known by a reprint of 1646. We are not aware whether the Independent editor then varied the text of 1614, but he added the information that Busher was a citizen of London, not making it clear whether that was already true in 1614. The minute researches of the Huguenot Society have brought to light more than a dozen references to Bushers in London, of whom the most conspicuous was Pieter de Busschere. His name in 1617 appears in the registers of the Dutch Church, with those of his wife and daughter; resident at St Swithin's Lane, but born in Flanders, under the sovereignty of the archduke,

h 2

now a merchant trading beyond seas. He can be traced as early as 1600, if not 1583, and as late as 1625, and was denizenated by 1617. Two Leonards appear, neither traceable to Pieter's circle. In 1562 Leonard Busshe, from the dominions of the king of Spain, was denizenated, as is recorded on the Patent Roll that year. It is conceivable, but not proveable, that the Leonard of 1614, who was 71 years old in 1642, was a descendant; if so, as a son of a denizen he would be an English subject. In 1636 on April 23, Leonard Bushen, born beyond seas, was denizenated, provided that he paid the same customs and subsidies as strangers; and this is recorded on the Patent Roll for that year; possibly he was son of the 1614 Leonard. It is somewhat singular that the Leonard who wrote in English during this year, from Holland, is next known as being at Delft in 1642, writing a letter in Dutch to the Mennonites in Amsterdam, then in 1647 as printing an English work, known by a manuscript reply from Toppe of Tiverton. Mr Burrage states that he quitted Holland soon afterwards. His Dutch writing does not conform to modern standards; but the language was not then standardised, and three letters of this period by Ries are very puzzling to his compatriots. It seems therefore unsafe to argue from the quality of Busher's Dutch; when we have his printed books of 1647 and 1614, we shall see whether his English was more up to the mark. In any case he is an interesting link between Mennonites and General Baptists, Dutch and English, the nascent and the established English Baptists.

When we examine his book for any allusion to Smyth, we find only such general references as that the king's subjects believing the apostolic faith, must depart the land to some free country; for to recognize antichrist in the bishops was a common-place. He complained that Robinson would not reply to a writing put into his hands nine months before writing, twelve months before printing, this book; he argued against Johnson; but Smyth is neither named nor glanced at in any way. The book however abounds in references to James burning heretics, as if the fate of Legate and Wightman in 1612 had struck him deeply; and if we are correctly informed as to his

Christological views, he may have had some faint sympathy with theirs.

There is one brief phrase in the 1646 edition of Busher which would be very surprising in 1614; that baptizing meant dipping for dead; the text refers both to 1 Cor. xv. 19 and Rom. vi. 4. There is no evidence that Busher at any stage of his life attempted to practise immersion; and as he and Smyth ignored one another, this solitary phrase has no bearing at all on Smyth's theory or practice. The custom was introduced from Poland by Geesteran at Rijnsburg in 1620 into a different circle, and it attracted attention in England from some early critic of Jessop's *Discovery of the Errors of the English Anabaptists*, 1623, for on page 68 of the copy in the Bodleian is a note including the acknowledgment that the word Baptism signified dipping.

John Hancock again may possibly be the London publisher of 1646, who issued the declaration of faith of the seven Calvinistic Baptist churches; if he in 1609 already held kindred views, we can understand why he had to stand aloof from everybody else.

Smyth and his company were thus isolated from all parties, English and Dutch. They continued their worship at the Bake-House, but also frequented the Waterlander meetings at the Granary. This betokens both a desire to keep the proposal for union in view, and an increasing acquaintance with the language. Smyth still kept his pen busy, stating eighteen reasons against infant baptism, and examining the confession of Ries. But realising how he had become entangled in one controversy after another, he decided to desist.

He therefore set himself to elaborate his views, and cast them into about a hundred articles. He repeated that "Original Sin" is an idle term, there being no such thing as men intend; that all infants under heaven are conceived and born innocent and sinless, and so dying are undoubtedly saved; that all sinners stand in the situation of Adam: that is, he denied the importance and even the existence of hereditary influence.

On predestination he spoke at some length, emphasising the love of God, but admitting that He casts away irrecoverable sinners. He noted, as the Paulicians had done, that the Lord entered on His prophetic ministry at His baptism; was quite clear as to the eternal pre-existence, and silent on Hofmann's theories. He emphasized the new life of the saint rather than the forgiveness of sins. He discriminated the baptisms of John and of Christ. A startling view was that while the scriptures and ordinances of the church were needed to lead to repentance, yet the regenerate man needs them not, having three witnesses within. Faith was still defined as a knowledge and assurance; the idea of its being trust being nowhere hinted at. The charitable view was expressed that all repentant believers are brethren in the communion of the outward church. It was expressly denied that the sacraments conferred or conveyed grace; they had the same use as the word, to teach; hence the corollary that they were not for infants. A curious touch was added to the duties of deacons, that they were to wash the feet of the saints; this was apparently due to the Mennonites, and it is an instance of Smyth's literary influence that the General Baptists adopted the practice. Succession was explicitly denied. Magistracy was commended as permitted by God, but not to believers, nor as extending to power over the conscience; believers were bidden compose their differences among themselves. Marriage was to be among believers only, and children to be trained and provided for: here again the General Baptists followed closely.

This lengthy confession shows that Smyth was true to his profession of willingness to learn: he had compared with the Mennonites, and while opposing some of their dogmas and passing by others, he modified some of his views very considerably, and to a large extent carried with him most of his fellow-emigrants.

Helwys was now entering the field of authorship on his own account, and did not refrain from one or two ungenerous allusions. Smyth therefore took up the pen once more, perhaps with a recollection of Augustine, to withdraw some of his earlier views, explain where others were misconceived, and restate a few more. With this last book, the university scholar is lost in the man;

logic disappears, and the heart speaks. Even as regards facts of the outer life, more is learned here than in all his other works; and here first we understand something of the charm he exerted in intercourse.

It was a swan-song, and unfinished. Residence in the fens of Cambridge and Lincoln had caused him to suffer from consumption, and the change to the Low Countries caused no improvement. The time came when he could spare not only his cloak to make clothes for one slenderly apparelled, but could have spared his coat also. Seven weeks he lingered, declining all debate, teaching his children, comforting his wife, cheering the brethren, "examining his life, confessing his sins, praying for patience, having always confidence in the mercy and favour of the Lord towards him in the end." He passed away triumphantly with the testimony, "I praise the Lord, He hath now holpen me, and hath taken away my sins."

On the first of September, 1612, his body was laid in the Niewe Kerke. That was burned down and rebuilt; the Bake-House has long since vanished, and no contemporary memorial remains. But the pilgrim who passes down the east side of the Kloveniers Burgwal and crosses the Binnen Amstel will see on his left facing the river, the site where John Smyth lived and died; he may amuse himself with the fancy that the Jan Smit whose bake-house stands there now, has the blood of the pioneer in his veins.

The leadership of the little band apparently devolved on Hugh Bromhead. Helwys and his friends returned to England, defining their position in four pamphlets, their Confession being distinctly moulded upon the Latin Articles accepted by Smyth's church. The other emigrants from the Gainsborough district had either joined the Ancient Church in Amsterdam, or had passed on to Leijden, where the new pastor, John Robinson, was taking a firm stand against Anabaptism and for Calvinism. The Ancient Church had yielded one or two adherents, such as Canadyne. The bomb discharged by Lawne was exploding it into fragments, some might be attracted into this orbit.

A bid for further support was made by Thomas Pigott of Axholme, who found a new publisher willing to put out Smyth's last book with his hundred Propositions; he added a few pages as to Smyth's last days, and prefixed an epistle to the reader. The little tract, wretchedly edited, is good evidence of Smyth's statement that he was too poor to publish any more, while it is also a striking testimony to the love he inspired; the closing words of the brethren who were eye and ear witnesses were: "His life and death being both correspondent to his doctrine, it is a great means both to comfort us, and to confirm us in the truth."

No fresh accessions came to the faithful band in the Bake-House, while John Robinson made an onslaught on Smyth's theology, showing that there was little hope of any further gain from England or Englishmen. Towards the end of 1614 they therefore requested the Mennonites to resume considering the application for membership. It would appear that the papers of 1610 were re-examined and brought up to date. From the signatures to the confession of Ries, fourteen names were crossed out, including Smyth's; and evidently others were added, for Mr Burgess points out that Dorethie Thomson, whose name stands last but one, was only married on 14 July, 1612, and her maiden name Dorothy Struth had not appeared on these documents. Then whereas in 1610 XX Latin articles had expressed the views of the church, the hundred English articles had since been published. It is in this connection that we interpret the fact of two manuscript versions of these into Dutch—remarkable Dutch, says Prof. Müller—being filed in the Mennonite library. There are a few variations from the English which show further attention to, and accordance with, the Mennonite beliefs, as if pains were being taken to arrive at harmony.

Four English could not accept all the Mennonite views, but after negotiation they sacrificed themselves and urged that the rest should not be held back. This was accepted as best, and agreement was reached. There were a few new-comers, Swithin Grindal of Tunstall having joined his parents, Solomon Thomson having sent for his father; these with two others were baptized, the baptism of the main company by Smyth was tacitly accepted, and on 21 January, 1615, all were admitted members of the Waterlander church.

For a time worship was maintained in the two buildings for the two groups, Dutch and English; Thomas Pigott was leader at the Bake-House till his death in 1639, and Joseph Drew followed till he died three years later. But the new generation naturally learned Dutch and acquired Dutch names, so that while in 1624 some correspondence was signed on behalf of "the Dutch and English churches," there seems to have been complete fusion twenty years later. Indeed there was a further sinking of differences, and amalgamation with the Fleming church which had worshipped on the N. Z. Achterburgwal under Abram Dirks, to whom Busher appealed in 1642. And when on the Consistory Wall of a new building on the Singel, the piety of a later generation inscribed the names of the officers, the list of the English teachers was headed by John Smyth, 1608–1612, while among the deacons are found Johannes Grindal, 1661–1666, Andries Busscher, 1679–1684 and 1689–1694. By that time the descendants of Smyth's company had thoroughly identified themselves with the political and religious life around, though two years later they welcomed a visitor bringing credentials from the great Assembly of churches sprung in England from the teaching of Smyth. Succession was not of outward men or institutions, but of ideas and spiritual realities; this they owned and rejoiced in.

The Man and His Work

When we look back over his career, the very obscurity of his origin is significant. He belonged to an age when new men were coming to the front, ushers like Cavendish, yeomen like Cecil. It is not strange that a Browne, a Smyth, a Robinson, graved their names deep in the history of thought and of church organization. But while the one class enriched by court favour made their way into the governing ranks, the others retained the

English love of local self-government, and applied it in a new sphere.

In Smyth's day, the universities, with all their limitations, still offered a career for all talented lads, irrespective of rank and resources. Merchants of Grimsby, clothiers of Guildford and Reading, could send their sons with a hope of their becoming the first peers of the realm. And Smyth used his twelve years at Cambridge to purpose; one critic owned that he was a scholar of no small reading, well seen and experienced in arts; a younger man that he was of able gifts and a good preacher; a generation later a far more caustic opponent admitted that he was a man of right eminent parts. If awhile he was somewhat slow to think for himself, he yet proved to be very rapid in his development when once he stepped outside the lines of convention. For some eighteen years he was receptive, and there is nothing to single him out from scores of other university men; but in the last eight years of his life he proved himself intensely original in his studies. More than that, he was perfectly fearless in acting on his beliefs. While the Cartwrights, Hildershams, Bernards, Brownes, Pagets, yielded a mutinous obedience and compromised with their convictions, he was

> One who never turned his back but marched breast forward,
>   Never doubted clouds would break.

More than that, he was distinctly original in the routes he explored. He found his way to truths others had discovered before, but he reached them on paths that he hewed out. He was one of the first in modern times to advocate that baptism was the peculiar privilege of believers, but he scaled that Matterhorn by a track that no one since has cared to use. More than once his breathless friends were startled at the audacity of his thought and the rapidity wherewith he translated it into action, and they lingered on the safer beaten roads.

Yet he was no solitary dreamer; he proved able to persuade men and to lead them. There were brave men before Agamemnon, but it was Agamemnon who inspired others. It would appear that in Holland, even in Amsterdam, others had anticipated Smyth in his new departure as to baptism; but no one cared. For him it was reserved to blaze a path along which he led others, to a position which is widely accepted. He was able both to pioneer and to persuade; it was no mere theorist who could influence a whole countryside, could organize men into a voluntary society with the knowledge that fine, prison and exile were the penalties, could persuade clergy and squires to relinquish their position, and could extort the admission that he was one of the "leaders who flee into foreign countries and free states and draw people after them to support their kingdoms."

An explorer inevitably loses his way at times; but Smyth showed himself ready to avow when he saw his mistake, frank to retract and to guide into a truer path. Again and again he invited discussion and declared himself ready to be convinced. Some of his neighbours took refuge from his keen reasoning in silence, but when they convinced him of error they found him meek enough to acknowledge and withdraw.

He had a remarkable power of winning affection. In the little sketch published by Pigott, it is said that he was well beloved of most men. The feelings of his closest associates are well expressed, and they show how he found his way to the heart. In administering physic he usually took nothing of the poorer sort; he was so mindful for the poor that he would rather live sparingly in his house than that any should be in extremity. Even more striking is the testimony of Helwys, after their separation: "Have we not neglected ourselves, our wives, our children, and all that we had, and respected him? and we confess we had good cause so to do in respect of these most excellent gifts and graces of God that then did abound in him; and all our love was too little for him, and not worthy of him."

To such contemporary evidence may be added judgments of modern students, all of other communions and not prejudiced in his favour. Powicke regards him as a beautiful character, and sees in his last book a noble utterance, proving that whatever else he had missed in his short life, he had won at length the mind of Christ. Dexter characterizes him as unselfish, benevolent and courageous, with many qualities of a great, as well as of a good, man; yet with a conscience morbidly sensitive about trifles. Perhaps the finest estimate occurs in a lecture, which however inaccurate in detail, is luminous in its perception of broad issues, and was fitly given by the Dixie Professor of Ecclesiastical History in that university church where Smyth had often worshipped. Said Prof. Mandell Creighton: "None of the English Separatists had a finer mind or a more beautiful soul than John Smyth. None of them succeeded in expressing with so much reasonableness and consistency their aspirations after a spiritual system of religious beliefs and practice. None of them founded their opinions on so large and liberal a basis."

Such a judgment of the man leads us on to value the results of his life-work. This may be summed in six respects.

The cause of Separatism, as it was then termed, or of the Free Churches, as we speak to-day, gained from him impulse sufficient to carry it on for a generation till it stood firm. To Englishmen the idea was all but inconceivable that religious societies could be organized independently of the State. Pamphlets had been published to ventilate the idea, but Harrison was executed and Browne was cajoled into silence. Societies had been formed at London and Norwich and near Trowbridge, but all had been driven out. Smyth wrote and organized and emboldened others so that a spark was kept alive, nay, sparks were struck off which kindled elsewhere, and little churches kept dimly twinkling till the day of repression ended. The Free Churches of England and America owe much to his writings and his example.

America. Smyth was the first to conceive a deliberate emigration, and to carry it out successfully. There had been ministers before, who had taken refuge in Dutch towns, and had continued their ministry as chaplains to recognized factories, or pastors of casual emigrants. But Smyth organized a systematic removal of his whole church at Gainsborough, to settle down complete as the same community in another land. The policy has often been copied; Blackwell moved on from Amsterdam to

Virginia in the same way, and presently new Bostons and Dorchesters arose by colonies from the home towns. But the old Greek plan had never before been acclimatized, and Smyth added to that plan the new touch, that the emigrants were bound together by their search for liberty. Some of his adherents from Nottingham went on via Leijden to New England, and the influence of his Gainsborough covenant has been traced in the covenant taken by the Puritans at Salem in 1629, "to walk in all His ways revealed or as they should be made known unto them." That final clause illustrates the truth of Roger Williams' sentence: "I am sure Mr Cotton hath made some use of those principles and arguments on which Mr Smith and others went concerning the constitution of the Christian church."

Smyth did not live to go beyond Holland. But there he met and solved a new problem, kinship of faith among those of differing nations and antecedents. English ecclesiastics were usually too insular to fraternize with foreigners; or to own indebtedness to them unless they had been dead a thousand years. Many chafed at correspondence with Luther, Bullinger, Hermann, Calvin; could not brook Erasmus, Peter Martyr, Bucer. Now Smyth came to Amsterdam with a very distinct prejudice against all Anabaptists. Yet he was willing to compare notes with them, under their influence to abandon many doctrines in which he had been trained and to study fresh points suggested, till he formally apologized for too hasty a new beginning when he might have joined those with whom he was spiritually akin. It is not often, even to-day, that a church of, say England, will seriously consider the possibilities of fraternizing with a church of Moravians, or of Sweden, or of other nations with differences of traditions or doctrine, even when there is no difference of opinion as to the essence of a church. Not till the nineteenth century was the Pan-Presbyterian Council formed, not till the twentieth did the Baptist World Alliance unite churches of twenty-four countries in all parts of the world, and make it clear among Protestants that barriers of race and language and politics were transcended by unity of faith and ideals.

This international feeling did not permit Smyth scope to display any strong love for his countrymen. This came out in two associates, of whom Busher is a remarkable link between Holland and England, pleading vigorously at this time for Religion's Freedom from James, while Helwys actually ventured back, scorning flight in persecution, and dared to take shelter close to his kinsman, the governor of the Tower, in Spitalfields, and thence to plead with the king for liberty to exist and to preach. Smyth himself threw in his lot with his adopted country, and was prepared to sink the individuality of his church in that of a Dutch church. This is the temper of a man whose grasp of his citizenship in heaven is so strong, that earthly distinctions and patriotism based on nationality, are of small account.

Smyth was the first to plead for full liberty of conscience. The honour clearly is not due to Browne or Harrison, nor even to Robinson, whose seven articles, sent to the Privy Council in 1617, acknowledge the power of the king to appoint bishops and bestow authority on synods and assemblies. It is equally clear that Helwys in 1612, Busher in 1614, Murton in 1615, were explicit in claiming it. But few have noticed that they learned it from Smyth, whose article 84 is most sweeping: "The magistrate is not by vertue of his office to meddle with religion or matters of conscience, to force and compell men to this or that form of religion or doctrine...for Christ onelie is the king and lawgiuer of the church and conscience." While that states the case as between subject and ruler, the practical consequence as to fraternization is put thus: "Difference in Judgement for matter of circumstance, as are all things of the outward church, shall not cause me to refuse the brotherhood of anie penitent and faithfull Christian whatsoever."

One thing remains to note, the vigorous propaganda initiated by Smyth. Even as a settled preacher at Lincoln he had declared that it was a Christian duty to bring to the knowledge of the truth, both Jews and Turks and all barbarous nations with whom there was trade. A year or two later he began practising what he preached, actually evangelizing in the lower Trent valley. His most effective work was however accomplished by his literature. The fact that his books are so extremely rare to-day easily obscures the fact that they exerted no small influence at the time. Not only did men of ability like Bernard, Hall, Johnson and Robinson, feel bound to notice his arguments, but their force was shown in the adoption of his principles and the formation of other churches. The knot of people who returned to England with Helwys formed the first Baptist church in the realm, which through many evil times held on its way in the city of London till the city was no longer a place of residence; its minute books repose to-day fittingly in the Guildhall library. An offshoot of that church was formed by 1624, worshipping south of the Thames; and to-day it may still be found, after an intricate history, in Church Street, Deptford. But there are others of an earlier date due more directly to Smyth. At Lincoln he was not forgotten, and some who had heard the Preacher to the City, and bought the sermons he had preached in the cathedral, bought his later works, acted on them, and formed a Baptist church. One or two members crossed the sea and threw in their lot with the Anglo-Dutch church, and in the library there survives correspondence between Lincoln and Amsterdam. At Coventry Smyth had sought to persuade Barbon and other Puritans, of the need to adopt a bolder policy; his optimism was justified when a similar church arose there. From the vales of Avon and Wiley many had emigrated to Holland and met Smyth; his books found their way back, and soon arose a church at Salisbury. The link with Devon is not so obvious, and it may be that Busher was an intermediary here, but the church at Tiverton testifies to the speedy effect of Smyth's reasoning in the west. These four churches, all flourishing to-day, were but the harbingers of many more which exemplify the power of truth to spread. These churches do not pay Smyth the poor compliment of adhering to any creed he ever drew up; they finely carry on the tradition of keeping the soul sensitive to new light. When in the middle of the seventeenth century we see the churches of Somerset, Wilts. and Devon declaring that it is an ordinance of

Christ and the duty of the church to send brethren and preach the gospel to the world, we see in this early avowal a natural corollary. When we find an order instituted of Messengers, whose duties included evangelizing certain counties assigned to them, we see a creed reduced to practice. When in the eighteenth century we note that the first English Missionary Society to the heathen originated among the Baptists, it is but the same conception set in a wider horizon. If the earliest officers of the Religious Tract Society and the Bible Society were Baptists, it is but another illustration of the use of the press to spread gospel truth. If to-day the Baptist Union puts as one of its three fundamental articles that it is the duty of every disciple to bear personal witness to the gospel of Jesus Christ, and to take part in the evangelization of the world, it is but the natural growth from that seed which was planted by John Smyth. Forty or fifty communicants he saw in his lifetime; three centuries later, seven million attest the fulfilment of the royal vision. The handful of corn has spread, the fruit thereof shakes like Lebanon.

THE
BRIGHT MOR-
NING STARRE:
OR,

The Resolution and
Exposition of the 22. *Psalme, preached*
publikely in foure sermons
at Lincolne.

By IOHN SMITH Prea-
cher *of the Citie.*

Apoc. 22. 16
*I am the roote and the Generation of David, and the
Bright Morning starre.*

[Ornament]

Printed by IOHN LEGAT,
*Printer to the Universitie of Cam-
bridge,* 1603.
And are to be solde at the signe of the Crowne in
Pauls Churchyard by *Simon Waterson.*

To THE RIGHT Worshipfull, religious, and *courteous Knight, Sir* William Wray, my approoued good *friend and benefactor, salut*ations in the Lord *Jesus.*

Sir : it seemeth a thing very reasonable to me, that seeing euery bald tale, vaine enterlude, and pelting ballad, hath the priuiledge of the Presse, the sermons and readings of ministers may challenge the same : the worlde is full of Guy *of* Warwicke, William *of* Cloudeslee, Skoggins, *and* Wolners *iests, and writings of like qualitie : and therein men take great delight to read, and so make themselues merrie with other mens sinnes, bestowing to this purpose much vaine time and superfluous expences : and I thinke the Stationers shop, and some mens shelues are better furnished with such trifles, which deceiue the minde and affection as the baite doeth the fish, then with wholesome writings of nature, arte, or religion. In which respect it seemeth to haue beene lesse hurtfull to mankind, if Printing had neuer beene inuented, sauing that the use of a thing is not to be forbidden because of the abuse : these things considered, haue imboldened me to publish my meditations and readings to the worlds view : and seeing that Printing is a trade wherby diuers good Christians maintaine their charge, & that for want of better imployment they sometime are compelled to prostitute their Presses to lies and vanitie : seeing also the trueth may better appeare by writings of diuers men, which perhaps one or two or more could not readily discouer : therefore I haue thought good in some part to preuent the danger of the one, and promote the benefit of the other. I haue not varnished my writing with the superficiall learning of words, and figures, tongues, and testimonies of men (which not withstanding I do not disalow) but because I purposed to apply my style to the understãding of the simple, I indeauour to utter matter with all plainenesse of wordes and sentences. Nowe because I haue experienced your selfe to be vnder the Kings Maiestie a principall professor and protectour of religion in these quarters : (for what a multitude of faithfull ministers are debters to you in the flesh?) and for that I among the rest haue rested under your shaddowe, your name came first to my mind in this writing : wherefore I beseech you vouchsafe to intitle it with your name, and I shall acknowledge my selfe graced therby. The Lord increase in your selfe and your vertuous Lady and childrẽ all manner of heauenly graces & blessings.*

Your Worsh. humbly
in all manner of
Christian affecti-
on,
Iohn Smith.

[*Ornament*]

The resolution of *the* 22. *Psalme, which may be* intituled the *Bright Morning Starre.*

The time when this Psalme was penned is unknowne in speciall : generally notwithstanding it may seeme to be, when the Prophet was in some great conflict of conscience, and temptation to despaire, whẽce he gathering consolation, recouereth at the length.

The Argument of the Psalme is a discription of the estate of euery true Christian and godly heart in the person of Dauid : also a type of the sufferings & glory of Christ.

The psalme cõtaineth two partes :
 The title or inscription.
 The matter or substance.

The title contayneth foure particulars.

1. The manner of writing, which is in forme of a *Psalme.*
2. The person that composed it, who was Dauid.
3. The person to whome it was committed to be kept, set, and song : who is called *the master musitian.*
4. The matter and argument of the Psalme, which is concerning the morning starre.

The matter and substance of the Psalme comprehendeth a : ˙ Complaint : Prayer.

The complaint contayned in the two first verses hath 2 things 1. the persō to whome he complayneth : (*God :*) amplyfied by an argument of relation. (*my God*)

2. The thing whereof he complayneth, which is that *God hath forsaken him.* Which the prophet auoucheth by 2. reasons.

The first, that seeing *God did not helpe him, but was farre from his health :* therfore he forsooke him.

The second, *that seeing God heard not the wordes of his roaring nor gaue audience to his prayer :* therefore he forsooke him.

This praier which the prophet professeth he made to the Lord, in the time of this his wofull desertion hath two adiunctes :

1. His prayer was feruent.
2. His praier was continuall.

The feruency of his prayer hath two partes.

{faith : (*my God*)
{desire : (*roaring crye.*)

The continuance of his prayer : (*day and night.*)

This is the first part of the psalme the complaint.

The second part of the psalme which is the prayer followeth.

The prayer hath a

1 Supplication : containing also a deprecation.
2 A Gratulatiō or thanksgiuing.

The supplication is continued to the 22. verse, wherein is exprest both the faith & assurance the prophet conceaueth to obtaine : and the desire : which are the two essentiall partes of a feruent prayer.

The faith of the prophet is grounded upon 4. arguments to the 11. verse : The first argument or ground of faith is in the 3. verse taken from the nature & office of God, which is to sanctifie and redeeme the Church that he may be praised & glorified by his church : concluded thus.

If thou wilt sanctifie the church and be praised by the church, then deliuer me the redeemer of the Church, without whose deliuerance, neither thy selfe can be glorified, nor thy church redeemed or sanctified.

But thou wilt sanctifie the Church (*for thou art holy*) & thou wilt be praised by the Church (*for thou inhabitest the praises of Israell.*)

Therefore *deliuer me vers.* 11.

Thus the argument is applyed to Christ: to Dauid thus.

Thou Lord art holy sanctifying thy children: therfore sanctifie me, and deliuer me from the power of sinne and thy wrath, that I may praise thee with al the true Israelites, whose praises are offered up to thee, as to the only owner and possessor thereof.

The second argument or ground of faith is in the 4. & 5. verses framed thus. If the fathers that trusted in thee, & called upon thee are saued & deliuerd and were not confounded: then saue me also who am their sauiour.

But *the fathers* of the olde testament &c. *are saued.*

Therefore also *saue and deliuer me vers.* 11.

The reason of this argument is: for that Christ necessarily must be saued and deliuered, seeing the fathers were saued by vertue of his sacrifice: whereas they could not so haue beene, if he had perished.

Thus the argument is applyed to Christ: to Dauid thus.

As God hath delt with others: so will he deale with me.

But God deliuered our fathers that faithfully prayed.

Therefore he will deliuer me also that pray faithfully: & so this argument is taken frō the experience of Gods goodnes to others.

The third argument or ground of faith is in the 6. 7. and 8. verses taken from Relation of Gods mercy to mans misery: disposed thus:

The most mercifull God wil releeue the miserable creature calling upon him faithfully.

But I am a most miserable creature. &c. and thou a mercifull God.

Therefore *releeue and deliuer me. vers.* 11.

The minour of this argument is amplified comparatiuely and simply.

The comparison is taken from a worme. As a worme

is exposed to all wrong and iniury, and of base account: so am I.

The simple arguments are the parts of Christs miserie, which are three: 1. he was shamed. 2. contemned. 3. derided.

He beeing God most glorious, was shamed and dishonoured by man, that is, Adam dust and ashes.

He that should haue beene accounted of, as the onely Sauiour of his people, was contemptible to the people.

He, whome men should haue gloried and reioyced in, was derided and mockt by all men that beheld him.

Christ was mockt by gestures, and speech.

The mocking gestures are two, mowing & wrying the mouth: & nodding the head.

The skoffing speech containeth an ironical cōtrarietie: for they say one thing that mocke Christ, and meane the cleane contrarie: thus they speake,

God will deliuer him that he loueth, and that trusteth in God.

But he is beloued of God, & trusteth in God: *ergo* God will saue him.

But their meaning is contrarie to this speech: which is this.

God will deliuer him that he loueth, and that trusteth in him:

But God doeth not deliuer him: *ergo*, he neither is loued of God, nor trusteth in God.

Thus the third argument is applied to Christ: to Dauid also in the same sense.

The fourth argument or ground of faith is in the 9. and 10 verses, taken from the experience of Gods goodnesse to himselfe in time past, framed thus:

As thou hast dealt with me before, so deale with me nowe.

But thou hast hitherto preserued and deliuered me: *ergo* doe so nowe.

The minor of the argumēt is amplified by a distribution or enumeration of parts, thus: thou hast preserued me in my life, birth, and conception.

Thus the fourth argument is applied to Christ: and in the same sense also to the Prophet.

Hitherto the Prophet hath uttered his faith, which is the first essentiall part of his praier : his desire which is the secōd essential part followeth.

The desire of the Prophet is exprest in the 11. verse : [*Be not farre from me*] and urged by a reason, *à relatis paribus*, thus :

If helpe be farre off, then thou wilt be neere to help thy seruants.

But helpe is farre off : *ergo* be neere to helpe. Or thus :

Thou wilt help the afflicted and helpelesse :

But I am afflicted and helpelesse : *ergo* helpe me.

Nowe furthermore, both the Prophets desire and this reason whereupon it is enforced are handled by inuersion of methode, for first the reasō is handled, then the desire.

The reason is handled to the 19. verse, where the desolatiō and extreame miserie of the Prophet is propounded in 2 kinds : First that which properly and immediately seazed vpon his soule, which by sympathie onely affected his bodie. vers. 12, 13, 14, 15.

Secōdly, that which directly and properly seazed vpon his bodie, and by compassion onely affected his sensitiue facultie. vers. 16, 17, 18.

The proper affliction of his soule is deliuered in three arguments, *viz*. the cause, the adiunct, and the effect.

The causes are the deuill and his angels, allegorically figured vnder the names of Bulls and Lyons.

These deuils are of two conditions : some ministers & seruants to their master the principall : other the cheife or master deuill.

The ministring deuils cōueniently are allegorized vnder the tearmes of Bulls, as beeing creatures inferiour in strength and rage to the lyon the king of the beasts of the forrest.

These deuillish Buls are described by their qualities and effects : their qualities are 3 : young, fatte, strong, vers. 12.

1 Young : *vz*. such as are not cicured or tamed, but are without the yoke, euē Belial : not subiect to any order.

2 Fatte and large limmed, such as were bred in Bashan, where was the largest breed, and the fattest fed cattel, Deu. 32. 14. which insinuateth the insolencie, arrogancy, & pride of these deuils.

3 Strong and mightie being principalities & powers, as the Apostle tearmeth thē, Eph. 6. 12. preuailing against the world of the vngodly.

These are their qualities; their effects are two, vers. 12, 13.

First they inclose him about with terror and temptation.

Secondly they gape vpon him with their mouths readie to swallowe him vp body and soule; the bodie in the graue or corruption: the soule in despaire and hellish torments, as much as in them resteth.

These are one sort of Deuills, that minister: the principall and Arch-deuill euen Beelzebub the prince of the deuils is termed a ramping & roaring lyon. vers. 13.

A lyon, as the king of all the hellish fiendes to whome they voluntarily become serviceable.

Roaring, as now ready to deuour the pray (for so is the vse of lyons Amos 3. 4. to roare when they are vpō the pray.)

Ramping, that is hunger-bitten and so most eagerly violent vpon the pray, as the lyons that were kept fasting for the deuouring of Daniell. These are the causes of Christs afflictions vpō the soule properly. The adiunct & effects follow.

The adiunct is the quantitie of his misery vttered by cōparison to water spilt vpon the ground, which cannot be gathered vp againe, euen so (saith the prophet) my misery is irrecouerable. v. 14.

The effects are in number fiue:

First effect is the dissolutiō of the Animall facultie, which is by this misery interrupted: verse. 14. the sinewes, ligamentes, brawnes, & tendons, which are the instruments of sense and motion beeing forsaken by the animall facultie of the soule, and so the bones which are as it were the studs of the bodie were laxed and vntied (for the disioyning of the bones is exprest, vers. 17.)

Second effect: that *his heart which* (as anatomie

teacheth) *is in the middest of the bowells, was melted like waxe:* that is the vitall facultie was interrupted: whose principall seate is in the heart, from whence vitall spirits by the arteries, whose originall is the heart, are diffused to euery liuing part. This vitall facultie was molten and quailed so as the soule ceased the execution thereof for a season.

Third effect: that *his strength was dryed up like a potsheard* that is, the *humidum radicale* or naturall moisture which is the oile to the lampe of life beeing the foundation of our strength and vigor, withered and spent, and so the naturall facultie decayed, ther being not much more moisture in the partes of the bodie then in a potsheard baked in the ouen.

Fourth effect: that *his tong claue to his Iawes*, he being scarse able through the fierce assaultes of Gods wrath to moue his tongue: so that here probably may be cōiectured that the faculty of reasō, whose instrument is the tongue, was suspended; though we denie not but also by this phrase the prophet may signifie his immoderate drought.

These foure are the speciall effects of the torment which now he suffered, now followeth one generall effect, vz. that he was brought *into the dust of death*, that is, vnto the graue. verse. 15. but this effect is solitarily here attributed vnto the Lord, and remoted from the former causes: for the prophet by Apostrophe, turneth his speech vnto the Lord: saying. *Thou hast brought me.* &c.

This is the affliction which immediately seazed vpon his soule, yet by simpathy also vpon the bodie, by these effects.

Now the affliction which entred vpō his bodie primarily, and by compassion vpon his soule follow: where cōsider also: the causes, & parts thereof. The causes are the wicked, Iewes and Gentiles which cōspired and procured his death, who are called dogs according to the custome of the scripture and expounded to be the wicked. v. 16.

The parts of this affliction are fiue.

First the wicked inclose him, that is whippe him, spitte vpon him, smite him with fist and rod, crowne him with thornes, and such like mentioned in the gospell (for here the signe is put for the thing signified, it being the custome of the people to flocke about the person vpon whome execution is done.) verse. 16.

Secondly they pierced or digged his hands and feet, when they nayled him to the crosse, which insinuateth the great woundes that were mad in his hands and feet, as if they had beene digged with the talentes or paues of a lyon, as the old translatour hath it frō the corrupt hebrue word. v. 16.

Thirdly they wrack him, & disioynt all his boanes, so as they may be nombred, and discerned seuerally each from other, as is customable to thē that are wracked: here is *signum pro signato :* v. 17.

Fourthly they behold and looke vpon him without pity and compassiō yea they mock and scoffe at him with taunting bitter floutes, and reuiling speech, here is lesse spokē and more signified : *signum pro signato.* v. 17.

Lastly they take from him his garmentes and strip him naked : a vild indignity : now his garments appertayned (as it is in vse with vs) to the tormentors, who were the souldiers : they therefore first deuide his vnder garments and euery one taketh, his part : but his vpper garment beeing without seame is not deuided or cut in pieces, but for it they cast lottes to whome it shall appertaine : and falling to one the other lost their partes. v. 18.

This is the affliction that immediately seazed vpon his body, but compassiuely also vpon his soule :

Thus the reason cōfirming the prophetes desire is handled.

Now followeth the prophets desire which is handled also v. 19. 20. 21. wherein cōsider foure particulars.

First the persō to whome he offereth this his desire, which is the Lord, whome he intituleth *his strength*, because he ministred vnto him strength to beare all that was laid vpon him.

Second : the thing he prayeth for, exprest in diuers phrases (*be not farre of : hasten to helpe, deliuer, saue, answer.*)

Third : the person for whome he prayeth exprest thus : *me, my soule, my desolate one.*

Fourth: the euill frō which he desireth deliuerance: exprest diuersly: *from the sword, from the power of the dogge, frō the lyons mouth, from the hornes of the vnicornes.*

Thus the prophets desire or request is handled: and so the supplication.

The gratulation or thanksgiuing, which is the second part of the prayer followeth.

This thankfulnes is 1. promised: 2. prophesied.

It is promised to the 26. verse:

This promise of thankfullnes is propounded and then repeated and concluded. It is propoūded & handled to the 25. verse, and that in the parts, or signes, or declarations of thankefulnes which are three.

1. Signe of thankefullnes: is Confession, which is a declaring of Gods (name or) attributes, as his mercy, and iustice &c. to the members of the Church which are Christs brethren according to the flesh Heb. 2. 12.

2 Signe of thankefullnes: is a commendation of the excellencie of these attributes to the honour and praise of God & that *in the open assembly.*

3 Signe of thankefullnes: is the Inciting and prouoking of them that feare God, the *seed of Iacob and Israel: to praise and magnifie & feare the Lord:* to be a meanes to bring others to god also.

These three parts or signes of thankefulnesse are amplified by a reason, enforcing the performance of the promise made before: which reason is taken *à paribus,* & is set downe Negatiuely and Affirmatiuely.

Negatiuely in 3. phrases: he hath not 1. *despised,* 2. *abhorred.* 3. *hid his face from the praier of the poore. ergo:* thankefulnesse must be performed.

Affirmatiuely: *he heard when the poore and humbled in spirit praied:* and therefore thankefulnesse must be performed.

Thus the promise of thankfulnesse is propounded & handled: It is also repeated vers. 25. and that in two parts thereof before handled, v. 22. The one part of thankefulnes, praise, and commendation of God is further enlarged by the circumstance of the place: *the great congregation.*

The other part of thankefulnesse, Confession is

exprest in a newe phrase [*paying of the vowes*] which were voluntarie sacrifices.

Thus thankefulnesse is promised.

Thankefulnes also is prophesied to the ende of the Psalme: which shall be performed by the subiects of Christs kingdome, who are in the sequele of the psalme described and distributed into their seuerall kinds.

First they are described by 6. arguments in the 26. verse.

1 Adiunct: *the poore*, that is, such as are poore in spirit, Mat. 5. 3.

2 Is an effect: *shal eate*, that is, beleeue in Iesus Christ. Ioh. 6. 35.

3 Adiunct: *shall be satisfied*, that is, shall haue peace & ioy spirituall, Mat. 5. 6. Ioh. 7. 38.

4 Is an effect: *shall seeke after the Lord*, that is, shall carefully vse the meanes of saluation, whereby God is sought and found, Mat. 7. 7.

5 An effect: *shall praise the Lord* by a godly life, and with heart and voice singing Psalmes of praise: Math, 5. 16. Coloss. 3. 16.

6 An adiunct: *your heart shall liue for euer ;* which is life euerlasting the reward of all the former. Ioh. 4. 14.

Thus the persōs of whome thankfullnes is prophesied are described.

Furthermore the person of whome thankfullnes is prophesyed, namely the members of Christ, and Subiects of his kingdom, are distributed into their seuerall sorts and kindes, thus:

Persons prophesied to be thankefull are,

Parents and progenitors.

Children and posteritie.

Parents (& so consequently children) are distinguished by two adiuncts:

1 Is their nation: they shal be Gentiles and not onely Iewes.

2 Is their condition: they shall be of the poorer sort, as well as of the rich.

The Gentiles are described both by the parts and cause of their thankefulnesse: the parts of the thankefulnesse of the Gentiles are three. v. 27.

1 They shall remember themselues, and take notice of their sinnefull and accursed estate, and so humble themselues.

2 They shall turne vnto the Lord forsaking their idols and other sinnes.

3 They shall worship the Lord in holinesse and righteousnesse.

The cause of the Gentiles thankefulnesse is exprest, v. 28. where there is the preuenting an obiection which might thus be made by a Iew.

Obiect. Shall the Gentiles also become subiects of the kingdom of the Messias, who were sometime execrable ?

Sol. There is nothing impossible to God: for seeing he is king, and so ruleth among the heathen, he is able to conuert the Gentiles also, and of stones to raise vp children to Abraham.

This is the first distinction of the persons by their natiō.

The second distinction is, that poore and rich also shall be thankefull: and that is exprest, v. 29.

The rich who are called the fat men of the earth haue their actiō of thākfulnes assigned thē: *eating, & worshipping.*

Poore or afflicted persons are of two sortes,

1 Such *as goe downe into the dust,* that is beggars and basse persons.

2 Such *as cannot quicken their owne soule,* that is persons condemned to die, or persons sick of deadly diseases &c.

All these afflicted persons haue their thankfull actions assigned them, which is that they shall *bow before him:* (*signum pro signato, Metonymia*) namely they shall worship him.

Thus the parentes which are the first sort of persons with their thankfull actions, are propounded.

The children and posteritie also haue their thankful actiōs & the reasō thereof assigned:

The thankfull actions of the posteritie are two.

1 They shall serue the lord in the obedience of his lawe, which is set out by the circūstance of time, *for euer they shall be reckened to him.* verse 30.

2 Action of thankfulnesse is that when they are come into the Church by effectuall vocation, *they shall declare his righteousnes ;*

The reason of these thankfull actions of the posteritie of the gentiles is for that God hath *wrought righteousnes for a people to be borne,* that is either for their posteritie, or some other straung people that as yet are vnborne by spirituall regeneration.

Thus thankfulnes is prophesied: and so the whole psalme is resolued.

In the Complaint and the Supplication Christs priest-hood is described both in his sacrifice and intercession.

In the promise of thankefulnesse, Christs prophesie is comprised.

In the prophesie of thankfulnesse Christs kingdome is comprehended.

Finis.

ANNOTA-tions and obseruations out of *the* 22. *Psalme*.
Of the Title of the Psalme.

A Psalme: THis Psalme containeth a pittifull complaint, a feruent praier, a promise and prophesie of thankefulnesse, and yet the Prophet penned it in the forme of a Psalme : whence thus much may be noted, that it is not vnlawefull to sing doctrine, exhortation, complaints, supplication, prophesies, and such like matters, as well as thankesgiuings : briefly to sing any portion of holy Scripture, so be that vnderstanding and edificatiō be not hindred : and this collectiō ariseth out of this place by analogie.

The Prophet Dauid is here to be considered. 1. in his owne person. 2. sustaining the person of a godly man. 3. as a type of Christ, whose Of Dauid. sufferings and glorie, whose priesthood in his sacrifice and intercession, with his propheticall office in teaching, and kingdome in gathering and guiding his Church in all ages, places, and times, are here not obscurely figured : whēce we may note that kings and mightie men of the earth are not to scorne religious exercises, as Dauid did not, the whole booke of the Psalmes witnesseth, but with the Prophet to acquaint themselues with holy meditatiōs, of their owne estate, howe the matter is betwixt God and their own soules : of the condition of the Church which shall suffer with Christ, before it be glorified with him, and of the doctrine of the Gospell in the offices of Christ, the summe of the Psalme.

The Musitians & Singers office principally consisted to the cheif in setting & singing the Psalmes of the or master Prophets, for the instruction and edification musitian. of the church : as also in keeping these holy writings safe for the vse of the Church in time to come, in regard of which office the Church is called the pillar and ground of trueth : wherefore when the Prophets had composed any Psalmes, they sent them to the singers and musitians, specially to the principal Musitian of any order, who had the ouersight of the rest of his order, that they might bring them in publike for the comfort and instruction of the whole church: whence this collection might be made, that if musicke were lawfull for the Iewes, it is now for vs: and if vocall musicke be lawefull by consent of all, why not instrumentall also? alwaies remembring that edification must not be hindered but furthered: for musicke beeing one of the liberall arts, why is there not vse of musicke in furthering vs in the worship of God, as wel as of Grammar, Rhetoricke, or Logycke, &c: and musicke is not a parcell of the ceremoniall lawe: and the Lord commanded it in the Church, and it was vsed by Christ and his Apostles.

Againe hence might be obserued, that it is lawful to pray the prayers composed by other men; which was customable to the Church of the Iewes: who vsed to bring other mens psalmes, which sometime were prayers, into the publique assemblie, as for example this psalme: and if it be said that they, were vsed only dogmatically; the answer is, that is not so: *for they praised God with the words of Dauid and Asaph, and they bowed themselues and worshipped* as it is euident. 2. Chron. 29. 30. where besides the meditation of the matter, no doubt they had holy desires & wishes sutable to the wordes of the prayers or thanksgiuings, as the wordes of bowing and worshipping do plainly import in the place alleadged: and therefore (howsoeuer some think) it seemeth to be very lawfull, to pray accordingly to a set forme: and so to say and pray the Lords prayer: so be that we insinuate our vnderstanding & affectiōs into the matter of that set prayer which we vse, making it our owne when we pray it.

To thinke these wordes (*aijeleth hasshachar*) to be the name of an instrument is neither warrantable nor reproueable, but coniectural: I know not what can be said for it or against it. <small>Concerning the morning starre.</small>

To think them the tune of a common song, or the tune of some ciuill ballad seemeth to be to accuse the holy ghost for not keeping decorum, which is when holy psalmes are song in the tunes of common, and it may be prophane ballads also.

To translate with *Tremellius* and *Iunius ad primordium auroræ*, is very good, for the words may beare that reading and then they import the time of vsing the psalme, the early morning, the time of the morning sacrifice, so that this psalme was an exposition and cōmentarie of the sacrifice: the sacrifice was a type of Christ; this Psalme teacheth the signification of the sacrifice: & so this Psalme annexed to the sacrifice did euery day traine vp the Church of the Iewes with a continuall meditation and expectation of the promised Messias, whose sufferings and glorie are in this psalme expressed.

Yet notwithstanding there is another exposition which may best befit the argument of the psalme, which is this (*concerning the Morning star*) and *aijeleth* signifieth *Stellam matutinā* as well as, *ascensum auroræ*. Nowe seeing that this Psalme is a prophecie of Christ, and that Christ is expresly called the *Bright Morning starre*, Apoc. 22. 16. the *day starre* by the Apostle, 2. Pet. 1. 19. and the *day spring from on high*, Luk. 1. 78. The argument of the Psalme, and this translation will very well sort together as we see.

Of the complaint the first part of the psalme.

In the complaint comprised in these two verses may be obserued these six seuerall points to be handled, which will cleare vnto vs the true meaning of the words, which are darke, and darkened more by some.

My God, my God why hast thou forsaken &c.

1 How Christ could pray vnto God, he beeing himselfe God equall to the father.

2 How Christ could pray in faith, seeing he could not beleeue in himselfe?

3 How it can be said that Christ was not heard by God when he prayed?

4 How Christ can be said to be forsaken of God?

These foure points appertayne to Christ, the other two concerne Dauid, & the godly.

5 How god forsooke Dauid, and how he may be said to forsake his children?

6 Lastly the properties of faith here exprest.

First how Christ God, could pray vnto God ? <small>Vers. 2.
O my God I cry.</small>

For the clearing of this point consider we that Christ was God, and so paraduenture could not pray vnto his father, for that might seeme to imploy some disparagement to God the sonne being equall to the father, & open a gap for the heresie of Arrius : but furthermore Christ also was man, and so made vnder the lawe, and so could and might, yea and ought to pray, as beeing a creature bound to worship the creatour : yet besides this Christ beeing the mediatour of the Church according to both his natures, he therfore prayed according to both his natures : thus : his manhood actiuely powring forth prayer, his godhead dignifying his prayer, and making it meritorious and purchasing audience.

Christ prayed to his father therefore, as man, and as the mediatour.

Now if it be alledged that seing himselfe was God hee must therefore pray vnto himselfe, which may seeme absurd, or els if he do exclude himselfe, then committ idolatry : the answer is that he prayed to his father directly and primarily, in respect of order the father being the first person in Trinitie ordine ; but indirectly, inclusiuelie, and secondarily he praied to himselfe, and the holy Ghost also : here the distinction of nature and person must be admitted necessarily : againe it may be supposed that no absurditie would followe, if we say that the second person in the trinitie did pray vnto the first, that is, did testifie his will to haue the Church saued : but that is abusiuely in a very hard Catachresis.

In summe : it is no absurditie to say that a man may pray to himselfe, that is, perswade himselfe to grant that which is for his owne aduantage : for as affectiō or desire sometime obtaineth of a man that which his iudgement disalloweth : (which is a kinde of praier or intreatie :) or contrariwise, as the iudgement perswadeth the affection that which it disliketh : so Christ-man may aske something of Christ-God : and no absurdity (as it seemeth) be admitted,

Secondly: how Christ could pray in faith?

For the further enlightning of this doubt a distinction of faith must be remembred. Faith is legall and euangelicall; of the law, and of the gospell.

V. 1, 2. my God

Faith required in the lawe Adam had in paradise and Christ had when he prayed whereby the creature relieth it selfe vpon the creatour for all manner of good things & deliuerance from all euill, if Christ had wanted this faith he had not presently obeyed the law, which to say were to blaspheme.

Euangelicall faith or the faith required in the gospell is that whereby the creature relieth it selfe vpon God, through Christ his mediatour: beleeuing to obtaine all good things from him, by the meanes of Christ: now although Christ were made vnder the lawe, yet he was not made vnder the gospell, for he was not bound to faith and repentance as sinners are, himselfe beeing without sinne: he is the matter and author of the Gospell: wherefore to tie Christ to the obedience of the law through and by vertue of the Gospell as we are tied, is to suppose him sinfull by making him his owne sauiour.

Wherefore to answer directly: Christ praied a legall prayer as Adam did but Christ praied not an euangelicall prayer: (except we vnderstand an euangeli[call] praier in this sense, that he made intercessiō for vs, which may rather be called a meritorious praier:) Christ praied in faith of gods infinite mercy, but not in faith of the pardon of sinne through a Sauiour, which he needed not: and which we neede.

Thirdly: Howe was Christ not heard when he praied?

There is no contradiction in holy scriptures: although there may sōtime seeme shew of opposition: we read in the Heb. 5. 7. that *Christ was hard from that which he feared :* here in this place we read that god did not heare Christ, but was farre from the wordes of his roaring: in shew here is an opposition, but in substance, things being aright distinguished, there is none.

V. 2. But thou hearest not.
V. 1. Farre frō the words of my roaring.

The art of reason teacheth that one rule of opposition

is, that the thinges opposed be opposite in the same sence: (*secundum idem* as the logicians say) now Christ was hard in one sence, and he was not heard in another sence: and so the prophet & the Apostle are not opposite: wherefore thus these two places are both verified, and may well be reconciled.

1 Christ was heard in that he was not swallowed vp of the wrath of god, but was deliuered from it, and from the power of our spirituall enemies: & again. Christ was not heard in that gods wrath lighted vpon him, and possessed his soule a competent season: or thus:

2. Christ was heard in regard of the conditions of his praier, (if it be possible, and if it be thy will:) and againe:

Christ was not heard in regard of the petition absolutely considered, without conditions: or thus.

3. Christ was heard, as the children of God are heard, to whome sometime the Lord denieth the very particular thing they aske, and in liewe thereof giueth them a thing as good or better then it: 2. Cor. 12. 8, 9. So the Lord did not deliuer Christ frō his wrath: for *he tasted the cuppe of his wrath,* as he saith, Math. 20. 22. But the Lord gaue him power and strength, and grace to beare it, and to vanquish it at the length: for euen then did hee ouercome the wrath of God when Gods wrath killed him.

These things beeing thus distinguished, we see the Prophet in this psalme, and the Apostle in the Hebrews are not at variance, & so we perceive also howe Christ was not heard when he praied.

Fourthly: howe Christ was forsaken of God?

That this point may the better be conceiued, let it be considered: Negatiuely, how he was not forsaken: & affirmatiuely howe he was forsaken. <small>My God, my God, why hast thou forsaken me: and art so farre from my health?</small>

Negatiuely thus: Christ was not forsaken any of these foure waies following.

First the essence of the godhead was neuer seuered or excluded from Christ the man, but it dwelt in him at all times fully: Coloss. 2. 9.

Secondly the personall vnion of the two natures was

neuer dissolued: and so the person of the sonne neuer forsooke the humanitie of Christ.

Thirdly, the power of the godhead also was alwaies present with him, enabling him to beare the full viall of Gods wrath.

Fourthly, the gratious assistance of Gods spirit was neuer wanting, inabling Christ without the least impatiencie, distrust, &c. to beare whatsoeuer was inflicted vpon him for our sins.

Thus Negatiuely Christ was not forsaken of the nature, person, power, and grace of God. Howe then was he forsaken?

Affirmatiuely therefore he was forsaken: both positiuely in that God the father powred vpon him the infinite sea of his wrath, which hee nowe felt: and priuatiuely in that he was bereft and forsaken of all comfortable presence; the godhead for a seasō shaddowing it selfe vnder the cloude of Gods wrath, that the manhood of Christ might feele the intollerable burden thereof: and thus Christ beeing destitute of consolation complaineth that he was forsaken. But Christ beeing thus forsaken, he sustayned the wrath of God, striued with it, and subdued it; that is, he deliuered both himselfe and vs from it, and so perfectly finished the worke of our redemption.

But if any man thinke it a thing vnreasonable, or rather a blasphemie, that it should bee auouched that Christ suffered Gods wrath which is commonly called the paines of hell, he must remember a distinctiō which ought to bee made betwixt the paines of hell, and the damnation of hell: Christ suffered not the damnation of hell but the paines of hell.

The paines of hell are only the sense of exquisite torments, and the want of all comfort and consolation: commonly called, *pœna* and *damnum*.

The damnation of hell are certaine necessarie consequents which followe the foresaid paines of hell in the meere creature: as for example, the soule of Iudas nowe in hell: besides that it is depriued of all comfort, which is a losse: and tormented with most exquisite tortures which is the paine: despaireth, wanteth faith, hope, loue, the feare of god, patience, and is affrighted with an accusing and gnawing conscience, and besides all this, is bound in euerlasting chaines to the iudgement of the great day in a certaine place which is called Hell.

Nowe for the application of the distinction : Christ if hee had beene a meere man, could not haue escaped part of the damnation of hel, when gods wrath was so fully powred out vpon him : but it should haue fallen out to him as it falleth out with the deuill and reprobates : but because Christ was God also, his godhead did infinitely strengthen and grace his manhood, so as none of all these accidents which necessarily growe vppon a meere creature, seazed vpon him, as despaire, impatience, &c. therefore to say that Christ suffered the wrath of God which may be called the paines of hell, is neither blasphemous nor vnreasonable, this distinction of hell paines and damnation beeing admitted.

Thus the foure points appertaining to Christ are cleared : now the other two concerning Dauid follow :

Fiftly : Howe God forsaketh Dauid and his children ? *Forsaken me.*

God forsaketh his childrē two waies principally.

First by giuing them to their own hearts lusts in part, and permitting them to the temptations of the deuill : and suffering them to fall into some sinnes which wracke & torment the conscience : against which Dauid praieth, Psal. 119. 8. And Christ teacheth vs to pray in the last petition of the Lords praier : *Lead us not into temptation*, &c.

Secondly by causing them to see and feele the wrath of God in some measure and for some time, till humiliation be wrought in them throughly for some sinnes. So Dauid was humbled Psal. 6. and 15. and so are all the children of God in some measure : and thus the Lord forsooke Dauid, both by permitting him to fall into sinne, and causing him to feele the smart of Gods wrath as a meanes of humiliation for that sinne : and thus the Lord forsaketh his children oft times, as they haue experience of : which may teach vs charitie in censuring men whome wee see straungly cast downe with fearefull humiliation, they may be neuerthelesse deere children of God, although it may bee also that they haue fallen into some greeuous sinnes as Dauid did : and yet happily also this humiliation may growe vpon infirmities with some tender heart : and for such vncharitable critickes that thus intemperately censure humbled consciences, they are to know that some kind of despaire is better then hardnes of heart.

Sixtly, what are the properties of faith here noted ?

Two properties of faith euidently appeare in the prophet. *My God, forsaken me.*

The first is, when God forsaketh, then to hold fast, when God killeth then to trust in him as Iob. 13. 15. who professeth that *though the L. should slay him yet he would trust*, and Dauid els where saith, *that though he was somtime affraid yet he trusted in god* for faith holdeth fast sometimes when all reason faileth as Abraham (Rom 4. 18. 19.) beleeued a thing in nature & reason impossible that a woman of nintie yeares, should conceiue with child of a man that was an hundred yeare old : so doth Dauid in this place : God forsaketh him, & yet he calleth him his god.

The second propertie of faith is particular application, whereby Christ with all his merittes are appropriated by the beleeuer to his owne soule in speciall and he is truly assured of the pardon of his sin & the salutatiō of his soule Ro. 8. 38. Ioh. 20. 28. some think it presumption for any man so to say : and none haue euer attained to this certen assurāce but those to whome god hath reuealed it : but wee are to know that there must be difference made between faith, and coniecture : Faith is knowledge which hath a certaintie in it whose *genus* is *scientia* : Coniecture is knowledge which hath vncertaintie in it, whose *genus* is *opinio* : wherefore they that denie the certaintie of faith and saluation, make faith coniecturall and confound faith and opinion which is absurd.

Now indeed faith is neuer without doubting, and yet faith is certain stil : for perswasion and knowledge is either a true perswasion, or a full perswasion : a true knowledge, or a full knowledge : as there is difference betwixt a true man, & a perfect full & complete man : a man wanting a hand is a man indeed : ὄντως but not τελείως : euen so of faith, and assurance : True perswasion is *fides* ἀνυπόκριτος where in there is no hypocrisie. Full perswasion is *fidei* πληροφορία which hath no doubting, which no man liuing hath or can haue till loue be perfected, when also feare shall be cast out, yet we are to striue against doubting, and still to pray : *Lord encrease our faith.*

That which some might comment vpon the ex-postulation of Christ, whereas he asketh a reason why God forsoke him also the two adiunctes of his prayer, that he prayed with roaring and crying, and day and night and had no ease, I omit as ordinarie matters : only thus much.

<small>Why forsakest, &c.</small>

Christ expostulateth and debateth the matter of his desertion with God, not for that he knewe not wherefore he was forsakē, but complaining most pittiously of his extream miserie : neither is here any suspition of impatiencie at all : no God forbid :

Againe Christs roaring & crying, that is, his feruent praier, also his continuance in praier day and night, are for our example in the like cases, that in our extremities we neuer cease crying till God give ease.

The groundes of the Prophets faith.

God is holy *Effectiuè* and *subiectiuè* : for he is both the worker of holinesse and the fountaine of holinesse : nowe both these are here signified by the Prophet : namely, that God is the author and worker of holinesse in the Church. And the Emphasis of the speech is to be obserued, in the pronoune *attah* (*thou*) which is exclusiue, as if the Prophet had said (*thou onely* :) which is the golden sentence written in the high Priests Miter, Exod. 28. 20. *Holinesse to the Lord.*

<small>V. 3. Thou art holy, & doeth inhabite the praises of Israel.</small>

The sanctification of the Church is the worke of God only : which doctrine for that it is a very materiall point, is first to be expounded, and then confirmed. It may be expounded or amplified by the particular causes of sanctification, wherein the Lord hath the maine stroke, or els the worke succeedeth not ; as by induction appeareth thus.

<small>Doctrine.</small>

1 God is the originall and fundamentall cause of the redemption, purgation and sanctification of the Church, who of his owne loue and compassion to mans misery prouided redemption for vs, there being nothing out of himselfe to mooue him there vnto.

2 Christs sacrifice is the meritorious and purchasing cause, for he paid the price of redemption for vs.

3 Christs kingdome that is his resurrection, ascension, session at the right (hand) of his father is the effectuall, operatiue, and working cause.

4 The word in the ministerie of teaching, praying celebrating the sacramentes and discipline ecclesiastical is the instrumentall cause, where if any man thinke that the meanes are any thing without God giue the increase he forgetteth the Apostles speech 1. Cor. 3. 7. for the word which is the power of God to saluation is not the bare sound or letter, but it is the inward spirit of powar and grace annexed thereto : which is Christs Scepter.

So that seeing the loue of God, the sacrifice, kingdome and scepter of Christ are the only causes of our sanctification, it is plaine that the redemptiō sanctification and clensing of the church is gods worke only.

The doctrine thus cleared may also be prooued and cōfirmed by induction of those things which are in or with sinne, the which none but God can take away and they are these foure.

1 Transgression which respecteth Gods lawe & iustice which in sinne is violated for *sinne is the transgression of the lawe* &c. 1. Ioh. 3. 4.

2 Corruption respecting the sinner; which followeth the transgression as the necessary effect thereof: as in Adam.

3 Guilt whereby the person transgressing and corrupted is culpable of iudgement.

4 Punishment the iust wages and desert of sinne, which is Gods wrath and the curse of the law Gal. 3. 10.

Now no creature can take away any of these, it is the worke of god alone therefore was it that our redeemer was God.

Remission of sinne, which is the taking away of the guilt and punishment of sinne is that worke of God onely. Micah 7. 18. Exod 34. 7. Mar. 2. 7. Esay. 43. 25. 1. Ioh. 3. 8.

Againe sanctificatiō which is the purgation of the staine of sinne which is imprinted in our soules (whether it be a qualitie positiue, or priuatiue) is the only worke of god. Iob. 13. 4. 1. Thes. 5. 23.

Seeing then the corruption, guilt, and punishment of sinne which are three principall matters appertaining to sinne are only taken away by god, because they conteyning the violation of an infinite iustice, are after a sort, infinite and so cannot be taken away but by some person infinite, Gods infinite iustice beeing able to ouerwhelme a meere creature euery way finit, it followeth therefore by ineuitable consequence that sin also is taken away by God only : for the corruption, guilt, and punishment of sinne being abolished, the anomie or transgression is remoued and reckoned as not done, which is also a fruit of remission of sinne, and of this the Lord saith that he wil cast it into the bottome of the sea, he will forget and remember it no more, Micah. 7. 19. Ierem. 31. 33. Ezech. 18. 22.

The doctrine thereof is thus confirmed and cleered : and it hath an excellent vse to vs not onely for confutation of the papists, which auouch temporall punishment sustained by the creature to be sufficient satisfaction for some sinnes and that good workes shall deserue grace, and that the priest can iudicially pardon sinne, all which are so many blasphemies against the mercy of God, the sacrifice kingdome and scepter of Christ, but especially it serueth for our instruction to teach vs to quake and tremble at the fearefull condition of sinne, which can no other way be abolished but by the omnipotent power of God encountring (as it were) the infinite wrath of God, and vanquishing it, to teach vs to take heed of committing the least sinne, which none but God can abolish : which also called the Lord Iesus Christ from heauen ; for this cause appeared the sonne of God that he might dissolue the workes of the deuill : for the papists deeme too lightlie of sinne that thinke some sinnes veniall in their own nature, & the profane multitude offer violence to Gods iustice in threatning kindnesse vpon his mercy, saying of small offences as Lott said of Zoar *oh it is but a little one ; and God is mercifull :* is it suppose we a small sinne that, for redeeming whereof, God must needes become man and die ?

God is the owner and possessor of his Church, and so consequently of the praise & worshippe which is in the church offred him continually : for God decreeing from all eternitie the glorie of his mercy and iustice, and the rest of his most excellent attributes (which are commonly called his Name) in the scripture decreed also to haue a Church ; and a sauiour for his Church : without whome neither could he haue a church, nor be glorified out of himselfe if hee wanted a Church : Wherefore Christ praieth thus : if thou wilt be glorified and praised out of thy selfe, thou must haue a Church : if thou wilt haue a Church, thou must haue a sauiour : if thou wilt haue a sauiour, then saue me who am appointed the Sauiour : and so the *sorites* is concluded : if thou wilt be praised, saue me.

But thou wilt be praised &c. *ergo* saue me.

Doctrine. Gods glory and praise is the ende of the worlde, the Church, and of Christ also. For to this ende hath God created the world, redeemed his Church, and appointed Christ the Sauiour of the Church, that he might be glorified : as the wise man saith : *God made all things for his glorie :* Prou. 16. 4. So saith the Apostle, 1. Cor. 3. 22. 23. *All things are yours, you are Christs, and Christ is Gods :* that is to say, Christ hath redeemed all things for your vse, that you may worship Christ, and God through Christ may be glorified.

The vse of this doctrine is to teach vs to glorifie God which is attained by a godly life, and two reasons may be alleadged for this purpose.

1. Necessity : for if we doe not glorifie Gods mercy by godlinesse and honestie in this life, he will be glorified by vs in his iustice in our vtter destruction after this life : for euery man shallbe either an instrumēt of glorifying god in his mercy, or seruing for matter of the glory of his iustice.

2. Analogie and proportiō : for we see all the creatures by naturall instinct without resistance and rebellion are caryed readily and speedily to there end, there place, and vse ; as the sunne &c. Psal. 19. 4. 5. and Psalme 104. *toto* : so that if we degenerate from this end which God hath apointed vs we are the onely irregular persons of the world, and indeed men and angels are so : wherefore if gods loue, Christs death, euerlasting life will not, yet lett feare & shame mooue vs to obedience.

To conclud this verse seeing god sanctifieth his church

and children, and will surely sanctifie them that he may be praised by them, hence doth arise matter of consolation & thankfullnes.

1 Of consolation thus ; if we be cast downe with the cōsideration of sinne committed and raigning in vs, so as that, though we pray and heare, & read, and partake in the sacraments, and discipline our own soules, and watch our hart & sences with all diligēce, yet we cannot obtaine cōquest ouer our sins, thē we may haue recourse vnto the Lord, & cōfort our selues with cōsideration of his holines ; that though we cannot ouermaster our own corruption, yet the Lord can and will in due time, for holines appertaineth to the Lord.

2 Of thankfullnes thus : therefore doth the Lord deliuer vs from the bondage of our spirituall enemies therefore doth he redeeme, purge, and sanctifie his Church that he might be glorified by his Church ; so doth the prophet reason psal. 103. v. 1. 2. 3. 4. & so doth Zachary. Luk. 1. 74.

V. 4. Our fathers trusted in thee, they called vpon thee, and were deliuered and not confounded.

God is immutable and vnchangeable in his loue and he remaineth as firme in his faith to the Church as euer he was : for he keepeth his fidelitie for euer and with him there is no variablenes, nor shadowe of change ; and seeing therefore the fathers in the old testament were deliuered through the mercy and truth of God through the promised messias, now also the posteritie, & namly Christ himselfe the promised seed must needs also be deliuered from perishing.

From this place then we learne diuers instructions.

First that Christ was the *lāb slain frō the beginning of the world.* Apoc. 13. 8. and he *by his blood purged the sinnes of the former testament :* Heb. 9. 15. and therfore howsoeuer the Papists teach and deliuer that there was *Limbus Patrum,* a certain skirt of hell, where the fathers were reserued vntill Christ had ouercome death, & opened heauē, yet we may confidently beleeue, and constantly auouch by this consideration that there was no such thing, for seeing the fathers trusted in God and called vpon him, they were therefore deliuered, and not confounded, as the text saith : but if they were in *Limbo,* they were confounded and not deliuered : for there as the Papists dreame is *pœna damni*, though not *pœna sensus*, it is a dungeon of darknes, and a pit that wil hold no water, as they will needs haue it.

Secondly : that by analogie and proportion the efficacie of Christs death also, must be stretcht to the worlds end, as wel as to the worlds beginning. For as the Apostle saith, out of the Prophet, Christ is a priest for euer, after the order of Melchizedech, as well as he was a lamb slaine from the beginning of the world:

<small>V. 4. Our fathers trusted in thee and were deliuered.</small>

<small>Psal. 110.</small>

& as his blood serued for the purgation of the sins of the former testamēt which liued before Christ was slain, so also it serueth for the clensing of the Church which nowe standeth vp after his death : for it is meere blasphemie to include the vertue of Christs sacrifice within the compasse of a fewe houres wherein he suffered his passiō : whence another popish opiniō hath the neck brokē also, which is, that there needeth a daiely sacrificing of Christ in the masse after an vnbloodie manner, which is as doltish a distinctiō as that other of a sacrifice applicatorie and not propitiatorie : for so farre forth as the Eucharist applieth, it is a Sacrament and not a sacrifice : and so farre forth as the sacrifice is vnbloodie it is Eucharisticall, and not propitiatorie : for without blood there is no propitiation.

Thirdly. Faithfull praier is neuer disappointed but alwaies obtaineth, as Christ saith, Mat. 7. 7. *Aske and yee shall receiue*, but we must aske in faith : for otherwise though we aske we shall not receiue, because we aske amisse, as Iames saith. Therfore faith is the necessarie conditiō of obtaining : and so of true praier : but faith is grounded vpon Gods word which is his will : and Gods word and will is, that we aske nothing contrary to his glory, the good of the church, or our own soules health ; for when we aske any thing derogating from gods glorie, our prayers are so many blasphemies : and when we desire any thing hindring the saluation of our owne soules, or the Churches good, we curse our selues & the church : Wherefore we must alwaies remember to examine our

<small>V. 5. They called vpon thee and were deliuered.</small>

petitions by gods word, that finding them agreeable thereto, we may be bold to present thē before God; finding them otherwise, we may learne to denie our selues, our wits and wils, and all we haue, and so cast down our selues at Gods feete, & say as Christ said, *Thy will be done and not mine*: thus if we doe in praier, we shall obtaine what we aske, as Christ also did when he praied that praier: Hebr. 5. 7.

Lastly, it is profitable for vs to obserue the dealing of God with his children in time past: and from thence to gather hope to our selues: for seeing God is as able, mercifull, and true, as euer he was, therefore we may assure our selues of helpe from god in time of neede beeing Gods seruants, as well as our forefathers: remembring alwaies the Apostles rule, Rom. 15. 4. that we may haue hope; But that we may obtaine hope, we must haue the consolation of the examples of Gods goodnesse reuealed in the scriptures to his children, and especially to Christ the head of the church, as that place importeth, and further also we must haue *patience, that whē we haue done the will of God we may obtaine the promise.* Heb. 10. 36. [v. 4. Our father, &c.]

v. 6. 7. 8. *But I am a worme and not a man: a shame of men and the contempt of the people.*

All that see me haue me in derision: they make a mowe, and nod the head: saying.

Hee trusted in the Lord, let him deliuer him: let him saue him seeing he loueth him.

The prophet Dauid was either annointed or crowned king without question when this psalme was penned, and yet we se he was thus shamfully abused by wicked men; Christ himselfe the most holy and righteous man and the most excellent and worthie persō that euer the earth caried, yet we se is exposed to the contumelious mocks of wretched mē; For this is the portiō of Gods children (as it was one part of Christs sufferings) to be dishonoured, contemned, and derided: the historie of the Gospell is plentifull in this point, they dishonor him in charging him with blasphemie, with breach of the Sabbath, with surfetting and drunkennesse, with Samaritanisme, which is to cast out deuils by the deuill, &c. when he was condemned to die they mocke him, attiring him despitefully as a king, with a crowne of thornes, with a garment of purple, with a scepter of a reede: as if he had beene a king amongest fooles, boyes, or Pigmies: they buffet him, they spit vpō him, they smite him, whip him, and in summe, they mocke at his kingdome and propheticall office: this befell Christ the head of the church, the master of the house: and shall his mēbers or houshold seruants thinke to escape? it is enough for the seruant to be as his master is: and the foote must not thinke to escape the piercing with nailes, when the head was crowned and wounded with thornes.

Now the reason why Christ was thus content to be abased was, that he might deliuer vs from eternall shame and confusion, which is the due desert of sinne: and to sanctifie the euill name and slaunder, which we sustaine now for his sake, and for our owne good, that though an euill name be euill, and a curse, yet the Lord hath by his reproach taken away the malignitie of reproch and slaunder from vs: yet he hath left shame for vs still to sustaine, that we might fulfill the remnant of the afflictions: he hath drunke the full cup, and we must pledge him in the bottome of the cuppe: we must therefore learne to deny our selues, and namely (as this argument implieth) our good name and fame: not that a mā may not by al good meanes preserue his good name, but that a man be not too popular without measure and by vnlawfull meanes to seeke a good name, many mē beeing too greedie (as Aesops dogge) catch at the shadowe and loose the substance, while they seeke fame and report, they leese a good name: for he that immoderatly and vnlawefully seeketh to get and keepe his credit with all sorts of persons, shall get a fame from the wicked, which is but the shaddowe, and leese a good name from the godly, which is the substance. A good name is the reward of humilitie and the feare of God: Prou. 22. 4. *and God will honour them that honour him:* 1. Sam. 2. 3. And by faith we shall obtaine a good report as the Elders did, Hebr. 11. 2. By such meanes we may seeke to get a good name, which will be a good ointment to the children of god refreshing them with comfort of a godly life,

Eccles. 7. 1. But if any of Gods children are too curious of their credit, and too much addicted to be popular, the Lord will really teach thē to denie themselues in this point, and by causing wicked men to slaunder them, will teach them by a reall sermon that which by the word and instruction they cannot learn : which is to forsake their credit for Christs sake, as Christ did forsake his owne excellencie, and deiected himselfe to the greatest indignities that a man could suffer, for our sakes : in so much as the scripture saith, he did annihilate himselfe, that is, he was content to be in no account, that we might be pretiously esteemed.

The wrying of the mouth, and nodding the head are vnciuill, foolish, and despitefull gestures, such as ciuil, discreet, and moderate men would haue beene ashamed to vse : but if malice haue got the bridle in the necke, howe will not wicked men transgresse the lawe of ciuill and courteous behauiour ? yea the sence of nature and humanitie they will trample flat to the groūd, as if they lost both ciuilitie and manhood : which point may further appeare in the mocking speeches which they vtter against Christ now hanging vpon the crosse : which mocking gestures and speeches shewe more then barbarous despight, and brutish malice : for a person that is condemned to die, yea nowe in execution is pittied and praied for by all the beholders, yea euen the hearts of Adamant then will soften to here a man in extremitie of paine readie to die, yet then these monsters of men and nature are neuer a whit asswaged towards him, but reioyce then at his woe, and scoffe at his fall : saying : God hath forsaken him, he loueth him not, he neuer did trust in god, as he pretended: for then surely God would not suffer him to perish, but would deliuer him : or if he himselfe were a sauiour he would saue himselfe and others and come downe from the crosse, that we might know him to be the sauiour and beleeue in him : but we are to know these things are otherwise, for God may loue a man, and a man may trust in God, and yet still continue in affliction : so we se the martyrs die for Christ and perish in regard of the outward man, & that they loue God, and God loueth thē

marginalia: Make a mowe and nod the head.

marginalia: Let him deliuer him, &c.

stil : and so was it with Christ : which may serue to mussel the mouths of the wicked worldlings, that presently think gods children forsaken of god, and that they are naughty persons because they sustain the crosse & sometime fall vnder it : nay cōtrariwise they should thinke it a signe of Gods hatred not to be vnder the crosse as it fareth with many wicked men, that thus the Lord fatteth thē for the day of slaughter.

But thou didst draw me out of the womb : thou gauest me hope at my mothers breast.
I was cast upon the euē from the womb ; thou art my god from my mothers belly.

Vers. 9. 10.

Howsoeuer these murderers of Christ delt with him, yet he assureth himselfe of Gods fauour and mercifull protection still, seeing that he had so graciously preserued him, euen from the birth, the womb, and the conception : For God did by an especial prouidence watch ouer Christ in all ages and times of his life, yea euen at his conception, when he was to be framed in his mothers womb : which thing may a litle be considered of in this manner following.

The Lord preserued Christ in his conception from the contagion of sinne, he beeing framed of the substance of the virgin by the power of the holy ghost without the helpe of man, by reason whereof the course of originall sinne was stayed which is deriued to vs in generation : wherefore in this sēce Christ had no father.

In his birth also hee was preserued by the speciall prouidence of God, that he perished not, though hee was borne in the stable and laid in the cratch, and wanted the other ordinary helpes which women in such cases haue for their childe at there natiuite : for it is probable they wanted a fire, the stable beeing no fit place for that purpose, besides the vnhealthsome sauor of the stable, &c.

In his education and nourishing, he was kept from the conspiracy of Herod that sought his life, when his mother fled into Egipt to saue his life : also when the innocents were slayne : when he was lost by his parents and found againe disputing with the doctors in the temple. In his life when he was called forth to the execution of the mediatorship after his baptisme, he was preserud from many conspiraces of the high priest and the pharises, and the rulers of the people, who sought to haue slayne him, but he was preserued by the Lords providēce till the appointed time.

Wherefore seeing god had watched ouer him all his daies hitherto hee nowe fully assureth himselfe of Gods protection and assistance at this brunt also.

And as this is true in Christ the head so also after a certaine manner is it true in his members, all the children of God, ouer whome the Lord watcheth by his gracious preseruation, and that in there conception. Iob. 10. 10. 11. and Psal. 139. 13. 14. 15. 16. which two places beeing viewed doe largely expresse this point : as also in there whole life : Psal. 121. *toto.* Which may serue to comfort the poore members of Christ, that peraduenture might think by reason of there base respect themselues vnworthy to be regarded by God, seeing the world so litle regard them, surely they are to knowe that he hath nombred there bones, and all there mēbers are written in his booke, yea he knoweth the nomber of the heares of their head : & therefore in this regard they may be comforted : Lazarus was poore and yet the Lords angels ministred to him. lu. 16.

Lastly from the force of the argument, vsed here to confirme the faith of the prophet in assurance of future mercy grounded vpon former experience thereof we are admonished to crōicle & record vp, and as it were hang vpon the file, all the fauour of Gods mercy vouchsafed vs, that from thence in time of need, we may gather faith & comfort : for our faith is weak, and a litle thing will not comfort vs in extremitie, we had need therefore to write a booke of remembrance of all the former experience of Gods mercy thereby to support our infirmity so Dauid did when he was animated to encounter with Goliah.

The request or petition of the Prophet propounded.

V. 11. Be not farre from me, because trouble is neere, and there is none to helpe, &c.

Out of this verse two things may be gathered: first that a Godly man may be troubled and helples: as was Christ, & the prophet in this place, All Christs apostles forsoke him, euen Peter that professed the contrary, and at the first seemed more forward then the rest by fighting for him: yea & Iohn whome Christ loued came away without his coate where Christ was apprehended: The Apostle Paul. 2. Tim. 4. 16 saith that *when he was to appeare before Caesar all men forsooke him:* for indeede there be very few or none to be found that dare and will stand out boldlie to helpe in time of neede, that dare cherish a man that is persecuted for the truth: although they wish the cause and the person well, yet they dare not be seen throughly in the matter, but then Christ shal shift for himselfe, if his life be once called in question: now therefore if we se gods children thus afflicted and helples, condemne them not, conclude not there vpon that they are naught, for the deare children of God, yea Christ himselfe was afflicted and desolate that is helplesse.

Secondly heare note we, that though the world offoard no helpe to Gods children, though all forsake them, yet the Lord will not forsake them: so saith the Apostle, 2. Timoth. 4. 17. So saith Christ, Ioh. 16. 32. though Christ were alone and desolate in regarde of mans helpe and comfort, yet he was not alone, but the father was with him, and though Paul was helpelesse when he appeared before Nero the Emperour, yet God deliuered him out of the Lyons mouth; for God wil either deliuer, or giue strength and patience to beare the affliction: which is matter of consolation: this the three children knew right wel, Dan. 3. 17, 18 which were threatned with the fierie furnace, which ministred comfort to them in deadly danger: with this the Prophet encouraged himselfe Psal. 23. *To walke fearlesly through the valley of the shaddowe of death,* considering Gods presence with him.

*The affliction that immediately seazed
upon Christs soule.*

Vers. 12, 13, 14, 15.

12. *Many Bulls haue compassed me, mightie buls of Bashā haue closed me about.*
13. *They gape vpon me with their mouthes, as a ramping and roaring lyon.*
14. *I am like water powred out, and all my bones are dissolued : mine heart is like waxe, it is molten in the middes of my bowels.*
15. *My strength is dried up like a potsheard, and my tongue cleaueth to my iawes, & thou hast brought me into the dust of death.*

The Apostle Peter: 1. Pet. 5. 8. calleth the deuill *a roaring lyon, who goeth about continually seeking whome he may deuour :* and in this place the Prophet saith, that his enemies gaped vpon him like a ramping and roaring lyon : whence probably may bee coniectured (the two properties of a lyon fitting so wel togither both here in the Prophet, and also in the Apostle) that the enemies that now afflicted Christ were, the deuill and his angels.

1 Pet. 5. 8. ὡς λέων ὠρυόμενος κȝ καταπίνων.

Psal. 22. 13. arich .. shoeg ... toreph.

Wherefore we will take it as graunted, that in this place the Prophet foretelleth the sufferings that directly and properly and primarily befell Christs soule : which may further be prooued by the strange effects which the prophet rehearseth, vers. 14. 15. that followed his affliction: as the dissolution of al the faculties of the soule, or the intermitting their functions, which the compassing and inclosure and gaping of his enemies, could not worke in him : & againe whereas in the v. 21. he desireth to be deliuered from the lyons mouth, how can this be expounded but of the power of Gods wrath, nowe vrged & enforced by the deuill against him : in regard whereof he desireth to be deliuered : all these things compared togither carie me easily to think that here the affliction proper to Christs soule is expressed. Therefore the might, malice, and mischeife of the deuils are here to be considered, who in this place are called mightie Bulls, and a rāping & roaring lyon, there being one deuil the cheife, and the rest consenting and conspiring with him.

The power of the deuils appeares in this, that they are angels, and although through their fall they haue lost grace and glory, yet their other qualities which the Lord endowed them with in their creation remaine : as namely their strength : now the strength of an angell is wonderfull great (though not infinite :) as may appeare, in that the angel ouerthrewe in the hoast of the Assyrians in one night, an hundreth foure score and fiue thousand, Esay, 37, 36. Also in the time of Dauid seauentie thousand in three daies, 2. Sam. 24. 15. And in Egypt euill angels destroyed all the first borne of Egypt. Psal. 78. 49. 50. 51. And as it may seeme in a peece of a night : yea surely it is likely, that if God should permit, the deuils were able to destroy all the men, and all the creatures in the world, and mingle heauen and earth togither.

The malice of the deuill is as great if not greater then his power, which may appeare in two particulars : first in that he setteth himselfe against God and Christ, whereas he knoweth he getteth nothing by it, but vengeance. Secondly in opposing against the Church of God, and his seruants : whereas he knoweth he cannot hurt them, nay rather he doeth them good : he afflicted Iob, and yet he knewe Iob by Gods own commendation to be Gods seruant : he tempted Christ, whome hee knewe to be the Messias and Sauiour of mankind.

The mischeife of the deuill also is as great, as it proceedeth from him, and as it seazeth vpon some persons : he brought Christ to death, Iob to beggerie : he worketh mischeiuously by the witch to destroy the goods and children of men both good and badde : he bringeth men into sinne and keepeth them in it, and so worketh their destruction and damnation, which is the greatest part of his mischeife, howsoeuer it is not so easily obserued.

As the deuil is thus mightie, malitious, and mischeiuous, so vndoubtedly he bestird himselfe with all his skil to afflict Christ, and he euen to the vtmost he could doe, no doubt wrecked himself vpon Christ, to spoile him if it had bin possible : & so doth he and wil do to all gods children : yea he carying an vniuersall hatred to mākind

& al Gods creatures, will worke what villanie he can vpon them : he carried the swine headlong into the sea : he caused the man that was possessed to beat himselfe with stones, &c. Here therefore we see the goodnesse of God towards vs, & toward mankind in generall, who represseth & bridleth the deuill, and chaineth him so as he cannot doe what he list : for thē we should not keep our cattel from his hands, nor money in our purses, nor any of our goods for our vse : nay our bodies should be sure to be tormēted strāgely, and worse then that, if god should lay the raines in his necke : all men therefore good and bad are to consider Gods goodnesse towardes them thus farre forth, that they are moderately preserued by him in their outward estates from the deuils tyrannie.

It may be demanded how farre forth the deuill could and nowe did preuaile against Christ in this place : or whether the deuils were the executioners of Gods wrath, now vpon our Sauiour Christ : whereto answer may be made thus, First it seemeth that the inflicting of Gods wrath vpon the creature is Gods worke onely, and there is no creature that can poure Gods wrath vpon another ; for the wrath of God beeing the curse of the lawe to be inflicted vpon the transgressors of the law, for the breach of the lawe, whereby Gods iustice is violated, and this curse, or this wrath of God beeing the effects of his iustice, it is not conuenient to assigne the execution thereof to the deuill. For the deuil being himselfe subiect to, and tormented with the sense and feeling thereof, and there being no superiour power to torment the deuill, but God, he himselfe must needs be the executioner of the deuils : and there beeing a kind of infinitnesse in Gods wrath, so as the deuill thereby is ouerwhelmed, howe shall it be said with reason, that he that is very vnable to sustaine it, should inflict it, he that cannot beare it himselfe should lay it vpon others ? and as he that is hanged cannot be hangman ; no more can the deuill that is tormented with Gods wrath, torment others therewithall. Therefore the Lord with his owne hand doeth immediately inflict his wrath vpon the creature, whether men or Angels : and as God had the helpe of no creature in the creation, redemption, iustification,

They compas, inclose, and gape vpon me.

sanctification, and saluation of the Church, no more hath he any helpe in the damnation of any creature.

Wherefore the deuils were not Gods instrumēts of powring his wrath vpon Christ, and yet Christ suffered immediately from the deuils, as it is here recorded, for they tempt him, and terrifie him, they compasse him about, and inclose him with temptation, they gape vpon him with their mouthes as readie to deuoure him and teare him in peeces, that is, they vrge and enforce the wrath of God with all possible argument and reason, aggrauating it to the vtmost of their skill. And it is euidēt that they tempted Christ, and no doubt Christ could not sustaine the vrging of the temptation without some sorrowe and griefe and vexation of heart, as euery godly man hath experience, when he resisteth a temptation: for conclusion of this point, the deuils did not execute Gods wrath vpon Christ, but the deuils did tēpt and terrifie Christ otherwise.

The effects that followed vpō the torture which Christ sustained, proueth the strāgenesse and extraordinarinesse thereof, to omitte the effects which are set downe in the story of the gospel, whēce should the dissoluing of the facultie of sense and motion proceede? in so much as that the bones beeing vntied were seuered each from other? surely euen as Baltashar when he saw the hand writing had his ioynts, through the feeling of some diuine power that in iustice smote him for his sinnes, loosed, so as his knees beate together, the animall facultie for a season beeing suspended, euen so was it in Christ. Againe whence came the melting of the heart like waxe, the drying vp of the strength like a potsheard, but from the intollerable heat of Gods firie wrath which nowe pearced our sauiour Christ, and consumed him as the fire that came downe frō heauen consumed the sacrifice into ashes: which was a tipe of this fire which thus dryed and scorched our Sauiour Christ and melted his heart, as waxe melteth at the sunne: How came it to passe that Christs tongue claue to his Iawes? was it immoderate drought that caused it? but then it should haue bene said: to the palate: but the prophet

I am like water powred out, my bones dissolued, &c.

My tongue cleaueth to my Iawes.

saith to the Iawes: according to the latine phrase *vox faucibus hæret*, Christ was not able to speake, but his words were halfe words, words sounding a farre of, faintly, his tongue faultred as it were in speaking it may be that Christ was drie but that drought signified in the Gospell when they gaue him viniger mingled with gal should haue beene mentioned in the 16. verse in due place when he suffered vpon the crosse, and not here where the effects of an other torture are repeated, namely of that which imediately affected his soule, as hath beene said; surely in all likelihood of reason some extraordinary tortures are here implyed which produce so strang effects, and make such deepe impressions in al the faculties of the soule, animall, vitall, naturall, reasonable: whereby the parts of the body seruiceable to the soule for the execution of her faculties are forsaken.

The vse of this doctrine is to teach vs carefully to auoid sinne which wrought such strange affectes in Christ satisfying for sinne, beeing god also: alas how shall wee vild wretches be able another day if it fall to our Lott for our sinnes to sustaine the least hellish torment? it is no maruaile though the rich glutton in hel crie out of his tong, & though Baltashars knees knocke together, though Iudas hanged himselfe, and Cayn blasphemed, and Saull fell vpon his sword, seeing there are such intollerable effectes followe the wrath of God euen in the sonne of God himselfe as are here mentioned.

Here the prophet turneth his speech vnto the Lord: & whereas before he had made a narration of the might mallice and mischeefe of his enemies how they had afflicted him, by terour and temptation, and how straungelie this affliction tortured him, that it caused the faculties of the soule to intermit there functions in there proper parts of the bodie, now he maketh an apostrophe as it were vnto the Lord, and telleth him, that it was he that had brought him to his death, for though his estate nowe was in all likelihood of reason irrecouerable and remediesse, beeing spilt like water vpon the ground, which cannot be gathered vp againe, yet all this sorrowe did not kill him, but he changeth his speech, and saith: thou hast brought me into the

Thou hast brought me into the dust of death.

dust of death : whēce two things may be obserued : the
one is, that God had a stroak in the death of Christ, not
onely by permitting the Iewes to kill him, which shall be
handled afterward in the 16. and 17. verses, but by pouring
his wrath vpon him, which hastened his death the sooner,
in so much as the historie in the gospell saith, he was dead
sooner then the theeues who died the same death with
him, as is likely : which hastie death of Christs was caused
no doubt by some inwarde cause, which was Gods wrath,
that had wrought the former strange effectes in Christ :
that it may be properly said that God killed Christ rather
then the Iewes, though the Iewes also tortured his bodie,
so as that in time he should haue died. The other thing
that we note here is, that all the might, malice, and
mischeife of the deuills, and the Iewes which was exprest
in the torturing and tormenting of Christ, could not haue
killed Christ, except God had killed him. For Christ
beeing God, could if it had pleased him, and if the decree
of god had not beene otherwise, haue retained his spirit,
cured his wound, or destroyed his enemies that they should
not haue beene able to wound him : in regard whereof hee
saith. Ioh. 10. 18. that *he had power to lay downe his life
and to take it vp againe*, and that his life was not wrested
out of his hand but seeing God had decreed it otherwise
therefore Christ must needes die, and yet the principall
crucifier of Christ (that I may so speake generally) was
God himselfe, who besides that he vsed the Iewes, and
the Deuills as his instruments to murder Christ yet he
retayneth in his owne handes one soueraigne torture, the
most fearefull wrath of God to bee inflicted vpon Christ
our surety, in regard whereof the prophet saith of Christ,
thou hast brought me into the dust of death.

Summarily (to ende the torments which immediatly
tortured Christs soule) wee may here obserue that Christ
was thus afflicted as is rehearsed alreadie, both willingly,
and necessarily : willingly in that he suffered the Deuills
thus to assault him with terour and temptation : necessarily in that God had a hand in killing him, and bringing
him to the graue which is deaths dust : and indeed Christ
did willingly and yet necessarily suffer all that hee suffered : hence then two consequents followe immediately.

1. Christs infinite loue that was content and willing to suffer such hardship for vs wretched caitifes: and.

2. That no lesse then that which Christ suffered was sufficient for our redemption & reconciliation to God, seeing that he suffered all that he suffered necessarily: for if it bee supposed that the least suffering of Christ had beene enough to haue appeased God towards vs, then it is superfluous and vnnecessary that Christ should come into the dust of death: should haue such straung effectes in his bodie before his death; should be subiect to the terour and temptations of the deuil: to the woundes and stripes of the Iewes: but because it was necessary that Christ should suffer all these things and so enter into his glorie, therefore the least suffering of Christ was not sufficient. This also might call into question the loue of God to his beloued sonne in that hee would bring him to the dust of death, if it were not necessary: and if it were necessarie that Christ should die & that by Gods owne hand (rather and more then by the Iewes woundes, and the Deuills worke) as is here noted, I would knowe what that hand of God was, if it was not the wrath of God working the former straung effectes in Christs bodie: and if Christ must of necessity die, why must he not of necessitie suffer Gods wrath properly? shall we say Gods loue would not suffer that? but Gods Iustice did require it: and Gods loue would suffer him to die: but necessitie vrged a despensation? what necessity I pray you? euen this perhaps that if Gods wrath had seazed vpon Christ, hee would haue bene forsaken of God: why? *he was forsaken of God* Psal. 22. 1. all comfort was secluded from him, and yet all grace was present with him: but it was impossible that Christ should suffer gods wrath? wherefore impossible? because he was God? therefore also it was impossible that he should die, but possibility admitted his death: and why not Gods wrath? for neither the Godhead died nor suffered Gods wrath, but the manhood only and the hypostaticall vnion was neuer dissolued & there is no daunger of fearing any absurdity to ensue vpon the suffering of Gods wrath rather then vpon the suffering of death: for despaire, want of faith, loue, &c. are not to be feared.

The affliction that immediately seazed vpon Christs bodie.

16. *For dogges haue compassed me, and the assembly of the wicked haue inclosed me, they pearced my hands and my feet.*   V. 16. 17. 18.

17. *I may tell all my bones, yet they behold and looke vpon me.*

18. *They part my garments among them and cast lottes vpon my vesture &c.*

These words containe that affliction which directly and immediately was inflicted vpon Christs bodie, which no doubt pierced the sensitiue part of the soule, which was inherent in the parts of the bodie wounded, for we see woundes in the parts of the bodie are sensible, and so very grieuous : the reason is, for that the obiect and the instrument of sense are ioined togither without a medium, whereas there ought to be a competent distance, and a cōuenient medium, which is called *Cuticula*.

Here in the first place the persons inflicting these bodily torments vpon Christ, are to be considered, who are called dogges, whereas the deuils in the former part of Christs torments were compared to Buls and Lyons : & the comparison hath in it excellent conueniencie & proportion, for as it is an easier matter to encounter a dog, then a mightie madde Bull, & a lyon, so the conflict which Christ had with the wicked, which were but a company of curre dogges, was nothing in comparison of the combate he had with the deuill and his angels, whose malice, might, and mischeife against Christ surpassed the villanie of the Iewes, as farre as the lyon rampeth and roareth more cruelly then the dogge barketh : and yet Christ suffered more then that also, which was the cōplemēt of al misery.

The wicked in the Scripture are compared to dogges in respect of two properties which dogges haue, wherein wicked men are answerable to them : the one is churlishnes the other is filthines : for the dogge will snarle at him that beateth him for his fault, yea though he be his master, Mat. 7. 6. and he will also turne againe and eate the carrion which he hath vomited, 2. Pet. 2. 22. which noteth out vnto vs two sorts of wicked men : one is open persecutors that reuile and persecute them that smite them with holesom reproofes, when they are faultie : another is temporizing hypocrites, that hauing made a shewe of godlinesse, as if they had vomited sinne out of their soules, yet at length returne again, & take vp their former sinnes, which only for a time in hypocrisie they forsooke.

Further this place warranteth (and innumerable more) that the assemble of wicked men that are temporizers or persecutors may lawefully be called dogges, or a kennell of hounds : men now a daies that serue times, and persecute the church take it in dudgin (as we say) that they shuld be called dogs, or swine, or lyons, or beares, &c. & yet they haue all the properties of these brutish creatures, as if bruite beastes were metamorphized & chāged into men, as the heathen haue allegorized : of such persons. I would demād this question ; whether is worse to be a dog, or to be called a dog ? may not a man call a dog a dogge ? Wherfore if such mē be dogs, I knowe no reason but they may be so called, especially the h. ghost going before, whose example is our instruction in the same case : either therefore lett such men cease to bee dogges, or if they still continue dogges let them be called dogges.

Againe some take the prick whē they are not prickt at all in the ministers intentiō- althogh they are prickt in the Lords disposition : for sometime the minister intendeth in his ministerie that which neuer pearceth : & sometime God causeth that to pearce in his ministerie that which hee neuer intendeth, that it may be knowne that Pauls planting, and Apollos watring is nothing except God giue increase : There are men called by the names of beasts, as lyon, fox, hart, hare, hound, or so forth, and these men are some good some bad, as our owne experience may informe vs well enough : nowe sometime it falleth out that the minister in his ministerie is occasioned by the scripture to vnfold the euill properties of wicked men in regard whereof they are cōpared to beasts as the lyons properties are prid and crueltie, the foxes craft and subteltie, the hearts fearefullnes, &c. and it may fall out that some wicked man called lyon hath the lions prid and cruelty, some wicked man called fox hath the foxes craft and subteltie &c. now if these men take themselues either named or aymed at in the ministerie, where as it may be the minister neuer dreameth thereof ; or if the minister intend such a thing, whence should a man say this proceedeth ? without doubt either grosse folly, or an accusing conscience, or meere mallice, or brutish ignorāce bring mē into these surmises : howsoeuer it be gods word, it is a sharpe two edged sword ; & the minister by gods prouidēce, which to him perhaps is chance medley, sometime shal woūd him whome he neuer aimed at, or harden him, whome he neuer thought of : for the word of God is both a sauour of life & of death to seuerall sorts of persons. These are the persōs that afflicted Christ, let vs further consider what afflictions befel him : they crucifie him, & mock him, they strip him naked, and dispoile him of his garments : all which are so many sufferings of Christ for our good : he was crucified, & suffered the most accursed death of the crosse, to deliuer vs frō the curse of the law, Gal. 3. 13 he was mockt to make vs honourable, he was robbed to make vs rich, & was stript naked to couer our nakednes : al these benefits we haue frō all Christs sufferings, though not each of them seuerally frō the like suffering in Christ, howsoeuer allegorically thus applied.

But one thing especially is here to be considered concerning the crucifying of Christ, in what sense Christ beeing vpon the tree, & there put to death, was accursed ? for expositiō wherof, we are to know, that to die vpon a tree is not a thing indeede accursed, either in nature *They pierced my hands and my feet, I may tell all my bones.* or ciuill constitutiō, or of it selfe. Nature doth not teach vs, that to hang vpon a tree is a thing accursed, more thē to be thrust through with a sword, or to be prest to death, or to be burnt, or so forth.

Againe no positiue or ciuill lawes of any nation vnder heauen haue accursed those persons that haue beene hanged vpon a tree vntill their bodies haue died, indeed the death is something more base and vilde then some other kind of death is, in reputation among some persons, whence in our nation it seemeth that noble men haue some priuiledge that way, that they die not as other sorts of persons die. And lastly, the death of the tree hath no curse in it selfe : we reade of diuers men that were godly men that died vpon the tree ; as the penitentiarie that died with Christ, & Christ himselfe also : and experience teacheth vs that euery yeare : for many men betwixt their condemnation and execution haue beene deepely humbled for there sinnes, and so haue died the true seruants of God : wherefore the death of the crosse (which Christ suffered) was not thus accursed : how then was it accursed ? surely by the iudiciall and ceremoniall lawe of Moses and not otherwise : that lawe which Moses gaue from God the lawgiuer of the Iewes Deut 21. 23. conteyneth a prohibition with a reason annexed thereto : The prohibition is in these words : *Thou shalt not suffer his bodie that is hanged vpon the tree to remaine all night vpon the tree :* and this prohibition is a meare Iudiciall law of Moses the which the people of the Iewes onely, were bound to obserue ; which lawe if the people of the Iewes had violated, they sinned so against God, that the land was defiled with the sinne, Deut. 21. 23. The reason of that prohibition is in these words : *For the curse of God is on him that is hanged :* and this reason is a meere ceremoniall lawe : (for it hath bin prooued, that neither by the lawe of nature, by ciuill or positiue lawe, or of it selfe, to be hanged vpon a tree is accursed ;) it is therefore a meere ceremonie : but we know that Christ is the substance of euery ceremonie : wherefore the Lord foreseeing that Christ should die vpon a tree, & vpō the tree suffer the curse of the lawe due vnto our sins, as our suretie : therefore he typically figured out this curse in the death of malefactours amōg the people of the Iews, that were hāged vpō the tree : so that euery malefactor that was hāged amōg the Iews, was a type of Christ, and therfore was accursed : not really (for it is want of charitie to think so) but ceremonially and typically, represēting vnto vs Christ, who was truely and really accursed for vs : in that he sustained gods wrath which is the curse of the lawe, which we should haue sustained : wherefore seeing

Christ was really accursed as hath beene prooued by this discourse, therfore he vndoubtedly suffered gods wrath which is the curse.

Whē they had nailed Christ to the crosse and wrackt his ioynts so as that his bones might bee numbered they heape vpon him all other indignities they can : and therefore first they behold & look vpon him : alas it was a pitifull sight for one that had any manhood in him, to see a man nayled hands and feete with great nailes (as they must needes be seeing the hebrue word signifieth such a pearcing, as was more like digging : or such a pearcing as a lyon maketh with his clawes) ; to see the blood issue abounly out of the woundes; to see his bodie strecht so as that one ioynt was seuered from an other which is an extreame torture, for a bodily torment ; and yet they behold and look vpon him without any pitty at all ; nay they mock and derid him as appeareth plaine in the historie of the Gospell, & when he would haue had a litle drinke to asswage his thirst, they gaue him viniger mingled with gaul to increase his thirst the more, gaull beeing a thing biter of it selfe ; all these shamefull outragies they offered to Christ nowe in dying ; whence we may cōsider ; not only the barbarous crueltie of these persons, but further the nature and property of sinne which is to grow one from degree to degree, till it come to an heigth and a fearefull excesse; these persons first contemned Christs doctrine, depraued his life, cōsented to his death, now most cruelly murder him, and yet that doth not satisfie them, but they mock at him in the middest of his misery : & will not affoard him any ease at al : It is good to gainstand sinne at the first, least if it get groūd of vs at length it conquer and subdue vs : for the Lord sometime accustometh to punish one sinne with another, and when men will not preuent small sinnes, they shall bee plunged into a sea of fearefull impietie : as the Gentiles because when they knewe God they did not glorifie him as God, fell to Idolatrie and after that to sinne against nature : and they in the seate of Antichrist because they receiued not the loue of the truth, therefore are giuen ouer to strang delusions to beleeue lies that they might bee damned. Rom. 1. 2. Thes. 2.

_{Yet they behold & looke vpon me.}

When they had thus shamefully handled Christ, they proceede to the deuiding of his garments (for they stript him of his cloathes when they crucified him) and here wee may obserue diuers points worth our noting : for what should be the reason that the holy Ghost should thus carefully expresse this practise of the souldiers in deuiding his garments & casting lottes for his vesture ? no doubt this is some speciall matter euen in this their practise, especially seeing the Euāgelist also testify the same thing to be done by the soldiers : some allegory the matter after this manner : the garmēts of Christ (say they) are the scriptures : the vesture of Christ is his Church, the souldiers are heretiques : For although the heretiques rend the scriptures with false exposition &c. yet they cannot dissolue the vnitie of the Church with there errours : This doctrine is true, but it is not intended in this place. It is a meere folly and dotage thus to abuse the scriptures, though the allegorie be neuer so wittie. But we are to knowe that one reason why the Euangelistes expresse these things is for the verifying of the prophecy : that the euent might declare the truth of the prophecy : other profitable considerations may hence be raised.

They part my garments and cast lottes one my vesture.

1 The souldiers deale as theeues which haue gotten a bootie : they make no conscience of robbing a man & yet they make a scruple in deuiding the spoile : the soldiers make no bones to kill Christ, and rob him of his garments, yet they are curious in the deuiding his apparrell amongst them : for it is a right propertie of an hypocrite to swallow a camell, and to strayne at a gnatt : to tith mint, cummin and annise seed, and to neglect Iudgement, mercy, and faith : the soldiers neuer strayne curtesy to iniury Christ, but they wil not iniury one another.

2 Againe the Holy Ghost seemeth to laie another fault among the soldiers that they cast lottes for trifles, as if men should card and dice for a coate : we neuer read in all the scriptures that lottes were vsed but in waighty matters, and it seemeth to be to take the name of God in vaine, to sport our selues with his immediate prouidence, as lots are.

3 Furthermore (if that bee not assented vnto) yet

here is another thing flatly reproueable, that by lottes (as it were cardes and dice) they would compasse parts of their maintenance, getting away from another mā by lott that which before was not theirs or wherto they had no title: for one of the souldiers must needes haue the whole coate (for seeing it was without seame they would not cut it) and so the other three soldiers lost their parts and he that gott the coat by lott, was a theefe to the other three: for god hath appointed men to get there goodes by labour and lawfull contractes not by carding and dicing and lotting, as the soldiers doe in this place.

4 Lastly: it seemeth that Christs coate was worth somthing, as also his garments for otherwise the souldiers would not haue regarded thē thus as they doe: and Christ was not so poore and beggerly, as some begging fryers might peraduenture suppose him to be: neither is begging a state of perfection, better then possessing & vsing riches: we read that Paull had a cloake which he left at Troas, & it is like he carried another with him, except we say he borowed one or went in his Ierkin: and though some mens riches are a snare vnto them, yet that is not in their riches, but in their corupt harts which are set vpon their riches: some mans pouertie also is a snare vnto him but that is in the wickednes of his owne heart also rather then in pouertie.

Of the request and petition of the prophet repeated.

19. *But be thou farre of O Lord my strength: hasten to helpe me.*
20. *Deliuer my soule from the sword, my desolate soule frō the power of the dog.*
21. *Saue me from the Lyons mouth, and answer me in sauing me from the hornes of the vnicornes.*

Hitherto the sufferinges of Christ haue beene discussed: nowe it followeth to intreat more largely of the prayer that Christ maketh, the substance whereof is here set downe by the prophet and it accordeth with the prayer which the Euangelist setteth downe Math 26. and Ioh. 12. *Let this cup passe from me. &c. saue me from this houre* &c.

where this question commeth to be scanned: what Christ praied for in this place, and in these two places of the Euangelistes: or what Christ praieth against: for the on of these include the other, and the supplication includeth the deprecation: for solution whereof: It must necessarily be granted that he praieth either against a bodily death, or against Gods wrath; if it be saide, that he praied against a bodily death, then also it must needes be that he prayed either that it should not light vpon him, or that it should not triumph ouer him; that is that the power of death should not hinder him from rising againe, that he should not be held of the sorrowes of death, Act. 2. 24.

Againe if it be said that he prayed against Gods wrath, then one of these three things must of necessity be graunted: namely that he prayed.

1 Either that Gods wrath should not light vpon him.

2 Or that it might depart from him beeing alreadie vpon him.

3 Or that it might not swallowe him vp and ouerwhelme him and eternally detayne him, and so cause him either to forfeite, or not to accomplish our redemption.

There beeing thus a sufficient enumeration of parts, let vs proceed further and inquire against which of al these he prayed.

First therefore he prayed not against death that hee might not tast it: for God had determined that hee should suffer death, and he knewe it very well it beeing figured in the sacrifices of the old law, whereof he was the substance prophecyed by the prophets, signified to the disciples by himselfe. Mat. 16. and to say that he prayed against that, for which he knewe he came into the world were to make him pray against his knowledge, & against the expresse will of God reuealed in the word, which were blasphemous to say of Christ in whose mouth there was found no guile.

Secōdly also he praied not against Gods wrath, so as that it should not light vpon him: for Matth. 20. 22. he saith plainely, *he must taste of that cuppe:* wherefore he did taste it when he praied it might passe from him,

Math. 26 & the conditiō which is exprest in this praier argueth so much : for in the place of Mat. 26. 42. Christ saith thus, *If this cuppe cannot passe from me, but that I must drinke it, thy wil be done:* which wordes plainely import thus much : that whereas before the first time he praied this praier, he directly said : let this cup passe from me, adding the conditions : Math. 26. 39. There was some opposition betwixt his naturall will and gods wil : nowe the second time he praied, Christs will is wholly submitted and subiected to Gods will, to drinke the cup prepared for him by God : as if Christ had said, Father if it had beene possible, and agreeable to thy will, I could wish that this cuppe of thy fierce wrath might passe away, so as that I might not tast it, but seeing it cannot passe till I haue drunke it, I submit my selfe to thy will. And this praier in the same wordes he vttereth the third time : Math. 26. 44. Where the changing of the wordes of the prayer in the verse, 42. is to be carefully noted : which change is retained the third time he praied, v. 44. as if Christ had now vanquished nature by grace ; for there was in Christ both nature & grace, and that this second praier was a correcting of the former : not as though his first praier were simply bad, but that nature seemed to carrie a greater sway in the first, then in the secōd, & grace throughly corrected nature in the secōd : other correcting I meane none : wherefore here Christ praied not that Gods wrath might not at al light vpō him.

Thirdly therfore, & for cōclusion, he praied against the other 3. parts of the distribution mentioned before : against the dominion and continuāce of gods wrath, and death. Against the dominion of death and gods wrath he praied vndoubtedly, and that properly as our intercessor, that neither himselfe the head, nor we cōsequētly the members, should be subdued & ouerwhelmed of them : but that himselfe, and we by him might conquer & vanquish them, & triumph ouer them : and so he was heard frō that which he feared. One Heb. 5. 7. doubt will here arise, howe Christ could feare the dominion of death & Gods wrath, for then Christ wāted faith, & doubted, which to say were blasphemy : for answer whereof, we must distinguish betwixt feare and doubting. A man may feare that which he assuredly knoweth shall not befall him : Adam in Paradise might feare the wrath of god, and feare his apostacie & falling from God, which was in him a vertue, & yet surely Adā had faith & a perswasiō of gods loue, & assurance to cōtinue in grace, if he would : so likewise Christ might feare least the wrath of God might ouerwhelme him and vs, and yet be fully assured of deliuerance from it : Feare is a naturall affection : and no naturall affection is contrarie to grace, but subordinate to it : and Christ feared these things naturally, and furthermore the word εὐλάβεια, Heb. 5. 7. signifieth a fearefull and carefull declining and auoiding some imminent danger, by reason whereof the minde is possessed with a great anxietie and sollicitude, intending it selfe, with all the powers thereof to gainstand the impendent mischeife : and thus Christ feared the dominion of death and gods wrath, and for this purpose praied against it, he beeing carefully and reuerently busied about the recouery of himselfe, and the redeeming of vs from the power of death and the sorrowes of hell : and because praier is one excellent meanes to furnish a christian captaine against the enemie for obtaining the victorie : therefore Christ prayeth with strong crying and teares vnto him that was able to saue him from death eternall, and was heard from that which he naturally feared, or rather from that, for declining whereof he was reuerently accumbred : nature working in him feare of it, and grace stirring vp praier against it : and there is no absurditie to say, that Christ praied against that which he certainely and fully knewe should neuer befall his Disciples.

And as Christ praied against the dominion of death and gods wrath, so he praied also that the wrath of God might not stay longer vpon him, he beeing now alreadie tormented therewithall, & so he saith, *let it passe from me : saue me from this houre.* For further explication whereof consider 3. propositions or axioms following.

1 Christ sustaining the ful wrath of God in his soule, was wholly busied in his whole soule, and all the faculties thereof in apprehending, feeling, and bearing it, so as the soule & faculties thereof were distracted from all

their obiects, & wholly applied herevnto : as appeareth by the strāge intermitting of the functiōs of the soule in the parts of the body, mentioned, v. 14. 15.

2 We must distinguish nature & naturall infirmities frō sin and sinful infirmities : it is a naturall infirmitie for a man to sleepe and be wearie, and so also sustaining Gods wrath, to desire to be released frō it : but it is no sinne at all.

3 We must knowe that Christ as he was man was ignorant of some things, as namely of the day of iudgment, Mar. 13. 32. for some ignorance is no sinne : as for a minister to be ignorant of the manuarie trades : for a man to be ignorāt where hel is, of the orders of angels, &c.

Now for applicatiō of these three axiomes : sure it is that when Christ praied, he praied without the least spotte of sinne : and either of these axiomes rehearsed will iustifie Christ praier from the least suspition of sinne : as it is thought.

The first axiome iustifieth a certaine obliuion or forgetfulnesse in Christ, when all the faculties of the soule were interrupted through the sense of Gods wrath : and wholly seazed with the intollerable paine thereof : this I dare not peremptorily say, euery way to be good and sound, neither doe I reprooue it : onely thus much, it may seeme to be a fault for a man to forget when he ought to remember ; and to say that Christ had nowe a holy forgetfulnesse, when he should most of all remember, euen when he was to make the vp-shotte (that I may so speake) of our redemption, is not presently without further inquisition to be admitted.

In regard of the second of these axiomes it may be more probably answered, that Christ sustaining the wrath of God, and hauing the nature of a man in him, which desired releife frō so extreame torment (which is a naturall sinlesse worke) said to his Father, *Let this cup passe, saue me from this houre, &c* and in the very selfe same moment of time that nature desireth, grace seasoneth and qualifieth nature, saying, *Not my* naturall *will, but thy will be fulfilled :* therefore came I into this houre. So here there is first a difference betwixt nature and grace ; then a subordinating of nature to grace : also it may be a correcting of nature by grace, not as if nature were euil simply but a lesse good : for it is good for the creature to preserue it selfe : it is better to obey gods wil by suffering according to his wil : especially considering the coincidence of nature & grace in the same time & praier : for nature maketh the request, grace addeth the conditions.

Nature saith thus :
Father let this cuppe passe from me : saue me frō this houre.
Grace saith :
If it be possible : & not my wil be done, but thine ; & therfore came I into this houre.

In regard of the third axiom aforesaid, it is thus answered, that as Christ was ignorāt of the day of iudgmēt, so without errour it may seeme, we may say he was ignorāt of the time how long or how oft he shuld suffer the wrath of god : and so beeing vnder the hand of God, & not knowing what space of time god in his euerlasting decree had set downe for enduring it, or how oft it should make incursion vpon him ; he praied, *Let it passe, &c.* that is, let it depart from me, I hauing now sustained it ; or let it not seaze vpon me againe, I hauing already suffered it ; sure it is, that Christ did vndergoe gods wrath a competent time, and diuers times, as Ioh. 12. Once Gods wrath like lightning did flash vpon his face ; also Math. 26. The secōd time gods wrath most furiously assaulted him, which wrought in him that strange agonie & sweat : lastly, hanging vpō the crosse, when he cried out, *My God, my God ; why hast thou forsaken me ?* & the third assault was the Cōplement of all his woes, for whereas before in the Garden an angell comforted, and so God had not cleane forsaken him, now God vtterly withdrewe from him all comfort ; and so there was nothing but wrath deuouring him & praying vpon him without all mercy and comfort : but exquesitely to determine howe oft, or how long at any time Gods wrath was vpon Christ, seeing the scripture hath not exprest it, is meere curiositie ; and if any man obiect that Christ prayed against Gods will neuerthelesse in praying thus ; it is answered that he praied against Gods secret will it may be and that is no sinne ; and his prayer had conditions, & so it was not against gods wil ; It is no sinne for the sonne to pray for the life of his father, which shall shortly die, hee praying cōditionally. Wherefore to end all this discourse of Christs prayer ; it is iustifiable as we see, in diuers respects by saying either he forgatt through the interrupting of the soule ; or that nature corrected with grace made this request ; or that he prayed through ignorance, contrary to Gods secret will conditionally.

These things beeing thus discoursed the meaning of these wordes in the psalme is very easie ; as if the prophet should haue said more plainly and without allegory thus all the powers of darkenes now rage against mee, (the dogge the lyon the vnicorne the sword) the Iewes, the deuill (which is the ramping & roaring lyon :) thy wrath and the curse of the lawe : nowe father I doe not desire that I may not incounter with them but that I may not be ouercome by them, saue me from the dominion of death & thy wrath (from the power of the dogge, frō the lyons mouth, from the hornes of the vnicornes) lette the Iewes (the dogges) crucifie and kill mee, let the Deuill and his angels (the lyō the vnicornes) tempt and terrifie me : let thy wrath and the curse of the lawe (the sword) seeing it must needes torture me : but yet father saue me, & by me thy whole Church from perishing vnder thy wrath : Yea father if I nowe haue sustained thy wrath long enough and often enough (as that is hidden from me, as is the day of iudgement) release me from it : but if it must needes still rest vpon me, I am content to beare it still patiently, and that for the full and perfect redemption of thy Church.

From these wordes paraphrastically thus expounded may arise a doubt : why Gods wrath is called a sword, or howe that exposition is iustifiable : for satisfying wherof we must cōsider the place, Zachar. 3. 7. *Arise o sword, and smite the sheapheard*, which place is applyed by the Euangelist, Math. 26. 31. to the death of Christ, also consider the phrase : the prophet prayeth that *his soule may be deliuered from the sword :* his soule doth not signifie his life, but his very soule indeede the fountaine of life : for Christ did not pray against death that he might not tast it : but

_{v. 20. Deliuer my soule from the sword.}

that his soule might not be swallowed vp of death : therefore this must needes be the meaning of the place : let not thy wrath ouerwhelme my soule : for we cannot say properly let not death ouerwhelme my soule, but let not death ouerwhelme my bodie. The soule dieth not but the bodie onely.

Summarily then to end ; this is not the meaning of the wordes : deliuer my life from death : *Supra probatum.*

Nor this ; deliuer my soule from death, for the soule cannot die, it is immortall.

Nor this ; deliuer my bodie frō the graue : for it is absurd and impertinent to this place.

Therefore this is the meaning : deliuer my soule from thy wrath (*my soule from the sword*) but the sword did smit the shepheard : *ergo* Gods wrath did torture his soule.

The meaning of this Epithet (*desolate*) is exprest v. 1. for Christs soule was desolate, because God had nowe forsaken him, and neither himselfe, man or angell or any creature did comfort him but all had forsaken him. v. 11. <small>Desolate (soule.)</small>

Although Christ was desolate of all comfort, yet he had strength and grace sufficient to beare whatsoeuer was inflicted vpon him by God as our suretie. And therefore neuerthelesse he intitleth god his strength, though he complaineth that God had forsaken him, and did not heare when he roared. vers. 1. <small>My strength.</small>

The promise of Thankefulnesse : and first of Christs Prophecie.

<small>Ver. 22, 23, 24, 25.</small> 22 *I will declare thy name vnto my brethren : in the midst of the congregation will I praise thee, (saying.)*

23 *Praise the Lord ye that feare him, magnifie ye him all the seed of Iacob, and feare yee him all the seed of Israel.*

24 *For he hath not despised nor abhorred the affliction of the poore : nether hath he hid his face from him, but when he called vnto him he heard.*

25 *My praise shall be of thee in the great congregation : my vowes will I performe before them that feare him.*

The Prophet hauing before set down the sacrifice and intercession of Christ both in the torments which he sustained partly in his soule directly and properly from the deuill, and from God himselfe, partly in his body frō the Iews that murthered him, as also in the vehement praier which he made, partly for himselfe, and partly for vs, seeing the fruite thereof wholly redoundeth vnto vs : now he proceedeth to the prophecy & kingdome of Christ: and first the prophetical office of Christ is exprest in these foure verses.

The principall worke of Christs prophecy is to declare Gods name, that is, his excellent attributes, and his whole wil vnto his brethrē the Iews, and so to the whole Church, for so this place is brought, Heb. 2. 12. to prooue the humanitie of Christ: whence we consider that Christ is designed by God the father for the onely Prophet, Doctour, and teacher of the Church, he is the great Bishop of our soules : God hath commanded vs to heare him : and he is the onely law-giuer that is able to saue and destroy: which is thus to be vnderstood, that he alone hath reuealed his fathers will to the Church by the ministerie of the prophets in the old Testament, by his own, & the Apostles ministerie in the new testament, who spake as the H. ghost directed thē, for Christ Iesus hath in his brest hid all the treasures of wisdome and knowledge, who is therefore called the wisdome of God : and therefore we are not to adde to, or detract any thing from the writtē word of god, or to alter any whitte thereof, which whosoeuer presumeth to doe, derogateth from the propheticall office of Christ : the scriptures indeede may be expounded, but they must not be altered, augmented or diminished.

Vers. 22. I wil declare thy name vnto my brethren.

Hence also followeth it by due proportion : that the ministers and Pastors of the Church, who stand vp in Christs stead (he being ascended vp on high, and hauing giuen gifts vnto men) are to open and publish Gods will (sufficiētly reuealed by Christ in the Prophets and Apostles writings) to the people of God for their conuersion & saluation. Finally also by like analogie Christians must without feare or shame confesse and professe the truth of Gods word, not onely before the friends of the Church, &

those specially ouer whome they haue charge, but also before the enemies of the Church being called and vrged thereunto.

This is the principal work of Christs prophecie to teach the Church: nowe the effects thereof follow, which are the praise of God, & the conuersion of mens soules: which are subordinate each to other: for by the conuersion of mens soules God is glorified.

The first effect of Christs propheticall office, and so of the ministery of the prophets, Apostles, and Pastors of the church, is the conuersion of mens soules: otherwise called the gathering togither of the Saints, the edification of the bodie of Christ. <small>V. 23. Let the seed of Iacob & Israel, feare, praise, and magnifie god.</small>

The second effect of the Prophecie of Christ, & so of the ministerie, is the praise of God, for therefore must ministers preach & teach that God may be glorified in the conuersiō of mēs soules: thus Christ saith, I honour my father: and again, I haue glorified thee on the earth: <small>V. 22. In the middes of the congregation I will praise thee.</small> Where the ministers, Pastors, and teachers of the Church are to learne in their functions to ayme at these endes, that they may saue soules which is a great point of wisdome, and gloryfie God which is the end of all things; where those pastours are reproueable that seeke rather to wine their own praise by inkhorne learning, by darkning and obscuring their preachings with the cloudes of phylosophy & the tongues, drawing as it were a vale before Christ crucyfied, and couering Moses face with a scarfe; that men should not with open face see the glory of God, then the prase of god, and the conuersion of mens soules, who are rather by this kind of preaching still kept in the dungeon of ignorance and palpable darkenes that the day starre Iesus Christ cannot arise in their hartes; so that this kind of preaching is rather to put out, then to open the eies of the blind.

Hitherto the prophet hath declared the propheticall office of Christ in reuealing Gods will to the Church with the two effectes thereof, the conuersion of mens soules and the glory of God (for the hardening of the wicked is no proper effect;) now the prophet rendereth a reason of Christs propheticall office, wherefore he will reueale his fathers will to his Church ; or wherefore the Church ought to praise God beeing conuerted because that when Iesus Christ beeing poore and in great humiliatiō sustaining the wrath of God for the redemption of the Church called vnto his father, hee heard: and did not abhorre or despise his affliction, but with a pitifull eie regarded him and at length when hee had satisfyed gods iustice deliuered him.

<small>V. 24. He hath not despised the affliction of the poore: but heard his prayer.</small>

Hence then we may learne two instructions.

First that the propheticall office of Christ is a fruit of his preisthood, of his redemption, sacrifice and intercession : for if Christ had not died for vs, he had neuer reuealed his fathers will vnto vs: according as the apostle (Eph. 4.) doth reason Christ ascended vp on high and led captiuitie captiue, and gaue gifts vnto men : but before hee ascended hee discended and suffered death for vs.

Secondly hence wee must learne euerlastingly to magnifie the worke of our redemption which is the fountaine of all our good : for without it we had still remained in blindnes & ignorance without the knowledge of Gods word, and so we had groped in the palpable darkenes of Ægipt : for the propheticall office of Christ principally reuealeth vnto vs the redemption of Christ which is the principall worke of his preisthood, so that Christs sacrifice is the halfe of the matter of his prophecy the doctrine of the lawe also through Christ prophecy is restored vnto vs sound and perfect which through the transgression of Adam was wonderfully defaced, and the condition of the lawe is qualified also by the conditions of the gospell, that the Lord doth not nowe require perfect obedience in quantity, but in quality : and so through the redemption of Christ. The Gospell is wholly reuealed, a matter altogether vnknowne to man by nature, and the law is restored, and qualified and made possible to the penitent and beleeuers.

Here a question may bee made how God heard Christ when he praied: seeing in the first and second verses it is said that god heard not: that doubt is answered before in the cōplaint: & therefore it is needelesse here to repeate it againe.

<small>He heard whē he called.</small>

In this 25. verse there are two phrases to be obserued: first what should be meant by the great congregation: it seemeth that the Prophet hath reference to that which should bee practised by Christ in his propheticall office: we reade in the booke of the Lawe, Deuteronom. 16. that all the males were commaunded to come vp to Ierusalem thrice in the yeare, nowe that was no doubt a great congregation when all the males came thither to worshippe: nowe there is an expresse place in the Euangelist, Iohn, 7. 37. that Christ preached and prophesied in the last and great day of the feast of Tabernacles, which was one of those three great assemblies: and so that place of Iohn and this of the prophet are parallell in sence: A second phrase doubtfull is: what is meant by Christes vowes? In the old testament vowes were of such matters and of such a condition as that before they were made, they were in a mans power, but after they were vowed they became necessary, Eccles. 5. 3. 4. Act. 5. 4. probably therefore it may be said that Christs vowes were that voluntary submission of Christ to become our mediator, our prophet and king and priest, which was most free & willing and vncompelled in him. Ioh. 10. 18.

Vers. 25. My praise shal be of thee in the great congregation.

My vowes will I performe.

Of Christs kingdome: or kingly office: and his subiects.

26. The poore shall eate & be satisfyed, they that seeke after the Lord shall praise him, your soule shall liue for euer.

27. All the ends of the world shall remember themselues and turne to the Lord, all the kindreds of the nations shall worshippe before thee.

28. For the kingdōe is the lords & he ruleth among the nations.

29 All they that be fatte in the earth shall eate and worship: all they that goe downe into the dust shall bow befere him: euē he that cannot quicken his owne soule.

30 There seede shall serue him, it shall be counted to him foreuer.

26. 27. 28. 29. 30. 31.

31 *They shall come & shal declare his righteousnes: because he hath done it for a people to be borne.*

In the kingdome of Christ the subiects are first to be cōsidered who are first described by two properties: which are indeed Properties euery way, wherein the wicked haue no part nor portion at all: which are these following.

1 Humiliation 2 faith 3 peace of conscience 4 desire of increase of grace 5 Glorifying God 6 life euerlasting: of each of them something.

Humiliation or contrition or sorrowe for sinnes is the first grace that appeareth sensibly in the soule of a Godly man, this is the sacrifice that is well pleasing in gods sight; & the Lord hath promised to dwell with the man that hath a broken and contrite heart; and blessednes is promised by Christ to them that are poore in spirit; and Christ inuiteth all those that are wery and laden with their sinnes to come to him for refreshing; and he came to call such sinners to repentance, whose hearts melt at the consideratiō of their sinnes whereby they offend a God that is most mercifull and iust.

<small>V. 26. The poore.</small>

Faith is the second grace which followeth humiliation, the property whereof is to eate Iesus Christ, to apprehend and apply the sacrifice of Christ particularly to it selfe: for faith is not a vast & indistinct apprehension of Christ, or a confused and indefinite conceipt of Gods mercy to the world: but a distinct appropriating & applying of gods mercie and Christs merit to my self, knowing in some measure, & beeing assured that Christ hath nayled, crucified, and buried my sinnes to his crosse, and in his graue, and to doe this is al the difficultie.

<small>Shall eate.</small>

Third property is ioy and peace and quietnes of conscience, when a man is assured of the pardon of his sinnes through faith, a man knoweth that God loueth him, and doth accept of his person, and watcheth ouer him to doe him good, hee knoweth that he is freed from death, and damnation through the redemption of Christ, that life euerlasting appertaineth to him, vnder hope whereof he reioyceth yea in the midst of affliction, though somtime this peace

<small>And be satisfied.</small>

bee disturbed through some sins wherin to the children of God fall through temptation: this is termed here *satisfying*, not for that a man that hath it, neuer desireth grace more: but because nothing in the world can satisfie him til he haue comfort in the assurāce of his sins pardoned, when a man is once throughly humbled; or because a man neuer is barren and drie, and cleane void of grace and comfort after, that once hath it.

Fourth propertie is desire of increase of grace, which is obtained by seeking the Lord where and howe he is to be found, that is, in the word and the meanes of grace: for he that wanteth grace can neuer desire it, onely he that hath it, and hath felt the sweetnes of it longeth for it still, like vnto the man that finding the treasure hid in the field, and the pearle, neuer resteth till he get both: by this also a man may knowe the trueth of grace in his soule: for he that neuer regardeth the word, neuer attēdeth vpon instruction, nor watcheth to praier, that man wanteth grace: for the heauēly couetousnesse and dropsie of grace is insatiable: and therefore the Church is sicke of loue vnto the Lord Iesus Christ in the Canticles. Seeke after the Lord.

A fifth propertie is the leading of a godly life according to gods commaundments, with a constant profession & confession of the trueth to the praise of God, that others may see our good workes, and glorifie God also. Also a thankefull heart whereby a man in himselfe blesseth God for all his goodnes, saying with the Prophet, *All that is within me praise his holy name.* Shall praise him.

Euerlasting life is the last propertie, which is the reward of all the former: and which is the complement of our happinesse and felicitie. Your heart shall liue for euer.

After the description of the subiects of Christs kingdome by their properties follow the seuerall sorts of them: Gentiles as wel as Iews, poore as well as rich: malefactors condemned to die, as well as guiltlesse persons; the childrē as well as the parents. Yea and the kingdome of Christ consisteth of all other sortes of persons that may be rehearsed: as bond and free, mā & woman, master and seruāt, &c. Generally hence may be noted two instructions.

First, wherefore the church is called Catholike; because it cōsisteth of al sorts of persons, it is in al places : it is at al times. v. 27. 29. 30, 31.

Secondly that grace is vniuersall no sort or estate of men excluded from Christs kingdom : ethe poore haue intrest to grace and Christ as- well as the rich, the gentill as- well as the Iewe, women as- well as men : yet wee must knowe that the note of vniversality must not be stretcht to euery particular man, but to euery estate and condition of man. For it is more then grosse absurdity to say that all and euery particular rich mā, and poore man shall bee a member of Christ, shall eate and worship, that is beleeue and serue God : wherefore this doctrine serueth to admonish first the welthie and fatt men of the earth not to contemne and despise the poore, and the leane & needie soule : and the poore not to enuie the rich, and malice the wealthie : but both to serue togither in their places, and to preserue the communion of saints mutually, remembring the Apostles rule, Iam. 1. 9. 10. that the poore is exalted, and the rich is made lowe in Iesus Christ : that though the rich be the poore mans master, yet he is Christs seruant : and though the poore man be the rich mans slaue, yet he is the sonne of God, and fellow heire with him, and with Christ of the kingdome of grace and glory. Besides these generall instructions, certaine particular obseruations also are here to be noted which followe.

V. 29. All that be fat: all that goe downe into the pitt.

The Prophet saith, that the Gentiles shal become subiects of Christs kingdome : which prophecie we see verified amongest vs at this day, wherevpon we are to be stirred vp to glorifie the mercie & truth of God, who hath cast off his owne people, and receiued vs, that were wilde branches of the wilde oliue, that were strangers and aliants from the common wealth of Israel : without God in the world : which must also teach vs not to be hie minded, but to feare, and looke to our selues that we stand fast.

Vers. 27. The ends of the world. The kindreds of the nations.

Againe, the conuersion of the Gentiles is here noted out vnto vs in the 3. parts thereof.

1 They shall remember themselues, that is, their

sinfull and accursed estate : they shall take notice of
<small>Shall remember.</small> it by the powerfull preaching of the Gospell : humiliation.

2 They shall turne to the lord : forsaking their false way of Idolatry and other sinnes and turning their feet into the truth, & walking in obedience of Gods lawes : obedience. <small>Turne to the Lord.</small>

3 They shall worship before God, by partaking al the meanes of saluation, as the word, prayer, sacraments. &c. publikely and priuately as good christians : adoration. <small>Worship before thee.</small>

Nowe because this may seeme a very straunge thing to the Iewes that the gentiles should be admitted into the fellowship of the Church, the partition wall beeing broken downe & one people beeing <small>V. 28. Kingdome is the Lords.</small> made of two : the prophet rendreth a reason hereof, designing out the principall worker of this conuersion of the gentiles and the meanes ? the workman is the Lord : who is able to raise vp children vnto Abraham euen of the stones : who is able to put life into the dead bones in the Churchyard : and the meanes whereby God will effect and <small>He ruleth among the nations.</small> bring to passe this great worke is his rule and dominion which hee exerciseth among the nations, by his word and spirit which breatheth where it listeth : whence that doctrine may be noted that was handled before. v. 3. that conuersion is Gods worke.

Furthermore not only we that now liue, but euē our <small>Vers. 30. Their seed shal serue him, &c.</small> seed & posterity that shal succeed vs in time to come shall serue the Lord : for the Couenant of grace stretcheth not onely to vs, but to our seede also : euen to the thousand generation of them that loue God, doth the Lord promise mercie : and the promise is made to vs, and our children, and to all that are afarre off, euen to as many as the Lord our God shal cal : which giueth vs hope for our children as well as for our selues, yea for our infants that die before yeares.

Yea and here is one thing more, wherein it seemeth we haue a priuiledge beyonde the Iewes, that the Church of God shall abide among the Gentiles to the worlds ende: not so though no particular Church shall be cast off, for we see that otherwise, but that the Church shall not vtterly faile among the gentiles for euer, as it did among the Iews; for although the church of Ephesus; Colossa; Gallatia &c. fayled, yet from the time of calling the gētiles hitherto there hath bin some church of the gentiles. And although the Iewes were cut of and we grafted in; yet wee shall not be cut of and they grafted in, but we shal remaine, and they shall be grafted to vs and both of vs stand and growe vp together: and as they were a meanes to bring vs into the Church, so we againe shall be a meanes to bring them vnto the fellowship of the gospell, as it were a recompence vnto them.

<small>They shall be counted to him for euer.</small>

Againe the church of the gentiles beeing gathered shall performe one principall office which is, beeing come home into the bosome of Christ, by effectuall vocation and true faith, shal declare the righteousnes of Christ God-man, that righteousnesse which he hath wrought for vs, in suffering and obeying the lawe: manfully auouching it against the Turkes and Papists that denie imputatiue righteousnesse, and mocke at a crucified Christ: which must cheere vs vp in this spirituall conflict against that man of sinne, that we faile not in defence of Gods righteousnesse.

<small>Ver. 31. They shall declare his righteousnesse.</small>

If any man list to vnderstand by righteousnesse that which God exercised in the whole worke of our redemption, shewing himselfe most righteous therein, he may for me.

The foresaid worke of the church of the Gentiles in auouching Christs righteousnesse must be performed euē to a people that is not yet borne by spirituall regeneration; to a people vnbaptized: for we are to labour by all possible means to bring home the Iewes and the Turkes, and all other barbarous nations where we traffique, to the knowledge and loue of the trueth: that they may partake in this righteousnesse which Christ hath wrought for as many of them as appertaine to his election.

<small>He hath wrought it for a people to be borne.</small>

If any man thinke better to expoūd a people to be borne, such as are not borne by naturall generation, we may obserue, that it is our dutie to teach our children and posterity especially the article of iustification by faith onely, least the subtill and crafty Iesuites the supporters and pillers of popery wrest it from vs, who labor to perswade the meritt of good workes and so to shoulder the Lord Iesus Christ his righteousnes out of dores.

Thus the kingdome of Christ also is described.

FINIS.

A PATERNE OF TRVE PRAYER.

A LEARNED AND COMFOR-
table Exposition or Commentarie vpon the Lords Prayer: wherein the Doctrine of the substance and circumstances of true inuocation is euidently and fully declared out of the holie Scriptures.

By IOHN SMITH, *Minister and Preacher of the Word of God.*

[Ornament]

AT LONDON

Imprinted by *Felix Kyngston* for *Thomas Man*, and are to be sold at his shop in Pater-noster row at the signe of the Talbot. 1605.

To THE RIGHT Honovrable Edmvnd Lord Sheffield, Lord Lievtenant, and President of his Maiesties Councell established in the North : Knight of the most noble Order of the Garter, &c.

IT is neither ambition nor couetousnes (Right Honourable) that moueth me to publish this Treatise to the view of all, which not long since I deliuered to the eares of a few, being then Lecturer in the Citie of *Lincolne*: but partly the motion of some friends, partly and chiefly the satisfying of some sinister spirits haue in a manner wrested from me that, whereto otherwise I had little affection. Credit through writing bookes, is a thing of such dangerous hazard, by reason of the varietie of censurers, that it is doubtfull whether a man shall winne or lose thereby : Gaine also is so slender, as that, for a booke of a yeeres paines and studie, it will be a verie hard matter to attaine, if it were set to sale in Pauls Church-yard, so much money as inck, paper, and light cost him that penned it : so as except a man should doate, hee must haue better grounds of publishing his writings, than either *credit* or *gaine :* especiallie considering the plentifull haruest of bookes of all sorts, amongst which there appeareth variable contention. In some it is questionable, whether wit or learning getteth the victorie : in others the strife is betwixt wit and the truth : some bewray dissentions betwixt conscience and policie : others contend after other fashions : All declare thus much, that except a man can adde something new of his owne, it is vanitie to write bookes : for otherwise a man shal sooner get mocks than thanks for his paines. Wherefore I doe professedlie renounce all ambitious affection of credit, and couetous desire of gaine : and betake my self to a better refuge, which is the cleering of my selfe from vniust imputations and accusations. I haue beene strangely traduced for the doctrine I taught out of the Lords Prayer : I haue been vrged to answere in defence of the doctrine I deliuered touching that subiect, before the Magistrate ecclesiastical : as if so be I called in question the truth thereof. For the cleering of the truth I am bold to publish this present Treatise: wherein (I protest before the God of heauen, and before your Lordship) I haue truly set downe the substance of all that which I deliuered in handling the Lords Prayer. I must needes confesse that it is not word for word the same (for that were impossible to me) yet to my knowledge it differeth not in any materiall circumstance : nay I doe verily thinke that if I misse the truth, it is rather in the writing than in the preaching. Howsoeuer it be, I most humbly beseech your Honour to vouchsafe the patronage of this traduced Pamphlet : I must acknowledge it is presumption in me to impose vpon your Honour the scandall of countenancing so suspitious a writing (for who knoweth whether it shal gaine the approbation of the godly learned, when it commeth to their censure ?) but for that your Lordship had the managing of the cause of difference betwixt my accusers and me concerning this occasion, and for that your Honour so wisely and charitably compounded the controuersie on both parts to the contentment of either of vs ; your Lordship might iustly challenge a greater title herein, than any other whatsoeuer : wherefore although it proue a troublesome burthen, I beseech your Honour not to refuse it : the rather for that the honourable interest which your Lordship hath in the affections and iudgements of men honestly disposed, will so farre preuaile, as to cleere your Honour from the least spot of dishonour, which perhaps might accrew through the patronage of so dangerous a tractate : yet thus much I may be bold to assure your Lordship, that this Treatise passeth with approbation to the presse ; and doth not shroud it selfe in *tenebris*, as if it either shamed or feared the light : which may be some reason to induce your Honour the rather to receiue it into your Honourable protection : for my selfe I freelie confesse, there is in me no abilitie to declare my thankfulnes to your Lordship, otherwise than by betaking my selfe by some such pamphlet to

your Honours safeconduct : which if it shall please your
    Honour to affoord, I shall at all times acknow-
        ledge my thankfulnes ; and instantly pray
            for your Lordships continuance
              and increase in al true honor
                  and happinesse.

Your Honours humblie at commandement,

IOHN SMITH.

TO THE CHRISTIAN READER.

BEloued, marueile not that after so many expositions vpon the Lords Prayer, this Pamphlet steppeth vp, as if so be it had some thing to say besides that which hath been alreadie spoken : to confesse the truth, I gesse it may occasion the iudicious reader to enter into a more inward view of Christs purpose in propounding that prayer : perhaps also the manner of handling the seuerall petitions may giue some light : but my intent was none of these, when I intended to publish the treatise : onely the cleering of my selfe from vniust accusations, and the satisfying of a few friends moued me therto : but whatsoeuer it be, and howsoeuer vttered, I pray thee of charitie to construe (a thing indifferently done) to the better part : especially those few questions resolued in the latter end of the treatise. I doe here ingenuously confesse that I am far from the opinion of them which separate from our Church, concerning the set forme of prayer (although from some of them, I receiued part of my education in Cambridge) for I doe verily assure my selfe vpon such grounds as I haue deliuered in the treatise, that a set forme of prayer is not vnlawfull : yet as Moses wished that all the people of God could prophecie, so doe I wish that all the people of God could conceiue prayer : the rather for that personall wants, blessings, and iudgements are not comprised particularly according to their seuerall circumstances in any forme of prayer possibly to be deuised : wherefore I desire that no man mistake me in this treatise : I doe iudge that there is no one doctrine or opinion contrarie to the doctrine of this Church in all this tractate : in respect whereof I hope it shall finde more indifferent censure at thy hands. And for that misconceit which some perhaps haue interiained at the hearing of the doctrine when I taught in Lincolne, I doe also as freely and truly protest, that I neuer durst admit (I blesse God for his mercie) so blasphemous a thought into my minde, as to surmise whether the prayer, commonly called the Lords prayer, be the prayer which Christ taught his Disciples, or no : for I doe with my soule confesse it to be the same prayer in substance which Christ deliuered to his Disciples: therefore I pray thee gentle reader, whosoeuer thou art, to accept this treatise, and to blame necessitie rather than me for publishing it: for the phrase and style it is homely, I confesse, and plaine; for I doe not intend the benefit of the style to the learned, but to the vnlearned for the better vnderstanding of the matter: the truth and homelines may well sort together, and the truth is not to be reiected for her plainnes, rather I wish that men in heauenly matters could frame themselues to the capacitie of the meanest, which is the surest way: seeing that learned men can vnderstand things plainly deliuered, but the vnlearned cannot conceiue the easiest doctrines, except they be deliuered also after an easie manner, with homely, familiar and easie speeches. Now if any man attribute this plainnes of mine vsed in this treatise to ignorance and want of skill, I will not endeuour to weede that preiudice out of his minde, seeing that I professe it to be a part of my studie to speake plainly: and I see no reason that seeing speech is the interpreter of the minde, the interpreter should need of another interpreter or commentary.

So crauing againe thy charitable censure, I bid thee hartily farewell in the Lord.

Pray for vs brethren.

Thine in Christ Iesus,

IOHN SMITH.

A PATERNE OF TRVE PRAYER:

OR

AN EXPOSITION VPON THE LORDS PRAYER.

Mat. 6. 9. 10. 11. 12. 13. Luk. 9. 2.
After this manner therefore pray ye, &c.

THese words containe two points: the first is a precept, whereby Christ inioyneth his disciples a dutie: and the second is a prayer or platforme of prayer.

The dutie which Christ enioyneth his disciples, is in these words: *After this manner pray yee.* Wherein wee may consider two things.

1 That we must pray, or the necessitie of prayer.
2 How we must pray.

First that we must pray, or of the necessitie of prayer. The necessitie of prayer may appeare vnto vs, partly out of these words; for that our Sauiour Christ therein giueth his disciples a commaundement to pray: all Gods commaundements binde the conscience, so long as they are in force: and his morall precepts being perpetuall, therefore binde the conscience to absolute obedience perpetually. Now this is a part of the morall law that we must pray: therefore we must pray of necessitie: if God should commaund a man, as he did *Abraham*, either to forsake his owne countrie and fathers house to goe to a strange nation and people, not knowing what might become of him: or to kill

<small>Necessitie of prayer.</small>

<small>Gen. 11. & 12.</small>

his onely sonne, he ought of conscience to this commaundement of God, presently without reasoning and disputing with flesh and blood, yeeld obedience simply: how much more then ought wee simply to obey the commaundement of prayer; for neglect whereof no reasonable excuse can be alledged, as might be for the other of *Abraham*? Againe, God that commaundeth, is the great lawgiuer that is able to saue and destroy: to saue thee, if thou obeyest his commaund, in calling vpon his name: to destroy thee, if thou disobeyest his will, in neglecting thy dutie. If thou wilt be saued therefore, thou must pray: if thou wilt not pray, thou shalt be destroyed: and this is a very great necessitie of prayer: saluation or destruction. Furthermore, we are to know that Gods will is the rule of mans will, and the will of the creature must be squared as it were and framed to the will of the Creator, which is the perfection of the creatures will: now Gods law is his reuealed will, and prayer is a part of his law commaunded in the second commandement. Wherefore that our wils and actions may be perfect, we must of necessitie frame them to the will of God, and therefore must pray.

Gen. 22. 1.
Iam. 4. 12.
Rom. 10. 13.

Secondly, the necessitie of prayer may also appeare vnto vs by other considerations, as namely of the vse of prayer: for prayer is that onely meanes in thee whereby thou procurest or obtainest from God sauing blessings: for Gods promises are conditionall: *Aske and it shall be giuen you: seeke and ye shall finde, knocke and it shall be opened vnto you:* If you aske not, you shall not receiue: you shall receiue, but you must first aske, seeke, knocke, pray. Now if it be alledged that many men haue abundance of Gods blessings, which neuer aske them of God, seeing that they cannot pray being wicked: it may be answered, that they be not sauing blessings, and so indeede they are not true blessings, if we will speake properly: for there is a secret poyson insensibly in heart in all the blessings of God, and in all the creatures, which we vse in the world, by reason of the curse wherewith God cursed the earth for mans sake: which poyson God

Matth. 7. 7.
Gen. 3.

neuer remoueth away till we beg it by prayer of him. Hence it commeth, that seeing wicked men doe not, nor cannot pray, therefore though they haue many blessings in shew, yet in truth they are not so, but rather curses, euen the verie poyson and bane of their soules, meanes to hasten their damnation, and to drench the deeper in the pit of hell another day: whereas contrariwise the godly asking blessings of God, he in mercie remoueth this curse from the righteous mans goods, and maketh his blessings sauing blessings vnto him. Wherefore if thou wilt be blessed of God, thou must of necessitie pray: otherwise thy blessings shall be accursed of God.

The third consideration of the necessitie of prayer, is the example of *Adam*, Christ and all the Saints of God that euer haue liued; whose example implieth a necessitie of imitation. 1. *Pet.* 2. 22. *Ioh.* 17.

The first *Adam* in the state of innocencie being free from sinne, notwithstanding had neede to pray, and no doubt did pray, for perseuerance, and cōtinuance in grace: for it must needes be graunted that during his innocencie he kept the law; and one part of the law is prayer, as was said before: wherefore if *Adam*, as yet free from sinne, and all the punishments of sinne, did pray, much more we haue neede to pray, vpon whom both sinne and Gods curse haue taken such fast hold.

The second *Adam*, Christ Iesus, who knew no sinne, neither was there guile found in his mouth, did pray and needed to pray, being made vnder the law for vs: and therefore he sometime continued a whole night in prayer, and prayed often a little before his apprehension. If Christ did pray, and had neede so to doe, lyeth there not a great and ineuitable necessitie vpon vs to pray? Finally all the Saints of God that euer liued did pray and needed to pray, as *Dauid, Daniel, Paul* and the rest; and yet the best of vs cannot compare with any of these: wherefore there is a great necessitie lying vpon vs, whereby we must be stirred vp to performe this dutie of prayer vnto God, especially considering that it is a principall part of Gods worship, and the propertie of a true child of God: wheras it is the propertie of a wicked man not to pray. Therefore it is not a thing indifferent or arbitrarie, left in our choyse to pray or not to pray, but it is a matter of meere necessitie, absolutely enioyned euery Christian vpon paine of damnation: and yet it is a wonder to see how this dutie is neglected by many, who passe ouer daies and yeres prophanely and Atheist-like, neuer calling vpon God in prayer, as if either there were no God, or no necessitie of worshipping this God by prayer.

Thus much of the necessitie of prayer, or that we must pray. Seeing then this dutie of prayer must bee performed, for the practising thereof these two circumstances must be considered; The time, and the place of prayer: for euery action must be done in time and place.

First of the time.

The time is threefold.

Time of prayer.
1. When we must pray.
2. How oft we must pray.
3. How long we must pray.

First circumstance of the time is: When.

The Apostle saith, *Pray continually*, 1. Thes. 5. 17. **When we must pray.** Which must not be vnderstoode as some heretikes haue deemed called *Euchitæ*, that a man must doe nothing but pray; but the meaning of it is, that there must neuer a day ouerpasse vs, but therein certaine times we must pray: more plainely and distinctly thus: 1. Pray at the enterprising and ending of all thy affaires, pray vpon all occasions. 2. Pray vnto thy liues end, neuer cease praying till thy soule part from thy body. Now although this bee generally true, that a man must pray vpon all occasions, yet it is not needefull that a man should vpon euery seuerall occasion fall downe vpon his knees and vtter a long prayer to the spending of time and hindering his affaires; but a man must from his heart send vp prayers to heauen, if it be but a wish or sigh or groane of the spirit, or such a short prayer as the publicane vsed, or the theefe vpon the crosse, vpon all our occasions. This we see warranted by the practise

A paterne of true Prayer 77

of *Nehemia:* who before he made his petition to the King for the repayring of Ierusalem, prayed vnto the God of heauen: no doubt this was inwardly with a sigh of the spirit vnto the Lord who knoweth the heart, as may be seene in the text. Furthermore, and specially we are to vnderstand that the principall occasions and times of prayer are these following. *Nehem.* 2. 4.
   1. The time of religious exercises.
   2. The time of affliction.
   3. The time of eating and drinking and vsing physicke.
   4. The time of sleeping and waking.
   5. The time of working and labour.
   6. The time of recreation and sporting.
   The truth of all these appeareth by that which the Apostle writeth, that *euery creature* or appointment *of God is sanctified by the word of God, and prayer, and thankesgiuing.* Gods word warranteth vs the lawfull vse thereof: prayer obtaineth the blessing from God, in the vse of it: thanksgiuing returneth the praise to God, who gaue the blessing. 1. *Tim.* 4. 4, 5.
   The second circumstance of time is, how oft we must pray. *Daniel* prayed three times a day, Dan. 6. 10. *Dauid* prayed seauen times a day, Psal. 119. 164. euen so oft as we alter our affaires and enterprise new busines: as hearing or reading the word: working and laboring in thy speciall calling, eating and drinking, sleeping, &c. also vpon all extraordinarie occasions: as iudgements, and blessings: all which are things of seuerall condition, and the condition of our affaires being changed, our prayers are to be repeated and renewed. How oft we must pray.
   The false Church of Antichrist hath deuised certaine houres which they call Canonicall; which are in number eight, as Father *Robert* rehearseth them: which must be obserued euery day, and cannot be omitted without deadly sinne, as he teacheth: but we are to know that Christians must stand fast in that libertie wherewith Christ hath made vs free: and seeing that we are redeemed with a price, we must not be the seruants of men, much lesse of times: *Galath* 5. 1. *Cor.* 7.

only thus much ; the Lords day of conscience, being Gods commandement, must be kept as oft as it commeth : and seeing the Church for order and conueniencie hath appointed certaine houres, when all the Church publikely may come together to worship God ; therefore we cannot breake that holy custome and constitution without confusion, and scandall, and breach of charitie : for priuate prayer, or priuate necessities, occasions, and opportunities may afford a godly heart sufficient instruction, alwayes remembring that there is no time vnfit to worship God in.

The third circumstance of time to be considered, is, how long we must pray. Our Sauiour Christ giueth vs this instruction generally by way of parable, that we ought not to waxe faint in prayer : the Apostle willeth vs to pray with all perseuerance and to watch thereunto : as Christ said to his disciples, *Watch and pray*. This then is the first rule for the length of our prayers : that we be not wearie. The second rule is, that we are to pray so long as the spirit of God feedeth vs with matter of prayer : for otherwise we should stint the spirit of prayer. Christ prayed till midnight ; our infirmitie will not beare that : wherefore it is better to cease praying when the spirit ceaseth to minister matter, than to continue still and babble : yet notwithstanding here we must know ; First, it is our dutie to striue against our corruption : Secondly, it is our dutie to strengthen our soule before prayer with premeditate matter ; that so comming to pray, and hauing our hearts filled with matter, we may better continue in prayer : for as a man that hath filled his belly with meate, is better able to holde out at his labour than being fasting ; euen so he that first replenisheth his soule with meditations of his owne sinnes and wants, of Gods iudgements and blessings vpon himselfe and others, shall be better furnished to continue longer in hartie and feruent prayer, than comming sodainly to pray without strengthening himselfe aforehand thereunto. To conclude this point, all prayers are either long or short : a long feruent prayer is best ; a short feruent

Marginalia: How long we must pray. Luk. 18. 1. Ephes. 6. 18.

prayer is better than long babling; a short prayer, containing all thy grace and matter in thy soule, is acceptable to God.

The second circumstance to be considered, needefull for practise of prayer, is the place where we must pray. As was said before, there is no time vnfit to pray: so there is no place vnfit for prayer. The world, and euery place in the world is fit for a Christian to call vpō the name of the Lord. *Paul* wisheth men in all places to lift vp pure hands, that is, to pray: Christ prayed vpon the mountaine, in the garden, in the wildernes; *Peter* vpon the house top; *Paul* on the sea shore; *Ionas* in the Whales belly in the bottom of the sea: but the superstitious papists will haue some place more holy than others: hence come there pilgrimages, to such a holy place, hoping thereby sooner to obtaine their petitions: therefore also they thinke the Church-yard holy ground, the Church holyer than the Church-yard, the Chancell than the Church, and the high altar more holy than the rest of the chancell. True it is indeed, that when the Church of God is assembled in the Church, the place is more holy: but not for any inherent holines in the ground, but because of Gods presence among his people, and because of holy actions there performed: in regard whereof it is sacriledge to offer violence to such places, or any way to prophane them; yet God will assoone heare thy prayer at home in thy closet, as in the Church; though the publike prayers are more effectuall than priuate. Finally, to shut vp this point: in regard of place, prayers are publike or priuate.

The place where we must pray.

Ioh. 4. 20.
1. *Tim.* 2. 8.

The place of publike prayer is the assembly of the Saints wheresoeuer it be, which sometime in persecution was in priuate houses, or in caues of the earth, or the wildernes, or mountaines.

Act. 1. 13.
Heb. 11. 38.

The place of priuate prayer is the house, or the closet, or some such fit place in secret: not the market place, nor the corners of the streete: though I doubt not but a man may sigh and groane to the Lord walking in the streete and making his markets; but the outward signes of prayer priuate must then be

Mat. 6. 5. 6.

concealed from the sight of men, least we appeare to men as hypocrites. Hitherto of the necessitie of prayer, with the time and place of performing that dutie.

The second generall thing to be considered in the dutie which Christ enioyneth his disciples, is, the manner how we must pray, which is expressed in these words: *After this manner pray ye.* The meaning of which words must needes be one of these things following, that is to say; Pray either

<small>How we must pray.</small>

1. These words onely: or
2. This matter onely: or
3. In this method onely: or
4. These words and matter: or
5. These words and method: or
6. This matter in this method: or
7. These words, and this matter, in this method.

Now which of these things our Sauiour Christ doth enioyne, shall appeare by the seuerall consideration of euery one of these seauen things.

First, Christ doth not commaund vs to pray these words onely: for then we should offend if we vsed any other words; and words without matter is babling: and Christ spake in the Hebrew tongue, the Euangelists wrote in the Greeke tongue: but Christ will not haue vs speake Greeke and Hebrew only when we pray: therfore it is euident, that Christ commaundeth not to say, and so tyeth vs not precisely to these words onely.

Secondly, he doth not enioyne vs to pray onely in this order or method: for then whosoeuer vseth any other order should sinne; and Christ commaundeth vs Matth. 6. *First* to *seeke the kingdome of God and his righteousnesse,* before our daily bread: but in this prayer Christ doth set the prayer for daily bread before remission of sinnes and imputation of Gods righteousnes: wherefore also this is plaine that Christ doth not commaund vs to vse onely this method. <small>Matth. 6. 33.</small>

Thirdly, he doth not commaund vs to pray this matter in these words onely: for then *Paul* and *Daniel* and *Dauid* should sinne that pray this matter in other words, and all the Churches that euer haue bin which haue vsed other words in prayer, <small>2. Cor. 13. 13. Dan. 9. Psal. 119.</small>

though they haue alwaies kept themselues to this matter: but it were impietie and blasphemie to say so: therefore Christ here doth not binde vs to this matter in these words onely.

Fourthly, he doth not commaund these words and method, as hath been prooued in the second and third parts.

Fiftly, he commaundeth not this matter in this method, as is proued in the second and third parts.

Sixtly, he commandeth not these words matter and method, as may appeare by all the former parts: wherefore in the last place it followeth necessarily, this being a sufficient enumeration of parts, that he commandeth vs to pray only this matter: as if when Christ said thus: *After this manner pray:* hee should haue said, pray: 1. the matter herein contained, and 2. with the affections here expressed. This then is the meaning of these words, and here Christ tieth vs to the matter and affections of this prayer. To proceed: Although Christ commandeth not these words and matter and method, yet he doth not forbid them; for in the whole Scripture there is no such prohibition: wherefore Christ leaueth it arbitrarie vnto vs, as a thing indifferent when we pray to say this prayer, or not to say it, so be that we say it in faith and feeling; or if wee say it not, yet to pray according vnto it: and this I suppose no indifferent man will denie: yet there are some (whom we wil account brethren, though they doe not so reckon of vs, seeing they haue separated from vs) which thinke it vnlawfull to vse the Lords Prayer as a set prayer, or any other prescribed forme of prayer: but that they are in a manifest error it may appeare by these considerations ensuing. *Whether a set forme of prayer be lawfull.*

For if it bee lawfull to vse the salutation of *Paul*, the Psalmes of *Dauid*, and the blessing of *Moses:* then wee may lawfully vse the Lords Prayer, or any other prayer in holie Scripture agreeable thereto for a prayer. For *Paul* himselfe vsed alwaies one manner of salutation; our Sauiour Christ, as is very probable, vsed one of *Dauids* Psalmes with his Disciples, after the first institution and celebration of his Supper; and the 92. Psalme was vsually in the church of the

Psal. 92.

Iewes sung vpon the Sabbath day: and *Moses* alwaies

<small>Numb. 6. 24. 25. 26. *and* 10. 35. 36.</small> vsed one manner of prayer at the remouing of the Tabernacle, and another at the pitching thereof: which euidently serueth for the ouerthrow of that opinion which they of late haue deuised, contrarie to the practise of the ancient Church, and all the reformed Churches in Christendome, who haue an vniforme order of publike prayer, one and the same almost in the very forme of words: and plainly confirmeth vs in the present truth wee hold, that it is lawfull to vse the prayers in Scriptures, or any other prayers made by the Saints of God to our hands consonant to the Scriptures: and yet notwithstanding, here are some cautions to be remembred.

1. That wee labour to insinuate our selues as much as may be into the grace and affections expressed in the prayers by the makers thereof: that so wee may pray with the same spirit they did indite and vse them, hauing by diligent consideration and vnderstanding of them as it were made them our owne.

2. This vsing of other mens prayers is rather allowed to young Christians that want the gift of conceiuing and vttering an orderly prayer: or to those that want audacitie and boldnes to speake before others, than to strong and exercised Christians, vnto whom God hath vouchsafed the gift of knowledge and vtterance and boldnes.

3. It is safer to conceiue a prayer, than to reade a prayer: for a man may reade a prayer, and neither vnderstand it, nor consider the matter thereof, nor affect or desire the petitions therein contained, hauing his minde pestred with wandring thoughts: but hee that conceiueth a prayer, though perhaps hee doe not desire the things he conceiueth, yet at the least he must haue attention, and so be free from many wandring thoughts, he must haue also memorie, and knowledge and consideration, needfull all for the inuenting of matter; and so there is lesse feare of babling in conceiuing a prayer, than reading one.

4. An vniforme order of publike prayer in the seruice of God is necessarie. Thus the Priests and Leuites in the old Testament praised God with <small>2 *Chro.* 29. 30.</small>

the Psalmes of *Dauid* and *Asaph :* which Psalmes were framed of those holie men and sent to the Musitions to bee sung vpon Instruments. Thus all the reformed Churches vse : thus the Church immediatly after the Apostles time vsed : yea thus in the time of the Apostles vsed the Church of Corinth : as may probably bee gathered by that which *Paul* speaketh concerning the bringing of a Psalme into the publike assemblie of the Church. 1. *Cor.* 14. 26.

5. Lastly, notwithstanding in priuate prayer when a Christian being alone calleth vpon the name of God, it seemeth most expedient and profitable that he powre out his soule vnto God with such a forme of words as hee can, for there and then the edification of other is no end of his prayer, as it is of publike prayer : and the Lord hee regardeth the heart, and hee knoweth the meaning of the spirit, though thy speeches bee neuer so ragged and broken, though thy sentences bee neuer so short and imperfect, though thy words be rude and barbarous : and yet a man ought to labour to glorifie God with the best of his lippes also. But here certaine obiections must be answered which are alleaged against the vsing of read prayers. For they say it is to quench the spirit, & to limit the spirit of God that teacheth vs to pray. For answere whereof we are to know, that as he cannot be said to quench the spirit that readeth a chapter of holy Scripture and no more, or that preacheth a sermon which he hath premeditate ; so also he cannot bee said to quench the spirit that prayeth a portion of holie Scripture, as the Lords Prayer, or the salutation of *Paul*, or a Psalme of *Dauid*, or any other prayer agreeable to the word which hee hath premeditate before and committed to memorie : for the spirit is not limited, though kept within the bounds of holy Scripture, as it ought to be. Againe, in a prayer which a man readeth, though a man doe not speake euerie thing that the spirit of God putteth into his heart, yet hee quencheth not the spirit : for to quench the spirit is to oppose against the voyce of the spirit. Neither is it to limit or stint the spirit, if a man pray it with his soule, though hee speake not the words. For example sake : I

say the Lords Prayer: yea when I speake these words; *Giue vs this day our daily bread*, there commeth into my soule by the motion of Gods spirit this petition: Grant me grace to be content with the mediocritie thou hast giuen me. If I pray this in my heart, though I doe not vtter these very words, yet I cannot bee said to stint the spirit: for the substance of that petition is comprehended in that fourth petition of the Lords Prayer. So likewise reading any prayer agreeable to holy scripture, and hauing attention to the matter read, though many motions come into my minde vpon consideration of the words of that prayer which I vtter not in particular speeches, yet I vtter them in generall, for they are all comprehended in the matter of that, otherwise they may iustly bee termed wandring thoughts, though good prayers at other times. Lastly, publike wants are alwaies knowne and may bee expressed in the publike Liturgie: also priuate wants and blessings are for the most part knowne; as at meate, labour, rest, recreation, Physicke, &c. Secret wants and blessings may be acknowledged in secret prayers: if any extraordinarie occasions occurre, extraordinarie prayers accordingly may bee had. They alleage

Obiection. also against set prayers, the speech of the
Rom. 8. Apostle: *We know not what to pray:* but in a set prayer a man knoweth what to pray: therfore set prayers are not prayers warrantable. For answere wherof, the speech of the Apostle in another place must 1. *Cor.* 2. 14.
be remēbred: the naturall man cannot dis- 15.
cerne spirituall things; but the spirituall man can discerne them: so may we say, the naturall man cannot tell what to pray, but the spirituall man can tell what to pray. Flesh and blood reuealed not the knowledge of Christ vnto *Peter*, but God the Father: so *Matth.* 16.
flesh and blood cannot reueale vnto vs what
wee ought to pray, but the spirit of God helpeth our infirmities; which spirit was in our Sauiour Christ that taught the Lords prayer, and in the rest of Gods seruants that wrote prayers: wee are not able of our selues to thinke any good, but God giueth vs abilitie:
so of our selues we are not able to pray, but 2. *Cor.* 3.
God giueth vs the spirit of prayer, which teacheth vs to

pray with sighs and groanes which cannot be vttered: when we haue this spirit of God, then wee know what to pray, and can teach others also. This may suffice for the answere of their maine obiections against set prayers. To conclude then: Christ hath not commanded vs to vse these words and no other, neither hath hee forbidden vs to vse these words, or any other holy forme of prayer: but hee hath left it indifferent and arbitrarie to vse them or not to vse them, as was said. Hitherto of the precept of prayer in the two general points thereof: first, that we must pray: secondly, how wee must pray. Now followeth the prayer it selfe.

In handling whereof we will first propound some generall considerations: after descend to the particular exposition of the words thereof.

In the generall consideration of the Lords prayer wee may obserue three things.

Generally of the Lords prayer.

1. The abuse of the prayer.
2. The true and holy vse thereof.
3. The qualities and conditions of it.

And first to entreate of the abuse of this prayer, and so of any other godly prayer, for this prayer is all prayers in vertue, and largenes, seeing that all prayers must be framed of the matter and affections herein expressed: it is abused especially by foure sorts of persons.

How the Lords prayer is abused.

1. By the ignorant persons that vnderstand it not.
2. By impenitent persons that practise it not.
3. By Papists that attend not the matter of it.
4. By witches, wise women or charmers.

The ignorant person abuseth it, for that he thinketh the very saying of the words, though hee vnderstand not the matter signified in the words, to be a good and acceptable seruice of God: which is very absurd.

How ignorant persons abuse prayer.

For first, hee that prayeth must pray in faith, if hee will haue his prayer granted: Iam. 1. for that man that wanteth faith shall not receiue any thing of the Lord: but where there is no knowledge of the maine articles of faith, there can be no faith: for faith commeth by hearing, learning, and knowing of the word of God expouned in the ministerie

Iam. 1. 6. 7.

Rom. 10. 14. 15.

thereof. Seeing then hee wanteth knowledge, hee wanteth faith, and wanting faith hee shall not obtaine that he asketh, and obtaining not he prayeth not aright: and so abuseth this prayer, for that hee vseth it not in faith and knowledge as is required.

2. It is expressely set downe by the Apostle, that a man must pray with the spirit and with the vnderstanding, that is, so that another may vnderstand him when he prayeth: if so as other may vnderstand, then much more must he vnderstand himselfe: if a man therefore pray, not vnderstanding the prayer hee saith, hee abuseth it; but ignorant persons pray without vnderstanding: wherefore they abuse both this and all the rest of their prayers. Therefore it were better for them to say fiue words with knowledge, than to say their *Pater noster*, or any other prayer tenne times as long, without vnderstanding.

1. Cor. 14. 26.

3. Finally, our Sauiour Christ out of the Prophet *Esay* reprooueth the hypocriticall Iewes, for that they did draw neere with their lips, but their hearts were a farre off, and requireth that they draw neere both with heart and lippes, when they come to worship God: but a man cannot draw neere with his hart, except the vnderstanding and the mind goe before as the leader of the heart (wherefore the vnderstanding is compared to the wagoner or coachman that directeth and guideth the horse with whip and bridle, that is, restraineth the headstrong and vntamed affections, and ordreth them aright by reason rightly ruled: they therfore that want vnderstanding of their prayers, although they may say they haue a good heart and affections, yet it cannot be that the hart should be right, except the vnderstanding bee right, which is by knowledge: wherefore all is wrong and amisse, and therefore thou abusest thy prayer, except thou vnderstand what thou prayest. To end this first point, prayer is the labour of the minde and heart, not of the lips: and all they that make it a liplabour onely, as all ignorant persons doe, abuse this and all other prayers. For foure things are necessarie to pray this prayer, or any other prayer in speech.

Matth. 15. 8.
Esay. 29.

1. Thou must vnderstand it, as alreadie hath bin said.

2. Thou must affect and desire the prayers.
3. Thou must vtter the words.
4. Heart, tongue and minde must accord in euery prayer, and euery seuerall matter : wherefore the tongue must not runne before our wits, as wee say in our common prouerbe : but first our hearts must indite good matter, and then our tongues must be as the pen of a readie writer : we must first beleeue, and then wee must speake. Thus then is this prayer abused by ignorant persons. *Psal.* 45. 2. *Cor.* 4. 13.

Secondly, the impenitent person though he haue knowledge, and so be freed from that kind of abuse of this prayer, yet abuseth it as bad, if not worse, in another kinde : for *How impenitent persons abuse prayer.*

1. God heareth not them that liue in sinne vnrepented of : for their prayers and sacrifices, and all their seruice of God is abominable, and is no better than iniquitie it selfe in Gods sight : for though God hath commanded prayer, and sacrifice, and incense, as was accustomed in the old Testament, yet he required that they should be offered by persons that were meete and fit for that purpose : and so though God now require that wee should pray, and heare the word, and communicate in the Sacraments, actions answerable to the former of the old Testament, yet God will not accept these actions performed by any man : but first a man must leaue his sins, and then pray : repent, and then heare the word, examine himselfe and finde himselfe worthie before he eate : otherwise his praying, hearing and eating are turned into sinne. If then the prayer of an vnrepentant person be abominable, if God heareth it not, if it bee iniquitie, surely the wicked man doth abuse it and make it so : for God would accept that of vs which hee commaundeth vs, if we would performe it as he requireth. *Psal.* 66. 18. *Ioh.* 9. 31. *Prou.* 15. 8. *Esay.* 1.

2. Againe, impenitent persons abuse prayer, because they doe not practise that which they pray : for euery prayer must be practised : otherwise there is hypocrisie and dissimulation. For if a man pray that Gods name may be hallowed, if hee by swearing vainly or falsely prophane the name of God, it is double dealing, for his

heart and tongue accord not in one, nay his tongue contradicteth it selfe : for he asketh with the tongue that he may not dishonor Gods name, and yet with a vaine or false oath his tongue doth dishonour Gods name: this his tongue speaketh contradictions : or else hee neuer meaneth to practise that which hee prayeth, and so his heart and tongue are at variance, which is hypocrisie : an impenitent person then doth abuse prayer, for that he neuer prayeth with his hart, though with his tongue he speake it.

3. Furthermore, the man that liueth in his sinnes, which he repenteth not of, doth curtoll and (as I may so speake) libbe this prayer, and so abuse it : for if we pray this prayer aright, we must pray euery petition thereof : but an impenitent person cannot pray euery prayer therein contained : for a swearer cannot pray, hallowed be thy name ; a persecutor cannot pray, thy kingdome come ; the impatient person cannot pray, thy will be done ; the couetous person cannot pray for his daily bread ; and so foorth of the rest : for how can they pray against those sinnes, wherein they haue resolued with themselues as it were to liue and die ? And therefore if the minister or any other Christian shall reproue them of those seuerall sinnes which they practise, they will hate him and persecute him for it; which argueth plainely that they neuer pray against them, for they cannot abide to heare of them.

4 To end this point, they abuse this prayer for that liuing in sinne, notwithstanding they take this prayer a part of holy scripture, and so Gods name in vaine ; for they haue nothing to doe to meddle with Gods word, seeing they hate to be reformed, and cast Gods word behinde them. For whereas they speake this prayer to God they are neuer a whit bettered thereby, and so it is in vaine to them : also they vse it without feare and reuerence, as euery part of holy Scripture should bee vsed, and therefore abuse it : whereby it appeareth euidently that wicked and hard harted and impenitent persons that purpose to continue stil in their sins, doe abuse this prayer, though peraduenture they vnderstand it, when they vtter it in the worship of God.

Psal. 50. 16.

Esa. 66. 5.

Thirdly, the papist also abuseth this prayer and that three wayes especially:
1. They say it in Latin, a tongue vnknowne to the common sorte of people.
2. They say it in number vpon their beades.
3. They say it as satisfactory and meritorious.

1 First they abuse it because they say it in Latin, a tongue which for the most part is not vnderstoode of them that say it, and hardly well pronounced by the multitude: but vnderstanding is necessarily required in prayer, as was said before: and whereas the Iesuites auouch that God vnderstandeth Latin or any language, and prayer is directed to God, and that instruction of the hearer is no end of prayer but of preaching: we answere that the Apostle saith flatly that all things must be done to edification: therefore prayer also, which is some thing, nay a chiefe and principal part of the publike seruice of God: hence we reade that the title of some of the psalmes, which are prayers, is to giue instruction: as Psal. 74. and 89. That therefore is but a forgerie of man contrarie to the word: for prayer is an excellent meanes of edification, it being as a whetstone to sharpen the grace of God in vs; especially if it proceed feruently from the heart and lips of the Minister, it doth rouze the drousie spirits of dull Christians: for there is no difference betwixt preaching and praying but this; that preaching is directed to men from God, prayer is directed from man to God, both preaching and prayer is the word of God, or ought to be so. Wherefore as preaching or reading the word are excellent meanes of edification and instruction; so likewise conceauing or reading prayer is a worthie meanes appointed of God to edifie the people of God, and prayer is a second hammer, or a second stroke with the hammer, to beate the naile to the head, that is to say, to fasten the holy doctrine, exhortation, admonition, reproofe, consolation, or what else, deeper in the conscience or vnderstanding: and this is the edification of prayer. Therefore herein the Iesuites are greatly mistaken that they thinke instruction and edification no end of prayer. *How papists abuse prayer.* *1. Cor. 14. 26.*

2 Secondly our Sauiour Christ requireth, and it is

the very summe of the first table of the law, that we loue God with all our heart, our soule, our mind, our thought, our strength; and all that is within vs must praise his holy name. But as was said before, prayer is commaunded in the first table, and is therefore a part of loue we owe to God: hence then it followeth as a necessarie conclusion, that we must testifie that we loue God with our minde and with all our minde in prayer, when our minde is busied about the vnderstanding and consideration of that holy matter which we vtter to God; but that cannot possiblie be, if wee vnderstand not what we spake, as they doe not that speake their prayers in an vnknowne language as Latin: they therefore abuse prayer that pray in Latin, not vnderstanding it.

Deut. 6. 5.
Matth. 22. 37.
Luk. 10. 27.
Psal. 103. 1.

3 Lastly, as hath been said, it is plaine babling to speake any thing with the lips in the presence of God, which a man vnderstandeth not, or desireth not in the heart and minde: for we must glorifie God with the body and with the spirit both, for they are both Gods by creation and redemption: now to pray to God is a principall part of the glorifying of God; therefore we must pray with the spirit, as well as with the tongue, which is a part of the body. For whereas the schoolemen teach that actuall attention is not needefull in time of prayer, but it sufficeth to come with a holy purpose to pray, it is as vaine a forgerie as the former of the Iesuites that held instruction no end of prayer: for whereas they alledge for confirmation of their opinion, that our heart is not in our owne power, and therefore we are not able to keepe it from wandering; surely we must needes graunt it to be so, and yet notwithstanding it is sinne for vs to suffer our hearts to wander: and who durst goe speake to his prince, his minde either not vnderstanding his matter, or wandering from it, which in effect are all one? Wherefore if babling be abusing of prayer, and they babble which vnderstand not or attend not their prayers: no doubt they that say the Lords prayer in Latin, not vnderstanding Latin, abuse it. Thus then the papist abuseth this prayer by saying it in Latin, a tongue vnknowne to the people.

1. *Cor.* 6. 20.

Secondly the papists abuse this prayer especially, by saying it in number, and numbering it vpon their beades: and hence it is that they say a whole beadrole of prayers; as for example 30. prayers, *Pater nosters, aue maries, creedes &c.* which will be proued to be a manifest abusing of the Lords prayer. For first, this is to babble: for it cannot bee that euery mans deuotion should last so long as the number of the prayers lasteth: for some weake Christians feruencie and zeale will not indure longer than the saying of the prayer twise or thrise ouer: at which time he must cease saying it; for if he still continue saying it without feruencie and deuotion and attention, in a word without sense and feeling, his saying is babling, onely a lip labor, which is abominable in the sight of God.

2 Againe, our Sauiour Christ condemneth vaine repetitions, and the wise Preacher requireth that our words should be few, because God is in heauen and we are vpon the earth: therefore we must not rashly and hastely huddle ouer ten or twentie prayers as a post horse runneth his post miles; but if in any action, surely in this holy and reuerent action, the calling vpon Gods name, our prouerbe is true, Hast makes waste: for God is in heauen, that is to say, a heauenly God, most wise, most holy, most iust, most mightie, and euery way most glorious, and therefore must be worshipped after the best manner we can possibly afford: againe, we are vpon the earth, that is to say, men, dust and ashes, subiect to sinne in the best actions, improuident and vnwise persons, especially in our affaires which are done sodainely and hastily: therefore we are not either with our heart to conceiue, or with our tongue to vtter a matter rashly and speedily before God, but we must be well aduised before hand, and in the action vse al solemne decencie: but to racket ouer the Lords prayer so many times as they doe, is nothing else but as it were to tosse it like a tennise ball, and to abuse it shamefully. Now our Sauiour Christ doth not condemne al repetitions, nor the Preacher simply forbid many words: but such repetitions and multitude of words as are vnreuerently, and without affection vttered, rather to perfect the number and hold

Matth. 6. 7.
Eccles. 5. 1. 2.

out the time, than expresse the affection: for repetitions and many words sometimes proceede from an ardent and vehement desire of obtaining something, which men desiring to haue, God doth, for reasons best knowne to himselfe, defer to graunt, and sometimes to stirre vp our feruencie and try our patience and perseuerance.

<small>Dan. 9. 19.</small>

<small>Luk. 18. 1.</small>

3 Againe, such repetitions are needles in regard of God, for he knoweth our wants and requests at our conceiuing of them in our hearts, seeing he knoweth the heart: or before wee thinke of them, because he knoweth our thoughts a farre off: much more then when we haue once vttered them, which God requireth not for that he needeth our speech to tell him what we want, but for that we must worship him with the whole man, body as well as soule, and tongue as well as any other part of the body: yea the tongue is the principall part in Gods worship, therefore called the glory of the Prophet, as the chiefe instrument of glorifying God: and as it is needles in regard of God to repeate so often, so in publike prayer it serueth not for edification, seeing it wearieth the auditory; and in priuate prayer it wearieth him that vseth it. Once therefore in feeling faith and feruencie is better than ten times in coldnes, dulnes, wearines and superstition.

<small>Act. 15. 8.</small>

<small>Psal. 139. 2.</small>

<small>Psal. 57. 8.</small>

Thirdly, the papists abuse this prayer and that very strangely, because they say it in opinion of merit and satisfaction: for so the arch Iesuite teacheth that there are three ends of prayer: namely, first obtaining, secondly merit, thirdly satisfaction: and that prayer doth not only obtaine but satisfie for sinne, and meritoriously deserue at Gods hands.

1 Now the truth is that as all our good workes are stayned with sinne, so especially our prayers, which are the weakest seruice we can performe to God, and hath most corruption in it: as may appeare by the manifold wandering thoughts that haunt our mindes in the time of prayer, withdrawing our hearts from that due attention and reuerence we ought to haue: wherefore the wise man for the terror of wicked men

<small>Prou. 15. 8.</small>

saith, that the sacrifice, euen the best seruice of the wicked, is abomination to the Lord : but contrariewise the prayer, that is the weakest seruice, of the godly man is acceptable, which maketh very much for the comfort of euery distressed conscience : now if our prayers be stained with so many corruptions, they cannot merit any thing except it be the punishment, neither can they satisfie the iustice of God, seeing they are not proportionable thereunto, nay they neede a satisfaction to be made for them : wherefore euery true humbled Christian finding the palpable experience hereof in his heart, crieth out with the prophet, *Enter not into iudgement with thy* *Psal.* 143. 2. *seruant O Lord, for no flesh shall be righteous in thy sight :* and prayeth continually, Lord pardon me my good deeds, that is, the imperfection of my good workes.

2 Besides, all our prayers are to bee made in Christs name, that is in the merit, mediation and intercession of Christ Iesus : and therefore the prayers of the Saints must be performed with the smoke of the odours which are giuen to the Angell, before they ascend vp before God : for in Christ Iesus God the Father is well pleased with vs, and with all our holy actions : but out of Iesus Christ he is displeased with vs : for wanting faith whereby wee are ingrafted into the true vine, we cannot please God. Wherefore if our prayers haue neede of Christs merit and satisfaction, how haue they any merit or satisfaction in themselues ?

Ioh. 16. 23.
Apoc. 8. 3. 4.
Matth. 3. 17.
Ioh. 15. 5.
Heb. 11. 6.

3 Lastly, all the arguments that are vsed against the merits of good workes in generall, serue sufficiently to ouerthrow the merit of prayers : and so to end this point, seeing the papists vse prayer for other ends than it is appointed, they abuse it ; as when a man vseth a sword to murther, which is appointed for iustice, he abuseth the sword. Thus we see how this prayer is abused by papists, saying it in Latin, in number, in opinion of merit and satisfaction.

The fourth sort of persons that abuse this prayer and others, are wise women, as they are termed, or good witches ; which are termed good, not for that they doe good by witchcraft and doe

How charmers abuse prayer.

no harme to their neighbours: these make the Lords prayer or other good prayers charmes: for by saying of prayers they can cure diseases, driue away the toothach, heale things forespoken, &c. Now that prayer is abused by them it is plaine.

1 God neuer appointed prayer to be a meanes to cure diseases or such like, being applied to the sore or disease or atch: for although it be needefull that we pray to God for the remouing of paines and sicknes from vs and ours; yet it doth not follow thereupon that God appointed prayer for a medicine, which being applied to diseases shall cure them: for then euery man would be a physition to himselfe whatsoeuer disease he had, by his prayers. Prayer doth sanctifie physicke vnto vs, it is no physicke it selfe: it obtaineth at Gods hands a blessing vpon our medicines that they may cure vs; it selfe by vertue inherent in it doth not cure vs: and as our meates and drinke by vertue in them doe nourish our bodies, which notwithstanding are sanctified by prayer for that end: so physicke cureth our diseases, prayer sanctifieth physicke. Wherefore seeing prayer is not Catholicum as the physitions call some of their medicines, that is an vniuersall medicine for all diseases, nay no medicine for any one disease, it followeth that these wise women that vse it as a meanes to cure diseases, abuse it. *1. Tim. 4.*

2 Againe, this was a miraculous gift in the time of the Apostles, whereunto was added vnction with oyle also; which continued in the Church but for a certaine season, so long as the doctrine of the Church had neede of extraordinarie confirmation by miracle: now the doctrine of the Gospell being sufficiently confirmed by witnes ordinarie and extraordinarie, of God and man, this gift ceaseth as all other miracles. Wherefore they that shall enterprise this miraculous course of curing sicknes, what doe they else but challeng this miraculous gift: and what are they else but imposters and seducers of the ignorant, or of those that receiue not the loue of the truth? *Iam. 5.* *2. Thes. 2.*

3 Besides this, you shall obserue these wise women, wizards, and charmers will with writing the prayer cure

the diseases and aches of men. As for example, they will write it vpon a peece of paper: or hauing written it, cause the partie diseased to weare it about his necke, and so they shall be cured: they will write it in cheese or vpon bread and giue it to mad dogges to eate, and their madnes shall depart from them: and other praƈtises of like folly and impietie: all which plainely argue societie and fellowship with the diuell, and the helpe of the diuell: for others cannot doe it, but themselues: and why I pray you cannot others doe it? forsooth say they, you doe not beleeue as we doe, no not though you say or write the same prayers that they doe. Surely wee beleeue that to be true which they say: for they haue either openly, or at the least secretly, contraƈted with the diuell, whose they are, whom they serue and honor; and in whom they beleeue. No maruaile then though others which worship the true God, cannot doe such charming trickes as they can, for indeede good Christians beleeue not in the diuell as they doe. Wherefore seeing they direƈt their prayers to the diuell, which should be direƈted to God alone, they doe greatly abuse their prayers.

If any obieƈt that these wise women vse medicines as well as prayers, and so their prayers doe only sanƈtifie their medicines which they vse to cure their diseases: the answere is, their medicines are not such as the art of physicke alloweth, but some foolish trumperie, which hath no qualitie or vertue sutable to the disease, as fit to draw the moone out of heauen, as to cure a disease: and both their medicines and prayers are nothing else but a colour of their charming, that so vnder such a shew of art and holines, they may the easier deceiue the simple people, who for the most part thinke that all is gold that glistereth: and who knoweth not that euen Sathan can transforme himselfe into an Angell of light? Also if it be obserued, these women and charmers are either ignorant, or profane persons, wanting the true knowledge of God, or leading lewd and vngodly liues: yet outwardly at performing of their cures they will make such a holy show of deuotion, as may bleare the eyes of vnexperienced people. In regarde whereof greater care and diligence ought to be vsed in examining

Obieƈtion.

and trying their actions: for the white diuell will sooner deceiue than the blacke diuell. It appeareth then plainely by this which hath been said, that the Lords prayer is diuersly abused by diuers sorts of persons, as namely the ignorant, the impenitent, the papist, the charmer.

The second point to be handled in the generall consideration of the Lords prayer, is, the true, lawfull and holy vse thereof, and so of prayer generally: which may partly be perceiued by that which hath alreadie been deliuered concerning the abuse; for the knowledge of one contrarie ariseth out of the knowledge of another, and he that knoweth wherein the abuse of the Lords prayer consisteth, knoweth also wherein the true and holy vse doth consist. Yet notwithstanding it shall not bee amisse to intreate briefely of this point; referring the further vnderstanding thereof, partly to that which hath been alreadie spoken of the abuse, and partly to that which shall be spoken afterward in the preface; and in the conclusion of the Lords prayer of the affections and dispositions in the time of prayer, and of the manner of prayer. To handle this point then of the true and holy vse of prayer: it consisteth especially in foure particulars.

The holy vse of the Lords prayer.

1. Knowledge: for a man must vnderstand what he prayeth.
2. Faith: which is an assurance of obtaining that we aske.
3. Repentance: which is bewailing our sins and wants, and a practizing of our prayers.
4. Deuotion: which is a due disposition in time of prayer.

For if vnderstanding the matter of our prayers, feeling our sinnes and wants, bewailing them, purposing to amend them, earnestly asking pardon and reliefe, reuerently carying our hearts in Gods presence, faithfully perswading our selues God will heare vs: if I say we thus aske, we doe truely and aright vse prayer.

Knowledge necessarie for the vse of prayer.

First, for knowledge that it is necessarie, shall appeare by consideration of the seuerall parts thereof: for there is a threefold knowledge required.

1. Knowledge of the words vttered.
2. Knowledge of the matter contained in the words.
3. Knowledge of the doctrine comprehended in the matter.

The knowledge of the words is opposed against prayer in an vnknowne tongue; which edifieth not, and therefore must be remooued out of the congregation: and in the congregation, the words of the prayer must be vnderstoode, else the speaker shall be a barbarian to the hearer, and otherwise the hearer cannot say Amen. Strange languages is a iudgement of God vpon the world, as may be seene by the history of the tower of Babell; the euidence whereof appeareth vnto this day, in that the paines we bestow about the learning of the tongues is so hard and tedious, and is a great impediment to the true knowledge of the Scriptures. If it bee a iudgement of God, why shall we not seeke to pray in a knowne tongue, and so to vnderstand what we pray, that we may be freed from that iudgement? The knowledge of strange tongues indeede is a blessing, but the strange tongue is vndoubtedly a iudgement.

1. Cor. 14.

Gen. 11.

The knowledge of the matter is a thing absolutely necessarie also: for shall we vtter we know not what to God, or shall we giue consent in publike prayer to that we are ignorant of? the prayer perhaps may containe Arrianisme, or Pelagianisme, it may be hereticall, or schismaticall, or sauor of some foule errors; which cannot please God seeing they are not agreeable to holsome doctrine of the word: all our prayers must be according to his will, but false doctrine, heresies or errors, are contrary to his will. Wherefore we must carefully know and search whether the matter of our prayers containe in them truth or falsehood; and so the knowledge of the matter is also absolutely necessary, if wee will haue our prayers accepted and graunted.

1. Ioh. 5. 14.

The knowledge of the doctrine comprehended in the matter, also is needefull, that a man in some measure know the fundamentall points of religion, which our Sauiour Christ requireth in the Samaritanes; for they worshipped they could not tell

Ioh. 4. 22.

what, but the Iewes knew what they worshipped: a man therefore must know God and himselfe, the law and the Gospell in some tolerable measure before hee can make acceptable prayers to God through Christ Iesus.

Ioh. 17. 3.
2. *Cor.* 13. 5.
1. *Cor.* 11. 28.

The second thing necessarie for the true and holy vse of prayer, is faith or an assurance of obtaining that wee aske according to his will: this faith or assurance is a fruite of iustifying faith, which laieth hold vpon Christ for pardon of sinne, and for all manner of good things for bodie and soule: so that whatsoeuer good thing wee aske, wee may certainly resolue our selues wee shall obtaine: for if God the Father hath giuen vnto vs Iesus Christ, how shall he not with him giue vs all things els that are good? If he giue vs the greater, hee will giue vs the lesser also: for temporall blessings are additions and dependants of heauenly blessings. More shall be said of this point afterward in the conclusion of the prayer, whither the reader is to be referred.

Faith necessarie for the holie vse of prayer.
1. *Ioh.* 5. 14.
Heb. 11. 30.
Rom. 8.
Psal. 34. 10.
Matth. 6.

The third thing requisite for the true and holie vse of prayer, is Repentance: for God heareth not sinners that liue in sinne vnrepented of, that regard wickednes in their hearts, that purpose to liue in knowne sinnes; al their prayers are abominable, for that they turne their eares from hearing of the law, as the Wiseman testifieth. Wherefore he that will haue his prayer heard, must in his hart bewaile his sinnes, hate them, renounce them, studie and striue to forsake them, pray against them, and then the Lord will gratiously graunt his petitions. Indeede sometime God graunteth wicked men that which they aske, or wish to haue from God, but that is in wrath and vengeance: for that which hee giueth them shall turne to their woe and miserie another day. And as it may be said of a godly man, that God heareth him by denying that he asketh: so also may it be said of a wicked man, that God heareth him not by granting that he asketh: the godly man is heard by denying the euill he asketh, and granting the good he asketh not: the wicked man is not heard by granting

Repentance necessarie for the holy vse of prayer.
Ioh. 9.
Psal. 66.
Prouerb.

the euill he asked, and withholding the good he asked not: for though none of Gods creatures are euil in themselues, yet through the abuse of the wicked and Gods curse, they may be euill vnto the euill man. Againe, though God heare what the wicked man saith when hee pray, and grant him that very selfesame thing hee asketh; yet God cannot properly bee said to heare his prayer and grant his request: for the wicked mans prayer is not a means of obtaining, neither doth God graunt him any thing by meanes or through instancie of his prayer: but God is truly said to heare the prayer and graunt the request of the godly, seeing that he graunteth that which they aske through the instancie of their prayers, they being the onely meanes of obtaining.

1. Tim. 4.

The fourth thing necessarie for the holy vse of prayer is Deuotion, which is the due regard and religious estimation a man ought to haue of Gods Maiestie and his owne miserie in time of prayer: which deuotion hath a speciall signification in this place, and containeth these foure things in it principally.

Deuotion necessarie for the true vse of prayer.

1. Attention in time of prayer.
2. Reuerence in regard of Gods presence.
3. Feeling of our sinnes and wants.
4. Desire to obtaine that we aske.

Attention is opposed against wandring thoughts, which vsually in the time of prayer creep into the minds of men: for expelling and auoiding whereof, it behoueth euerie carefull Christian to watch ouer his vnderstanding, and affections, that by-thoughts either rush not into the minde; or if they do, that then presently they be thrust out againe.

Attention a part of deuotion.

This attention is threefold.
1. Attention to the words of prayer.
2. Attention to the matter contained in the words.
3. Attention to God, to whom prayer is directed.

Attention to the words, is when a man doth so watch ouer his tongue, that no words vnsanctified, or vnfit for the holy matter of prayer, doe vnawares breake out of his mouth.

Attention to the matter, is when a man doth so busie his vnderstanding in conceiuing, and affections in pursuing the substance of his petitions, as that by-matters take not place to disturbe the course of his prayers. *1. Cor. 7.*

Attention to God, is when a man doth so conceiue of God as the words of prayer affoord, according to the seuerall names, titles, attributes, properties, and workes wherewithall in time of prayer wee intitle God according to his holy word: as, Father, mercifull, iust, &c.

Reuerence is opposed against either a common or base estimation of Gods excellencie and glorious maiestie, before whom wee appeare when wee come to pray. When a man commeth to make a supplication to a Prince, he is striken with a reuerent feare of so excellent a person as the Prince is: much more ought wee so to bee affected comming before the Prince of all the Princes in the world: wherefore the Psalmist counselleth vs to feare when wee serue God, and to tremble when we giue thankes. *Psal. 2. 11.* This reuerence will be increased, if we consider who God is before whom we come, and what we are that come before God: God is in heauen, and we are vpon the earth: wee are dust and ashes, as *Abraham* spake to God, and God is the Creator and maker of vs all: we are vile, and to be abhorred, to whom apperteineth shame and confusion of face: but God is excellent, admirable and glorious. If these things possesse our affections throughly, a holy reuerence also wil enter vpon our soules. And as it befell *Iacob* when he slept at Bethel; which is by interpretation, *Gods house*, that hee was afraid, saying, it was a fearefull place, and no other but the house of God, and the gate of heauen: euen so ought we to bee affected, by faith seeing God spiritually present which is a spirit and inuisible, searching the hearts, and knowing the thoughts of all the sonnes of men.

Reuerence a part of deuotion.

Eccles. 4. 1.
Gen. 18. 27.
Psal. 95.
Iob. 42.
Dan. 9.

Gen. 28. 17.

Feeling of sin is opposed against hardnes of heart, both that generall obduration which is contrarie to repentance; and a more speciall, which the children of God sometime are cumbred with for want of a continuall renouation of repentance, and growing by occasion of lapse into some sinnes, whence issue hardnes of heart and a carelesse securitie

Feeling of sin a part of deuotion.

and affections benummed for the time. This feeling of
sinne is called by our Sauiour Christ a heauie
load, and wearisome burthen. For as a man
that hath a burthen or load vpon his backe, doth sensiblie
feele it, and is thereby greatly wearied, oppressed and
compelled to bow and stoope through the waight thereof,
his strength being not sufficient to match and ouercome
the weight of his load : euen so the man that once feeleth
the heauie burthen of sinne, which is the wrath of God
euery way intolerable and insupportable of man, is thereby
so surcharged and oppressed, as that hee
cannot looke vp, and then his heart beginneth
to faile as a man in a swoune : and therefore the Prophet
in the Psalme complaineth and confesseth his
sins vnto God, after hee had knowne his
iniquitie and viewed his sinnes, being alwaies placed in
his sight : and they only are fit to come vnto Christ by
faithful prayer that feele this burthen of sinne
vpon their backs; that thinke themselues vile
and abominable sinners : for God resisteth the proud, as if
hee were his speciall enemie: but he giueth grace
vnto the humble as vnto his beloued friend.

Matth. 11. 28.
Psal. 40. 12.
Psal. 51. 3.
Luk. 4. 18.
Iam. 4. 1.

Desire to obtaine that we aske is opposed against cold,
lukewarme or faint affections : when men
aske, but care not greatly for obtaining that
they aske : true deuotion hath feruencie annexed
thereto. For as a begger is very earnest
to get his almes, if hee bee hungrie : so the deuout person
is full of crauing and begging affections, if he haue once
felt the spirituall hunger and thirst of a barren
and drie soule voide of the grace of God.
Thus much briefly of the right and holy vse of prayer,
whereof more shall bee spoken afterward.

Desire to obtaine a part of deuotion.
Iam. 5. 16.
Matth. 7. 7.
Matth. 5. 6.

The third point to be handled in the generall consideration
of the Lords prayer, is the qualities and
conditions thereof, which are these fiue following.

The qualities of the Lords prayer.

1. First, it is a platforme of prayer.
2. Secondly, it is most excellent.
3. Thirdly, it is most perfect and absolute.
4. Fourthly, it is onely a generall forme of prayer.
5. Fiftly, it is hard to be vsed aright for a prayer.

The first qualitie or propertie of this prayer is, that as it is a prayer, so also and that more especially it is a direction and platforme of prayer. For as a man going to build an house, will first haue a platforme or an idea in his head, according whereunto he will frame his house : so the Lords prayer is an idea or paterne whereby euery true prayer is framed : and as the holy Scriptures are termed Canonicall, for that they are the canon or rule of faith and manners ; so the Lords prayer may bee called Canonicall, for that it is the canon or rule of all other prayers : for there is no prayer in the holy Scripture but it may bee referred vnto this prayer : and all the prayers which haue been, are, or shall be made, must be measured by this prayer, and so far forth are they commendable and acceptable as they are agreeable hereunto. For as a circle containeth al figures, a sphere all bodies, and an infinite line all lines : so the Lords prayer containeth all prayers : resembled to a map which at once to the view offreth the consideration of al the world, so this is the synopsis of all prayers.

The Lords prayer is a platforme of prayer. Matth. 6. 9.

The second qualitie of this prayer is the excellencie thereof : for it is Gods word, a portion of holy Scripture. The prayers which wee make may be, and ought to be agreeable to the word, but Gods word they are not : wherefore it is most excellent : for if all the men liuing in the world should studie all their daies to frame a prayer, they were not able to make a prayer comparable hereunto : Iesus Christ the wisedome of God framed it, and that purposely teaching how to pray : therefore excellent must that prayer bee which was framed by the excellencie of Gods wisedome : and as there is no proportion betweene the finite and the infinite ; so is there no comparison betweene the infinite excellencie and capacitie of this prayer, and the prayers of all other men liuing.

The excellencie of the Lords prayer. Luk. 11. 49. & 11. 1.

The third propertie of this prayer is the perfection therof : other prayers are imperfect, either for that they are stained with manifold wants and corruptions, as all our prayers are ; or for that they containe but some portion of the matter

The perfection of the Lords prayer.

contained in this prayer : as the prayers of holy men mentioned in the Scriptures. This prayer containeth the whole Scripture : for it is an Epitome or abridgement of the whole Scripture, a Catechisme in forme of a prayer, containing all the vertues of the Law and Gospell, and all the good we can pray for, all the graces and blessings wee can giue thankes for, all the euill we can pray against : and to these heads may the whole Scripture be referred.

The fourth propertie of this prayer is, that it is onely a generall prayer or forme of prayer : for all the good things we want are not nominated here, nor all the euill wee pray against ; yet they are here included, either simply and naturally as the speciall in the generall, the part in the whole : or else figuratiuely and by proportion, as one part vnder another. For example sake, prayer for health, patience, faith, the King, the Counsell, the Minister, the afflicted, &c. are not here expressely named ; yet they may euery one of them be referred to some one petition or more : therefore this generall prayer may be compared to the Commandements, and the Articles of faith : to the Categories and predicables in Logick, where the heads and generals are propounded onely, or the chiefe or principall matters : the speciall and lesse principal are by proportion and discourse of reason to be referred thereto, or reduced thence.

<small>The Lords prayer a generall prayer onely.</small>

The last qualitie or propertie of this prayer is, that it is very hard to vse this prayer aright for a prayer. Now it is not denied but that it is a prayer, and may be vsed lawfully for a prayer : but to vse it aright as it ought to be vsed, there is the difficultie. For the words of the prayer being so short as they are, and the matter contained in the words both so large and diuers ; euen as large and ample as all things we stand in need of and can pray for, as all things we can pray against, as all things we can giue thankes for : how is it possible that a man praying this prayer should in any mediocritie with his minde conceiue, and his affections pursue the thousand part of the things comprehended in this short forme ? especially considering the vnsearchable depth of our Sauiour Christs conceipt, when he vttered this prayer ; whereinto wee

<small>The Lords prayer hard to be vsed aright for a prayer.</small>

are in some measure to conueigh our conceipts in time of vsing it for a prayer; otherwise it will be the abusing of it.

Againe, it being a portion of holy Scripture very hard to be vnderstood, & being diuersly by diuers persons expounded; also it being doubtfull which is the true exposition thereof: if we perhaps light vpon a false exposition, and so a false meaning of the words, we do not pray it aright as we ought to pray; for we must giue the same sense vnto euery petition, which our Sauiour Christ gaue whē he did pray it; if we do otherwise we wrest the prayer & abuse it: hence therfore appeareth the difficultie of vsing it aright for a prayer.

Out of the consideration of this last propertie of this prayer ariseth this consectarie or conclusion; that there is lesse daunger of sinne in conceiuing a prayer agreeable to this prayer, than in vsing this prayer for a prayer; which may bee verified thus: when wee conceiue a prayer, wee know our owne meaning certainely; so doe wee not certainely know the meaning of euery point in the Lords prayer: againe, when we pray we attaine the depth of the meaning of our owne words; so can we not possibly attaine the depth of the meaning of our Sauiour Christ, when he vsed these words: Finally, our words in prayer conceiued are as large as our matter and affection; but here in the Lords prayer, the matter being as large as the whole Scripture, the words are scant the thousand part thereof: wherefore the conclusion and consectarie is verified. To end this point then, although this be the most excellent and perfect platforme of prayer, and prayer, that euer was deuised; yet considering that it is onely a generall prayer, and hard to be vsed aright, as Christ himselfe vsed it, therefore it may seeme that a prayer conceiued according to this prayer, is as acceptable, if not more accepted of God, than this prayer: for though the Lords prayer is better than any other prayer, yet a man may, and can, and doth vse his own conceiued prayer better than he can vse the Lords prayer: and prayer is accepted or not accepted of God, according as it is rightly vsed or abused: and this is profitable for the ignorant people to thinke vpon, considering their intolerable abusing of the Lords prayer. Thus much may suffice to haue spoken of the generall consideration of the Lords prayer in the foresaid three points, the abuse, the vse, and the conditions thereof.

<small>Specially of the Lords prayer.</small> Now it followeth, that we also consider thereof specially.

This prayer containeth three things.
1. The first is the persons to be considered in prayer.
2. The second is the matter of prayer.
3. The third is the manner of prayer.

The persons which are to be considered in prayer, are <small>The persons to be considered in prayer.</small> comprehended in that which is ordinarily termed the preface of the Lords prayer, or the compellation, contained in these words.

Our father which art in heauen : or
Our heauenly father.

Now the persons we are to consider in prayer, are foure.
1. First, who is to pray. *Quis.*
2. Secondly, for whom we are to pray. *Pro quo.*
3. Thirdly, to whom we are to pray. *Ad quem.*
4. Fourthly, in whose name we are to pray. *Per quem.*

All they are to pray that can call God father, or the children of God brethren : *Our Father.*

We are to pray for others as well as for our selues, namely for all that are or may be our bretheren. *Our.*

We are to pray to God onely, who is the Father of the creature, and our Father in Iesus Christ. *Father.*

We are to pray in his name, who hath made God, of an enemie a friend, yea a father, that is Christ Iesus. *Our Father.*

The first of those persons that are to be considered in prayer, is who are to pray, which may be thus distinguished.

First, who must pray : or who is bound to pray.
Secondly, who may pray : or who may lawfully pray.
Thirdly, who can pray : or who can pray aright.

For the first : all men must pray, that is to say, all men are bound in conscience to pray vnto <small>Who must pray.</small> God, for prayer is a morall precept, which bindeth all men, as all the commaundements of God doe :

for all the commaundements were written in the heart of *Adam*, in the state of innocencie; and that not onely for himselfe, but for all his posteritie: wherefore the very gentils which knew not the law giuen by *Moses*, yet shew the effect of the law written in their hearts, when their consciences accuse them, or excuse them. *Rom. 2. 15.* Seeing therefore that prayer is a commaundement of the morall law, and all the commaundements of the morall law binde the conscience of all men to obedience, therefore all men must pray, otherwise they incurre the penaltie of the breach of the law, which is the euerlasting curse of God.

Here it may be obiected concerning this and all the rest of the commaundements, that all men are not bound to pray, or to keepe the law, seeing *Obiection.* that it is impossible we should keepe the law, or that all men should pray: for God commaundeth not impossibilities, say the papists: seeing therefore it is impossible for all men to keepe the law, or to pray; all men therefore are not bound to pray, or all men must not pray.

To this, answere may bee made by a distinction, that things may be termed impossible two waies, either for that they are impossible in their *Answere.* owne nature, or for that they are impossible by accident or some outward occasion: examples of things impossible in their owne nature are these; that a stone of it owne accord should moue vpward; that iron or leade of it owne accord should swim vpon the water, and not sinke: examples of things impossible through accident, or by reason of some outward occasion are these; that a man that hath his tongue cut out, should speake, or that hath his eyes put out, should see: now the application of the distinction answereth the obiection sufficiently: Gods commaundements, and so the commaundement of prayer is not impossible to be performed of it owne nature, for *Adam* was able to keepe it continuing in that estate of innocencie, wherein God had created him, and so all mankinde in *Adam*: but *Adam* transgressing, and all mankinde in him, by accident and occasion, the commandement of God (and namely that of prayer) is *Rom. 8. 3.* become impossible vnto vs: we are not able to pay our debts, for we haue made our selues bankerouts; we cannot see, for we haue put out our owne eyes. Wherefore God doth not commaund things impossible by nature, when he requireth obedience to his law, although now through our owne defaults, we are not able to obey.

Yet God seemeth to deale hardly that exacteth obedience of vs, now we are not able to performe it.

Obiection.

It is no hard dealing at all: for if the creditor may iustly require the debt of the debter, though he be not able to discharge it, or otherwise cast him in prison for default of payment; much more may God deale so with vs: either exact obedience of vs, or cast vs in prison till we pay the vtmost farthing: neither is there any reason that God should change his righteous law, and square it to our corruption, no more than because there are theeues and malefactors, therefore the law that commaundeth such persons to be hanged, or punished, should be altered: the workeman squareth his crooked timber to his rule, and he doth not frame his rule to his crooked wood; so we must frame our actions to Gods law, and Gods law must not yeelde to our corruptions. Wherefore prayer being one of Gods commaundements, all men therefore must pray, or are bound in conscience to pray, though now it be impossible to pray aright.

Answere.

Thus we see the first point, who must pray.

The second followeth, which is, who may pray.

Who may pray.

Though the commaundement of prayer be directed to all men, and therefore all men are bound to pray: yet notwithstanding there are some men which may not pray, for if they doe, their prayer is turned into sinne. Incense is abomination vnto me, saith the Lord by the Prophet, it is iniquitie: now in the old Testament incense was a type of prayer, and was commaunded by God as a part of his outward worship: so also the sacrifice of the wicked man is abominable, that is, all the worship of the wicked (for the part is put for the whole) and yet God had

Esa. 1. 13.
Psal. 141. 2.
Pro. 15. 8.

Pro. 28. 9.

commaunded the sacrifices: he that turneth his eare from hearing of the law, his prayer is abominable; and yet prayer is Gods commaundement: whence it is necessarily collected, that there are some sects of men, who if they pray, sinne in their prayer, and therefore though they must pray, yet notwithstanding they may not pray: they are bound to pray, yet if they pray, they sinne.

These two propositions seeme to be contradictorie: and therefore cannot both be true, as nature it selfe teacheth: All men must pray: and this: Some men may not pray. How can these things agree? *Obiection.*

Here we see that which the Apostle speaketh in another sense, that sinne is out of measure sinfull: sinne peruerteth the whole order of nature, causeth contradictorie propositions to be both true; for certaine it is that all men are bound in conscience to pray, and therefore must pray; and this is certaine also, that all men may not pray; for if they doe, they sinne and breake the law of God. Now the Lord of his goodnes hath found out a meanes to dissolue this absurditie, and breake the contradiction: wherefore he commaundeth to repent and forsake our sinnes, and then to pray. And here we may note into what an intricate labyrinth or maze, sinne hath brought mankinde, consisting of three bywaies. *Answere. Rom. 7.*

First, we must pray that we may keepe the second commaundement,

Secondly, we liuing in our sinnes must not pray, lest wee transgresse the third commaundement.

Thirdly, we must repent (and that is a thing altogether impossible to flesh and blood) before we pray aright. We being thus included in the maze, the Lords sheweth vs the way out by the power of his spirit in the preaching of his word, working repentance in the hearts of his children that they may pray aright, and so all his commaundements are made easie vnto vs, which before were impossible; and so that sentence of the Father is verified: *da quod iubes, & iube quod vis:* giue me power to doe thy commaundements, and then commaund what seemeth good vnto thee.

A paterne of true Prayer

Thus also the second point is handled, who may pray. The third is, who can pray, or who can pray aright?
Who can pray.
Rom. 8. 15.
They onely can pray aright, that haue the spirit of prayer which teacheth vs to cry Abba, that is father, which is the spirit of adoption, and sanctification. But for the further cleering of this point, a distinction is to be admitted betweene three things, which the world thinketh either to be all one, or very neere of kindred: namely, first saying a prayer, secondly wishing a prayer, thirdly praying a praier.

For the first, we must remember that all men can say
What it is to say a prayer.
prayers; there is not any man so ignorant, so impenitent, or so wicked, but he can and doth sometime say his prayers: and this is no better than the prating of a parret in Gods eares.

Secondly, to wish prayers is one thing, and to pray is
What it is to wish a prayer.
another: for a wish is a sodaine, earnest, wandering, inordinate desire of hauing something, which a man either greatly regardeth not, or is not perswaded to obtaine.

Thirdly, a prayer is a continuall, setled, ordered, and
What it is to pray a prayer.
feruent desire of obtaining that which a man both greatly prizeth, and is perswaded in some measure he shall haue.

1 A wish is sodaine, as a flash of lightning, or the stay of a ball cast at a wall, which reboundeth backe so soone as it toucheth: so a wish quickly shineth in the affection and by and by is extinct; but a prayer is continuall, which doth so possesse the heart that a man neither can nor will be voyded of it; hence we reade of some that prayed all night.

2 A wish is earnest and vehement out of measure, especially in temporall blessings, when the affection is caried as it were with a whirlewind for the present; yet in spirituall matters, there is an exceeding great coldnes and frost of affection, but a prayer is feruent in spirituall matters, and moderate else where: yea and in spirituall matters, there is not that snatching vehemencie in prayer, as in wishes, but rather a sober and moderate equability permanent and increasing.

3 A wish is wandering and rouing, for a wicked man

would haue that he wisheth, howsoeuer he come by it, whether by hooke or crooke he care not; and therefore when he wisheth his heart is not set vpon God, nor knit vnto him: hence it commeth to passe that his wishes are either wicked, euen the transgression of the tenth commaundement, or else God must worke wonders for the graunting of them: as hee will wish to haue a thousand pound land by the yeare: here there is a secret implication either of iniurie to some man from whom it must be had, he coueting another mans goods; or else God must miraculously create so much new earth or space of ground in the world, &c. But a prayer is setled and grounded vpon God and his word: hauing patience and expiration, waiting Gods leasure without the aforesaid rouing and runagate wishes.

4 A wish is inordinate, for the wicked man he neither will vse the meanes to obtaine that he wisheth, nor referre the thing wished to the right end: for example, a wicked man may wish heauen, but he wil neuer vse the meanes to come to heauen, as *Balaam*; he may wish to haue the gifts of the holy Ghost, as *Simon Magus*, but he would haue vsed or rather abused them to his owne gaine, and he would haue bought them with money. But the prayer of the godly man is ordered aright intending Gods glory, the good of others, his owne edification, carefully vsing the good meanes which God hath sanctified for that purpose: hence it is that *Iames* saith that many aske and receiue not, seeing they aske amisse for the satisfying of their lusts. *Iam.* 4. 3.

5 A wicked man sometime wisheth grace by fits, but he doth not greatly regarde it: therefore it is with him as with a woman that longeth for some vnholesome thing, as tar, &c. desiring it eagerly for a fit, and afterward abhorring it: but the godly man he prayeth and prizeth grace inualuable, for obtaining whereof he will sell all that he hath, and separate himselfe to seeke it, and occupie himselfe in all wisedome. *Matth* 14. 44. *Pro.* 18. 1.

6 A wicked man wisheth, but hath no assurance to obtaine; for his wishes are driuen away with desire, as the dust by the winde: but the godly man prayeth, and saith in some measure with the man in the Gospell,

I beleeue, Lord helpe my vnbeliefe. Thus wee see how a wish differeth from a prayer: and that there is a great distance betweene wishing a prayer, and praying a prayer; and that they onely can pray that are qualified as is aforesaid. And thus we see who are to pray.

The second sorte of persons to bee considered in our prayers, are, for whom we are bound to pray: the summe of the doctrine, that concerneth this second sort of persones, shall be comprehended in certaine propositions following, whereof some are affirmatiue, some negatiue: the propositions affirmatiue are these sixe ensuing.

<small>For whom we must pray.</small>

1 First, we are to pray for all the seruants of God, for all them that in present beleeue in Iesus Christ, and repent of their sinne.

2 Secondly, we are to pray for all the elect, that as yet do not actually beleeue nor repent: and these two propositions are confirmed vnto vs by the example of our Sauiour Christ, who hath gone before vs in the practise of them both; though he prayed in another kinde, namely as the onely Mediator of redemption and intercession betwixt God and vs: his prayer being satisfactory and meritorius; ours onely dutifull and charitable.

<small>Ioh. 17.</small>

3 Thirdly, we are to pray for all the members of the visible Church, whom in the iudgement of charitie we are to account Saints by calling: so the Apostle writing to the Romanes in his salutation prayeth for them.

<small>Rom. 1. 7.</small>

4 Fourthly, we are to pray for all men, that is, for all sorts or states and conditions of men, according to the Apostles counsell, Iewes and Gentiles, bond and free, rich & poore, Magistrate and subiect, man and woman; and if there be any other distinction of states and conditions of life.

<small>1. Tim. 2. 1.</small>

5 Fiftly, we are to pray for any one particular person that shall be noted out vnto vs, as standing in need of our prayers: as an excommunicate person, the Turke, the Pope, heretikes and schismatikes, and vitious persons of all sorts: so wee reade that Christ prayed for his persecutors: so did *Steven* the first Martyr. For although

wee must not pray with them, as being persons out of the communion of Saints; yet nature bindeth vs to pray for them, they being of our owne flesh; and we know not how God hath disposed of them for their finall and futuer estate: and it may be that our prayers shall be meanes of obtaining at Gods hands remission of their sinnes, and their conuersion and saluation, as it is probable *Steuens* prayer did further *Pauls* conuersion.

6 Sixtly and lastly, we must pray for our very enemies that wish euill vnto vs, and deuise mischiefe against vs: according to the precept of Christ and the practise of all the Saints, that so we may do good for euill, and heape coales of fire vpon their heads. *Matth.* 5. 44. *Rom.* 12. 20. 21.

Thus we see affirmatiuely for whom we are to pray. Now negatiuely we must also consider who they are for whom we must not pray: and they are comprised in fiue propositions following. For whom we must not pray.

1 First, we are not to pray for all mankinde, that is to say, for all the men that haue liued, do liue, and shall liue in the world. For although wee may pray for any particular person that is nominated and pointed out vnto vs, yet to pray for all that proceed of the roote of *Adam*, is against Gods will. For Christ did not pray for the world, neither is it Gods will that all *Ioh.* 17. that issue from *Adam* should be conuerted and saued: yet because we know not which man is reprobate, therefore by the generall rule of charitie wee may pray for any particular man; excepting some, which afterward shall be excepted.

2 Secondly, wee are not to pray for the dead: for wee will take it graunted for this present that there is no purgatorie (there being here no fit opportunitie to dispute the question) for all the dead are either in heauen, and so thy prayers cannot mend them; or in hell, and thence thy prayers cannot fetch them: wherefore seeing prayer auaileth not, there is no reason it should be vsed for the dead. I will not discusse the quidditie that some of late haue deuised, that wee may pray for the dead thus farre foorth, that their bodies at the last may bee ioyned to their soules to their full and perfect blisse.

3 Thirdly, we are not to pray for the diuels.

4 Fourthly, wee are not to pray for them that sinne the sin against the holy Ghost.

5 Fiftly, we are not to pray for them that are reprobates, if we could know them: the reason of all these things is most apparant, for that therein wee resist Gods reuealed will: hence we reade that God rebuketh *Samuel* for praying for *Saul*: howsoeuer some may thinke that *Samuels* prayer was onely for enioying the kingdome, and not for the pardon of *Sauls* sinne; which hath little probabilitie: hence it is that we pray against the diuell by the example of the Apostle, that God would tread Satan downe vnder our feet: hence it is also that *Dauid* in the Psalmes by the spirit of prophecie oft times prayeth against his enemies, whom he knew were reprobates, or irrecouerable from their sinnes: and if the Church hath the spirit of discerning one that sinneth the sinne against the holy Ghost, and hath adiudged that person so to haue sinned, we are not onely not to pray for him, but to pray against him for his vtter ouerthrow and present damnation, yea though it were *Iulian* himselfe the Emperour.

<small>1 Sam. 16. 1.</small>

<small>Rom. 16. 20.</small>

Thus negatiuely also we vnderstand for whom wee are not to pray: onely there remaineth this point neere vnto the former, against whō we may pray, which being shortly handled, this second sort of persons also is limited.

<small>Against whom we may pray.</small>

Generally therefore we may pray against al the enemies of our saluation: absolutely against the diuell, the world, the flesh, and all reprobates, whether sinning the sinne against the holie Ghost, or otherwise, if they may bee knowne. Also we may pray against wicked men, these cautions obserued.

1 First, that our prayer be *in concreto, non in abstracto*, as the Logicians speake: that is to say, we must direct our prayer not against the creature of God, but against the creature corrupted with sinne and rebelling against God.

2 Secondly, in our prayers wee are not to intend the destruction of the creature which God hath made, but the execution of iustice in the deserued punishment of sinne, which is the will of God most righteous and iust.

3 Thirdly, wee must take heede that our owne priuate reuenge bee not the motioner of our prayers: for wee must not seeke to auenge our selues; but the cause of God and of the Church, which are matters publike, ought to stirre vs vp in imprecation.

4 Lastly, because wee know not what God hath decreed of them, finally wee must alwaies remember to pray distributiuely and conditionally: as for example thus: If they appertaine to thy election, conuert them, and in the meane time represse them: if not, confound them. Thus the second person, for whom we are to pray, is distinguished.

The third person to be considered in prayer, is, through whom, or in whose name we are to pray: and that is in the name and through the mediation and interposition (that I may so speake) of Iesus Christ, who doth mediate our cause with the Father. And here two points are to be remembred and handled. The one is affirmatiue or positiue: wee must pray in Christs name. The other is exclusiue, containing in it a negatiue: we must pray in Christs name onely, and not in the name of any other.

First, wee are generally to remember that the name of Christ signifieth Christs merit, mediation, redemption, intercession, obedience, or what else Christ did or suffered for our reconcilement and reuniting vnto God, and that to pray in Christs name is to desire the Father to graunt that wee aske, through and for the dignitie and worthines of Christs person, and actions which he vndertooke and performed in our behalfe.

What it is to pray in Christs name.

This generally promised of the signification of Christs name: the first point to be handled, is, that we must pray in Christs name: for Christ being the meane betwixt God and vs he is the fittest to be our Mediatour: for therefore is Christ Mediatour, because he is *medius*: now Christ is *medius*, the meane betwixt God and vs in diuers respects obseruable.

We must pray in Christs name.

Christ is a meane in diuers respects.

1 First, in regard of his person which is compounded (let not this word be misexpounded) of two natures, the deitie and the humanitie; so that Christ Iesus is God

and Man: in that hee is God, hee hath the nature of God: in that hee is man, hee hath the nature of man; and so hee being Godman, is a meane person betweene God and man: and so fit to be interposed as Mediatour on both parts.

2 Secondly, Christ is *medius*, a meane, in respect of his fauour and loue: which in regard of God is passiue, and in regard of vs is actiue: for he is beloued of God, as being the onely begotten sonne of the Father: and we are beloued of him, as being parcels of his owne flesh. In that he is beloued of the Father, hee is fit to obtaine things needfull for vs: in that hee is louing to vs, we are likely to obtaine good things through him: so that Christ being fauoured of God, and fauourable to vs, is perfectly qualified for the office of a Mediatour.

3 Thirdly, Christ is also *Medius*, or a meane, in respect of his actions or workes, which in his owne person out of his loue he hath wrought for vs: his actions are compound, as his person and his loue is: they are works not of a meere man, nor of God alone, but of a person hauing the qualification of God and man, that the Godhead might dignifie, and the manhood might fit the worke, that in respect of the Deitie the worke might be propitiatorie, deseruing mercie of God; and in regard of the Manhood applicatorie, fit to bee imputed to vs, that wee being inuested therewith, Gods iustice may bee satisfied, and wee reconciled through the worke. Seeing therefore that Christ Iesus is the onely Meane person betwixt God and vs, he is the only Mediatour betwixt God and vs: and therefore in his name wee must pray: so saith the Euangelist, *Aske in my name, and ye shall receiue.* And againe in another place, He is the true Aduocate with the Father, and in him God is well pleased with vs: and the Father doth alwaies heare him whatsoeuer hee asketh, as hee himselfe witnesseth, because he is so dearely beloued of his Father. Wherefore for conclusion of this point, as it is impossible that a thing should moue, *ab extremo in extremum sine medio,* from one place to another without a meane way; as for example, from earth to heauen, and not passe through the ayre: euen so cannot

Ioh. 16. 23.
1. *Ioh.* 2. 1.
Matth. 3. 17.
Ioh. 11. 42.

our prayers, which are sinfull, come into Gods presence, who is most iust, without the meanes and mediation of Iesus Christ: and thus the first point is plaine that wee must pray in the name of Iesus Christ. The other followeth, which is negatiue and exclusiue, that we must pray in his name onely, and in the name of no other: and here are excluded foure sorts of persons who are not to bee mediatours of intercession. <small>We must pray only in Christs name.</small>

    1. The first sort is the Father and the holy Ghost.
    2. The Angels are the second sort.
    3. The third sort are the Saints departed: and liuing.
    4. The fourth sort is our selues.

For the first: we are to know that the first and third persons in Trinitie are excluded from the office of intercession: for though each person in Trinitie hath his seuerall office in all the workes which are termed *ad extra*, wrought vpon the creature, as creation, redemption, sanctification, &c. yet there are some particular acts and motions in these seuerall workes, which are proper to some one person and incommunicable to the rest, as namely such actions which are relatiue between person and person: for example sake, the Father sealed and sent the Sonne into the world, the Sonne was sent of the Father: the Father did not send the holy Ghost to take our nature: neither did the holy Ghost take our nature, but the Sonne onely. So in the case propounded: the Father doth not make intercession with the Sonne, but the Sonne maketh intercession with the Father: so neither doth the holy Ghost. For neither the Father nor the holy Ghost were incarnate, suffered or merited for vs, but the Sonne onely. The Father accepteth our prayers: the holy Ghost teacheth vs to pray, which is called intercession by the Apostle, Rom. 8. 26. but in a generall signification: the Sonne onely meriteth and deserueth and obtaineth our prayers, hauing onely assumed our nature, and therein merited and prayed and obtained. Seeing then of all the three persons in Trinitie the Sonne onely is our intercessor, therefore in the name of Christ alone wee must pray. <small>The Father and the holy Ghost are not our intercessors.</small>

For the second: the Angels are excluded also from this work of intercession, as being not persons qualified thereto sufficiently; which conīsideration groweth vpon the former: for if the Father and the holy Ghost, then much more the Angels cannot performe this office: for as hath been, so the office of intercession and propitiation are dependants and conuertible: so as the person that is to bee our intercessor, must also be our sacrifice of propitiation: and contrarily our propitiator is our intercessor. Hence it is that the Apostle *Iohn* hath ioyned them toīgether by way of answering an obiection, or rendring a reason, which implieth this exclusiue doctrine: the Apostles words are following: *Though a man sinne, yet wee haue an Aduocate with the Father, Iesus Christ the iust, and he is the propitiation for our sinnes:* which sentence may admit this Resolution: because Christ is our propitiation, therefore hee is our intercessor, and therefore wee neede not despaire of pardon, if wee sinne through infirmitie: or thus by way of question and answere.

The Angels are not our intercessors.

1. Ioh. 2. 1.

Q. What is the end of preaching the Gospell?
A. That Gods children may be kept from sinne.
Q. If we doe sinne, what comfort is there?
A. We haue an Aduocate to make intercession for vs.
Q. But how may we be assured that he shall obtaine?
A. Because he is sufficiently qualified for the purpose, both for that he is iust, hauing perfectly fulfilled the law: and he is also a propitiation for our sinnes, or sustaining the punishment and meriting for vs: so that by this Scripture it is manifest that the person which is fit to make intercession for vs, must also haue abilitie to make satisfaction for our sinnes: which power, because it is not incident to the Angels, therefore the Angels are excluded from this office of intercession.

For the third: the Saints, whether departed this life, or liuing, are excluded from this office of interīcession, as it is proper to Christ, and that by the same reasons before recited: yet neuertheīlesse, neither the Angels, nor Saints departed, or liuing, are excluded from all manner of intercession or

Saints deīparted or liuīing are not our intercesīsors.

prayer for vs: for seeing the Angels and Saints haue loue to the Church of God militant, themselues being triumphant in heauen, no doubt they wish and desire and pray earnestly after their manner, for the prosperitie and welfare of the Church vpon earth: and the Saints liuing doe in their prayers continually recommend to God their brethren yet liuing, and militant against the common enemies: but there is difference to be made betwixt the one and the other.

1 For Christs intercession is deseruing and meritorious: but the intercession of the Angels and Saints is onely dutifull and charitable.

2 Christs intercession is distinct and particular for euery one seuerally: the Angels and Saints make their intercession generally and confusedly for the whole number of the elect.

3 Christs intercession is in his owne name: theirs in Christs name. For if the Angels and Saints obtaine any good things for the Church, it is by meane of Christ, and not for their owne worthines. And here in deepe silence without further confutation we will passe by the two opinions of the Papists: the one blasphemous, That Angels and Saints are mediators of intercession, as Christ is in the same kinde, though not in the same degree: the other foolish, That by reason of their merits they obtaine for vs of God: and therefore the popish crew in their seuerall necessities haue recourse to seuerall Saints for reliefe: whereunto a third may bee added, That the Angels and Saints departed in God, as in a glasse see the seuerall petitions of their clients here in earth; and so are readie to mediate for them in their neede: which is as very a fansie, as the former blasphemie or folly.

For the fourth and last sorte of persons excluded from the office of intercession, we must know, that seeing Angels and Saints are disabled to this worke, our selues cannot possibly partake therein, being sinfull, needing a mediator, and an intercessor, and wanting merits of our owne; howsoeuer the false Church of Antichrist hath forged the contrarie, thereby dispoyling Christ of his office, by foysting in their owne merits: for Christ will be all or none, our merits

We must not pray in our owne name.

cannot stand with his, they shoulder out one another. Hence then followeth the conclusion; That Christ is onely the intercessor; and therefore in his name onely must we pray.

And this is the third person in whose name wee must pray.

The fourth person is, To whom we must pray. To God: and to him onely: and this is a consectarie of the former matter; for seeing the Angels and Saints are no intercessors for vs to God; therefore there is no reason we should pray to them: for this is the supposed end of the inuocation of Saints and Angels, that they may obtaine of God for vs, that which we cannot obtaine for our selues; they being, as it is presumed, more gracious in Gods eyes than we are, and more familiar with him being in his presence or priuie chamber, as Nobles about their Prince. But here two propositions must be distinguished, as in the former.

<small>To whom we must pray.</small>

First, that we must pray to God: secondly we must pray to him onely.

Concerning the first there is little doubt of that in the word, sauing that we reade in the booke of Daniel that there was an act made that no man should pray to any God for the space of thirtie dayes, but to the King onely: this act the Princes made against religious *Daniel* in policie, through flattery accomplishing their murtherous designes: but this was only a mouths atheisme. We finde it also by most fearefull experience, that there are some Atheists, or Naturalists, who because they would banish the memorie of God out of the world, by blind-folding their owne conscience, haue denied prayer to God: but these men rather neede our prayers, than our confutations, who are euery day and night confuted, and confounded in their owne thoughts.

<small>We must pray to God. *Dan.* 6. 7.</small>

Leauing this first point, we descend to the second, That our prayers are to be directed to God alone; which may be confirmed by two reasons: the first reason is the words of Christ alledged out of *Moses: Thou shalt worship the Lord thy God, and him onely shalt thou serue:* which sentence affoordeth this argument: that seeing prayer is

<small>We must pray to God alone. *Matth.* 4. 10. *Deut.* 6. 13.</small>

a principal part of Gods worship and seruice, therefore it is due to him onely : for to him only we must pray, whom we must worship and serue : but we must onely worship and serue God ; therefore to God onely we must pray : now if that thredbare or motheaten distinction of *Latria*, *Dulia* and *hyperdulia* be still obiected, as though *dulia* and *hyperdulia* might be giuen to Saints, and the Virgin ; but *latria* onely to God : the answere will euince, that by comparing of *Matthew* with *Moses*, *latria* and *dulia* are all one : for the Hebrew word *Gnabad*, which is translated *Latreuein* by *Matthew*, doth properly signifie *duleuein :* but this quircke hath bin so sufficiently answered by diuers of our learned countrimen, that I dare scarse attempt any thing in it. *Deut.* 6. 13.

The second reason, therefore followeth which may be collected out of the Apostles word : *how shall they call vpon him on whom they haue not beleeued*, which may be framed thus : To him only we must pray on whom we beleeue, but we onely beleeue in God ; therefore we must only pray to God : for seeing prayer hath two parts, desire, and faith, if faith be wanting, prayer is imperfect. Now I doe suppose that there is no papist dare say ẏ we may trust in the Saints or Angels, which were flat idolatrie ; and cursed is he that putteth his trust in an arme of flesh. Wherfore for conclusiō of this fourth point, seeing we are only to beleeue in God, and to serue God, therefore we must onely pray to God. *Rom.* 14.

Furthermore, this fourth person, to whom we must make our prayers, which is God, is expressed vnto vs two waies.

First, by a name of relation, in that he is intituled *Father*.

Secondly, by the place he inhabiteth, *Heauen*.

For this title, *Father*, which is here mentioned, it is to be enquired whether it is *Naturæ* or *Personæ nomen*, that is to say, whether it is to be referred to the first person in Trinitie, or to the whole Trinitie : whether we speake to God the Father of his onely begotten sonne Christ : or to God the Father and maker of all his creatures : for answere whereof thus much ; it seemeth that there is no absurditie to take it

Whether Father be a word of nature or person.

either way, or both waies rather: if Christ prayed this prayer (as it is probable he did) then without doubt it was directed to the first person in Trinitie, and it signifieth personally; if Christ prescribed it to his disciples for a forme of prayer, then (in all likelihoode) it signifieth the whole Trinitie, who is to be called vpon by the creature. Now as I coniecture, for that Christ did both pray it, and prescribed it to others for a forme of prayer, therefore I incline to thinke that there is a compound meaning of the word, signifying both the first person in Trinitie, and the whole Trinitie; which affordeth vs this instruction: That when we pray we are so to direct our prayers to the Father, as that we do not exclude the other persons of Trinitie, who with the Father are equally to be worshipped, being God equall with him. And here it shall not be impertinent to consider, how we are to conceiue of God in prayer, which ariseth partly out of the title which is giuen to God, partly out of the place where he dwelleth: this point may be comprehended in fiue positions, which followe.

1 First we must not think God like any creature, as the Papists haue painted him: for in the fourth of Deuteronomie *Moses* expresly forbiddeth the Israelits so to doe; and he rendreth a reason in that place; because they saw nothing when the law was deliuered: and therefore the practise of many now adayes is reproueable, who, though they will not paint God, yet they paint two hands giuing the two tables, one to *Moses*, and another to *Aaron:* which is false, monstrous, and idolatrous: false, because the tables were giuen only to *Moses*; monstrous, because there are hands without a body; idolatrous, because there are hands, whereas God hath no shape at all, any way sensible. *(How we must conceiue of God in prayer. Deut. 4. 15.)*

2 Secondly, although in the holy Scripture figuratiuely there are hands, armes, feete, face, eares, and other manly parts attributed to God, yet we must not thinke that God hath any of these parts properly: indeede God hath something answerable to these parts, or rather something whereunto these parts in the creatures are sutable: for God made man not onely according to his image, which consisteth in holines and righteousnes, but also according to his similitude (for the words may aptly be

distinguished) so that man is a similitude of God : Gods armes and hands, and fingers, argue his power and actiuitie; his feete argue his vbiquitie; his face, eyes, and eares, declare his wisedome and fauour, &c. and proportionable to these attributes of God, there is a configuration of the lineaments of the body in man, wherein man is like God : wherefore we may say, and so we must conceiue of God, contrarie to the *Psal.* 115. gods of the heathen : *They haue eyes and see not*; but God seeth, and yet he hath no eyes : *they haue feete and walke not*; but God walketh euery where, and yet hath no feete : and so of whatsoeuer other part may be applied to God ; which figure is called Anthropopathia, being a speciall metaphor.

3 Thirdly, we must conceiue of God as he hath reuealed himselfe in his word and workes : namely, most mightie, iust, mercifull, wise, true, holy, simple, and euery way infinit, eternal, and blessed Creator, Redeemer, Sanctifier, and Sauiour of all his creatures, &c.

4 Fourthly, we must so direct our prayers to one person, as that we doe not exclude the other ; for that is idolatrie to diuide the persons, which are onely distinct.

5 Lastly, for order sake we must pray to the Father directly and primarily; and that through the merit and mediation of the Sonne, with the instinct and inspiration of the holy Ghost : yet it is not vnlawfull to direct our prayers to the Lord Iesus Christ ; or to the holy Spirit personally, according to the example of the Apostle, who blesseth the Corinthians from the Father, Sonne, and holy Ghost ; which blessing is a prayer : and by the example of *Iacob*, who prayeth that the Angell which deliuered him from all euill (which Angell was Christ) would blesse the sonnes of *Ioseph*. We see then to which person of Trinitie our prayers are primarily to bee directed ; with the manner how we are to conceiue of God in time of prayer.

2. *Cor.* 13. 13.

Genes. 48. 16.

This may serue for the title, Father. Now followeth the place which God inhabiteth, which is the second argument descriptiue : and that is vttered in these words (*which art in heauen*) which also doth impart vnto vs his condition, that hee is heauenly: of which two points a little in order.

First, God is in heauen: not circumscriptiue, as though he were included within the compasse of heauen; for he is infinit, and therefore euery where: neither is he in heauen definitiue, as though when he were in heauen, he were no where else, for he is euery where at once; for God is in euery place, and yet not included in any place, he is out of euery place, and yet excluded from no place: but God is in heauen, first because that in heauen he doth especially manifest himselfe in his mercie, grace, and glorie to the elect Angels and Saints through the humanitie of Christ Iesus which is exalted in heauen: secondly, because that from heauen he doth visibly manifest himselfe to the creatures in the works of his prouidence and preseruation, and especially to mankinde in manifold blessings and iudgements; but most especially to the Church in the meanes of saluation: and in these respects God is in heauen. *How God is in heauen.*

Secondly, God is also heauenly: that is to say, free from all corruption, mutation, or alteration whatsoeuer; whereby he differeth from the creatures, which in time of their owne inherent infirmitie corrupt, vanish and perish: in which sense the Prophet saith, *They all waxe old as a garment, and as a vesture they shall be chaunged:* whereas *God is alwaies the same, and his yeeres doe not faile.* *Why God is heauenly. Iam. 1. 17.* *Psal. 102. 26.*
Againe, also God is heauenly, for that hee is most excellent and glorious, full of incomparable and incomprehensible maiesty: not as though God his essence or substance were of the same nature and condition with the heauens; for they are created bodies: but for that there is no creature more excellent and glorious to sense than the heauens, therefore God is compared to them: whereas indeede the essence of God doth as farre surpasse the heauens, as the Sunne shining in his brightnes doth the blacke and palpable darknes of Egypt, or of hell it selfe.

Thus much may be sufficient for the fourth person to be considered in the preface of this prayer, with his title and place of habitation, expressing also his condition, which is glorious and heauenly.

Furthermore, out of the consideration of these foure sorts of persons signified in the preface of the Lords prayer, arise certaine holy affections and dispositions, whereby the heart is prepared to prayer, and aright composed in time of prayer: and they are in number sixe following. *The disposition of the heart in prayer.*

The first is boldnes, in that we direct our prayers to him that is a Father. *Boldnes.*

The second is charitie, that wee pray not in particular, but in common, intituling God our Father. *Charitie.*

The third is humilitie, that we direct our prayers to him that in Iesus Christ is made of an enemie a father. *Humilitie.*

The fourth is reuerence, that wee come to him that is an heauenly father, most mightie and glorious. *Reuerence.*

The fifth is heauenly meditations: for wee direct our prayers to a heauenly father. *Holy meditations.*

The sixth is faith, that ariseth from all the former: of each of which something shall be spoken in the discourse ensuing. *Faith.*

And first of that boldnes and confidence which Gods children haue, in that they direct their prayers to him that is a father, who pitieth his children more than an earthly father can, yea more than a most naturall and compassionate mother doth or can pitie the fruite of her wombe, which she purchaseth with so much sorrow and paine: which boldnes is to bee distinguished from presumption and impudencie, a thing too common to impenitent persons, who come into the presence of God, as a bard horse rusheth into the battell, or as a mad desperate ruffian challenging his enemie into the field, where they receiue their mortall wound through their foolehardines: so these presumptuous persons either not regarding Gods iustice, or loosely perswading themselues of his mercie, still liuing in their sinnes, inconsiderately prease into Gods presence: who afterwards receiue the iudgement of presumption in their owne consciences, if euer the Lord discouer to them their palpable hypocrisie through true repentance: whereas the children of God

1. Of boldnes.
Psal. 103. 13.
Esay. 49. 15.

approch with confidence to the throne of grace, hoping assuredly to obaine mercie, and to finde grace to helpe in time of neede, because that God is our Father full of compassion and mercie, and Iesus Christ is our high Priest, who hath a sympathie and fellow feeling of our infirmities partaking flesh and blood with vs, and so with bowels of pitie yearneth toward vs complaining in our miserie. Wherefore when we come before the Lord in prayer, we must learne to distinguish between this filiall boldnes, and foolish presumption, least we iustly incurre the reproofe of blind and bold bayards through our inconsiderate rashnes: for it is not lawfull for euery ruffling hackster to rush into the Princes presence; but if he doe, he shall be accounted a presumptuous person, and punished deseruedly: but it is lawfull for the children of the Prince, who for so doing, passe not vnder the censure of rashnes or impudencie.

Heb. 4. 16.

Secondly, charitie is here inclusiuely suggested vnto vs, seeing that Christ teacheth vs to say, not as in the Creede (*I beleeue*) singularly, but respectiuely and charitably, *Our Father:* for euery man shal liue by his own faith only, but not by his own prayers only: *Pray one for another*, saith *Iames:* but wee doe not reade it written, beleeue one for another, (though one mans faith may bee an instrument of conueiance to another of externall sanctification, which is an outward title to, and participation of the meanes of grace and saluation). Wherefore seeing in our prayers we include our brethren, yea our enemies also, it is apparant that our prayers must be made in loue and charitie; so the Apostle teacheth, that wrath & malice must bee abandoned, when we lift vp our hands in prayer to the Lord: so that the practise of many is reproueable that bring their prayers in one hand, and malice in another, being compounded as it were of strife and contention, of railing and reuiling, of slaundering and backbiting, of malice and enuie, putting a kinde of felicitie in these fretfull and deuouring affections; who are to remember the condition of the fifth petition of the Lords prayer gathered by consequence: that if we do not forgiue others, the Lord himselfe will not forgiue vs.

2. Of Charitie.

Iam. 5. 16.
1. *Cor.* 7. 14.

1. *Tim.* 2. 8.

Mat. 6. 14.

Thirdly, humilitie or humiliation and contrition is here presupposed, whereas we come to God as to a father, who was an enemie sometime, but now through the intercession and propitiation of our Sauiour alone is become a father vnto vs. This therefore putteth vs in minde of Christs merits, and therefore of our sinne and miserie: which consideration is auaileable to perswade humiliation: surely that person which commeth before the Lord with a proud heart, and haughtie affections, shall want entertainment from the Lord: because God resisteth the proud person that neuer was humbled: and hee sendeth the rich away emptie: and the boasting Pharisie shall depart home vniustified: but he that commeth into Gods presence, repenting in dust and ashes as *Iob* did; with a rope about his necke (and sackcloth about his loynes) as the messengers of the King of Aram: he that in his owne eyes is most vile, most wretched, most miserable, most abominable, is most acceptable to God, who giueth grace to the humble, filleth the hungrie soule with good things, and iustifieth the despised Publican.

3 Of Humility.

Iam. 4. 6.

Luk. 1. 53.
Luk. 18. 14.

Iob. 42. 6.

Fourthly, reuerence also is intimated vnto vs when wee intitle God an heauenly Father: for children come into their parents presence with reuerence: so also it behoueth vs religiously to reuerence before so great a Maiestie as he is; who though he be a father, yet is also a consuming fire, to fall into whose hands is a thing most dreadfull. This honourable estimation, and reuerent feare, the Lord challengeth by vertue of his Fatherhood, as the Prophet *Malachie* pleading the Lords cause, reporteth; which will arise in our hearts vpon these grounds, duly prepondered.

4. Of reuerence.

Heb. 12. 29. & 10. 31.

Mal. 1. 6.

First, if we consider that God is the Creator of vs all, and that it is hee that hath made vs, and we are his workmanship; then as *Abraham* confessed, so shall we: let not the Lord be offended that we are bold to speake vnto him, being but dust and ashes: and as *Iob* saith, Behold we are vile when wee speake vnto the Lord, that maketh answere out of the whirlewinde.

5. Of holy meditations.
Psal. 95. 6.
Genes. 18. 27.

Iob. 39. 37.

Secondly, if wee seriously weigh with our selues that God knoweth the inward disposition of the soule; that he searcheth the hearts, and trieth the reines; and that the bowels of the soule are seene of him, and requireth spirituall seruice of vs, himselfe being a spirit, it will work in vs religious feare and reuerence with sinceritie, which is opposed to pride, rashnes, and dissembling with God.

Heb. 4. 13.

Ioh. 4. 24.

Thirdly, if wee consider with our selues the wonderfull attributes of God, as his heauenly omnipotencie, his exquisite iustice, his incomprehensible Maiestie, and glorie euery way infinite; it may cause in vs rather astonishment and horror, than a bare and naked feare.

But of this doctrine ariseth a reproofe of their practise that come into Gods presence, either with common & ordinarie affections, or with vile and base estimations, vpon whom the censure of irreligious and prophane persons may in some degree be charged, for that they look not vnto their feete when they come into Gods house: for there are some that come before God, 1 as men that goe to the market to buy or sell, or to dispatch other ciuill businesses; or it may bee with lesse circumspection: for worldly men for the most part follow worldly affaires with great diligence, desire, and warines: but wee must be otherwise affected: for seeing prayer is a matter of religion, and directed to God our heauenly father, for our euerlasting good, therefore we must put on reuerence, and religion, in regard both of God, of our selues, and of that holy action, and doffe off ordinarie and common affections, as it were a paire of foule shooes of our feete with *Moses*, when wee come to talke with God, who is in the midst of the fire.

A reproofe of carnall affections and thoughts in time of Prayer. *Eccles.* 4. 17.

Thoughts of ciuill matters reprooued.

Exod. 3. 5.

2 Others there are, more vile and base in their estimations, who bring before God the price of a dogge, or of an harlot: for this is the practise of many, who come to pray as the theefe to steale, the drunkard to the Ale, the leacher to the stewes: or as men that come from stealing, drinking and whoring: for when they haue wearied themselues with these sinnes,

Vile and wicked thoughts reprooued.

then they drop out of the stewes or Alehouse into the Church to prayer: these men say as the Priests and people said in the Prophet *Malachies* time, *The table of the Lord is not to be regarded:* wherefore before we appeare before the Lord, some time must bee spent in preparing our hearts to prayer, that all carnall and fleshly affections may be set apart, and wee throughly possessed with an honourable and reuerent regard of that holy busines: wherefore the Prophet exhorteth the true *Iacob* or *Israelite* to lift vp the heads of the euerlasting doores, that is, the cogitations and affections of the soule which is eternall, that Christ the King of glorie may come in; for sensuall and worldly thoughts and desires doe barre and lock the doore against him. And in the next Psalme the Prophet himselfe practiseth his exhortation (like a good Teacher) lifting vp his soule vnto the Lord when hee speaketh vnto him in prayer: for seeing we pray to God our Father which is in heauen and heauenly, therefore wee must haue heauenly affections and meditations in time of prayer. Christ saith, where our treasure is there will our hearts be: If God bee our treasure who is in heauen, our hearts and mindes will be there also: wherefore wee must pitch our affections on things which are aboue, and not on things which are below: so that here falleth to the ground all wauing and gadding thoughts and desires in time of prayer, besides or contrarie to the matter vttered in prayer: as about our dinner, our money, our cattell, our pleasures, our suites and aduersaries, and a thousand of like qualitie: so that if our prayers were written as wee conceiue them, and our by-thoughts as parentheses interlaced, they would be so ridiculous, as that wee might very well bee ashamed of them: and yet alas God must haue such prayers of vs, or he must haue none; for wandrings will creepe into the prayers of the most godly and vigilant, though in time of prayer they watch their hearts with double diligence: which ineuitable infirmities being disliked and bewailed, shall not be imputed to Gods children.

Mal. 2. 7. 8. 13.

Preparitiue before Prayer needfull.

Psa. 24. 6. 7.

Psal. 25. 1.

Mat. 6. 21.

Collos. 3. 2.

Wanderings reprooued.

And thus the fourth affection, *viz.* reuerence, is requisite, by occasion whereof the fifth holy disposition also hath been handled, which is (as hath been said) heauenly meditations and affections, seuered from the world and worldly matters. Now therefore the sixth and last of these holie dispositions is Faith, which is grounded vpon the former foundation: for seeing God is our Father, therefore wee may be assured of his loue; and seeing hee is in heauen or heauenly, we need not doubt of his power; and seeing he is so in heauen as that hee is euery where else (as hath been said) wee may bee sufficiently perswaded of his presence: adde hereto his truth and fidelitie, which will assure vs of performing his promises, and wee may haue full assurance of faith: which may thus be singled out.

<small>6. Of Faith.</small>

<small>Foure grounds of faith, loue, power, wisedome, truth of God.</small>

1. First, God is euery where, and so knoweth our wants.
2. Secondly, God is powerfull and omnipotent, and so able to doe whatsoeuer he will.
3. Thirdly, God is louing and mercifull, and therefore hath will to doe for vs what is best.
4. Lastly, God is true, and therefore performeth his promises, and keepeth his fidelitie for euer. So that if these meditations frequent our mindes, our faith will marueilously bee confirmed, which is thus grounded out of this preface. And these are the persons & affections of prayer.

Hauing thus discussed the preface, which is the first part of the Lords prayer: now it followeth in like manner to intreate of the petitions, which are the second part thereof, and may bee termed the matter of prayer: in handling whereof generally this method shall be obserued.

<small>The matter of this prayer.</small>

First, because the petitions are propounded by our Sauiour Christ in due order, some first, and some last; therefore the reason of this order shall be searched out.

<small>Rules for expounding the petitions.</small>

Secondly, for that the words of some or all the petitions are doubtfull, therfore the sense and meaning of the words in the next place is to be scanned.

Thirdly, seeing the words of euery petition are so short, the contents are also to be obserued: for better inuention whereof, certaine rules must be remembred.

Whereof the first is, that seeing the petitions are as the Commandements, certaine generall heads, or places, whither the specials are to be referred, or else some speciall put for the rest, therefore a particular enumeration will be requisite of such matters, as by Rhetoricall discourse may arise: and here the figures *Synecdoche* and *Metonymia* haue speciall vse in most of the petitions. <small>Rules for the contents of each petition.</small>

A second rule is, that where good things are prayed for euill things of the same kinde, as the hinderances and impediments of the good, are prayed against: and so the petitions containe supplications, and deprecations.

A third rule also is, that seeing this prayer is a perfect platforme of prayer or inuocating of God, therfore of necessitie there must place of thankfulnes be had in this prayer: and hereupon it followeth, that in each petition, as we pray for good things, so we giue thankes for them: and as wee pray against euill, so wee giue thankes for immunitie and preseruation from euill.

Hence therefore it followeth, that in euery petition fiue things are to be considered: which are these following. <small>Fiue things to be considered in euery petition. 1. The order. 2. The sense. 3. Supplication. 4. Deprecation. 5. Thankesgiuing.</small>

First, the order of the petitions.

Secondly, the sense and meaning of the words of each petition.

Thirdly, the good things we aske, called supplication.

Fourthly, the euill we pray against, called deprecation.

Fiftly, the good wee giue thankes for, which is either in blessings conferred, or euill preuented, called thanksgiuing.

Out of which consideration appeareth also the difficultie of vsing the words of the Lords prayer for a prayer: namely, for that it is an instrument for seuerall purposes opposed each to other: as for good and against euill: in asking and praising, and that in euery petition: so that we had neede <small>The difficultie of vsing the Lords Prayer aright.</small>

vse great leisure in vttering the words, deep meditation in searching out the contents, and contrarie affections in respect of contrarie obiects, good and euill, and so foorth : or else very likely wee shall in no mediocritie diue into the depth of the matters therein contained : and yet neuerthelesse I thinke it may lawfully bee vsed for a prayer, for ought that I yet conceiue. These things being generally prefixed, as materiall for the vnderstanding of each petition, it remaineth that we descend to a particular discussing of them : and first they admit this distinction : Some of them respect God simply and meerely : others respect vs also : now these prayers which concerne God directly and simply, without any respect of vs, are propounded first of all : the reason whereof is diuers.

First, for that God is the absolute Lord of all the creatures, and hee must absolutely bee regarded, all respect of our selues set apart : wherefore, if wee wanting our daily bread, and remission of sinnes, God thereby might gaine glorie, we ought to be content therewith. Hence we see how vehemently Gods children haue bin carried with fierie zeale of Gods glorie : The zeale of Gods house consumed Christ, famished *Elias*, and vrged the Prophet *Moses* to reiect his owne saluation; and caused *Paul* to wish himselfe *Anathema :* or at least to be content so to be. *Ioh.* 2. 17. 1. *King* 19. 14. *Exod.* 32. 31. *Rom.* 9. 3.

Secondly, God in creating the world intended his owne glorie, which was the first and chiefe end ; and all other things, all Gods creatures and ordinances are but meanes to that end, as our daily bread, remission of sinne, strength against temptation, Christ himselfe the Mediatour, with all his workes and sufferings, the Gospell, Magistracie, Ministerie, the creatures and whatsoeuer else : that therefore which was first in Gods intention, must also bee first in our intention, if we be zealous of his glorie aright. *Pro.* 16. 4.

Thirdly, Gods glory, kingdome, and will are most deere to himselfe, he loueth them as he loueth himselfe : wherefore if wee will be like God, and approue our selues to bee the sonnes of our heauenly father, and his faithfull seruants, wee must loue and procure, and further that which God our Father and Master prizeth so highly.

Fourthly, God will be honoured, his kingdome shall be enlarged, and his will shall be fulfilled, let all the men and diuels in the world striue to the contrarie neuer so long or so much. Wherefore it is better for vs voluntarily to become seruiceable to his glorie, kingdome, and will, than by resisting to take the foyle, and procure iudgement to our selues.

Lastly, Gods glorie is the end of the creatures creation, and all the vnreasonable creatures in the world aime at this end: wherefore the Prophet exhorteth all the creatures, of all kindes; and mankinde of all ages and sexes, by necessarie consequence of an argument from the lesser to the greater, to laud and praise God. True it is that men and Angels of all the creatures onely are irregular and degenerate from the end of our creation, wherein we are inferior to the bruite beast that perisheth: we are the end of the vnreasonable creatures, and God is the end of man: wherefore as the creature is seruiceable to vs; so ought we also to be to God: for because we are rebellious to God, the creature prooueth rebellious to vs.

Psal. 148.

Psal. 49. 20.

Thus we vnderstand the reason of this order, which the holy Ghost vseth in the petitions, preferring God before our selues, as reason requireth; which instructeth vs many waies. First, to the deniall of our selues, which is the maine doctrine of mortification; the full measure whereof, is the perfection of Christianitie, which consisteth both in affection, and that is continually to resolue to part with all, rather than to deny the truth, or to offend God; and in action, which is the confession of the truth vnto death: wherefore Christ in the Gospell teacheth, that he is not worthie to be his Disciple, that doth not in affection at the least, and resolution intend so to doe: viz. to forsake father and mother, wife and children, liuing and life it selfe for Christs sake: for he must be our best beloued, as we are his, and therefore his honor and praise must specially be intended and procured; which cannot be, if we loue any thing more than him: wherefore this order insinuateth this selfe-deniall, which is opposed to selfe-loue.

Luk. 14. 26.

Cant. 2. 16.

Secondly, this order teacheth zeale to Gods glory, for

procuring whereof we are to spend our selues, and all we haue. The light account wherof deserueth a very sharpe reproofe. *Iohn* the Diuine, prophesieth of a great haile, which like talents shall fall from heauen vpon men : and Christ he prophesieth, that because iniquitie shall abound, the loue of men shall waxe colde : this colde haile and colde loue is now apparant in the world : it is marueilous to see how furiously the world flameth with contention about worldly profits and preferments, and yet how frozen their affections are to the obedience of Gods will, the enlarging of his kingdome, and the aduancement of his glorie : whereas indeede the zeale of Gods glory should so possesse vs, as that in comparison thereof our care for daily bread should occupie a very meane place.

Apoc. 16. 21.
Matth. 24. 12.

Lastly, this order teacheth vs the end of our daily bread, remission of sinne, and strength in temptation, namely the obedience, kingdome, and glory of God : for to this purpose doth God bestow vpon vs riches, honor, gifts, and graces, that we might imploy them to the best aduantage of God who gaue them. The rich man must so vse his wealth, as that thereby God may gaine glory : the honorable personage must account it his chiefe honor to honor God : the man of learning, and speech, and counsell in like manner ; and so forth of the rest. Hence it is that in the olde Testament, the Lord requireth the tenth of all the encrease, whether of the earth, or of cattell, for the maintenance of his worship; which by proportion must also be enlarged to whatsoeuer God bestoweth vpon vs ; as the tenth of our learning, honor, wit, children, and the rest, if they were increaseable, and communicable : but beeing otherwise, the Lord requireth and accepteth that which may bee had, a carefull imployment of them all, to the further enlarging of his praise in the world. This may suffice in generall for the order of the petitions. Now more specially, the petitions which concerne God simply, and meerely admit this distribution : for they respect either the end or the meanes procuring the end : Gods glory, mentioned in the first petition, is the end : the kingdome and will of God, mentioned in the second and third

Exod. 22. 29.
Leuit. 27. 30.
& 32.

petitions, are the meanes procuring the end : for God is glorified when his kingdome is aduanced, and his will fulfilled.

The first prayer : *Hallowed be thy name.*

1 The first thing to be obserued in this prayer is the order why the end is before the meanes, why Gods glory is first prayed for, seeing that the meanes are in nature before the end : for it is impossible that God should be glorified, except his kingdome come, and his will be done : and vpon the aduancing of his kingdome, and the obedience of his wil, his glory is purchased. The reason of this order is to be fetcht from the Lords predestination, and the Churches intention : for the Lord in his eternall counsell first propounded his glory, vttering as it were this euerlasting decree in the first place : *viz.* I wil be glorified by the creature : this being set downe, the Lord in the next place predestinateth the meanes whereby this end must be atchieued : & thereupō he vttereth this second decree : *viz.* I will aduance my kingdome, and cause my subiects to obey my will, that by this meanes I may be glorified by them. And as this is the order of Gods predestination, so Gods glory is first in the Churches intention, who in all their actions and endeuors propound Gods glory, whether it bee eating or drinking &c. they doe all to the praise of God. Which is the instruction that ariseth from this order ; whence this exhortation is to be deduced to all sorts of persons, whether the publike officer of the common-wealth, or Minister of the Church, or the priuate man : the Magistrate so ought to gouerne, as Gods glory may best be procured : and not to administer iustice for rewards, or of affection, whereby it sometime falleth out that the iust and righteous man hath his righteousnes taken from him, and the wicked and vngodly are iustified, and so Gods honor is obscured. The Minister ought so to vse his gifts that God thereby may gaine glory, and not to seeke himselfe by ostentation of knowledge, which puffeth vp, and edifieth little without loue. Euery man in his place and calling must so demeane himselfe, as that he

The order of this petition.

1. Cor. 10. 31.

Esa. 5. 23.

1. Cor. 8. 1.

may credit the Gospell, and adorne his profession, and that no aduantage be giuen to the aduersarie to blaspheme the name of God: but we must so shine by our good workes, that God may be glorified in all things: yea the man of trade and occupation in the exercising thereof, must seeke to honor the Lord, when as his worke and wares are such as may carry the commendation of honestie and truth, yea euen in the iudgement of malice, and testimony of enuie it selfe.

<small>Matth. 5. 16.</small>

2 Thus much for the order of this petition. The next is the sense and meaning of the words: they containe two things: first, the action: secondly, the obiect where about the action is conuersant or occupied: the action appertaineth to vs; the obiect of which action is the Lords; for we must sanctifie, and his name must be sanctified: Gods name is any thing whereby he is knowne vnto man, as one man is knowne vnto another by his name; for in the first institution of names, whereof mention is made in the historie of the creation; euery creature had his name out of his essence or essentiall properties; as is very probable by the imposition of the name to the woman who is so called in the Hebrue of her matter, as *Adam* also had his name by God of his matter: the earth being the matter of the man, the man of the woman. So then although God is not nor cannot be knowne of vs by his essence, yet he may be knowne of vs by his properties and actions, which may be conceiued and seene of vs in some measure. Now the things whereby God is knowne, are his workes, and his word; his workes manifest vnto vs diuers things of God, as the Apostle teacheth; namely, his eternall power and God-head: but his word doth fully and sufficiently discouer whatsoeuer is needful for vs to know of God: and that which is darkely and imperfectly shrouded as it were vnder a curtaine in the creature, the same cleerely and throughly is exposed to the view of all those that will search the Scripture: now Gods word doth describe God generally by titles and attributes. His titles are such as partly teach what God is not, as

<small>Sense of the first petition.</small>

<small>What Gods name signifieth.</small>

<small>Genes. 2. 19. 20. 23.</small>

<small>Gods workes are his name.</small>

<small>Rom. 1. 20.
Gods word is his name.
Ioh. 5. 39.</small>

<small>Gods titles are his name.</small>

infinit, immutable, incorruptible, inuisible, incomprehensible, and such like : partly teach what God is, as God, Lord, *Iah*, *Iehouah*, *Elohim*, Father, Master, King, Creator, Preseruer, Redeemer, Iustifier, Sanctifier, Sauiour, &c. Whereof the latter are affirmatiue, teaching something of God ; the former are negatiue remouing something from God. These are the Lords titles. Gods attributes are in

Gods attributes are his name. like manner, his name ; as his Power, Wisedome, Mercie, Truth, Goodnes, and such like ; which doe not import in God any qualitie or accident ; howsoeuer the resemblance of them in vs are onely qualities, in God his wisedome is himselfe, and so of the rest. Yet these attributes teach vs many things

Gods workes are his name. of God : his workes are nothing else but effects of these and other his attributes and titles : as Election, Creation, Preseruation, Redemption, Iustification, Sanctification, Saluation, Reprobation, Occecation, Induration, Damnation, Creatures, Ordinances, blessings, Iudgements : all which enlightened by the word, doe wonderfully declare what may be conceiued of God. Thus we see what is the name of God. Further we are

What it is to hallow Gods name. to inquire what it is to hallow or sanctifie Gods name. For further cleering whereof we must know, that Gods name is not prophane or vnholie, though here we pray it may be sanctified, and hallowed ; for all the wicked men and Angels in the world are not able any whit to blemish the name of God in it selfe, for God and his name are out of their gunshot : but because men doe meruellously prophane & dishonor the holy and reuerend name of God in themselues, and before others ; it is hence that wee pray that Gods name may be vsed of vs and others, with all holy reuerence and honorable estimation, as beseemeth the name of so great a Maiestie as is the Lord. A pearle or pretious stone, cast into the ditch or myre, is still pretious ; but being set in golde or goodly vestiments, shineth very beautifully : so though wicked men cast dirt and myre vpon the glorious and pretious name of God, by blaspheming, and cursing, &c. yet Gods name is still most excellent, though it doth not so appeare to vs : but when Gods children with religious reuerence handle Gods name, as in preaching,

A paterne of true Prayer

and praying, and deposing, being lawfully called, then Gods glory and maiestie, glistereth brightly to the view of all the beholders. And this is to sanctifie or hallow Gods name. Wherefore as the Sunne is alwaies in it selfe, the fountaine of light, and shineth most cleerely, howsoeuer sometime we see it not so, being either eclipsed by the interposition of the moone, or shrowded vnder a darke cloud, or couered from our sight by the earth: in like manner the name of God alwaies is full of excellencie and glory; howsoeuer the darkenes of sin, and the foggie mist of ignorance and error doth obscure the same, and conceale it from our eyes. Summarily therefore, we pray in this petition, that as Gods workes and word are good and holy in themselues, so by thought, word and deede, we cause them to appeare to our selues and others.

3 To sanctifie Gods name then is, first, to thinke, secondly to speake of, thirdly to vse the workes, and word of God reuerently. So that in this prayer we aske these things following principally, which may be reduced to fiue heads. *The supplication of this petition or prayer.*

1. First, knowledge.
2. Secondly, acknowledgment of Gods excellencie in his word, and in his workes.
3. Thirdly, religious and reuerent affections according to the kinde of the worke, or part of the word.
4. Fourthly, religious speeches.
5. Fifthly, religious actions.

Fiue things needfull to the sanctifying of Gods name.

First, that knowledge is necessarie to the sanctifying of Gods name, will easily appeare, for that it is a necessarie precedent to reuerence and high estimation: for to know the excellencie of any thing, is a good preparatiue to a due valuation thereof: this knowledge is commended vnto vs as the way to life eternall: which if a man wanteth, he is but a refuse as yet: herein *Adam* excelled, who is thought to haue knowne the essentiall properties and formes of the creatures: herein *Salomon* excelled, who spake of all plants, beasts, foules, creeping things and fishes; which knowledge of the creatures must needes stir vp in them a marueilous admiration of the Creator, who had printed

First knowledg.

Ioh. 17. 3.
2. *Cor.* 13. 5.

1. *King.* 4. 33.

such excellent impressions of his Maiestie in his workes. Wherefore the Prophet entring into consideration of Gods name in his workes and word, breaketh foorth into wonderment; as if so be that a man could not know but he must needes wonder also at the excellencie of them. *Psal.* 19 & 8.

Next vnto knowledge followeth the acknowledgement of that which wee know: which is a thing as materiall to the sanctification of Gods name as knowledge: for a man may know and resist his knowledge, and smoake out the eyes of his conscience, and set his knowledge and approbation together by the eares; as it fareth with many, who seeing, doe not perceiue, and hearing, doe not vnderstand. Wherefore though the Gentiles knew God, yet because they regarded not to acknowledge him as God, they could not glorifie him, as the Apostle witnesseth. This assent then to that wee know, is meerely requisite to the sanctification of Gods name.

2. **Acknowledgment.**

Esa. 6. 9.
Rom. 1. 21. 28.

In the third place the affections are to be moued according to the qualitie of the matter knowne: for as wee must sanctifie Gods name in our mindes, so also with our hearts and affections, and that especially. Hence it is that we reade of diuers sanctified affections in Gods Saints, according to the diuersitie of the worke exhibited: as in a miracle, admiration, as it is apparant in the curing of the creeple: in a blessing, thankfulnes; which is called the praising of God: in a iudgement, feare and humiliation, and trembling: in all the workes of God, loue: and so foorth as Gods works varie, so our affections must moue. In like manner we must bee stirred with Gods word, as to feare at the threatnings of the law: to reioyce and be comforted with the promises of the Gospell, generally to beleeue, and to loue euery part of Gods word: thus if our hearts and affections bow and bend at the workes and word of God, we sanctifie the Lord in our hearts, as the Apostle willeth vs. For it shall be needlesse to shew how vpon occasion of meditation in the attributes & titles of God, our affections are to moue:

3. **Religious affections.**

1. *Pet.* 3. 15.

Act. 3. 10.
Psal. 116. 13.
Psa. 119. 120.
Psal. 139. 17.

Esay. 66. 5.
Iob. 33. 25.
Psal. 119. 97.
Heb. 4. 2.

for euery religious heart can sufficiently instruct it selfe therein. And thus God is sanctified within vs.

Now in the next place we must consider how the name of God must bee sanctified before others, and the instruments thereof are our speeches and actions.

In the fourth place therefore we are by our speeches also to hallow Gods name: which is performed partly in such speeches wherein Gods name is not mentioned, partly in such wherein God is named: of the first sort are Assertions, and Asseuerations: of the second sort are, Confessions, Vowes, Oathes, Adiurations. In each of which it shal not be impertinent to insist a little for better declaration of this point. *4. Religious speeches.*

Although there bee no better words than the names of God, yet all our speeches are not fit to entertaine all good words: if wee speake of ordinarie and common matters, ordinary and common words will sort them well enough, and then it is good with a reuerent silence to honor Gods name. Wherefore the Iewes superstition may iustly challenge our prophanenes: they did forbeare to reade the name of God in the Scriptures, and we in our trifling talke doe not forbeare to vsurpe the weightie names and titles of the most glorious God: Yea, yea, or nay, nay, were enough for our trifling speeches: and if wee debated matters of better importance, verily or certainly, or assuredly, might fit our purpose well enough: *Religious silence.* *Assertion. Mat. 5. 37. Iam. 5. 12. Asseueration. Matth. 25. 12.*
but we offer that dishonour to God, which a Prince would not endure, that in euery toyish and vaine sentence wee should foyst in his name: for when we speake to a Prince or of a Prince, wee commonly giue titles of reuerence and honour to so excellent a personage; but the prophane multitude doe varnish their ribald and scurrilous talke with the fearefull names of a most iealous God, who will not beare that indignitie at their hands another day. Wherefore we in reuerence of the holy names and titles of God, which are most honourable and fearefull memorials of his excellencie, in our ordinarie speech must with sanctified silence forbeare the mentioning thereof. Indeede sometimes it falleth out that wee either by calling from others, or from our selues, vse Gods names and titles

140   *A paterne of true Prayer*

in our speeches lawfully: as when we are called foorth by the enemies of Gods truth to giue testimonie thereto; which is a confession to the glorie of God before his and our enemies: or when the Church requireth it, or Gods blessings bestowed vpon vs deserue it: or els when the Magistrate imposeth an oath of God vpon vs to speake the truth in matters otherwise vndeterminable, yet of necessarie importance: wherein we glorifie God with the witnesse of truth, and knowledge of secrets: or otherwise when wee impose a charge vpon another with an imprecation from God for neglect thereof, adiuring men to their duties, with the consideration of Gods iustice which thereby is glorified: or finally when we either vpon conscience of our owne infirmities, whereof we desire mortification, impose vpon our selues voluntarie penance in abstinence from certaine matters, which pamper the flesh, being in our owne power to performe; for strict obseruation whereof wee binde our selues to the Lord, thereby honouring his holinesse: or else in way of thankfulnes to the Lord for blessings desired or receiued. Promise vnto God, to the praise of his mercie, matters acceptable vnto him, called in the old Testament freewill offrings. Preaching and praying also are excellent instruments, whereby God is honoured in our speech; but they may generally bee comprehended vnder confession, and therefore I forbeare to speake of them particularly. Thus is God glorified with the tongue, which the Prophet calleth his glorie, as that principall instrument wherewith God is glorified, the effect being put for the cause by a *Metonymia*.

Marginal notes: Confession. 1. Pet. 3. 15. Matth. 10. 32. Psal. 40. 9. 10. Oathes. Ierem. 4. 2. Adiuration. 1. Thess. 5. 27. Vowes. Eccles. 5. 3. 4. Iudg. 11. 30. Psal. 119. Psal. 108. 1.

    In the fifth and last place wee are by our actions also to glorifie Gods name: which are of three sorts, naturall, ciuill, and religious. Naturall actions are such as wherein we communicate with the beasts and plants of the field, as eating and drinking, sleeping, procreation, and recreation: which actions are not so to bee vsed of vs as bruite creatures practise them, to whom the Lord hath giuen no limitation

Marginal notes: 5. Religious actions. Naturall actions.

nor law, and therefore cannot sinne in excesse, or the manner of vsing, they being no causes nor subiects of sinne properly for themselues: but we to whom the Lord hath giuen reason and religion, as moderators of nature and naturall actions, are so to demeane our selues in the exercising thereof, as that wee faile not in the proportion either by excesse or defect, nor swarue in the manner of their lawfull vse, but that we alwaies hedge our selues within the compasse of those bounds which the Lord hath limited to vs: and here expressely the Apostle mentioneth eating and drinking, being naturall actions, to bee done to the glorie and praise of God.   *1. Cor.* 10. 31.

Now ciuill actions are of another condition, *viz.* such as wherein the bruite beast partaketh not with vs, such as are buying and selling, borrowing and lending, giuing and taking, letting and hiring, and other affaires of like qualitie, whether Ethicall appertaining to ciuill and mannerly behauiour; or œconomicall respecting the familie; or politique in the Common-wealth: in all which Gods name must bee glorified through vs. Hence it is that the Apostle prescribeth rules to Masters and seruants, husband and wife, Magistrate and subiect, Ministers and all sorts of persons how to demeane themselues, as that the Gospell of Christ, and the name of God bee not blasphemed; but that euen they which are without may bee wonne by our godly conuersation euen in these our ciuill affaires: for falsehood, rebellion, and tyrannie, giue aduantage to the vnbeleeuer and mock-god to contemne true religion, and to dishonour God; when those that professe the feare of God, deny the power of godlinesse in their liues, causing their profession and practise to contradict each other. Wherefore as the Apostle counselleth, we must walke worthie of the vocation whereunto we are called, that we may be a credit to our Master.   Ciuill actions. Ethicall. Œconomicall. Politique.   *Colos.* 3. 18. 19. 20. 21. 22. &c. 1. *Tim.* 3.   *Ephes.* 4. 1.

Now religious actions directly aime at Gods glorie, as being appointed by God to that purpose, and to no other: of which sort are the exercises of Gods word, and administration of the Sacraments, and all the parts of Gods worship publike or priuate;   Actions meerly religious.

of which point because it needeth no proofe nor illustration, I forbeare of purpose to speake.

Thus it is manifest that both our thoughts and affections which are inward, as also our words and actions which are outward, are to bee instruments of Gods glorie to our selues or others, according as their seuerall conditions may affoord : and so it appeareth also what things we aske in this first petition or prayer.

4   Those things which we pray against are in the next place to be considered, and they are opposite to the things wee pray for, and they may be referred to fiue heads also: which are these following.

<small>The deprecation of this petition or praier.</small>

First, ignorance and errors.
Secondly, vanitie of minde.
Thirdly, a prophane heart.
Fourthly, prophane speeches.
Lastly, prophane actions : all which are so many meanes to obscure or deface, or abolish the glorious name of God out of the world.   Of these in order.

First, ignorance either of Gods workes or word, is the cause of prophaning Gods name : for as pearles cast before swine or dogs; so are ye works and word of God amōg ignorant persons : swine or dogs will trample pearles vnder their feete in the durt, but skilfull Lapidaries will vse them carefully, and set them in gold and costly garments : so the ignorant people that know not the works or word of God wil contemne & reiect, or at least neglect the excellent instructions and documents of Gods glorie therein exhibited, and so prophane the name of God : but they that know them may vse them aright, and glorifie God in them.   The dunghill Cocke, as the fable moralizeth, regardeth a barly corne, more than a pretious pearle, knowing the profit of the one, but not the price of the other : so the blind dunghill people of the world, Atheistlike through light estimation, because of their ignorance, preferre the dirtie commodities of this life, before the glorious footsteps of Gods Maiestie imprinted in his workes and word, thereby marueilously disparaging the Lord himselfe and dishonouring his name.

<small>Ignorance dishonoreth God.</small>

Againe, ignorance being the cause of superstition and errors, as Christ teacheth : saying, *Ye erre, not knowing the Scriptures,* and *ye worship ye know not what :* therefore it must needes bee a maine cause of blemishing Gods glorious names and memorials; for errors and heresies, are so many lies against the truth of God, charging false and slanderous imputations vpon God, making him the author of that which he abhorreth and condemneth : and as it is blasphemous to make God the cause of sinne, so is it of error : for it is to call God by a false name and to belie God, which is a great dishonour to God. For as it is a disgrace to a Prince to bee belied, or blasphemed, or backbited : so is it much more inglorious and dishonourable to God to make him the master and teacher of lies : for it is customable with false teachers and their followers to father their doctrines vpon Gods word, which God himselfe inspired to his Church : and so by necessarie consequent, in that they are found liers against the truth of God, they shamefully dishonour God.

<small>Error dishonoreth God. *Matth.* 22. *Ioh.* 4.</small>

In the second place also we are to marke how vanitie of minde prophaneth the name of God. The Apostle defineth this sinne to be the withholding of the truth of God in a lie, that is, to make a false consequent or vse from a true doctrine : to know God, and not to glorifie him as God : for example, to know God to bee inuisible, and yet to make an image of him ; to know God to bee incorruptible, and yet to resemble him to corruptible creatures, as beasts, birds, creeping things, &c. and thus the Gentiles thinking themselues to bee wise, hauing some truths of God, became starke fooles in deducing foolish consequents from that truth, & so through their vanity of mind defaced that truth with a lie : and this is a great indignitie offered to Gods truth. For as a subiect knowing his Prince, yet making as though he knew him not, and so vsing himselfe vnreuerently before him, doth disgrace the prince : so they that know God, and his workes and word, yet notwithstanding doe not glorifie God, but become vaine in their imaginations, and discourses, and conclusions from Gods word, and workes, thereby occasioning and

<small>Vanitie of minde prophaneth Gods name. *Rom.* 1.</small>

encouraging themselues in licentious liuing, and by their liues denying the power of their knowledge, which otherwise might haue been auailable to their saluation; do shamefully abuse their knowledge, & iniuriously dishonor the truth reuealed vnto them, which they should haue glorified.

As blindnes and vanitie of minde, so prophanenes of heart also, which in the third place commeth to be considered, doth greatly dishonor God; which is when mens affections are not stirred according to the qualitie of Gods workes or word, his titles or attributes: and that is especially of three sorts. <small>*A prophane heart dishonoreth God.*</small>

The first is an Atheists heart, which is the extinguishing of al affections in respect of God; for as an Atheist laboreth for a perswasion that there is no God, so also he desireth that the feare of God may be cleane taken away; also that the loue of God, the hatred of sinne, the loue of vertue and of the word of God may be put out; and that he may liue as he list, without any conscience, or difference of good and euill, which is to bury the memorie of God, and to banish his name out of the world, which is the greatest indignitie that may be. <small>*Atheisme dishonoreth God.*</small>

The second is a worldly heart, when a man is so estranged from heauenly matters, and so wholy possessed with the loue and liking of worldly things, as that he careth not for God, nor any goodnes further than he may gaine thereby; which men doe greatly dishonor God and his truth, making it a meanes of compassing the world; whereas indeede we should make the world a meanes of religion: for to this purpose hath God created and bestowed the world vpon man, that thereby they might be the better prouoked and furthered to the worship and glory of God; hither are to be referred all couetous persons that minde nothing but their goods; all proud persons that minde nothing but the trimming of themselues, gay apparell, and the credit of the world; all wanton persons that minde nothing but the pleasures of the flesh: generally all such as dishonor God by presuming any thing in their estimation, and affection before God: for seeing God is <small>*Worldlines dishonoreth God.*</small>

the chiefest good, and the most high, he therefore ought to bee the chiefest and most highly esteemed of vs, otherwise we honor the creature more than the Creator, and dishonor God by communicating his glory to another. *Rom.* 1. 25.

The third is a secure heart, when men that haue the grace of God in them, notwithstanding doe not so carefully and diligently stirre vp the grace of God, in the meditation and application of Gods workes and word, as the condition thereof doth require; for sometime it falleth out that euen Gods children slumber and sleepe: so we reade that the Church in the Canticles complaineth or excuseth her sluggish disposition: so we reade that *Dauid* slept in securitie, almost a whole yeere; in which time no doubt hee vsed the word of God, and the rest of Gods worship, though with dulnes and great flatnes of spirit; whereby it came to passe, that much of Gods honor and glory fell to the ground, vnrespected of the Prophet: but then God is dishonored, when he is not honored in that measure as the meanes affoord, and our grace may permit. *Securitie dishonoreth God. Cant.* 5. 2. 3. 2. *Sam.* 12.

Hauing hitherto intreated how Gods name is inwardly profaned in our mindes and hearts, it followeth now in the next place to speake how by our words and actions we dishonor God: and for our speeches, which is the fourth generall head, we must remember that they are especially of sixe kindes. *Prophane speeches dishonor God.*

1 First to speake of Gods workes or word without reuerence and feare, and attentiue respect to the matter: whether it be in prayer, or preaching, or conference, or howsoeuer else; for Gods word being so reuerend and honorable a name of God, must with proportionable reuerence and honor be handled: and therefore the Apostle would haue Preachers so deliuer the word, as that the matter and words be of the same nature; for sanctified matter, must haue sanctified words, and spirituall matter spirituall speeches: otherwise the matter is dishonored by the words: therefore the Scriptures phrase and rhetoricke is to be obserued of Preachers, that their sermons may sauor of them as much as is possible. Here *Vnreuerent speech of Gods word or workes dishonorGod.* 1. *Cor.* 2. 4. 13.

also they are to be reprooued that make prayer a lip-labor onely; for they speake to God of his word, and adde no attention and reuerence, which is to dishonor that graue and solemne exercise of inuocation. Hither also appertaine those curious schoole-disputes, interlaced with philosophicall quiddities, whereby Gods word is miserably stretcht, and rackt, and rent in peeces, and disfigured; as Christ was vpon the crosse by the souldiers: in summe, whatsoeuer vndecent, homely, and vnmannerly metaphors or comparisons, whatsoeuer false glozes and expositions, whatsoeuer railings and reuilings shall be vsed in disputations, sermons, or tractats vpon the word; fall within the compasse of abusing the holy word of God: and the Apostles counsell is reiected, who willeth, that if any man speake, he should speake as the words of God.

1. Pet. 4. 10.

2 Next to vnreuerent speech, are such as giue approbation to error or false worship, whether by word, or writing, as subscription to poperie, Mahometisme, or any other false doctrine or superstition. For if it be alleadged that though they by word or writing, may seeme to approoue that profession whereto they subscribe; yet they keepe a pure heart, free from any assent or allowance thereto. The answere is, that God will be glorified with the whole man, and not with the spirit onely, though that be chiefely regarded of him, himselfe being a spirit as Christ teacheth the Samaritane. The reason which the Apostle vseth to disswade the Christian Corinthians from presenting their bodies at idolatrous feasts, least thereby the weake be enboldned to doe so likewise, is sufficient to enforce this conclusion, that no outward approbation must be giuen to superstition, least others be deceiued thereby, and so Christ be dishonored. For that which may be alleadged of *Elishaes* approbation to *Naaman* the Syrian, is altogether impertinent, if the place be truely translated: for *Naaman* doth not desire indulgence from God, for idolatrie which he purposeth to commit, as though hee spake in the future tense; but for that idolatrie which he had formerly committed; for indeede

Approbation of false doctrine by word or writing dishonoreth God.

1. Cor. 6. 20.
Ioh. 4. 24.
1. Cor. 8. 10. 11.

2. King. 5. 18.

the words may aswell be translated in the time past, and so they are directly in the originall. So then whatsoeuer may be alledged to the contrarie, it is manifest that all outward approbation of false doctrine, or worship by word or deede, is dishonorable and scandalous to our weake brethren. Let vs take heede therefore how wee receiue the marke of the beast in our fore- *Apoc.* 13. 16. heads, or our right hands, that is, that we by our gestures or subscription doe not approue the doctrine and superstition of the Pope, or the Turke, *Vers.* 3. least by this meanes we worshipping the beasts, and dishonoring God, our names be not found in the booke of life.

3 After superstitious subscription, or approbation of false worship, follow mocking and iesting at or Scoffing
with Gods workes or word, a thing very com- speeches
mon now adayes; for euery wittie, or rather about Gods word or
indeede witles braine, wil be deuising and belch- workes dis-
ing out the scum of their wit, in iesting and honor God.
scoffing at Gods workes, or with Gods word, or other holy writings agreeable to the word, and consecrated to the worship of God. These men in truth mocke God himselfe in that they mocke Gods workemanship: for the disgrace of the worke tendeth to the dishonor of the workeman: for the world hath Nick-names for euery one that hath either a great head, or wry necke, or long nose, or crooked backe, or lame legge, or that wanteth a hand, or an eye, or so forth: these deformities should stirre vp in vs humiliation, as being so many prints of Gods wrath in man: and if we be free from them to acknowledge with thankfull memorie, the mercie of God to vs that haue deserued as much: that so wee might glorifie God in his iustice and mercie: also the world, and especially the stage, which is a little world of wickednes, is full of Scripture iests; it would cause a mans hayre to stand vpright to heare how some please themselues in this kinde of Rhetoricke, which the diuel deuised and suggested into
2. *King.* 2. the mindes and mouthes of mocke-gods. We
24. reade how seuerely God punished young
children that mockt the Prophet, for his infirmitie of baldnes, and his ministerie of prophecie: and the Apostle

condemneth iesting, which notwithstanding the heathen man counted a morall vertue. Now if it be a fault for one man to mocke another; it is likewise a fault, and much more, for a man to mocke with the word of God: it is a great sinne also for vs to make our selues merry with the simplicitie of a naturall borne fooles: in all which Gods workes and word, and so God himselfe is dishonored.

4 Furthermore vaine oathes diminish Gods glory, when men vpon no necessitie, hauing no calling, in vaine toyes vsurpe the name of God, or the name of Gods workes, as by this light, fire, salt, bread, or the name of false gods or worship, as the Masse, our Lady, Saint *Anne*, &c. In al which God is dishonored either directly or immediatly, as in vsing Gods titles or attributes, or the parts of Christs body or soule, idlely and fruitlesly, or indirectly and by consequence in calling to witnes the workes of God, which are so many memorials and testimonies of God; as faith, troth, &c. Or lastly in calling to witnes false gods, or false worship, which is to rob God of his honor, and giue it to another which is no god; a matter of most fearefull blasphemie.

<small>Vaine swearing dishonoreth God.</small>
<small>Matth. 5. 34.</small>
<small>Matth. 23. 16. 17. 18. 19. 20. 21. 22. Psal. 16. 4. Exod. 23. 13.</small>

5 After vaine swearing, as an higher degree of dishonoring God, followeth periurie or false swearing, when we cloake false witnes vnder the Lords skirt: wherein, as much as in vs lieth, we make God the voucher of a lie, who is notwithstanding the God of truth: how great a dishonor is offered to God by this course, is so apparant as that it neede no illustration.

<small>Periurie dishonoreth God.</small>

6 In the last place, blasphemie occurreth, thā which a greater despite or disgrace cannot bee offered vnto the Lord, which is to reuile and raile vpon God, called in the Scripture, cursing God; a sin so great, as that it was dreadfull to the holy Pen-men of Scripture to vse the word, and therefore they vse the contrarie word, blessing in stead of cursing, as the wife of *Iob* said to him, *blesse*, that is, *curse God and die:* howsoeuer some expound the place otherwise.
The haynousnes of which sinne is so great, as that the

<small>Blasphemie dishonoreth God.</small>
<small>Iob. 2. 9.</small>

Lord hath punished one degree thereof, called blasphemie
against the holy Ghost, with the most fearefull *Matth.* 12. 32.
punishment of finall impenetencie, in regarde
whereof the sinne commeth to be vnpardonable.

Thus also we see how, and how many waies we dishonor God by our prophane speeches; not that there are no more, but these are the principall. Now it followeth in the last place shortly to consider of those prophane actions whereby God is dishonored. Concerning which it must be knowne, that all our euill deedes doe in some measure staine Gods glory, either directly or by consequence; but yet some are more properly said so to do, and they are these ten which shall be handled in order following.

Prophane actions dishonor God.

1 The first is idolatrie, which is the making of an image of God: the worshipping of that image made; or the making and worshipping of an image of a false god: by all which meanes God is dishonored in the highest degree: for to resemble God in an image, is 1 to make the Creator like the creature, betwixt whom there is no comparison, the one being infinite, the other finite: and therefore euery image is a lie of God, and so dishonorable to God. Againe, to worship that image made, is 2 to honor a lie; and to giue to the workemanship of man, that which is due to God onely; and this is to rob God of his honor, and to impart it to a stocke or stone. 3 Lastly, the making and worshipping of an Idol, which is the image of a false god, is most shamefull, for therein we forsake the true God, and follow our owne inuentions, and worship the picture or shape of that which is nothing in the world, as the Apostle speaketh, or else is the diuell: for indeede when we doe worship Idols we worship diuels. 1. Cor. 10.

Idolatrie dishonoreth God.

2 Superstition followeth in the second place, which is the worshipping of the true God after a false manner: as the Turke worshippeth the true God, according to the tradition of *Mahomet*: the Papist worshippeth the true God, but with mixture of much draffe of mans inuentions, fearing and making scruple where there is no cause of feare: and taking libertie to inuent and deuise meanes and waies of

Superstition dishonoreth God.

worship where they should not: and thus they blemish Gods glorie in taking vpon them authoritie to prescribe and impose such a worship vpon the Lord which his wisedome neuer determined, thereby controlling Gods wisedome with their inuention and will worship.

To Idolatrie and superstition may be annexed, as neere of kinne, all Witchcraft, Sorcerie, Magicke, Charming, Southsaying, Figure-casting, Palmistrie, Necromancie, and whatsoeuer other diuellish arts the idle braine of curious Naturalists haue deuised; al and euery whereof containe in them a secret idolatrie and superstition at the least, if they haue not openly contracted with the diuell, whom they adore, or pay tithe to of their blood; or recompence some way or other for his obedience, suggestion and seruice performed at their becke: wherefore all those that had vsed such curious Arts to the dishonor of God, after their cōuersion burned their books at Ephesus, as the Euāgelist reporteth in the Acts: in which storie there are diuers points very worthie obseruation to this purpose; as that they were learned men that vsed these Crafts, and that their learning was out of bookes, and their bookes were worth eight hundreth pounds: which declare plainly that they were writings of Astrologie or Magicke, or Southsaying and the like, and not of witchcraft only, which vsually is not committed to writing, but learned by obseruation or tradition: further it is to bee considered, that they did not sell but burne their bookes, as it were preuenting the vse of them to others, because they were conuicted in their consciences of the dishonour which came to God thereby.

Curious arts dishonoreth God.

Act. 19. 19.

3 In the third place, after Idolatrie and superstition, which respect God and his worship, succeed sacriledge and simonie, which respect the meanes of Gods worship. Sacriledge is when violence is offered to holy places, things, persons, or times, &c. as if men should take away Churches, and Church liuings, and so ouerthrow the callings of Churchmen, and conuert the times appointed to Gods seruice to Faires and Markets: by which practises it commeth to passe that Gods worship perisheth, and prophanenes preuaileth, and the

Sacriledge dishonoreth God.

Lord is either forgotten, or dishonoured. Thus did the King of Babel commit sacriledge, when hee destroyed the Temple, and carried away the vessels of the Lords house to Babylon, and vsed them to common offices, as in banquetting: thus did Christ prophecie after *Daniel*, that the abomination of desolation should bee set in the holy place: thus did the people prophane the Temple, making it a market place in our Sauiour Christs time. *2. Chro. 36. Matth. 24. 15. Ioh. 2. 15.* Diuers other examples there are in the Scriptures of this kinde: but these may suffice, to shew that such sacrilegious practises greatly dishonour God, as being meanes to abolish or defile Gods worship.

4 Simonie also is no small cause of defacing Gods glorie, which is when offices Ecclesiasticall are set to sale: whereby it commeth to passe, that vnworthie persons by money prepossesse the places of Ministery and maintenance, which should be conferred vpon persons whom God hath qualified competently to such functions. Hereby it commeth that ignorant and wicked Ministers creep into the Church, which are fitter to keepe swine, than to feede the flocke of Christ, meeter to be Masters of misrule, than rulers of Gods heritage: and so the people perish for want of knowledge, or goe astray after their blinde guides, and God is greatly dishonoured, by people and Pastors: besides the indignitie which the Ministerie ecclesiasticall sustaineth, that it should be valued with money, which is the means of conferring the inualuable gifts of the holy Ghost, which are not to be bought with all the worlds good.

<small>Simony dishonoreth God.</small>

<small>*Act. 8. 18. 19. 20.*</small>

5 Hauing spoken of those sinnes which respect God and his worship, or the meanes whereby God is worshipped: now followeth a sinne which is committed vpon the persons that worship God: which generally is termed Persecution, and that either of the Preachers or professors of the truth: which is a manifest indignitie offered euen to God himselfe: for the Ministers are Gods Embassadors, and euery true professor is a member of Christ: wherefore as the Prince is then disgraced, when his Embassadour is shamefully

<small>Persecution dishonoureth God.</small>

intreated; so is the Lord dishonoured in his Ministers and messengers: and as Christ was abused when his bodie was crucified vpon the crosse; so is he also now when the members of his mysticall bodie are persecuted.

And these are the fiue grand-sinnes of Gods dishonour in action and practise: there follow fiue other of lesser disgrace, whereby notwithstanding God is blemished in his glorious name.

6   In the next place therefore wee must consider that God is dishonoured, when his Word and Sacraments &c. are vnreuerently vsed, which falleth out sundrie waies: sometimes by want of attention our minds and hearts and eyes are in the corners of the world, about our worldly affaires, so that the matter handled in the word and Sacraments passeth into the ayre without our attention and consideration: otherwhiles through the sleepie & sluggish disposition of the flesh a great drowsines of the soule and body falleth vpon vs, so as either we heare not at al, or else we heare onely as the man in the Gospell saw men walke like trees: at other times wee carpe at the word, and blame the Preacher: some come to catch and to intrap: none of vs all do so heare as that there is no fault in our hearing: for the best of vs neglect some, forget other, dislike this, or do not applie that doctrine or exhortation, reproofe or consolation: whereby Gods word losing part of that reputation which it ought to haue of vs, is in part also disgraced by vs.

[margin: Vnreuerent vsing Gods word and sacraments dishonoreth God.]

7   After the vnreuerent vse of Gods word, followeth the vnreuerent vse of Gods creatures and ordinances, which hee in mercie permitteth vnto vs for the refreshing of our bodies and the inferiour faculties of the soule, wherein we communicate with the bruite beast: for seeing therein God manifesteth his mercie and loue, and goodnes to the creature, we are not to neglect the same, but with due animaduersion obserue all those his attributes, and further take heede that wee doe not immoderatly glut our selues with the creatures and ordinances of God, but with a necessarie and pleasonable sobrietie, as occasion serueth, relieue and comfort

[margin: The vnreuerent vse of Gods creatures and ordinances dishonoreth God: as meates and marriage.]

nature, and prouoke our hearts to the glory of the Creator, who hath made the infinite varietie of the creatures to refresh and delight man. *1. Tim. 4. 4. 5.*

8 Amongst the creatures and workes of God there are some extraordinarie, as miracles, and wonders: others ordinarie, whereof some are iudgements, some blessings; all which seeing they teach vs excellent things of God, are not to be ouerpassed inconsideratly: for miracles *Inconsideration of Gods workes dishonoureth God: of wonders and miracles.* and wonders being strong impressions of Gods power and Godhead, ought to smite deeply by extraordinarie affections, as admiration and astonishment into our hard hearts, least God thereby be dishonored: 9 and euen the workes of God which ordinarily befall, are so many witnesses of Gods prouidence to mankinde, which are not sleightly to be ouerpassed: *Of ordinarie workes of Gods prouidence.* for he that cannot see and acknowledge the glory of God in the heauens, and the interchangeable course of day and night, Summer, Haruest, Spring, and winter, &c. is as blinde in not seeing Gods prouidence, as the mote is to the Sunne: and so through his negligent or wilfull inconsideration Gods glory is darkned at noone day: whereas in them all the attributes of God shine most cleerely, as his power, mercie, wisedome, iustice: and to this purpose the Prophet hath composed whole Psalmes. *Psal. 104. and 136.*

10 Amongst Gods ordinances lots obtaine a special place, which as it seemeth must not bee vsed but in weightie and serious busines, for so the examples of Scripture where lots haue been *Lots in sport seeme to dishonour God.*
Pro. 16. 33.
1. Sam. 14. 41. 43.
Ios. 7. 14.
1.Sam.10. 20.
Act. 1. 16.
Num. 26. 54. &c.
Mat. 27. 35.
vsed doe certifie vs: as about life and death, election of Ministers, distribution of inheritance, and matters of like consequence; and the Scripture expressely noteth the abuse of lots in the souldiers that cast lots for Christs coate without seame: and as it seemeth for men to sport and play with lots is to dishonour the immediate prouidence & direction of God, where the wit and arte of man hath no place: but in this point I doe not delight to bee long, seeing it is a matter something controuersall.

Thus wee see these prophane actions whereby God

especially is dishonoured : and so the deprecation of this petition is in some sort opened, to bee against whatsoeuer wants, thoughts, affections, speeches and actions are any way dishonourable to the Lord. Now the last thing to bee considered in this first petition is the thanksgiuing.

5 We giue thanks vnto God for these good things which he hath bestowed vpon vs and others his children : as

<small>The thanks-giuing of the first prayer or petition.</small>

1. Knowledge of his word and workes.
2. Acknowledgement of the same.
3. Religious affections, speeches and actions.

Also we giue thanks for that he hath mortified the contrary sins in some measure both in vs and our brethren : as first, ignorance : secondly, error : thirdly, Vanitie of minde : fourthly, prophanenes in affection, speech, and action : the particulars of all which may easily be collected by the former tractate in the supplication and deprecation. And this also in briefe may suffice for the thanksgiuing.

For a conclusion of this petition let this generall rule be remembred, that whatsoeuer vertue is commanded in the three first commandements, that is here desired : whatsoeuer sinnes are forbidden in the same, are here also prayed against : for the vertues appertaining to Gods worship are worthie meanes of honouring God, and the contrary vices are so many cloudes that hinder the cleere Sunneshine of Gods glorie in the world : wherefore whosoeuer listeth more particularly to search into these matters, let him search the writings of the learned, expounding the commaundements. This is the first petition concerning Gods glory, which is the end of all : now followe the two petitions which inferre the meanes of his glory : and first that of the Kingdome of God.

Thy Kingdome come.

1 This petition in order of nature goeth before the third, as the cause before the effect : for Gods Kingdome is that onely meanes which enableth vs to obey his will. First, God must erect his Kingdome in our hearts, and we must be his subiects

<small>The order of the second petition.</small>

before we can yeeld obedience to his lawes: from which order ariseth this instruction: That a man can neuer obey Gods will till he haue Gods grace; or a man can neuer keepe Gods lawes till he be Gods subiect, and God be his Lord and King, to rule and ouerrule him; or (which is all one in effect) good workes proceede from grace; or without faith (which is the roote of grace) it is impossible to please God; or whatsoeuer is not of faith is sinne: or the end of the commaundement is loue, out of a pure heart, and a good conscience and faith vnfained: and the necessarie consequence of this doctrine is: that whatsoeuer a man doth, wanting grace, is sinne: whether they be actions naturall, ciuill, or religious: for some Preachers, and Prophets in the day of iudgement shall bee found workers of iniquitie. *Heb.* 11. *Rom.* 14. 1. *Tim.* 1. *Pro.* 15. 8. *Esa.* 1. 13. *Matth.* 7. 22.

Here notwithstanding wee must remember to distinguish betwixt the action and the manner of performing the action: the agent, the ouerseer, and the matter the action is naturall: the manner of performing the action morall: the agent is *terminus à quo*, the efficient cause: the obiect is *terminus ad quem*, or the patient vpon whom the action falleth. Now to all those must be added the matter or the thing moued. This destinction being remembred, let vs take for examples, preaching and almes. Fiue things in euery action. 1. Actio. 2. Agens. 3. Modus agendi. 4. Res mota. 5. Patiens.

The vttering of the voyce in preaching, is action, good in it one nature; the matter of preaching is good, the holy word of God. The obiect whereupon the action is occupied is a godly man, the hearer of the word: all which make the action so farre forth good: but the agent, and the manner of performing the action may turne it to sin: for if the agent, that is, the Minister or Preacher be a man out of Christ, wanting faith and grace, being no member of Christ, nor subiect of his Kingdome, he cannot possibly obey his wil, but the fountaine being vncleane, the streame flowing from the fountaine is vncleane also. Againe, if the Preacher erre in the manner of doing the action, though he be in Christ, as if he preach Christ of contention How preaching is good or bad.

or malice, and so forth, his preaching may proue sinne: sinne I say, not to the godly and carefull hearer, nor in it selfe, but onely to the Preacher. In like manner, the reaching faith of the hand in giuing almes, is good in nature; the money or matter giuen is Gods creature; the person to whom the almes is offered, a godly man: but if either the person that giueth the almes, or the manner of distributing be vitious as aforesaid: as if the proud Pharisie should cause a trumpet to be blowne for ostentation and vaineglorie, he being not qualified with the foundation and forme of a good worke; all his almes, if it were all his substance, were abominable in the sight of God, as it came from him, and as good as nothing, as the Apostle teacheth. This distinction then being remembred, will cleere this doctrine, that the good deedes of wicked men are sinne: from whence the conclusion also will follow, that the wicked in the day of iudgement shall be condemned for their good deedes. This besides that it thwarteth the doctrine of the Church of Rome, which teacheth good workes before grace, and their merit of congruitie: it teacheth vs further to labour for two things: first, that we haue the foundation of a good worke, which is faith in Christ, by and through whom our persons and actions are accepted of God. Secondly, that in all our good workes we haue the forme and manner of doing, which in generall, the Apostle calleth loue, not onely to God, ayming at his glory, which excludeth vaineglorie and hypocrisie; but also to man, intending the benefit of him, to whom the good worke is extended. And this is the doctrine and vse which ariseth from the order of this petition before the third.

<small>How almes is good or bad.</small>

<small>1. Cor. 13.</small>

<small>1. Tim. 1. 5.
1. Cor. 13. 1.
2. 3.</small>

2 The sense and meaning, which is the second thing to be obserued, followeth; wherein these two things are to be considered, as before in the first petition, viz. the obiect, and the action, that is to say: First, what Gods Kingdome is: Secondly, how Gods Kingdome is said to come.

<small>The meaning of the second petition.</small>

Gods Kingdome, which is the first point, is the heauenly politie or regiment, which God through Christ exerciseth in the hearts of the

<small>What Gods Kingdome is.</small>

faithfull by his spirit and word in this life, and by glory and blisse in the life to come : in regarde whereof the Kingdome of God is called the Kingdome of grace, when it is begun in the consciences of the faithfull, and continually cherished and increased by all the holy meanes of saluation ; and it is called the Kingdome of glory, when it is consummate and perfectly accomplished, the Saints yeelding absolute obedience to the will of God in heauen ; whence issueth the glorious happines of the creature. For better vnderstanding of this point, what the Kingdome of God is, consider shortly these twelue points which followe.

1 Who is the King ? Christ Iesus as he is God and man ; where we must know that the Father, and the holy Ghost are not excluded : but all the creatures, of what excellencie soeuer. Heb. 2. 5.

2 Who are the subiects ? They are of two sorts : true subiects, who are the whole companie of beleeuers wheresoeuer : and counterfeit subiects, who though they be in the Church, yet are not of the Church ; which distinction is grounded, 1. Iohn. 2.

3 What are the lawes ? They are the law of nature, which is the decalogue : and the lawe of grace, the summe whereof is contained in the Gospell, namely, faith and repentance ; and obedience, which is the summe of the decalogue.

4 Who are the enemies ? They are these ten following. First, Sathan : secondly, sinne : thirdly, death : fourthly, hell or the graue : fifthly, damnation : sixtly, the world : seauenthly, the flesh : eightly, the Pope and all Papists, and heretikes : ninthly, the Turke and all Pagans : tenthly, the hypocrits, Atheists, and all prophane and professed wicked men.

5 What rewards to the subiects ? They are in this life, all good things that may profit them, and freedome from all euill which may hurt ; and in the life to come, euerlasting happines in heauen.

6 What punishments or chastisements ? The punishments are all taken away in Christ, who hath vndergone them for vs : yet there remaine corrections of diuers sorts to nurture and discipline vs, and to keepe vs in awe and so forth.

7   What weapons to resist our enemies ? The weapons are spirituall, namely, faith, hope, loue, righteousnes, the word, prayer.

Ephes. 6.

8   What is the time of this kingdome ? It lasteth so long as the world endureth in that outward polity, and forme of gouernment established by the word. 1. Corinth. 15. It lasteth for euer, euen so long as God is God, in the most gracious and glorious regiment thereof in heauen, these outward meanes ceasing.

9   What is the place of this Kingdome ? There are two places, the one is this world, where the Church is militant, fighting against her enemies : the other is heauen, where the Church is triumphant raigning for euer.

10   What are the offices and officers of this Kingdome ? The offices and officers, (besides these that were temporarie and extraordinarie, as Prophets, Apostles, Euangelists) are these following.

The first office is teaching, and that officer is called a Doctor.

The second is exhorting, and that officer is called a Pastor.

The third office is ruling, and that officer is called an Elder ; in the Church of England, he is called a Bishop.

The fourth office is distributing, and that officer is called a Deacon.

The fifth office is shewing mercie, which officer is called a widow. These are all set downe. Rom. 12. 7. 8.

The questions that are betweene the reformed Churches concerning these offices and officers, I of purpose spare to handle, being both vnfit to debate them, and loth to offend : onely I wish that such controuersies might be ended by Councels, and that the peace of the Church might be kept.

11   Who is the Deputie or Vicar of this King ? There is no one person Christs Lieutenant : for wee renounce the Pope, who is Antichrist ; but we acknowledge euery King in his Kingdome, the supreme Gouernor in all causes, and ouer all persons, aswell ecclesiasticall, as ciuill, next and immediatly vnder Christ : which Prince hath authoritie to substitute ecclesiastical Magistrates according to the word, for the polity of the Church, in the exercising

of iurisdiction, visitation of Churches, and ordination of Ministers; which persons in England are called Bishops.

12 What are the properties or qualities of this Kingdome? It is spirituall, not worldly, and exercised vpon the conscience: wherein it differeth from the ciuill state.

Thus we see what Gods kingdome is: now we are further to enquire how Gods Kingdome is said to come, namely. *How Gods Kingdome commeth.*

1. When it is erected or established where before it was not.

2. When it is enlarged and increased where before it was.

3. When it is repaired or restored from some former decayes.

4. When it is perfected and accomplished fully: of each something.

First, Gods Kingdome is erected and set vp generally and specially: generally when it is entertained by publike consent in a countrie or Kingdome; and that is when the Magistrate by law doth *How Gods Kingdome is erected.* establish the worship of God according to the word: and execution is done accordingly: and when the Ministers, in their ministerie teach and minister the word and worship of God established. Specially the Kingdome of God is established or erected, when men by the word of God are conuerted to the faith, and outwardly make profession thereof. Thus Gods Kingdome is set vp.

Secondly, Gods Kingdome is enlarged; both when *How Gods Kingdome is enlarged.* there are new subiects made, when as before they were enemies, that is to say, when there are added to the Church, such as shall be saued, or when they that are ordained to life euerlasting beleeue: as also when the former subiects are confirmed and bettered, that is, when such as are within the Church, and doe beleeue, grow in grace, and in the knowledge of our Lord Iesus Christ.

Thirdly, Gods Kingdome is repaired from two great *How Gods Kingdome is repaired.* ruines and downefals especially: the one of doctrine, the other of manners, and they are both of them vniuersall, and particular; for there are some which depart totally from the whole doctrine of the faith of Christ, as when a Christian becommeth a Turke, and some depart onely from some particular doctrines: as they in the kingdome of Antichrist. Againe, there are some which being baptized and professing Christ, powre out themselues afterward to all manner of licentious wickednes: others fall into some particular sinnes, as adultery with *Dauid.* Now if a man recouer againe from false doctrine, as from Turcisme, or Papisme, that repayre is dogmaticall: but if a man recouer by repentance from lapse into sinne, that repaire may be called morall: all which kindes both of Apostacie, and backsliding, and of repairing and restauration, may sometime befall a whole kingdome or common-wealth, aswell as particular families or persons.

Lastly, Gods Kingdome is perfected and fully accomplished at two times: The first time is the day of a mans death: the second time is the last and general day of iudgment. *How Gods Kingdome is perfected.*

The day of death is the speciall perfection of this kingdome in the subiect that dieth, for then grace is perfected and consummated.

The day of iudgement is the generall perfection of this kingdome in all the subiects thereof, which shall either die, or be changed suruiuing at that day. The speciall perfection of this kingdome, is the glorie of the soule only in sanctification and saluation: the generall perfection of this kingdom, is the glorie both of bodie and soule, of the whole man, which then shall perfectly, according to the measure, be sanctified and glorified. Thus we see how the kingdome of God commeth.

Hauing now deliuered the meaning of this second petition, it followeth according to the order propounded to speake of the contents thereof, in the supplication, deprecation and thanksgiuing: and first of the supplication, which is the third generall.

3 The things which wee aske at Gods hands in this petition, are these following: the first concerneth the Common-wealth, *viz.* *The supplication of the second petition.*

1. Godly Magistrates, for whom the Apostle willeth to pray: teaching that it is a thing good and acceptable in the sight of God our Sauiour so to doe: and the Wiseman *1. Tim. 2. 3. 1. Godly Magistrates further Gods kingdom.*

forbidding to curse the King, and the rich, on the contrary signifieth that wee should pray for them and blesse them: for the negatiue includeth the affirmatiue and contrarily: for Magistracie is an excellent meanes to further the kingdome of Christ: and therefore they are compared to nursing fathers and nursing mothers by the Prophet: for as parents doe both beget and bring vp their children; so godly Magistrates doe erect and maintaine the faith and true religion by the sword: hence it is that the Kings and Queenes of England are intituled *Defenders of the Faith:* which is the most royall part of the title royall.

Ecles. 10. 20.

Esay. 49. 23.

2 Wee pray in this petition that the godly Magistrates may make godly lawes, and establish the whole truth of the word, and see that both the tables of the Commandements be obserued: for the Apostle in the former place to *Timothie* expresseth the substance of the Magistrates dutie, which is to procure that the subiects may leade a peaceable and quiet life in all godlines and honestie; where there are three things appertaining to the Magistrate, which he must endeuour for his subiects: Peace, Godlines, Honesty, which doe comprehend the substance of the whole law of God: such Kings were *Dauid, Iehosaphat, Ezechias, Iosias, Nehemiah, Zorobabel, Hester,* and *Mardochai,* with others: whose care was to establish holesome lawes, to ouerthrow Idolatrie and superstition, and to procure the peace of the Church and Common-wealth. Such lawes did *Darius* and *Artaxerxes* procure to bee made, for restoring the worship of God in Ierusalem, although they were Heathen Kings, who in some sort did helpe forward the kingdome of God.

2. Godly lawes with due execution further Gods kingdome.

1. *Tim.* 2. 2.

Dan. 6. 26.
Nehem. 2.

The second thing we aske appertaineth to the Ministerie of the Church.

1. Able and faithfull Ministers, which both haue gifts, and willing mindes to employ their gifts in their Ministerie to the glorie of God, and the edification of the bodie of Christ. This is that which Christ teacheth his disciples to pray for, that seeing the haruest is great, and the

1. Able Ministers further Gods kingdom.

Mat. 9. 37. 38.

w.

labourers few, therefore the Lord of the haruest would send foorth labourers into the haruest: and the Apostle willeth the Thessalonians to pray for him and other the Ministers of the Gospell: for next vnto godly Magistrates are godlie Ministers, the one establish Gods worship, the other teach Gods worship: hence it is that as Magistrates are called nursing fathers and mothers, so Ministers are called Gods fellow-workmen, builders, shepheards and such like: for that they feede the flock, build the citie, and performe the worke of the Ministerie outwardly as God doth inwardly: yea there are more excellent titles giuen to the Ministerie in the holy Scripture than to Magistracie, as that they are the light of the world, the salt of the earth, Christs Ambassadours: indeede there is one onely title giuen to Magistrates before Ministers, that they are termed *Gods*; which is not so much in regard of their office, as of their superiority and authoritie ouer all persons: whereas the titles of the Ministerie are rather giuen to the office than the person.

_{2. *Thess.* 3. 1.}
_{1. *Cor.* 3. 9.}
_{*Psal.* 82. 6.}

2. Wee pray also that these Ministers may faithfully, powerfully, and zealously exercise their offices ministerial, not onely in preaching, but also in gouerning the Church: as in teaching the ignorant, reprouuing, suspending, excommunicating the obstinate, comforting the comfortles, confirming the weake, confuting errors and heresies, and generally in building vp the kingdome of Christ, according to their seuerall functions delegated vnto them by the politie Ecclesiasticall. Thus *Moses* prayeth for *Leui*, that *Vrim* and *Thummim* might be with him, and that he may teach *Iacob* the law and iudgements of God. So the Apostle *Paul* wisheth the Ephesians to pray for him, that a doore of vtterance may bee giuen vnto him to speake boldly as hee ought: for the powerfull Ministerie is as it were horsemen and chariots to ouerthrow the kingdome of the diuell, that so the kingdome of Christ may take place; it is the spirituall weapons which are mightie through God to cast downe the holds of mans imaginations, and of euery high thing that is exalted against the

A powerfull Ministerie furthereth Gods kingdome.

_{*Deut.* 33. 8. 10.}
_{*Ephe.* 6. 19. 20.}
_{2. *Cor.* 10. 4. 5.}

knowledge of God, and bringing into captiuitie euery thought to the obedience of Christ.

3. We pray also that these godly Ministers may be preserued and kept from the persecution of tyrants and wicked men, whom the diuell enrageth against them especially, as we see by euident experience that no sort of men is so much maligned and exposed to the despight of malitious men, as the faithfull Ministers. Yea and the more faithfull and powerfull they are, the more doth the diuell in his members outray against them. Thus did *Moses* pray that the Lord would smite through the loynes of them that rose vp against *Leui* to persecute him: so the Apostle willeth the Thessalonians to pray that he might be deliuered from absurd and euill men: for persecution is a great discouragement to a Minister, and it driueth many a godly man to his dumpes, and interrupteth his Ministerie, or at the least his cheerefulnes in his Ministerie, and so by this meanes the efficacie of his Ministery being hindred, Christs kingdome receiueth hindrance also.

<small>3. Preseruation of Ministers from the persecution of the wicked, furthereth Gods kingdome.</small>

<small>Deut. 33. 9.</small>

<small>2. Thes. 3. 2.</small>

Thus we pray for Magistracie and Ministerie, which are the two generall and maine pillars of Gods kingdome. Now follow the fruites and effects of them both, which are, reformation, and conuersion.

In the third place wee pray that by godly Magistrates inacting wholesome lawes, and causing due execution of them: and by godly Ministers powerfully exercising their ministeriall actions, men may bee reformed from their errors and misdemeanour, and bee truly conuerted to the faith, and brought to repentance out of the snare of the diuell, or at the least by outward punishment from the Magistrate and ecclesiasticall censures from the Ministerie be restrained and repressed, so as they breake not out to open prophanenes: and also that those which are alreadie conuerted and reformed, may bee further built vp in the spirituall building of Gods temple. The substance of this point is, that God would vouchsafe to adde the operation of his spirit, to the outward meanes both of Magistracie and

<small>Reformation and conuersion further Gods kingdome.</small>

Ministerie. This the Apostle calleth the kingdome of God: when he teacheth that the kingdome of God standeth not in meate and drinke (or any outward meanes by consequence) but in the effectuall operation of the spirit which worketh in vs righteousnesse, peace, and ioy in the holie Ghost: which three things are principall parts of this kingdome.

Rom. 14. 17.

1 Righteousnes is twofold: first imputatiue, which is the righteousnes of Iesus Christ the Mediatour and Redeemer purchased through his doings and suffrings for the church, and imputed to euery beleeuer by the holy Ghost: which righteousnes is apprehended and applied by faith.

Righteousnes a part of Gods kingdome.

The second is righteousnes inherent & resident in vs, as a qualitie really qualifying the subiect, which righteousnes is an effect of the former righteousnes of Christ imputed, whereby sinne daily is crucified and weakened: and we are enabled to yeeld obedience to the will and law of God in some measure acceptable to God through Christ: from which inherent righteousnes, as from the bodie of the tree, (Christs righteousnes imputed being the roote) spring manifold branches, which bring foorth fruites worthy repentance and true conuersion.

2 After righteousnes followeth peace, which is peace with God, who of an enemie is made a friend through the mediation of Iesus Christ: and peace with our owne consciences, which before were either ouerwhelmed with despaire, or puft vp with presumption and senselesse securitie: and peace with all the creatures, so farre forth as that they shall not hurt vs, but become seruiceable to vs.

Peace a part of Gods kingdom.

3 After peace followeth ioy in the holie Ghost, arising from righteousnes and peace: for being once through faith made partakers of the righteousnes of Christ, and qualified with the manifolde graces of Gods spirit, and being at peace with the Creator and the creatures, then we reioyce with ioy vnspeakable and glorious, receiuing the end of our faith, which is the saluation of our soules: whereby also wee reioyce in the afflictions which befall vs for Christs sake.

Ioy spirituall a part of Gods kingdome.

1. Pet. 1.
Rom. 5.

A paterne of true Prayer 165

These are the principall things we pray for in this petition appertaining to this life: some thing also appertaining to the life to come is here desired, namely the speedy comming of Iesus Christ to iudgement, and so the perfecting of the number of the elect, the resurrection of the bodie, and the euerlasting ioyes of heauen: so in the Apocalyps the Spirit and the Bride say, *Come: come Lord Iesus, come quickly.* And this may suffice for the supplication.

<small>The last iudgement furthereth Gods kingdome.</small>

<small>Apoc. 22.</small>

4 The things which wee pray against follow in the next place to bee handled, which may bee gathered out of the supplication, and are to be handled according to the order there vsed: and in the first place things concerning Magistracie.

<small>The deprecation the 4. part of this petition.</small>

1. Anarchie: which is want of Magistrates, whence issueth disorder and confusion, that euery man may do what him listeth, a fault taxed in the Common-wealth of Israel: whereby it commeth to passe not onely that the second table of the Commandements concerning iustice and equitie is transgressed; example whereof is brought of the Leuite, whose wife was abused vnto death: but that the first table also is violated, which respecteth the kingdome of God, as the example of *Micah* and his idolatrie teacheth. For it is a thing that the diuell would wish principally that Magistracie were abolished, and therefore hee hath inspired that diuellish doctrine into the confused heads of the Anabaptists, who take away all rule and authoritie and all superioritie among men: for if hee could compasse that, then the feare of punishment being abandoned, and the hope of rewards taken away, which are the two sinewes of the Common-wealth, he might easily prostitute men, women, and children to all impious and dishonest behauiour: whereby the kingdome of God should be banished out of the world. Hence it is that the light of nature teacheth, that it is better to haue a Tyrant than no King: for nature is not so extinct in any man, no though he were an Atheist, but he would, if not of loue to order and ciuilitie, yet in policy prescribe lawes to his subiects, wherby peace may be maintained and

<small>Anarchie hindereth Gods kingdome.
Iudg. 19.</small>

<small>Iudg. 18.</small>

some forme of moderation, least the bruite beast should controll man, to whom nature hath prescribed and limited a compasse, as wee see labour in the Pismire, chastitie in the Turtle, curtesie in the Elephant, and the like in other creatures: and although a Tyrant might doe and suffer much impietie and iniquitie, yet some good must needes proceed from him, though he were neuer so great a monster of men: in regard whereof Tyrannie is better than Anarchie; there being some order in the one, and none in the other.

2. Next vnto Anarchie is Tyrannie, when euill Magistrates are in place, which seeke by all meanes to erect and set vp the kingdom of Satan, in Gentilisme, Mahometisme, Papisme, or Atheisme, or any other superstition and heresie, whereby persecution is raised against the true worshippers of God and true religion: or else when there is a Toleration of many Religions, whereby the kingdom of God is shouldered out a doores by the diuels kingdome: for without question the diuell is so subtill that hee will procure, through the aduantage of mans naturall inclination to false doctrine and worship, more by thousands to follow strange Religions, than the truth of Gods word: wherfore the Magistrates should cause all men to worship the true God, or else punish them with imprisonment, confiscation of goods, or death as the qualitie of the cause requireth. Here notwithstanding a doubt ariseth: how it is lawfull to pray against the euill Magistrates, when as the Apostle doth wish prayers to bee made for Heathen Princes and Magistrates, which then were persecutors. The answere is very easie, that we may pray for their saluation and conuersion, but against their tyrannie and persecution: for it is not vnlawfull to pray for the Turke, Pope and Spaniard that they may be conuerted and saued: but it is lawfull also to pray against their proceedings against the truth, that God would discomfit them in battel, bridle their corruption, abate their pride, asswage their malice, and confound their deuices. Thus wee see the Prophet prayeth against the enemies of the Church.

Euill Magistrates hinder Gods kingdome.

Toleration of strange religion and worship hindreth Gods kingdome.

1. *Tim.* 2. 2.

Psal. 68. 1. 2.

Thus also did *Deborah* and *Barak* pray that all the enemies of God might perish as *Sisera* perished: and so in another Psalme prayeth the Prophet. *Iudg.* 5. 31. *Psal.* 83. 9. 10.

3. Lastly, wee pray against all wicked and irreligious lawes and statutes, that God would hinder the making of them, or at the least the execution of them: such as was the law made against *Daniel*, that contained a months Atheisme, that no man for thirtie daies should worship any God but the proud King: such as was that which *Haman* procured to be made and ratified against the Iewes, that all the true worshippers of God should be destroyed & slaine: such as were enacted in the time of the bloodie persecutions by Heathen Emperours, that whosoeuer said he was a Christian should bee put to death: for by such lawes the very foundation of Gods kingdome is shaken, and greatly endangered. *Euill lawes hinder Gods kingdome. Dan.* 6. *Hester.* 3.

Againe, in the second place wee pray against certaine sinnes and enormities incident to the Ministerie: which are these.

1. Ignorance: for ignorant and vnlearned Ministers pine the soules of men, being not able to teach and instruct the people committed to their charge: the Priests lips should preserue knowledge, and the law should bee required at their mouthes: and the Lord he refuseth such Priests as refuse knowledge: for they are the lights of the world, and therefore they must haue light in them whereby they may giue light: they are the salt of the earth, and therefore must haue sauour in them to season withall: wherefore by law established in this land none ought to bee admitted into the Ministerie, but such as can render a reason of their faith in Latine, and can teach the Catechisme allowed by law containing the summe of Christian religion, so as the people may vnderstand, and at their ordination haue authoritie giuen them to expound the Scriptures being called thereto. Wherefore seeing there can be no faith without knowledge, and no knowledge without teaching, and no teaching without learning: therefore the Ministers that want learning cannot teach, so as the people may know and beleeue and be saued: *Ignorant Ministers hinder Christs kingdome. Malach.* 3. 7. *Hosea.* 4. 6.

and by this meanes the people perish for want of knowledge, and Gods kingdome is diminished in the number and qualitie of good subiects.

Hosea. 4. 6.

2. After ignorance followeth error, which poysoneth the soule: for hereticall and erroneous teachers broaching erroneous and false doctrine, infuse poison into the minds of men: for such doctrine fretteth and infecteth like a Gangrene, as the Apostle teacheth: and therefore hee willeth that men should auoyde such teachers and heretikes after once and twise admonished: for as all men will auoyde him that hath the plague, or any other contagious disease; so erroneous and hereticall teachers must bee shunned as being such as haue the plague of heresie vpon them, which is almost incureable, whereby they infect those that are of sound iudgement, and so pull them from subiection to Christ their King and Prophet.

False teachers hinder Christs kingdome.

2. *Tim.* 2. 17.

3. In the next place, idle and vnprofitable teachers follow, which eate the milke, and cloath themselues with the fleece of the flocke, but feede not the flocke. The sinne of these men is so much the greater, for that they can, and will not teach their people: and as idle persons in the common-wealth are called theeues by the Apostle, not because they violently steale, but for that they are caterpillers and drones, eating that which they neuer sweate for: so these men that liue idly in the Church, incurre the iust rebuke of spirituall feloney and theft; in that they eate and worke not: in that they reape temporall things of the people, and doe not minister their spirituall things to the people. And so it commeth to passe that the people being vntaught, and vnfed, their soules pine away and are famished and perish, and the Kingdome of Christ is depriued and robbed of subiects.

The Ministers hinder Gods Kingdome.

Ephes. 4.

4. After idle Ministers which can teach, and will not, followeth another sort, which wil teach, but cannot: whose seruice is therefore refused of God, for that they take vpon them that whereto they haue no competent abilitie. For there are certaine bounds and limits wherein consisteth a sufficient

Vnskilfull Ministers hinder Gods Kingdome.

qualification to the office of the Ministerie, whereto if any man be found defectiue, although he may be profitable to the furthering of Christs Kingdome in another calling, yet therein he doth harme, in that he hindereth another, that might doe good : these men may be called manglers and hackers of Gods word, for they cannot deuide the word aright, as the Apostle speaketh, neither are they apt to teach. A skilfull carpenter can by line and leuell square his timber, but a man not brought vp to the trade, will hacke and mangle and mare the timber: so the Apostles compareth Ministers to skilfull builders, and not to them that cleaue and chop wood, rending and cutting it in peeces, they care not how so it be done. For a Minister must be a master of his profession and mysterie, as well; yea much more than other men. Againe, it is one thing to be learned, and another thing to be apt to teach, the one is contemplatiue, the other practicall ; for a man may haue knowledge how and what to teach : and yet want gifts of speech to vtter significantly, and profitably, as experience teacheth. By reason whereof it falleth out that some men hauing good learning, do not edifie others: or hauing speech and wanting learning, are no better than sounding brasse, and a tinckling cymball.

5. Now further let it be graunted that a man haue the qualification of learning, sound iudgement, paines, skill, and vtterance; yet neuerthelesse if his life bee vitious, he doth not builde with both hands, but pulleth downe as fast as he buildeth. Wherefore the Apostle requireth that Ministers should be both apt to teach, and vnreproueable, and Christ himselfe willeth his disciples to haue a double light in them, both of sound doctrine, and a godly life. Such Ministers may very well be compared to images, placed in crosse wayes, which point the way to the towne, but neuer set foote to goe thither : or like to the sermon bell that calleth men to the sermon, which is the meanes of saluation, but neuer heareth nor profiteth by the sermon. And these Ministers greatly hinder the Kingdome of Christ, for howsoeuer they preach and may be meanes of conuersion and edification to those that are conuerted : yet surely their euill life doth scandalize and

Vitious Ministers hinder Gods Kingdome.

1. Tim. 3.
Math. 5.

offend many, not onely that are without, but some weake ones also within the compasse of the Church. For howsoeuer it be a fault for a man to stumble at a blocke wilfully and of purpose, as these men doe: yet surely it is a great fault for to lay the blocke in his way, which we know will stumble at it; it is as if we should giue a sworde to a mad or desperate man, that would kill himselfe.

6. In the last place those Ministers that seeke to please men, that sow pillowes vnder euery elbow, that say peace, peace, when there is no peace, that daube with vntempered morter, that out of a policie securing themselues from daunger, refraine holsome doctrine and application, not daring to say with *Nathan* to *Dauid*, thou art the man: nor with *Elias* to *Ahab*, it is thou and thy fathers house that troubleth Israel, nor with *Iohn Baptist* to *Herod*, it is not lawfull for thee to commit incest, nor with Christ to the Scribes and Pharsies, woe be to you Scribes and Pharises, hypocrits, serpents, generation of vipers: these Ministers, I say, walking fearefully and politikely in their ministerie, hinder the building of Christs spirituall temple: for they doe not hew, and sawe the rough stones, nor plane and polish the knottie timber, but rub them with a smooth flickstone, and wipe them with a soft foxe skinne, and so by this meanes the rubbish stone, and knottie timber, is vnfit for the spirituall edifice: whereas the Ministers should be such as *Iames* and *Iohn* were, the sonnes of thunder, which should with the thunderbolts of Gods iudgements pearce the flint-hard hearts of secure and carnall men, that they might be turned into soft and fleshie hearts. *A Flattering Ministery hindereth Gods Kingdome.*

Hauing spoken sufficiently of the faults incident to the magistracie and ministerie, which hinder the Kingdome of Christ, other vices follow which in this petition we pray against.

First against infidelitie, impenitencie, and raigning sins, the subuersion whereof is an effect of good Magistracie, and Ministerie, and the nourcing and cherishing whereof necessarily groweth from the foresaid vices in the Magistracie and Ministerie. These sinnes, howsoeuer they are incident to some *Generall sinnes hindering Christs Kingdome.*

Magistrates and Ministers, yet they are generall sinnes that indifferently possesse the hearts of all men of all estates and callings.

1. Infidelitie is one leafe of the yron gate that barreth the Lord Iesus Christ out of the soule: who being kept out, it is impossible that his Kingdome and scepter should there be erected. *Infidelitie hindereth Gods Kingdome.* So long as the diuell, who is the strong man, keepeth possession, all things are safe: but when faith entereth into the soule, then one leafe or head of the euerlasting gate is lifted vp, and the King of glory commeth in: then that man Iesus Christ, which is stronger than the diuell, spoileth him of his castle and furniture, and taketh possession of the spirituall fort, and aduanceth his scepter and Kingdome, proclaiming himselfe the King and Lord of that subiect.

Psal. 24.

Matth. 12.

2 Impenitencie is another leafe of that yron gate, which excludeth Christ Iesus, and causeth the owner to rebell against his soueraigne Lord and King; which must be opened and lifted vp before Christ will enter. Repentance may be termed the Haruenger of the King, as *Iohn* the *Baptist* was of Christ, who taught the baptisme of repentance, for the remission of sinnes, whereby the Lords way was prepared, and his paths made straight. This is the doctrine which Christ himselfe taught: *Repent, for the Kingdome of God is at hand:* for Gods Kingdome being at hand is admitted into the soule by repentance, and excluded by impenitencie.

Impenitencie hindereth Gods Kingdome.

Luk. 3.

3 Raigning sinnes also may be termed the locke vpon the gate, or the barre, or the port-culles, whereby the yron gate is further fortified and strengthned against an entery. For so long as any one sinne raigneth in the soule, the Lord Iesus cannot, nor will not raigne there, who will haue all the place of the soule, or none: for Christ can indure no consort or copartner in his Kingdome, especially his enemie: and no man can serue two contrary masters; or be a good subiect to two Kings, inioyning contrary lawes.

Raigning sins hinder Gods Kingdome.

4 Secondly, we pray against al the Kingdome of darkenes, as against Gentilisme, Mahometisme, Iudaisme, Papisme, and against the proceeding of all those, or any other false doctrines and superstitions: for by all these false meanes, the Kingdome of Antichrist, and of Mahomet, the two eldest sonnes of the diuell, is aduanced; and the Kingdome of Iesus Christ is deiected and cast downe.

<small>False doctrine and superstition hinder Gods Kingdome.</small>

Lastly, we pray against wicked men and Angels, that God would hasten their iust destruction and damnation: and in the meane space represse and bridle their malice and rage, that they doe not preuaile against the truth of God and professors thereof: and if wee doe discerne any man to be a reprobate, as namely, one that committeth the sinne against the holy Ghost, directly and particularly to pray for his speedy damnation, and all the meanes effecting the same. Finally, that God would shortly tread downe Sathan vnder our foote.

<small>Rom. 11. 9.
Psal. 69. 22.
Rom. 16. 20.</small>

5 This is the deprecation. The thanksgiuing followeth; which how it is to be made, may be gathered by the particulars of the supplication and deprecation.

<small>Thankesgiuing of the second petition.</small>

This is the first of these two petitions which concerne the meanes of Gods glory: from whence this may be obserued; that one and the selfe same vertue and vice may be referred to diuers petitions in diuers respects; which is agreeable to the rules of reason, which teacheth that the respect being chaunged, the argument is also chaunged. To this petition the fourth commaundement is to be referred.

Now followeth the second of these petitions, which respecteth the meanes of Gods glory, which is the obedience of his will.

Thy will be done in earth as it is in Heauen.

1 This petition followeth consequently vpon the former, for when men are subiects of Christs Kingdome, then they begin to obey his will, whereas before they were rebels and traytors, and the slaues of sinne and Sathan; whence this instruction

<small>Order of the third petition.</small>

ariseth. That obedience to Gods will are the fruites of Gods Kingdome. Or that good workes are the effects and signes of grace, and the Kingdome of God in vs: or that good workes iustifie, that is declare that we are iustified, and that they argue faith, and grace in the heart. The tree is knowne by the fruite saith Christ: and *Iohn* <small>Mat. 12. 33.</small> *Baptist* willeth those that came to bee baptised, <small>Mat. 3. 8.</small> to bring forth fruites worthie amendement of life; or worthie conuersion; as if it had been said by Christ and *Iohn Baptist:* Euill fruite argueth an euill tree, and good fruite commendeth a good tree: so euill workes shew an euill heart, and good workes shew a gratious heart. Repentance or conuersion appeareth in godlines and righteousnes, and not in prophanenes and wickednes. And therefore if you will approue that you haue repentance, which is the inward baptisme; whereof the outward baptisme of water is a signe, bring forth such fruites of a holy and righteous life, which may euidently declare the same: for the inward disposition of the heart is outwardly ingrauen in the life: *Shew me* <small>Iam. 2. 18.</small> *thy faith by thy workes, and I will shew thee my faith by my workes,* for we cannot otherwise iudge one of another, but by the outward practise; for God onely is the searcher of the heart.

This doctrine will minister vnto vs a touchstone whereby we may try a sound and substantiall Christian from a foggie and bumbasted hypocrite: the life of the one is <small>Psal. 45. 2.</small> religious and righteous full of good workes, his <small>Ephes. 4. 29.</small> lips are full of grace, and rotten communication proceedeth not out of his mouth: whereas the life of the other is either grosely vitious or meerely ciuill; who though perhaps he doe no harme, yet he doth no good, especially he will be dissolute in religious exercises, and worldlines tainteth his life: and though happily himselfe will not talke corruptly, yet he can either with patience or delight, heare others. Againe, <small>1. Cor. 4. 5.</small> although wee may not clime vp into Gods iudgement seate, to giue the definitiue sentence of his election, or reprobation vpon other men, for that were to rob God of his honor, yet without breach of charitie we may censure the present estate of other men, leauing the issue to the Lord; neither ought men thereat to be offended, considering that Christ hath left vs a most certaine rule of direction, ye shall know them by their fruites: and howsoeuer a godly man may sometime be censured for a wicked man, he *Mat.* 7. 16. being in some grosse sinne a long time, as *Dauid* in adultery without repentance; yet though the censure bee false, it is charitable, because it is according to the rule: *By their fruites yee shall know them.* And contrariwise, though sometime a wicked man may play the hypocrite so kindly as that he may by the shew of good workes, wring from the Church, the charitable censure of a godly man, he being nothing lesse; yet that censure also is due being false, and in charitie, and iustice hee can haue no lesse, for the heart is vnknowne to man, and we can know them only by their fruits. And this may serue for the order of the petitiō.

2 For the meaning of this petition, consider three things.

  1. What is Gods will.
  2. What it is to doe Gods will.
  3. How Gods will must be done.

The meaning of the third petition.

For the first we are to know that Gods will is partly reuealed to the Church in his word and workes, partly kept secret to himselfe in the closet of his owne eternall counsell; which distinction is grounded vpon that speech of *Moses: The secret things to the Lord, the reuealed things to vs.* For example, these are things secret: Which man is a reprobate amongst vs? (if he haue not sinned the sinne against the holy Ghost) Where hell is? How the Angels are distinguished? When the day of iudgement is? which things God hath concealed from vs as impertinent for vs to know: and to search whereunto, were to passe the bounds of a modest and sober inquisition. Now things reuealed are such as are contained in the world, *viz.* All that holy doctrine of the law and Gospell contained in the writings of the Prophets and Apostles: as also whatsoeuer other things the workes of God ordinary or extraordinarie discouer vnto vs. As for example, the howre of this mans death is vnknowne till he be dead, then it

What is Gods will.

Deut. 29. 29.

is knowne, &c. And thus God doth daily reueale new matters to vs, which before were hidden: thus by the obseruation and inquisition of wise men the course of heauen and the whole order of nature was discouered.

For the second thing, which is the doing of Gods will, *What it is to doe Gods will.* wee must consider thereof according to the distinction of Gods will before set downe: and first for the reuealed will of God, that is done two waies: either by obeying the commandements willingly, or suffering the chastisements patiently: for the chastisements which befall vs are parts of Gods reuealed will, of what kinde soeuer they bee: and here are two vertues suggested vnto vs, when wee pray let thy reuealed wil be *Deut.* 6. 1. 2. done: Obedience, which is so often vrged in 3. Deuteronomie: and Submission, which is insinuated in the emphasis of the word, *Thy will*, containing a negation of our owne wils, as Christ said in his prayer, *Mat.* 26. 39. *Not my will, but thy will be done.* Secondly, for the secret will of God we doe also in part pray that it may be done: I say in part: for example sake, we pray that God would daily more and more reueale vnto vs Antichrist, which to the Primitiue Church was a secret, and in part is a secret to vs. So also we pray, *Apoc.* 22. *Come Lord Iesus, come quickly,* and yet the second comming of Christ vnto iudgement, in regard of the time, is concealed: so we pray for patience to beare the crosses which God shall inflict; which of what kinde they are, and when they shall befall vs, is vnknowne.

Thirdly, Gods will must be done *in earth, as in heauen:* *How Gods will must be done.* which words are diuersly expounded by Interpreters.

Some say: Let the bodie, which is earthly, obey Gods will, as the soule and spirit, which is heauenly: 1. *Cor.* 6. 20. but that is as good as nothing, for the soule is sinfull as well as the bodie, yea is the author of sinne to the bodie which is only the instrument.

Others say: Let the earthly minded men bee conuerted 1. *Cor.* 15. and yeeld obedience, as the heauenly minded 47. are and do: but this also is as good as neuer a whit, being neuer the better: for the heauenly minded are imperfect, and wanting in the best of their obedience.

But the better sort of Expositors say thus : Let men vpon earth obey the will of God, as the Angels doe in heauen : and this seemeth to bee the true exposition of the words : now the Angels obey Gods will readily and perfectly. The willingnes and readines of the Angels doth appeare by the similitude and shape which is giuen them ; they are said to haue wings by the Prophet *Esay*: and the Cherubims imbroidred vpon the vaile of the Tabernacle, and the two Cherubims vpon the Mercie seate had wings : yea further, the two Cherubims vpon the Mercie seate did looke with their faces to the Mercie seate ward, which is by our Sauiour Christ expounded of their willingnes, where he saith, that *the Angels alwaies behold the face of my father which is in heauen*. Now it is apparant that the beholding of the face signifieth in a seruant readines to bee imployed about his masters busines, according as it is in the Psalme, *The eyes of seruants looke to the hands of the masters and mistresses :* by which phrase the Prophet signifieth not onely confident hope and expectation of deliuerance, but in the meane season till deliuerance come, patience to beare contempt, mocking and despightfulnes, and readie obedience to Gods will, yea in these great extremities, which in that Psalme is insinuated by the Prophets prayer. The Angels also obey Gods will perfectly, who are therefore called holy Angels, for that they haue no spot of sinne or disobedience in them : for howsoeuer the Angels being compared with God haue in them imperfections, in regard whereof *Eliphaz* speaketh in *Iob*, that hee found no stedfastnes in his seruants, and laid follie vpon his Angels : and therefore in *Esay* the Seraphims with two wings couer their feete ; yet neuerthelesse if the Angels bee compared with Gods law, which is the rule of their obedience, they are able, and doe perfectly euen in the strict and exact measure and manner of obedience yeeld obedience thereunto, otherwise they could not continue in that estate of grace and glorie wherein they are now, and so shall abide confirmed for euer. So then

Psal. 103. 20.

Gods will must be done readily.
Esay. 6. 2.
Exod. 36. 35.
Exod. 25. 20.

Mat. 18. 10.

Psal. 123. 2.

Gods will must be done perfectly.

Iob. 4. 18.

Esay. 6. 2.

the meaning of these words is thus much: Graunt that wee may willingly and perfectly obey thy will, as thy holy Angels doe.

But here in opposition to this last propertie of the Angels obedience it may bee obiected, that seeing it is impossible we should perfectly obey Gods will, therefore we must not in our prayers aske that at Gods hand: for shall it be thought lawfull and reasonable to aske impossibilities? For answere whereto thus much in briefe: Impossibilities are of two sorts, *viz.* alwaies impossible, and impossible for a certaine time. Now although it be for the present impossible that Gods children should perfectly obey Gods will, yet it is not so for euer: for when wee shall bee perfectly regenerate, then shall wee perfectly obey Gods will: which we are here by way of implication taught to pray for, and so to long after.

Three kinds of perfit obedience.
Esay. 38. 3.

Furthermore, perfection is of three sorts: First perfection opposed to hypocrisie, and so is *Ezechias* said to haue walked before the Lord in truth and with a perfect heart, and this may bee termed *perfectio qualitatis:* when our obedience is perfect in qualitie, and not dissembled.

Secondly, perfection of number, when obedience is not performed to some onely, but to all the commandements of God, as *Zachary* and *Elizabeth* are said to haue walked in all the commandements and ordinances of God without reproofe: and this may bee called *perfectio partium ac numero[rum]*, when obedience is complete in all the members thereof, whereto one kinde of imperfection is opposed.

Luk. 1. 6.

Thirdly, perfection of degree, when obedience in the highest and exactest measure is exhibited: so Christ onely, and *Adam* in the state of innocencie, and the holy Angels and Saints in heauen doe obey Gods will: of this Christ speaketh, alleaging the sentence of the Law: *Thou shalt loue the Lord thy God with all thy heart, with all thy soule, with all thy strength, and with all thy thought:* this is called *perfectio quantitatis ac graduum:* whereto another kinde of imperfection is opposite. Of all these kindes of perfection the Apostle speaketh in one place, denying in himselfe the

Mat. 22. 37.

Luk. 10. 27.

perfection of degree and contending to it: but affirming of himselfe and others the other two kindes of perfection: for although hee was not perfect in the highest and absolutest degree of obedience; yet hee and other of the Philippians were vpright in regard of the qualitie, and complete in respect of the parts of obedience. The distinction being thus warranted must be applied to the purpose: Although then as yet it is impossible for vs to yeeld the perfect measure of obedience to Gods commandements with the Angels; yet wee may endeuour and desire to attaine vnto it with the Apostle, and in the meane season we must performe, and endeuour to performe, and pray to performe true & complete obedience with the Angels, which is a thing possible to bee performed by Gods children, as hath been declared in the examples of *Ezechias*, *Zachary* and *Elizabeth*, and the Apostle *Paul*.

Phil. 3. 12. 15.

Verse 12.

This may suffice for the meaning of this petition, whereby there is a doore opened to the contents thereof, which now follow in order.

3 The third thing to bee considered in this third petition or prayer is the things which wee here aske of God, which are these.

Conuersion, commanded in the Gospell, which is one part of Gods reuealed will, a thing so often vrged by the Prophets, and the want thereof so sharply censured, especially the Prophet *Ioel*, and *Amos* are vehement in the matter: *Amos* spendeth a whole chapter in vpbraiding the induration of the people. For hauing repeated certaine grieuous punishments inflicted by God vpon them iustly for their sinnes, as famine and pestilence, and an ouerthrow like the destruction of Sodome and Gomorah, hee endeth diuers verses with this foote or burden: *Yet haue ye not returned vnto me, saith the Lord.* In like manner *Ioel* hauing threatned famine and the sword against the rebellious people, diuers times, but especially in the second chapter vehemently exhorteth to conuersion, that by this meanes they may preuent Gods fierce wrath. *Ezechiel* also spendeth an whole chapter to this purpose.

The supplication of this petition. Conuersion a part of Gods will.
1. *Thes.* 4. 3.
Rom. 12. 2.
Ephes. 5. 17.
Amos. 4.

Ioel. 2. 12.

Ezech. 18.

This conuersion is vrged also by *Iohn Baptist*, and our Sauiour Christ in their Ministerie as the first lesson: *Repent, for the kingdome of God is at hand:* and, *Repent, and beleeue the Gospell.* And the signification of the word implieth these two things especially, *viz.* First, turning from the wrong way wherein a man wandreth. Secondly, entring into the right way from which a man erred: the word in the Latin and Hebrue being borrowed from trauellers in their iourney, and referred to the bodie and outward act; but in the Greeke applied to the purpose and disposition of the minde, which in conuersion is altered. Conuersion in the new Testament in certaine differing respects hath diuers appellations; as Renouation, Regeneration, Sanctification, the first Resurrection, Obedience to the Gospell, and such like: and the parts of conuersion also are diuersly intituled: as the first is called Mortification, crucifying the old man, the crosse of Christ; the second, viuification, newnes of life, new obedience. To conuersion appertaineth diuers excellent affections and dispositions mentioned in the Scripture, as Humi[l]iation, sorrow for sinne, hatred of sinne, loue of righteousnes, consolation, feare, ioy, and such like: diuers whereof the Apostle mentioneth writing to the Corinthians: and others may easily bee obserued in reading the Scriptures: but to make any tractate of conuersion is not the purpose of this tractate, which onely by way of capitulation pointeth out a fit place for euery matter.

Mat. 3. 2. & 4. 17.
Mark. 1. 15.

Shub.
Conuertere.
Metanoein.

2. *Cor.* 7. 10. 11.

Obedience, commanded in the Law, succeedeth next in order of nature to the obedience of the Gospell. For the obedience of the Law issueth from the obedience of the Gospell, as the Apostle saith, *Loue commeth from faith vnfained:* for although the Law bee a schoolemaster to whip vs to Christ, yet Christ doth send vs backe againe to the Law for direction, when he hath once admitted vs into his schoole by conuersion.

Obedience a part of Gods will.

1. *Tim.* 1. 5.

Obedience is either generall or speciall.

Generall obedience is that which appertaineth to all Christians.

Generall obedience respecteth God or man. *Mat.* 22. 37.

Generall obedience respecting God is called holines or godlines, or religion sometime. *Luk.* 1. 75.

Generall obedience respecting man is called righteousnes, one branch whereof is sobrietie. *1. Tim.* 2. 2.

Speciall obedience is that which appertaineth to some sorts of persons.

Speciall obedience is either of a ⎰ Speciall commandement. ⎱ Speciall calling.

Obedience of a speciall commaundement is, when the Lord inioyneth something contrarie to the morall law: as *Abraham* was commanded to sacrifice his sonne; and it is obeyed. *Genes.* 22. 2.

Obedience of a speciall calling is manifold, as of the Magistrate, the Minister, &c.

The rules of all these kindes of obedience are these shortly. **Rules of obedience.**

Obey God absolutely as the only law-giuer that is able to saue and destroy: but man must not bee so obeyed, but conditionally.

Worship God as hee hath taught, not as thou thinkest good: for God knoweth best what is best, and what best pleaseth him. *Mat.* 15. 9.

Loue thy neighbour as thy self: whatsoeuer thou wouldest that men should doe vnto thee, euen so doe thou vnto them. *Matth.* 7. 12.

A speciall commandement ouerthwarting a generall must be obeyed: *In Antinomia lex posterior obligat.* *Genes.* 22. 2.

The duties of our speciall callings must bee performed in conscience to Gods commandements. *Ephes* 6. 1.

After actiue obedience, which consisteth in doing Gods commandements, followeth passiue obedience in suffering his chastisements, which generally may be termed submission, that is, when the creature is content to resigne himselfe ouer wholy to the will of the Creator: and to say as *Dauid* said, *Behold here am I, let him doe to me as seemeth good in his eyes:* this vertue doth especially respect the time to come, and the Lords secret will: that if the Lord **Submission a part of Gods will.**

2. Sam. 15. 26.

haue in his secret counsell determined such and such euils and afflictions to befall vs, we can be content with patience to beare them, how many and how great soeuer they be, so be that thereby God may be glorified.

After the kinds of obedience follow the qualities of obedience, *viz.* cheerefulnes or willingnes ; and sincerity or perfection.

Cheerefulnes or willingnes is highly regarded of God, and accordingly endeuored of the children of God. God loueth a cheerefull giuer, saith the Apostle : and God himselfe giueth freely, and vpbraideth no man, saith *Iames:* and he liketh that in his children, which himselfe practiseth.

Cheerefulnes in obedience a part of Gods will.
2. *Cor.* 9. 7.
Iam. 1. 5.
Ioh. 4. 34.

Christ saith that it was meate and drinke to him, to doe the will of his heauenly father : yea and in suffering for our sinnes, he protesteth great willingnes : for he did willingly lay downe his life, and it was not taken from him against his liking ; and therefore *Dauid* prophecieth of him, that seeing it was written of him in the volume of the booke that he should doe Gods will, therefore he was content to doe it. And this is that eccho which *Dauids* heart gaue to Gods voyce : God said, *seeke ye my face : Dauids* heart answered : *Lord I will seeke thy face :* and although it cannot bee denied, but that the flesh is very weake, yea repugnant and refractary, yet the spirit is willing, and the children of God do delight in the law of God according to the inner man.

Psal. 40. 8.

Psal. 27. 8.

Rom. 7. 22.

Finally, perfection or sinceritie also is required as another necessarie qualification of obedience ; which consisteth in a true purpose of the heart, ioyned with an earnest endeuour to the vtmost of grace, to obey euery one, yea the very least of Gods commaundements ; making conscience of idle words, and vaine thoughts, yea of the stirring of concupis[c]ence, and, which is most of all, of originall sinne, and *Adams* transgression imputed. This vertue of sinceritie is much despised and persecuted by the world, when men intitle it by straunge names : as humor, spiced conscience, precisenes, puritanisme : alas that euer the diuell should so preuaile ! For example,

Sinceritie in obedience a part of Gods will.
Psal. 119. 106.
1. *Cor.* 4. 4.
Rom. 7. 24.

take a man that is very well content with the state, obeying the Magistrate, ciuill and ecclesiasticall in al the ceremonies of the Church ; yet if he doe not sweare, and drinke, and quarell and so forth ; but reproue the swearer, the dronkard, the hackster, and the rest : This man is as odious to the multitude, as the veriest disciplinarian in the land, and he shall partake as well in the foresaid titles of disgrace as the other.

4. Now in the fourth place follow the things which in this petition are to be prayed against: whereof the first is obstinacie, which is a purpose and resolution to continue in the course of wickednes, wherein a man liueth : the sinne of the drunkards, of whom the wise man speaketh, which are resolued still to seeke after drunkennes : also the sinne of the Shepheards and Watchmen of Israel, of whom the Prophet *Esay* speaketh, Who say, To morrow shall be as this day, and much more abundant in wine and strong drinke and couetous oppression. The extremitie of this sinne is recorded in the rebellious Iewes, by the Prophet *Ieremie*, who being admonished of their sinnes, and of obedience to Gods commaundements, made answere, that they would not heare the word of the Lord which *Ieremie* spake, but they would doe what themselues listed. The Apostle calleth this sinne a hard and irrepentant heart, and the despising of Gods bountifulnes, patience, and long suffering, which is directly opposite to the obedience of the Gospell.

<small>The deprecation of this petition. Obstinacie opposed to Gods will. *Pro.* 23. 35.</small>

<small>*Esay.* 56. 12. *Ierem.* 44. 16. 17.</small>

<small>*Rom.* 2. 4. 5.</small>

In the second place followeth disobedience, which is euery transgression of the morall law, or of any other speciall precept. Disobedience hath foure specialties.

<small>Disobedience opposit to Gods will.</small>

1. Vngodlines, irreligion, or prophanenes, when men regarde not Gods worship, but liue as if there were no God, no heauen, no diuell, no hell, no conscience : of such Atheists the world hath millions, who make no more account of Gods Sabbaths, than of the market or faire, no more reckoning of a sermon than of a fable of *Esop*, that for gaining a peny sweare and forsweare, and what not ? those impious wretches are more fearefull and

damnable sinners than the world esteemeth them, seeing they by their practise declare themselues directly to forget God, who is then especially remembred, when hee is worshipped. Against this sinne Gods wrath is reuealed from heauen.

Rom. 1. 18.

2. Vnrighteousnes, or iniustice, which is when any violence or wronge is offered to our neighbours person or gifts, as his dignitie, goods, life, or chastitie.

3. Rebellion, when men peremptorily resist Gods will knowne particularly, and euidently vrged vpon their conscience; or performe not obedience to a speciall precept. Example hereof wee haue in *Saul*, who was commaunded by God vtterly to destroy the Amalekites, and all their goods: now he saued *Agag* the King, and the fattest of the sheepe and oxen, and so flatly rebelled against this precept: the punishment of this sinne was most fearefull vpon him, which argueth the fearefulnes of the sinne. And the Prophet *Samuel* saith, that it is a sin as great as witchcraft, or idolatrie: and although now the Lord giueth no speciall precepts to men, yet hee doth particularly vrge vpon the conscience of some men generall commaundements: as when in the Ministerie of the word, the spirit of God cryeth aloude in the heart of the drunkard to forsake his drunkennes: and for that sinne hee is prickt in conscience, and perswaded to forsake it; the which sin, if he still practise and doe not forsake, then he rebelleth flatly against God, and is obnoxious to a fearefull punishment.

1. *Sam.* 15. 23.

4. Vnfaithfulnes, when men in their speciall callings doe not seeke Gods glory, nor the benefit of the Church or common-wealth, or the good of some societie, or when men liue idly or negligently. This sinne the Apostle taxeth in the Thessalonians, that they liued disorderly; and in the Ephesians, whom he termeth theeues for that they did not labour.

1. *Cor.* 4. 2.
1. *Cor.* 10. 31.

2. *Thes.* 3. 6. 11.
Ephes. 4. 28.

These are the specialties of disobedience.

In the third place is Selfe-will, Peeuishnes, Repining, Grudging, Murmuring, Complaining, Discontentment, Frowardnes; all which containe seuerall circumstances of one and the same sinne: when men will not become seruiceable to Gods

Selfe-will opposed to Gods will.

prouidence, but will choose what they list themselues, as though they knew what were best for them, thereby controlling Gods wisedome, and causing it to yeeld to their wilfull corruptions: for this sin the diuell did calumniate *Iob*; but *Iob* proued him a lyer, being content to receiue euill at Gods hands aswell as good; howsoeuer there appeared in *Iob* (though he be propounded as a patterne of patience to the Church) a little spice of impatiencie. *Iob.* 2. 5. 10. *Iam.* 5. 11.

In the fourth place followeth Backwardnes in obedience, and wearines of well doing, the fault which the Prophet *Malachy* reproued in his time, when men say, it is a wearines, and suffe at the paines and cost of Gods seruice; which in those dayes was a fault more tolerable than now, by how much Gods seruice was more chargeable and painfull than it is now, in regarde of the outward ceremonie, the yoke of the ceremoniall law being intolerable, as the Apostle speaketh. This sinne the Apostle preuenteth by admonition in the Galathians, vsing an argument for the purpose. *In due season we shall reape, if we faint not: therefore let vs not be wearie of well-doing.* (Backwardnes opposed to Gods will. *Mal.* 1. 13. *Act.* 15. 10. *Gal.* 6. 9.)

In the last place followeth hypocrisie, or a false and dishonest heart, when men purposing to liue in sinne, neuerthelesse make shew outwardly of godlines and honestie, for aduantage sake. Christ calleth it drawing neere with the lips and remouing the heart farre off; a sinne so odious in Gods sight, as that it seemeth he hath assigned it a speciall place in hell, because Christ ioyneth the euill, oppressing, and drunken seruant together with the hypocrite and dissembling mocke-God in the portion of such a punishment where is weeping and gnashing of teeth. (Hypocrisie opposed to Gods will. *Mat.* 15. *and Esay.* 29. *Mat.* 24. 51.)

This may suffice for the deprecation.

5. The thanksgiuing, which is the last thing to be considered in this petition, may easily be collected out of the supplication and deprecation: for we blesse God that he hath bestowed vpon vs and others his seruants these graces following. (The thankesgiuing of this petition.)

First, conuersion : Secondly, obedience to the law, in godlines, righteousnes, speciall obedience and faithfulnes in our callings : Thirdly, submission : Fourthly, cheerefulnes, and fifthly sinceritie.

And againe, we praise God for that he hath preuented and mortified in vs and other his children the contrarie sinnes : as first, obstinacie, or impenitencie, and infidelitie : secondly, disobedience to the law in vngodlines, vnrighteousnes, rebellion and vnfaithfulnes : thirdly, selfe-will : fourthly, backwardnes : fifthly, hypocrisie. This shall be sufficient for this petition, and so for those petitions which directly concerne God in his glory, and the meanes thereof, his Kingdome and will.

Now follow the prayers which directly concerne our selues, both in regarde of matters temporal for the body, and also of matters spirituall for the soule : from which order vsed by our Sauiour Christ, there is offered vnto vs this instruction ; that our good dependeth vpon, and issueth from Gods glory, and is a necessarie consequent thereof ; or thus : when men are carefull to glorifie Gods name, to aduance his Kingdome, and to obey his will, then our daily bread, and all other good followeth thereupon : and contrarily, when men dishonor God, hinder his Kingdom, and transgresse his commaundements, thence issueth all woe and miserie. This doctrine is the summe of the law, in the promises and the threatnings annexed to the obedience or disobedience thereof. The summe of this doctrine is expressed by *Moses* largely in Deuteronomie : especially, Cap. 28. And the Lord commaundeth *Moses* to cause sixe Tribes to proclame the blessing and promises to obedience vpon mount Gerizim, and other sixe Tribes to stand vpon mount Eball to pronounce the curse to the disobedience of the law : the which two mountaines were two strong witnesses (as it were) to the people of their consent to obey and to receiue the promise : or else disobeying of the curse of God deseruedly to befall them : Christ teacheth that the Kingdome of God and his righteousnes hath all temporall blessings annexed thereto : and the Apostle *Paul* saith, *Godlines hath the promise of this life, and the life to*

Deut. 28.
Leuit. 26.
Deut. 27.

Mat. 6. 33.
1. *Tim.* 4. 8.

come : and by Christs speech to the man that was sicke of the palsie, he doth plainly signifie that sinne is the cause of all sicknes, and the remission of *Mark. 2. 5.* sin the meanes of remouing the curse : which doctrine yeeldeth a profitable vse for the time of Gods iudgements vpon vs : that then we are assured that the cause is sinne : and therefore wee are carefully to enquire what sinnes raigne most, and to assure our selues that those sinnes are the greatest cause : and that there is no reason wee should thinke that Gods iudgements shall be remoued, till those sinnes bee reformed : this especially concerneth the Magistrates, who may with the sword and authoritie ; and the Ministers, who by the power of their Ministerie may worke conuersion and reformation, that the curse may cease from the land. And this is the doctrine and vse which groweth from the order of the three first petitions concerning Gods glorie, before the three latter respecting our good.

Now these three latter petitions admit this distribution also: for they respect blessings temporall or spirituall: the petition which is made concerning temporall blessings, is this.

Giue vs this day our daily bread.

1 Concerning the order of this petition for things temporall, before the other two which intend things spirituall, this question may bee mooued: *viz.* Whether temporall blessings are first to be asked in prayer ; or else why should Christ prescribe this order of prayer for things temporall, before spirituall ? To which question or doubt, answere may be made in this manner following.

Order of the fourth petition.

First, Christ rather signifieth vnto vs our corruption, telling vs what wee doe, than instructeth vs in our dutie, teaching vs what wee should doe, although this latter ariseth from the former (for a reproofe of our fault implieth an intimation of our dutie.) For first wee should seeke for the pardon of our sinnes, then after and in the second place for daily bread, so Christ expressely teacheth : yet we contrarily doe seeke earthly things more a great deale and in the first place ; the reason whereof is, for

The order of the fourth petition reprooueth our Corruption.

Mat. 6. 33.

A paterne of true Prayer 187

that wee liue by sense, and not by faith; whereas we
should (as the Apostle saith) liue by faith, and not by
sense: and so this order reproueth our corruption, and teacheth vs our dutie, which is
not to make worldly things our greatest care.

2 Cor. 5. 7.

Secondly, some men trusting in God for the pardon of
their sinnes, yet distrust God for the prouision
of their bodies; and so Christ in regard of
their infirmitie and want doth in this order
condescend vnto them, teaching them first to
pray for that which they most neede, *viz.* grace to depend
vpon God for outward matters: a thing wherein Gods
children faile mightily. Hence it is that Christ doth so
earnestly labour with his disciples to cast away
immoderate, distrustfull, and distracting care
for outward prouision, sending them to learne of the
fowles of the ayre, and of the lillies of the field. And the
manner of the Apostles argument in the Epistle to the
Romanes doth import as much, saying, *If God giue vs
Christ, shall hee not giue vs with Christ all things
else?* As if so be that when wee had Christ, we
doubted whether wee should haue other things needfull:
and indeede so ordinarily wee doe. For, besides that
Gods children are regenerate to the enduring of the crosse,
which is an inseparable concomitant of Christianitie, it is
true also that they are straightned in their consciences,
being not able to vse those indirect and vnlawfull meanes
for the supplie of outward wants, as the wicked worldlings
can, and doe vse, without any present sensible disturbance
of their peace: and therefore the godly wanting many
meanes of their daily bread, and being by Gods predestination called to some scarsitie thereof, no marueile though
they bestow their cogitations and affections more liberally
in the prouision of outward needes by lawfull meanes,
therein in part bewraying their infirmitie, and
little faith in Gods prouidence for the world:
which little faith Christ in this order partly rebuketh,
partly confirmeth by instruction. The same thing is to
bee obserued by our Sauiour Christs mandate
and commission deliuered to his disciples when
hee sent them to teach: neuer a whit strengthening them

The order of the fourth petition strengthen-eth our infirmitie.

Mat. 6. 24. 25. 26. 27. &c.

Rom. 8. 32.

Mat. 6. 30.

Mat. 10. 9. 17.

in the assurance of the forgiuenes of their sinnes, but many waies encouraging them against persecution and want of daily bread, insinuating their infirmitie herein.

Thirdly, Christ by this method doth traine vs vp as it were by certaine rudiments, and teacheth vs to ascend to the great and maine matters, as it were to the top of the staiers by these lower degrees. For as it is impossible for a man to come to the vpper roome but by staiers; so it is impossible for a man to attaine fulnes of faith for pardon of sinne, but by these inferiour exercises of faith, which are to depend vpon God for the lesser matters, as our daily bread. For howsoeuer to Gods children, hauing grace in some small measure, and assurance of pardon of their sin, the want of outward matters seemeth the greatest trouble, and therein they bewray their greatest infirmitie: yet indeede and in truth the pardon of sinne, and the assurance thereof when the conscience is possessed with the feeling of sinne and Gods wrath, is the greatest matter, and at that time the trouble for daily bread is nothing, or not sensible in comparison of the feare and doubt of the forgiuenes of sinne.

The order of the fourth petition teacheth vs some meanes of faith.

This three-fold reason of the order of this petition for daily bread before the petition for grace, affoordeth one doctrine, which may be distinguished into three branches.

First, our greatest care must be for spirituall matters.

Secondly, we must learne to depend vpon God for our daily bread, and temporall matters.

Thirdly, the temporall blessings which God vouchsafeth his children, ought of them to be vsed as arguments and meanes of the assurance of remission of sinnes.

Of each of these doctrines something.

In the first place seeing (as hath been said) this method reprooueth our corruption in the immoderate care for the world, by consequent it discouereth our dutie, which is to busie our selues more in obtaining pardon of sinne and grace than in seeking the world. *Dauid* opposeth the worldlings care and his care, saying: *Many say, Who will shew vs any good?* but Gods people say: *Lord lift the light of thy countenance vpon vs:* signifying their greater desire

Grace must be first and principally sought.

Psal. 4. 6.

of grace than of the worlds good : seeing that wee are risen with Christ (as the Apostle saith) let vs set our hearts on heauenly things, and not on earthly things. For the soule being the principall part of the man, those things which appertaine to the soule must be principall also, and so principally regarded : now in the Scriptures wee see oft times the soule onely named, as if that were onely to bee regarded, for indeede the soules health is the fountaine of the bodies good, and the good of the bodie is a necessarie dependant of the good of the soule : for when the soule is saued the bodie cannot perish. Hence it is that Christ and *Steuen* being readie to die, bequethed their soules onely into Gods hands : for they knew right well that hee that receiued the soule, would not reiect the bodie appertaining to the soule.

Colos. 3. 1. 2.

1. *Pet.* 1. 9.

Luk. 23. 46.
Act. 7. 59.

In the second place, howsoeuer wee are chiefly to seeke the soules good, yet wee are not to cast off all care for the bodie ; because God in giuing vs a bodie giueth therewithall a signification that it ought to bee prouided for : and in that God hath created fruites, and herbes, and flesh, and other parts of our daily bread, hee insinuateth the vse of them, and a care to be had for them : and seeing he hath inspired into men diuers artes manuarie of preparing and fitting our daily bread for our vse, the moderate vse wherof is lawfull, as of the Cooke and Apothecarie, &c. thereby the Lord doth giue vs to vnderstand that sometime, and therefore some care may bee bestowed to that end. Here two extremities occurre : carelesnes, and that in the defect ; and carefulnes in the excesse : The one, that is, immoderate and distrustfull care, distracting the minde from the chiefe care equallizeth vs with the Heathen, and argueth little faith : the other, *viz.* no care, no prouision, no foresight and prouidence for our daily bread maketh vs worse than Infidels, and is a plaine argument that we haue denied the faith, which establisheth the meanes of life : for God will haue vs liue ordinarily by bread : and the Pismire shal teach the sluggard labour and prouidence, as

The body must be prouided for.

Exod. 30. 23. 25.
Exod. 35. 30. 31.

Mat. 6. 32. 30.

1. *Tim.* 5. 8.

Pro. 6. 6.

the Wiseman morallizeth: wherefore as a moderate care argueth faith in Gods prouidence; so an immoderate care, or no care, denieth faith, and maketh men brutish or heathnish.

In the third place: As wee are to seeke the good of the body aswell, though not as much, as the good of the soule; so the good things we obtaine of God for the bodie, ought of vs to bee applied as arguments of confirming our faith, for the obtaining the best things for the soule, and we must make them so many pledges and seales of Gods loue and mercie to vs in Christ Iesus: for otherwise wee partake in Gods blessings, which respect our daily bread no otherwise than the bruite beasts or the wicked, who haue many good things from Gods generall bountie and liberalitie, but not from his speciall goodnes and mercie. Wee reade that the land of Canaan was by faith inherited of the Israelites, that by faith they passed through the red sea, and many other temporall blessings were through faith receiued by them: which is thus to be vnderstood, *viz.* by faith they receiued these temporall deliuerances and blessings, and vsed them as seales and pledges of heauen and heauenly blessings, whereof the former were types onely. And this is to rise from earth to heauen; from the daily bread of the bodie, to the spirituall bread of life; to support and vnderprop our faith in Christ for the remission of our sinnes, and the saluation of our soules, with the earthlie pillars of meate, and drinke, and apparell, and what other things are the staffe and stay of our bodily life. This doctrine the outward shape of the Sacrament seemeth to teach vs: for there is bread and wine, the nourishers and comforters of our life: whereby the Lord doth seale vp vnto vs the spirituall nourishment and comfort of our soules, heauenly matters in earthly creatures. In like manner by analogie and proportion, though not sacramentally, yet by discourse of reason and by a worke of faith wee may allegorize all outward matters. As for example; God giueth vs clothes for to couer our nakednes, therefore hee will giue vnto vs the wedding garment of Christs righteousnesse to couer our sinnes: God giueth the light of the Sunne for

Temporal blessings must be pledges of spirituall grace.

Heb. 11. 30. 31.

our comfort, therefore he will giue vs the light of his countenance in mercie to lighten our darknes and affliction. And thus we may ascend from things visible, sensible, and palpable, to things inuisible, insensible, and intelligible: and with the Apostle *Iohn* say, that wee see, feele, taste, and handle the Lord Iesus Christ: yea and grope him in these outward matters, as *Paul* saith the Gentiles might haue done God. And this may bee sufficient for the three particular branches of that doctrine which riseth from the order here vsed by our Sauiour Christ, in preferring the petition for daily bread to the petition for grace.

1. *Ioh.* 1. 1.

Act. 17. 27.

2 Now followeth the second thing to bee considered in this petition, which is the meaning of the words: for the discussing of the particular words we are to remember this distinction.

The meaning of this petition.
What bread signifieth.

This prayer containeth, *Rem, & rei circumstantias,* the subiect and the adiuncts: that which is desired, and the circumstances thereto appertaining.

That which is here desired is generally called *Bread.*

The circumstances hereto appertaining are fiue following.

First circumstance is, *Modus acquirendi:* the manner of obtaining the bread: which is by free gift (*Giue.*)

Second circumstance is, *Persona,* the persons for whom wee aske this donation or gift of bread (*vs*) viz. our selues and others.

Third circumstance is, *Tempus,* for how long time wee begge this bread (*this day*) for the present.

Fourth circumstance is, *Qualitas,* the condition of that bread which we aske (*daily bread*) for repairing our life.

Fifth circumstance is, *Dominus,* the owner, or to whom the bread appertaineth (*ours*) to the children of God.

Of all which circumstances, with the subiect thereof, something must be vttered. First therefore of *Bread.*

Bread, as some of the ancient Fathers interpret, signifieth Christ Iesus, which is that bread of life, or liuing bread, that bread that came downe from heauen, or heauenly bread: and so they expound that other word *supersubstantiall,* that is, celestiall or

What bread signifieth.

heauenly: according as Christ saith: *I am the liuing bread which came downe from heauen.* To this exposition some of the new writers incline. *Ioh.* 6. 51.

Others, and namely the greater and better part of ancient and new writers (to whose iudgement as it is meete we subscribe in such a matter of doubt not determined in Scripture) expound the bread here named the corporall bread, the foode of our bodies: yet so as the word containeth a *Synecdoche*, bread being put for all outward prouision: so that bread here must signifie three things.

First, *bona corporis*, the good things of the bodie: which may be generally called health, or the due constitution and temperature of the bodie: whereto appertaineth Nourishment, Apparell, Recreation, and Physicke. *Bona corporis a part of bread.*

Secondly, *Bona fortunæ* (if the word fortune may be tolerated) namely such outward good things as doe indifferently befall good and bad men: viz. *Bona fortunę, a part of bread. Eccles.* 9. 11.

1. Wealth, 2. Honour, 3. Libertie, 4. Peace, 5. Plentie: whereto appertaine, 6. Labour in our callings, 7. Magistracie, 8. Fruitfull seasons.

Thirdly, the blessing of God vpon all the former good things, whether inherent in the bodie, or adherent thereto. Now that bread may generally signifie all these things, it is apparant by that excellent speech of *Moses*, repeated by Christ; that, *Man liueth not by bread only, but by euery word which commeth out of the mouth of God:* but more especially this signification of bread may bee collected out of the Prophet *Esay:* where the Lord threatneth to take away the stay of bread, and then as it were exemplifying or particularizing the matter, hee threatneth to take away the strong man, the man of warre, the Iudge, the Counsellor, the Artificer, and the Orator, &c. as if al these were parts of bread: but the Prophet *Moses* in Leuiticus doth plainly signifie, that Gods blessing is a most essential part of bread: saying, that because the Lord shall breake the staffe of bread, therefore they shall eate and not be *Gods blessing a part of bread. Deut.* 8. 3. *Mat.* 4. 4. *Esay.* 3. 1. 2. 3. *Leuit.* 26. 26.

satisfied. Summarily therefore bread signifieth euery outward helpe, and the blessing of God helping the said outward helpe, that it may effect that for which we vse it. For example sake, after Physicke health, through Gods blessing vpon Physick; warmth by apparell; wealth through our labour: in wealth libertie, peace and plentie, mirth and ioy of heart, with a quiet minde voide of feare. All which, with many other, are our daily bread here signified.

But before wee leaue this first point, this doubt is to bee cleered: wherefore Christ nameth bread rather than any other particular part of outward prouision. For answere whereof wee are to vnderstand, that of outward matters some are absolutely necessarie for our being, as foode; others not so, but onely requisite for our better and more happie being, as apparell: now of those things which pertaine to our being, and the continuance of our life, bread is the chiefe: for wee can bee better without flesh, or fish, or whit[e] meate, than without bread: for water is only the outward moistning of bread, & hath no nourishment in it self, but onely as it doth partake bread, that is, the substance of corne, or so foorth. Hence it is that the word in the Greeke tongue hath the notation from sustaining the frame of the bodie: as though without it the frame of the bodie could not continue. To conclude this point therefore: seeing bread is the thing most needful for our life, Christ teacheth vs to aske that, thereby confining our inordinate and infinite affections: and this is the subiect of the circumstances. Now follow the circumstances: first, *Modus acquirendi.*

<small>Wherefore Christ nameth bread.</small>

The meanes of obtaining this bread, is by the free donation and gift of God: for whatsoeuer we haue to enioy, it commeth from the meere liberalitie of God, yea though wee haue gotten it by our labour or industrie; though it come by inheritance, or wee haue it by the gift of friends: for as *Moses* saith in the booke of Deuteronomie, God giueth vs power to get substance, and it is Gods gift that we are descended of parents that haue great substance, and God stirreth vp the hearts of our

<small>We obtaine bread by gift from God.</small>

<small>*Deut.* 8. 17. 18.</small>

benefactors to bestow their gifts vpon vs. Here therefore pride is rebuked: for what haue we that we haue not receiued? and hauing receiued it, there is no reason we should boast as though wee had not receiued it. *Pride rebuked. 1. Cor. 4. 7.*

Now for more euidence of this circumstance, a double obiection must be answered: for first it may bee thought vnnecessarie for him to aske bread that hath bread: now there be many men that haue bread enough, namely, such as abound in the riches and honour of the world: wherefore it may rather seeme needfull for poore people to make this prayer, that want their daily bread, than for all sorts of persons indifferently. For answere whereof wee may consider, that there is a double interest and title to the creatures, or to bread: namely, ciuill, and religious. Rich men, many of them, haue a ciuill title to the riches which they possesse: for amongst men hee that robbeth the rich man shall be counted a theefe, as taking another mans goods, seeing that by the law of the nation where he dwelleth, euery mans goods are ciuilly confirmed vnto him in the proprietie thereof: but neuerthelesse euery rich man hath not in the Lords sight and estimation a religious interest vnto his goods: for if he be a wicked man, out of the communion of Saints, no member of the Church Catholike, he is but a meere vsurper of all his substance, and therefore hath need to aske this second interest to his goods of God, whose is the earth and all that therein is, and who only giueth his creatures through Christ Iesus to the faithfull his friends, and not to the wicked his enemies. *Psal. 24. 1.*

Secondly, it will further be obiected, that Gods seruants that are rich neede not aske their daily bread of God, seeing they haue before men the ciuill title to their goods, and before God a religious interest also, they being Gods friends, and members of Iesus Christ, through whom they are made the heires of all things. But for answere of this obiection also wee must remember to distinguish betwixt the title to the bread, or the vse of the bread, and the benefit or commoditie which is reaped by the bread, or by the vse of the bread: for the children of God oft times vse bread, and yet haue no benefit by

A paterne of true Prayer

the vse thereof: as they vse mariage, and want children; they vse Physicke, and recouer not their health: therefore Gods children are taught to aske a staffe to their bread, Gods powerfull word or blessing vpon the meanes, without which man cannot liue: and hence it is that all Gods creatures and ordinances must bee sanctified by prayer, as the Apostle teacheth.

<small>1. Tim. 4.</small>

This prayer then includeth these foure particulars following.

First, Lord giue vs a ciuill title to bread.
Secondly, Lord giue vs a religious title to bread.
Thirdly, Lord giue vs leaue to vse the bread.
Fourthly, Lord giue vs comfort by the vse of the bread.

The first is opposed to pouertie: the second to vsurpation: the third to the taking of Gods name in vaine: the fourth to the curse or withdrawing the staffe of bread.

This is the first circumstance; the second followeth, which is *Persona*, the person for whom wee aske bread.

<small>For whom we aske bread.</small>

We desire bread for others aswell as for our selues: euen as in the next petition we desire forgiuenes of sinne for other men aswell as for our selues: whence wee learne to suppresse enuie, which Christ calleth an euill eye: and as the Apostle saith, *to reioyce with them that reioyce:* and as Christ teacheth, to pray for our enemies, and persecutors: but especially for them that are in the communion of Saints: not to fret our selues at the prosperitie of the wicked: nor to maligne Gods gifts or graces in other men, as *Iosua* for his masters sake did enuie the gift of prophecie in *Eldad* and *Medad*.

<small>Enuie supprest.</small>
<small>Mat. 20. 15.</small>
<small>Rom. 12. 15.</small>
<small>Psal. 37. 1.</small>
<small>Numb. 11. 29.</small>

The third circumstance followeth, which is *Tempus*, the time how long, and so consequently how oft we aske this bread: for the latter groweth out of the former, as shall easily be perceiued. For seeing wee aske bread but for the day, when the next day commeth we are to aske it againe, and so as God renueth the day, or occasion of vsing bread, we in like manner renew our prayers for a blessing vpon the bread. The word expressing this circumstance thus

<small>When we aske bread: also for how long: and how oft.</small>

distinguished, is (*semeron*) to day: or (*to cath emeran*) appertaining to the day; the one being the exposition of the other: which word or phrase of speech importeth two things. *Matth.* 6. *Luk.* 11.

First, that euery day wee neede the vse of the bread, because that Christ doth teach vs euery day to aske bread with the sanctified vse thereof, and Gods blessing therevpon. *Bread is alway needefull.*

Secondly, that seeing wee aske bread onely for the day, therefore wee must be content with our present estate, and depend vpon God for the time to come, for euery day hath care enough. *Contentment: and faith. Mat.* 6. 34. And here two questions are to bee discussed, which follow.

First, whether may not a man aske riches at Gods hands? This question ariseth necessarily from the circumstance, whereas Christ teacheth vs to aske bread only for the day: it may bee doubted therefore whether it be lawfull or not to aske bread for the time to come: whereto answer may be made Negatiuely, that a man must not desire to be rich, and so must not aske riches at Gods hands: which may be prooued by many reasons. *Whether it be lawfull to aske riches.*

1. First, the Apostle saith, that a desire to be rich occasioneth temptations and snares, many daungerous and noysome lusts, which drowne men in perdition and destruction: and our Sauiour Christ in the same sense saith, that riches are snares to intangle men in the diuels net: but we are not to pray for the occasions of sinne, seeing that wee must auoide the occasions of sinne. *1. Tim.* 6. 9. 10. *Mat.* 13. 22.

2. Againe, a desire to bee rich argueth discontentment: but this is a fault, for we must be content with that portion of our daily bread which God giueth vs, yea though it bee but meate and raiment, as the Apostle saith. Now that, whose fountaine or cause is euill, cannot be good: wherefore discontentment being an euil cause impulsiue of desiring riches, the desire of riches is a sinne also. *1. Tim.* 6. 8.

3. Further, couetousnes is a sinne: but a desire to be rich is couetousnes: for the two Greeke words in their

notations differ not in substance and signification, how-
<small>Pleonexia.</small> soeuer they differ in letters and pronunciation:
<small>Philargyria.</small> the one signifieth a loue of siluer, the other a desire of hauing much.

4. Besides this, in the Prouerbs *Agur* prayeth only
<small>Pro. 30. 8.</small> for food conuenient for him, that is, for daily
<small>To pray for a competency lawfull.</small> bread, & he doth by negation remoue from him the desire of riches: which example being not contradicted by any rule of Diuinitie, is a perpetual rule of direction for vs: and the Lord himself testifieth in granting *Salomons* petition, that hee was
<small>1. King 3. 11.</small> pleased that *Salomon* asked not riches: and
<small>1. Tim. 6.</small> it seemeth the Apostles scope in the former place of *Timothy* affoordeth thus much; that a desire to be rich is sinne.

The conclusion then followeth, which is the solution of the doubt, that wee must not pray for riches, nor against them: but we must proceede in the practise of the duties of our callings, intending Gods glory, the benefit of Societies, and prouision for those that appertaine to vs: and if God blesse vs with riches, to bee thankfull and to bestow them well; if hee send pouertie, to beare it patiently and thankfully, as a part of our daily bread, or an adiunct thereof.

The second question to bee handled is: whether a man may lay vp any thing in store for time to come, and so by this meanes care for the time to come: which question also riseth from this circumstance: for when Christ teacheth to aske bread for the day, it may seeme we should not respect the morrow: whereto this answere may bee made: That a man may lay vp in store for a time to come, and therefore may haue some prouidence and respect to the time to come: for God hath giuen man reason and foresight, which is to be vsed for the preuenting of euill, and the procuring of our good, not only for the soule, but for the body also: And Christ himselfe in the gospell by *Iohn* willeth his Disciples to gather vp the broken meat, and in that it is <small>Ioh. 6. 12.</small>
reported that *Iudas* caried the bag and was <small>Ioh. 12. 6.</small>
Christs purse-bearer, and that at other times <small>Ioh. 6.</small>
they caried loaues and fishes with them, it is plaine that

the familie of Christ had a regard of the time to come: also the Apostle *Paul* signifieth this laudable custome of parents treasuring vp for the children. Hence it is that in the Scripture there are diuers precepts of frugallity, thrift, or parsimonie: and all that good huswifery mentioned in the prophecie of *Bathsheba* apertayneth to this place: and the Apostle saith that this is one end of labour that we may haue something to bestow vpon them that neede. But here it may bee obiected, that Christ forbiddeth to lay vp treasure in store, because the moth and rust wil corrupt, and theeues wil breake through and steale: but that is easily answered; for Christ doth not speake simply, but comparatiuely, as if Christ should haue said; Seeke not worldly treasures, chiefly, immoderatly, onely: nay, they must not be sought for at all, but treasure them not vp so as that yee neglect the heauenly treasure, *viz.* inordinately.

2. Cor. 12. 14.

Prou. 27. 23.
& 31. 16.

Ephes. 4. 28.
Matth. 6. 19.

Againe, it may be obiected that Christ expresly forbiddeth the care for the morrow, for euery day hath sorrow enough of it owne, and we must not aggrauate it with future care and sorrow: but the answere thereto also is apparant by the intendement of Christ: for Christ in that place laboreth to suppresse distrustfull, and distracting care which deuideth the minde from God and Gods seruice: but Christ forbiddeth not prouidence, or foresight, or prouision for the time to come, which the Apostle doth directly require in the gouernor of a family: yet neuerthelesse concerning this laying vp in store and moderate prouident care, some cautions must bee remembred: as first, that our goods which we treasure vp, be gotten with our honest labor, or that we come by them by inheritance or gift, or by some such lawfull meanes; not by gaming or cosoning. Secondly, that if our riches increase we trust not in them.

Mat. 6. 34.

Merimne.

Pronoia.
1. *Tim.* 5. 8.

Ephes. 4. 28.

Psal. 62. 10.

Thirdly, that wee doe not treasure them vp when wee should spend them in the needfull vses of the Church or common-wealth: for such times are vnfit times for storing vp. And in this respect the Apostle commendeth the Church of the Macedonians, for that they were liberall in their extreame pouertie, the necessitie of other Churches requiring it.

2. Cor. 8. 1.
2. 3.

Lastly, when we haue treasured vp riches, we must not keepe them niggardly, but we must bestow to the good of our selues and others, such a portion of our treasure as shall be requisit, and befitting our estate, wherein sometime we are to passe the bounds of our abilitie; in which respect Christ also commendeth the widowes almes of two mites.

Mark. 12. 44.

It is apparant then, these cautions obserued, that storing vp, and prouident care is not vnlawfull, but very meete : which serueth to ouerthrow that ouerlashing and swaggering disposition of riotous vnthrifts, which like vnto the prodigall sonne consume all their substance, so as at length they are brought to a morsell of bread, and charge others with themselues and theirs; whereas their patrimonie being moderately ordered according to their estate, might haue not onely been preserued entire with the maintenance and reliefe of many poore, but also out of the encrease and vse thereof much might haue been treasured vp, for their posteritie. For a conclusion therefore of this circumstance, couetousnes is a sinne, and so is prodigalitie: liberalitie and magnificence are vertues, so are also parsimony and frugalitie, which by this consideration are insinuated vnto vs.

The fourth circumstance followeth, which is *qualitas*, the condition or vse of the bread. The greeke word expressing this circumstance is translated (*daily*) *epiousion* : which the Etymologist expoundeth, *befitting our substance or being:* namely, such a bread as is meete and conuenient for the preseruation of our being: and the bread we aske hath this epithite adioyned in two respects.

What vse the bread hath.
O epi te ousia armozon.

One is : for that our essence and being is in a continuall flux, and, as I may so say, a naturall consumption : for mortalitie, which is inflicted vpon vs by God, draweth vs euery day to corruption, and we doe as naturally incline thereto, as the fire goeth vpward : wherefore the Lord in his mercie hath prouided bread, which shall stay this declining of our nature in

Genes. 2. 17.

part, and repaire the ruine of our essence; that as the naturall lampe of our life, consisting of fire and oyle, spendeth and wasteth; so there may be a new supply made by the fat of wheate, as the Prophet speaketh; till at the length the light of our life be extinct or suffocated, either by old age, when the wicke is spent, or by disease and sudden death, when the heate is choked, or wanteth oyle. Calor natiuus
Humidum radicale.
Psal. 81. 16.

Another respect why the bread is so intitled, is, for that this bread can neuer bee added to our substance for the repaire thereof, except the Lord giue a blessing thereto: for as the Prophet saith, we may eate and not haue enough, drinke and not bee satisfied, vse marriage, and want children, earne wages and put it into a bottomles bagge: for howsoeuer the faculties of nourishment doth naturally worke in the stomacke and other parts, and howsoeuer the bread hath in it a foyson or iuice fit for nourishment, yet the Lord he can suspend the one and the other, so as they shall neither of them performe their offices: for he can stay the worke of all the secondarie causes: and hee can worke without the helpe of any secundarie cause. Hence therefore wee are taught, both to vse the bread, it being the meanes God hath appointed for our preseruation: and also not to trust in the bread, seeing that it cannot helpe vs if God suspend the vertue thereof: more plainely, two sinnes are here discouered, and secretly reproued. Leuit. 26.
Hag. 1. 6.

First, tempting of God, which is drawing too neere God.

Second is a secret idolatry, withdrawing our selues from God.

All they tempt God which neglecting the bread, which is the ordinary helpe of our life, doe cast themselues vpon the immediate prouidence of God: as the diuell perswaded our Sauiour Christ to cast himselfe downe headlong from the pinacle of the temple, when hee might come downe the staires: for God will not haue vs neglect or despise the meanes which he hath giuen vs. Mat. 4. 6.

All they withdraw themselues from God which make idols of the bread, which vse the bread, and neuer aske a blessing at Gods hands vpon the bread, as if God were tied to giue his blessing to the bread necessarily: this is the sinne which is oft times reproued by the Prophets: for example, to trust in chariots and horses: to trust in Princes, to trust in the Physition, generally to trust in an arme of flesh.

The fifth and last circumstance followeth, which is *Dominus*, whose the bread is, or the owner of it. Christ calleth it our bread, and that in diuers respects.

<small>Whose the bread is.</small>

1. For that it is so indeede, wee hauing gotten it by our labour and industry, or hauing it by inheritance or gift of friends: and according to this construction the Apostle willeth the Thessalonians to eate their owne bread which they haue earned with the labours of their hands: this is the ciuill title which is called *ius adrem*.

<small>2. Thes. 3. 12.</small>

2. For that it is the childrens bread, according as Christ saith to the Canaanitish woman: which was through *Adams* fall lost, but now through Christs redemption is restored to vs againe, as appeareth plainely by the Prophet in the Psalme. And this is called *ius in re*, the religious title.

<small>Mat. 15. 26.</small>

<small>Psal. 8.</small>

3. For that we desire no more of the bread than is fit for vs, as *Agur* prayeth in his prophesie: and the Lord sutably doth bestow vpon vs onely, and all that part of the bread which is good for vs: for we see that diuers of Gods children haue seuerall and different portions of this bread: *Abraham* hee had abundance: *Lazarus* was scanted; yet each of them had his bread, euen a portion conuenient for him. So that this last circumstance insinuateth vnto vs three vertues.

<small>Prou. 30.</small>

<small>Psal. 34. 10.</small>
<small>Rom. 8. 28.</small>

1. Industrie, which is in some honest calling to get our liuing with the sweate of our browes: and not to walke inordinately, yea though thou haue great liuing and possessions of thine owne. For although it may seeme needles for him to labour which is wealthie, yet indeede there is an ineuitable necessitie thereof. For besides that God hath imposed this yoke vpon all in *Adam* to eate the labours of their hands, and the sweate of their browes, and so they which doe not labour

<small>Genes. 3. 19.</small>
<small>Psal. 128. 2.</small>

walke inordinatly, *viz.* as a souldier out of his ranke; the Apostle also saith that he which doth not labour, should not eate: and one end of laboring in a calling is, that we may haue the more to bestow vpon them that want: therefore *2. Thes. 3. 10. 7.* *Ephes. 4. 28.* euen the King himselfe, the Iudge, and the Counsellor, and the Minister is to sweate for his liuing, though he dig not with the spade: which is when the mind laboreth and trauelleth in thought, and counsell, and care, and prouidence, and instruction, dropping as it were an inuisible sweate from the browes of the vnderstanding, and the inward parts of the soule.

2. Thankfulnes to the Lord, that he hath restored to vs that interest which was lost through *Adams* fall: that we may freely and with good conscience vse any part of the bread which is our owne; not onely for our necessitie, but euen for our moderate delight and comfort, seeing that God hath giuen wine to comfort the heart, and oyle to make the face shine, *Psal. 104. 15.* *Psal. 23. 5.* and *Dauid* had his head annoynted with oyle.

3. Contentment in our estate whatsoeuer, seeing that is the best estate, and that part of the bread is most fit and meete for vs: for howsoeuer perhaps we doe not so thinke, yet surely if wee finde in our selues the markes of Gods election, and if we labour to obserue the worke of God vpon vs at that time, wee shall be compelled to say from our owne experience, that then God in wisedome saw such a portion was best for vs. *Psal. 119. 71.*

These are the circumstances annexed to the bread.

3 Next in order followeth the third thing to bee obserued in the petition, which is the Supplication: the things therefore which wee here aske of God, are these following.

The supplication of the fourth petition.

First, things generall, whereof some are causes, some effects: causes are especially these sixe.

1. Fruitfull seasons, with all the meanes procuring them: as the first and latter raine; frost, and snow, mist, and dew, and whatsoeuer other creatures God hath appointed for that purpose. *Deut. 28. 12.*

2. The due simpathy of the creatures consenting

together, as when the heauens heare the earth, the earth heareth the corne, wine, and oyle, and they heare Gods people.

Hosea. 2. 21.

3. Wise and prouident Magistrates that may enact holsome lawes, for the peaceable gouernment of the common-wealth, and by lawfull and iust warre defend the subiect and countrie.

1. *Tim.* 2. 2.

4. Learned and conscionable Iudges and Lawyers, that may iustly and mercifully execute iudgement, accusing, defending, pleading, and iudging according to the aforesaid good lawes.

Numb. 16. 16. 26.

5. Valiant and Christian Captaines and Souldiers, which may resolutely fight the Lords battels against his enemies, such as were the thirtie seauen worthies in *Dauids* Kingdome.

2. *Sam.* 23. 39.

6. Conscionable and experienced and learned physitions, for the health of the body: and generally all good manuary arts and trades with their skilfull professors, which labour for the preparing of meate, apparrell and their instruments: and in making weapons for warre, &c.

Exod. 30. 25. & 35. 30. 31.

After the aforesaid causes follow certaine effects which we pray for in this petition.

1. Peace: when euery man may quietly sit downe vnder his vine and figtree, when there is no leading into captiuitie, no complaining in our streetes of women that leese their husbands, or of orphanes leesing their parents in warre.

Psal. 144. 14.

2. Plentie: that our sonnes and daughters may bee as the young plants which come vp thicke out of the ground; that our garners may be full with corne, that our sheepe may bring foorth thousands and ten thousand; and that we may lend and not borow.

Psal. 144. 13. *Deut.* 28. 13.

3. Health: that there bee no feeble person among vs, that our oxen also may bee strong to labour, that our sonnes and daughters may bee as the polished corners of the temple.

Psal. 144. 12.

The generals being numbred, the specials followe: which being handled before in the meaning of the words of the petition, shall onely neede in this place to be shortly repeated.

1. The staffe of bread, or Gods blessing vpon the bread.
2. Humilitie, seeing God giueth vs the bread.
3. Contentment with whatsoeuer estate we be in.
4. Faith in Gods prouidence for things meete for vs.
5. Prouidence or moderate care for the time to come.
6. Painfulnes and labour in our vocation and calling.
7. Thankfulnes that God permitteth vs the vse of the bread.
8. Ioy of heart at the outward prosperitie of others.
9. Frugalitie or parsimonie to spare when we neede not spend.
10. Liberalitie, to bestow of our abundance to supplie others wants.
11. Magnificence to bestow bountifully vpon Church or Common-wealth, as in erecting Colleges, Hospitals, making high waies, &c.

These are the principall things we pray for in this petition.

4 The things that we pray against may easily be gathered by the contrary: yet for plainnes sake it shall not be amisse for to number them thus.

<small>The deprecation of the fourth petition.</small>

1. Vnfruitfull seasons, as a wet and cold summer, a hot and drie winter: no raine, no frost, no snow, &c.
2. The Antipathie of the creatures, when the heauen becommeth brasse, and the earth iron, &c. Deut. 28.
3. Foolish, childish, and improuident Magistrates or tyrants, that make pernitious and hurtfull lawes, Esay. 3. Eccles. 10.
4. Vnlearned and wicked Iudges and Lawyers, Esay. 3.
5. Vnskilfull and vnconscionable Physitions, as wise women, Witches, or Wizards, professing Physick and Empiricks, that gesse onely and want skill.
6. Cowardly Captaines, and dastardly souldiers, when as tenne flie before one, and a hundred before tenne, &c.
7. Warre. 8. Scarsitie or famine. 9. Sicknes, as the plague or other mortall diseases epidemiall.
10. Breaking the staffe of bread.
11. Pride. 12. Discontentment. 13. Immoderate or no care for things needfull.

A paterne of true Prayer 205

14. Idlenes. 15. Vnthankfulnes.
16. Enuie. 17. Couetousnes. 18. Prodigalitie.
19. All vnlawfull Arts and Trades to get bread.
20. All gaming to get our liuing by, 2. Thess. 3. 10.
This also may suffice for the deprecation.

5 The thanksgiuing may easily bee collected out of the supplication and deprecation : for wee are to praise God for the good things vpon vs, and the euils kept from vs. Wherein wee may easily runne through all the aforesaid vertues and vices, good and bad.

The thanksgiuing of the fourth petition.

For conclusion of this petition therefore, hitherto appertaineth the fifth commandement especially. Againe, these places of Scripture following, are as it were Commentaries to this petition, or rather indices thereof.

The whole 28. chapter of Deuteronomy.
The whole 26. chapter of Leuiticus.
The beginning of the third chapter of *Esay*.
Psalme the 144. the 12. 13. 14. 15. verses.
The sixt chapter of the first epistle to *Timothy*.
The sixt chapter of the Gospell by *Matthew*.
Prou. the 31. the whole chapter, and such like.

Now after the petition for things temporall, follow the petitions for things spirituall, namely for grace and perseuerance in grace. The fifth petition is for Grace.

Forgiue vs our debts : as we forgiue our debtors.

1 This petition for grace or remission of sinne is in nature before the petition for perseuerance : for first a man must haue grace before he can perseuere in grace : whence ariseth this doctrine : A man must be a righteous man, before he can leade the life and die the death of a righteous man : A man must first haue remission of sinne, and the righteousnes of Christ iustifying and sanctifying him, before hee can resist temptation, fight the spirituall combat against the spirituall enemie, and be deliuered from the euill of sin and the curse. More distinctly and plainly these particulars doe arise from this method.

Order of the fifth petition.

First, he onely that hath grace can resist temptation.
Secondly, though a man hauing grace to resist, be

sometime foyled by the temptation ; yet he shall be freed from the euill of the temptation, from the euill of sinne and the curse : but contrariwise therefore by necessarie consequences.

Thirdly, hee that wanteth grace cannot resist temptation, but shall bee foyled by the Tempter.

Fourthly, hee that wanteth grace, being foyled by the temptation, shall fall into euill.

These particular doctrines shall afterward bee handled in the sixt petition, whither the reader is to be referred.

2 The second thing to be considered in this petition followeth, which is the meaning of the words.

Meaning of the words of the petition. The prayer hath two parts : {The thing asked. The condition.

The thing asked is (forgiuenes of our debts)

The condition whereupon it is asked (our pardoning others.)

For the better vnderstanding of the first part of the petition, these fiue things are to be considered.

First, *Quid*, what we aske (forgiue)

Secondly, *Cuius*, whereof we aske forgiuenes (debts.)

Thirdly, *Pro quibus*, for whom we aske forgiuenes (vs)

Fourthly, *Quorum*, of whose debts we aske forgiuenes : (ours)

Lastly, *Per quem :* through whose merits, which consequently doth arise from the word (*forgiue*)

What we ask? forgiuenes. The first point is, what wee aske : that is, pardon or forgiuenes. Debts or sinnes are discharged two waies.

1. When the debtor himselfe doth satisfie in his owne person : thus the damned men and Angels discharge their debt to God, who for that they are neuer able to pay the vtmost farthing, are therefore kept in prison, and damned euerlastingly.

2. When another person doth satisfie for the debtor, and the debt is forgiuen the debtor by him that satisfieth. Thus the debts of Gods children are discharged through the satisfaction of Christ, who hath paied the vtmost farthing to the creditor, to God his Father for vs. This may be called remission or forgiuenes.

1. In respect of vs that receiue it, we
conferring no merit thereto, nor any way
purchasing it.

Rom. 11. 6.

2. In respect of Christ that satisfied the debt for vs,
wee being not able to gratifie him againe in
any measure.

Psal. 116. 12.

3. In respect of God the Father, who of his free mercie
and meere loue to mankinde sent his only be- *Ioh.* 3. 16.
gotten sonne to discharge the debt. *Rom.* 6. 23.

This point then hath this vse : It teacheth vs to cast
down all pride in our hearts, and to emptie our selues of
all opinion of our owne merits and excellencie,
and to come with ropes about our heads before 1. *King.* 20.
the King of Israel. 31.

The second point followeth : whereof we desire forgiuenes : namely, of our debts, that is, of our   Whereof we
sinnes : for sinne containeth in it a threefold   aske pardon ?
debt : first, transgression, or disobedience,   of our debts.
which is the priuation of obedience, by reason whereof
wee still are indebted obedience to God : for they that
doe obey Gods law, notwithstanding still are indebted
obedience, and therefore much more they which disobey
Gods law are indebted obedience through their disobedience. The Apostle speaketh according to this
sense concerning the summe of the second   *Rom.* 13. 8.
table, calling loue a debt which wee alwaies owe vnto our
neighbour ; and so by consequence vnto God : wherefore
the neglect of loue is much more a debt.

Secondly, sinne containeth in it the punishment,
which, by reason of our transgression, wee are indebted
to vndergoe : and according to this our Sauiour Christ
calleth sinne a debt, saying, that they whom the Sergeant
at the commandement of the Iudge cast into
prison, shall not come thence till they haue paied   *Matth.* 5. 26.
the vtmost farthing, that is, sustained the due punishment.

Thirdly, sin is a debt in regard of the corruption which
accompanieth the transgression : for God requireth of vs puritie and sanctimonie, which   *Psal.* 51. 6.
we are indebted vnto God alwaies ; but much more are
wee indebted holines when our hearts are full of impietie,
and dishonestie. Briefly then, because all sinne is a

transgression of the law, binding the transgressor in guiltines to suffer punishment, and corrupting the transgressor with vncleannes: thence it followeth that the sinner is so greatly indebted to God.

The vse of this poynt is to stirre vs vp diligently to seeke pardon of our debts, which doe so greatly indanger vs to Gods iustice and wrath: and whereby we are triple debtors vnto the Lord, but we are for the most part like vnto prodigall dingthrifts, we neuer regard how much we goe vpon the score, we neuer thinke that the day of reckening or payment will come: it were good for vs (according as Christ aduiseth vs:) to agree with our aduersary quickly, euen while we are in the way with him: it is the Lord with whom we must agree, who is a fearefull aduersarie, that will prosecute law against vs before a iudge that will accept no mans person, that hath thine owne conscience as good as a thousand witnesses to proue the debt: yea, it is wisedome to agree quickelie being in the way with him, whilest he doth reason and dispute the matter friendly in the Ministerie of the word, least if death and hell, the Lords sergeant once lay hold vpon vs, and arrest vs, we be cast into perpetuall imprisonment.

Matth. 5. 25.

Antidicos.

The third poynt followeth, for whom we aske forgiuenes, namely for our selues and others, our friends and our enemies.

For whom we aske pardon? for our selues and others.

1 For our selues, yea though we know we are the children of God, and haue already obtained pardon at Gods hands for our sinnes: for Christ teacheth his disciples to make this prayer, who no doubt had their sinnes pardoned before: but it may be obiected, that it is needles to aske that which a man hath alreadie, and will it not be accounted mockerie to deale thus with God? This knot is dissolued two waies: (first) some answere that Christ teacheth vs to aske forgiuenes, not as it commeth from God, which is graunted already to Gods children, but as it commeth to vs, and as we apprehend and applie the merit of Christ for forgiuenes: as if this should be the meaning; Lord giue me grace more effectually to apply to my soule by faith, the righteousnesse of Christ for the pardon of my sinne: others, and

Pardon for our selues.

that more fully, answer (secondly) thus; that it is in the worke of iustification or remission of sinne, as in the worke of creation: for as when God had created *Adam*, he was continually present with him by his prouidence to support his being, and to stay and preserue his substance and nature, which prouidence is nothing else but as it were a continuall creation; euen so when God hath iustified a sinner, and forgiuen him his sinnes, he continually is assistant to the partie iustified, vpholding his iustification: this cannot be termed properlie a second iustification, but a continuall supporting of iustification, no more than preseruation can be termed a second creation. Now further this continuall supporting of iustification is performed by the application of the salue to the sore, of Christs righteousnes to the wounded soule of the sinner: which application is the worke of Gods holy spirit principally, and not of faith onely instrumentally. For further declaration of this poynt we are to know, that when God iustifieth a sinner, he giueth him whole Christ and all his merits for euer, so that the partie iustified cannot possiblie leese Christ: yet the Lord doth onely applie Christ and his merits, as it were the salue, to those sinnes and sores that are alreadie in his soule burst out, for the which he seeketh the salue, and for which he asketh pardon and is humbled: afterward as new sinnes and sores grow, and hee espieth them, feeleth them, and asketh the salue for them, the Lord applieth Christ the salue vnto them. Wherefore directly and fully to answere the obiection, Gods children aske at Gods hands that which they haue not: for although in the counsell of God, in the redemption of Christ, in the donation of Christ to the partie iustified by the Father, at the very first moment of iustification it may truly bee said, that all his sinnes are forgiuen, past, present, and to come: yet in regard of the particular application of Christs stripes to the sores of sinne in the soule, it cannot be said that the godly mans sinnes are pardoned, or forgiuen, or cured, or couered, till they be committed, till they be espied, till the pardon thereof be asked. Gods children therefore doe not aske a primarie iustification, but a secondarie application: they doe not desire to be

Act. 17. 28.

Esay. 53. 5.

made righteous of persons wholly vnrighteous, but to bee made righteous from some particular vnrighteousnesse: As a man that is, desireth God still to preserue his being by daily bread; so a man that is iustified, desireth God still to support his iustification by a continuall application of the salue to the sore. Wherefore to conclude, Gods actions in iustification are two: first, the donation and gift of Christ: secondly, the application of Christ giuen. As a Chirurgion giueth a boxe of salue to a wounded person, and after applieth plaisters of the salue to the wounds as they breake out in the bodie. And sometime the Lord doth deferre and suspend the application of the plaister of Christs blood to the sores of sin in the soule, that he may prouoke vs the more earnestly to consider of the hainousnes of sinne, more seriously to bewaile sinne, more carefully to auoide future sinnes, seeing the smart of former sinnes is so sharpe, more feruently and with greater perseuerance to pray vnto God for pardon thereof, and with greater ioy and thankfulnes to receiue the pardon of sinne from our gratious God.

The vse of this doctrine then in briefe is thus much: to teach vs daily to obserue our sinnes and particular lapses, and accordingly to descend to a particular confession and penitencie for them, and particularly to desire forgiuenes with the application of Christs righteousnes, according as we doe euery day desire bread for our nourishment.

Psal. 51.

2 Thus we pray forgiuenes for our selues: we pray also pardon and forgiuenes for others, yea euen for our enemies, according to the example of Christ, *Stephen*, &c. but this point hath alreadie been handled in the preface of the Prayer, to which place the reader is to bee referred: onely thus much wee are here to learne, pitie and compassion to them that pitie not themselues, that seeing it is vnknowne vnto vs how the Lord will deale with men that liue in impenitencie and grosse sinnes, wee are therefore to hope the best in charitie, and seeing they are of our owne flesh to haue commiseration of them, it may bee that the Lord will at the instance of a godly mans prayer, which auaileth much, haue mercie vpon them; as

Pardon for others.

Iam. 5. 16.

it is supposed hee had mercie vpon *Saul* at *Stephens* prayer, and the Centurion at Christs.

The fourth point followeth, which is, whose debts and sinnes they are whereof wee aske pardon. They are called ours in a double respect: first, for that they are ours properly, wee hauing committed them against the Maiestie of God, and for that we cannot lay our sinnes vpon God, the diuell, or other men: for God hee doth not compell vs to commit sinne, neither doth hee inspire wickednes into vs, seeing he tempteth no man to sinne: and howsoeuer the diuell or wicked men may tempt vs, yet wee willingly and freely yeeld to the temptation, and take a delight and pleasure in the committing of sinne: and though a wicked man be a seruant and slaue to sinne and Satan, yet hee is so willingly, and he selleth himselfe for a slaue, as it is said of *Ahab*. For whose sins we aske pardon? ours. *Iam.* 1. 13.

2 Sinne is called ours emphatically, to signifie thus much, that seeing the soule that sinneth shall die, and that euery one shall beare his owne burthen, therefore we especially seeke for the pardon of our owne sinnes, howsoeuer wee are not to neglect our dutifull and charitable prayers for other men. *Ezech.* 18. *Gal.* 6. 4. 5.

The last point is, through whose merits we aske forgiuenes: which is implied in the word *pardon* or *forgiuenes*: for which purpose we must know that God is a iust God, and therefore he will be satisfied wherein his iustice is violated, and God can no more forgiue sin without any satisfaction done vnto his iustice, than he can cease to be iust or cease to be good: wherefore in that Christ teacheth vs to aske forgiuenes, there is necessarily insinuated some satisfaction to bee made to Gods iustice: and therefore some person to make that satisfaction: which person is Christ Iesus God-man, in whose name wee are to pray, and through whose satisfaction and obedience we obtaine forgiuenes: and so God continueth iust, because hee pardoneth not before he be satisfied, and yet is most mercifull also in prouiding a meanes for the discharge of our debt, whereas we were *non soluendo*, vtter bankerupts, neuer able to pay our debt: and so the Prophets speech For whose sake we aske pardon? Christs.

is fulfilled: *Mercie and truth are met : righteousnesse and peace kisse.*

<small>Psal. 85. 10.</small>

The vse of which point is to teach vs, that when wee come to aske discharge of our debts, we bring our acquittance with vs, otherwise we can neuer be discharged. And here there is some difference betwixt the paiments of men and Gods paiment: for with men the creditor giueth an acquittance to the debtor; but here the sinner, who is the debtor to God, giueth an acquittance to the creditor, which notwithstanding before the creditor freely gaue vnto him vpon the discharge made by the suretie Christ Iesus: briefly and plainly thus much, when we craue pardon of our sinnes we must bring with vs faith to applie Christs righteousnes; which being applied vnto vs, our debts are discharged in Christ.

This is the first part of the petition, *viz.* the thing wee aske. The second followeth, the condition whereupon we aske pardon.

<small>The condition of the petition.</small>

As we forgiue our debtors.

These words are an instrument seruing to seuerall purposes: wherein wee may consider both the meaning and vse of them. For the meaning of the words two points must be noted.

1 How other men are our debtors.
2 How we forgiue other men their debts.

First, to know how other men are our debtors, wee must consider that sinne containeth alwaies an offence to God, sometime also an offence to man. The offence which is against God is the violating of his holy and righteous law which is the rule of his iustice. The offence which is against man, is the iniurie which is done against the person, honor, life, goods, good name or honestie of any man, whereby any of them is diminished or abolished in our neighbour: as in murther, the life of a man is diminished; in theft, his goods; in slaunder, his good name; in fornication, his honestie, &c. Now the offence and iniurie of our neighbour containeth the debt which wee owe vnto him: for first, in that we haue wronged him, we haue not loued him, and so we owe loue vnto him: secondly, we owe a

<small>How other men are our debtors.</small>

satisfaction or amends, which in equitie must be made to the partie iniuried : thirdly, we owe vnto him a certaine punishment also, which in equitie may bee exacted and inflicted vpon the partie offending. And in these respects other men are our debtors.

Secondly, we forgiue other men their debts, when wee remit, not the transgression of Gods law, for that wee cannot, for none can forgiue sinne but God: but either the wrong, the satisfaction, or the punishment : sometime all three, sometime two, sometime one onely, namely the wrong or iniurie done vnto vs; which wrong we doe here professe our selues readie to forgiue, and thereupon desire God to forgiue vs. How we forgiue other men.

But for further declaration of this matter wee are to remember these things.

First, when man forgiueth the wrong, God doth not alwaies forgiue the sinne : for there bee many persecutors whose sins are neuer forgiuen of God, and yet Gods children that are persecuted by them forgiue them the wrong, which through their persecutions they sustaine : so Christ and *Stephen* prayed for their persecutors, some of whom (as is probable) God neuer pardoned.

Secondly, though man doe not forgiue the wrong, yet the Lord sometime may and doth forgiue the sinne : for if there be any man found so cruelly mercilesse as that he wil not forgiue his enemies, his sinne is the greater, and his charitie is the lesse, and hee can haue little or no comfort that God will pardon him : but if the partie that hath done the wrong, doe craue pardon at Gods hands, and satisfie or make restitution according to equitie to the partie wronged, the Lord forgiueth the sin and the wrong both to himselfe and to man : for God can forgiue, and doth forgiue both, vpon performance of the condition of true repentance, which containeth in it satisfaction or restitution or amends.

Mat. 5. 24.

Thirdly, though God forgiue the sinne, and man also forgiue the wrong, yet man may vrge the partie culpable to satisfaction and punishment according to the law of God, and of the nation where they liue : yea sometime the partie wronged ought so to doe necessarily, otherwise hee shall sinne against God and the Common-wealth. This wee see euidently in the theefe vpon the crosse: God forgaue him his sinne, and yet he confesseth he was iustly punished: and *Achan* was punished according to Gods commandement, and yet it is very probable by his confession of his fault that hee repented: and certaine it is that *Iosua* forgaue the wrong: and if *Moses* had spared any murderer or adulterer from death, hee had offended God, and damnified the common good, seeing that such sinnes doe defile a nation.

Luk. 23. 40. 41.

Iudg. 7. 19. 20.

All which hath this vse, that though a man doe prosecute a felon, or a murderer to death, yet hee may forgiue him: and therefore the guiltie persons want charitie, in reuiling and making outcries against the persecutors of iustice, as if they were blood-suckers, and so foorth: for sometime the qualitie of the offender is such, as that if hee bee suffered to liue, the Common-wealth is in daunger to sustaine much detriment, besides the great offence done to the righteous law of God, which hath awarded death to some sort of sinners. Againe, much more therefore is it lawfull for a man to commence suite of law, and to be the plaintife in a manifest iniurie thereby to recouer his right, and to obtaine satisfaction, and that without any breach of charitie: for there is a difference to be made betwixt an Enemy & an Aduersary: the one is caused of hatred to the man: the other of a loue to iustice; and a man may retaine loue and be another mans aduersarie; so can hee not and be his enemie: wherefore if a man haue a controuersie with another, and retaine loue and charitie with his neighbour, (as hee may very well) notwithstanding the suite, hee may worthily partake in the Sacrament of the Lords Supper, though some bogle at it: wherein they bewray either their malice, ignorance or superstition.

Echthros.
Antidicos.

Thus we see the meaning of the condition: now the vse thereof is three-fold.

1 It is a probation of our charitie and loue to our brethren, whereby wee may gather comfort of pardon from God, or be terrified and humbled through despaire thereof. This is euidently expounded by our Sauiour

Christ, saying: If you forgiue others, God will forgiue you: or if you will not forgiue others, neither will God forgiue you. Mat. 6. 15.& 18. 33.

2 It serueth for a profession of our loue and charitie to others, yea towards our enemies by forgiuing them: for by this speech publikely vttered in the assemblie of the people we proclaime to all the hearers our inward disposition, which certainly doe possesse the hearts of all those, whose sinnes the Lord hath pardoned.

3 It serueth for an argument enforcing the petition for remission of sinne: as if this were the sense: Lord forgiue vs, for we forgiue others: as if this were the argument: The mercifull shall ob- Luk. 11. 4. taine mercie.

But we Lord are mercifull in pardoning others:

Therefore Lord be mercifull in pardoning vs.

And for this latter vse wee are to know, that none of all the petitions haue a speciall argument particularly fixed to the side of it but this, as if our Sauiour Christ would signifie vnto vs thereby the weakenes of our faith in that matter which most concerneth vs, *viz.* the pardon of our sins, and the meanes whereby we might best fortifie our weaknes by forgiuing our enemies.

3 This is the second thing considered in this petition, the meaning of the words: now followeth the third thing, which is the Supplication. The supplication of this petition.

The things which wee aske in this petition are specially three.

1 Humiliation, and that is insinuated by consequent.

2 Iustification, and that is expressed in one part, *viz.* forgiuenes.

3 Charitie, and that is included in the reason.

First Humiliation, which necessarily is implied in that we aske pardon: for a man will neuer aske that which hee needeth not, or whereof he feeleth no want: he that is sick, and seeth and feeleth his sicknes, will seeke and aske the meanes of health: he that is in health, as he feeleth no sicknes, so he will seeke for no cure: Humiliation containeth these particulars. Humiliation.

Mat. 9. 12.

1 A sight and knowledge of our sinnes, and of the curse of the law due vnto sinne, which is the theoricall or speculatiue knowledge in the braine.

Sight of sinne.

2 A sense and feeling of the heinousnesse of sinne, and the intolerable burthen of Gods wrath due vnto sinne, which is a further impression in the heart and affection. Now both these befall some of the wicked, as *Caine* and *Iudas*, who because they felt their sinne, no doubt knew them: and from these two sometime in the wicked the Lord wringeth,

Sense of sinne.

Genes. 4. 13.
Mat. 27. 4.

3 A confession of sinne with the deserued punishment. This confession ariseth from a double fountaine and cause: in the wicked it groweth from despaire and murmuring, and it is ioyned with blaspheming and much outrage, as in the former examples of *Iudas* and *Caine*, who were compelled to confesse their sinnes against their liking, for they desired to hide them.

Confession of sinne.

In the godly and penitent and honest heart, this confession ariseth from hope of ease and pardon, from hatred and wearines of his sinne, and it is ioyned with Gods glorie, and it is performed willingly, and vndertaken voluntarily without compulsion: and howsoeuer there be a little strife with the shame of the world which might perhaps befall him vpon the confession of his sinne to others, yet he is content therein also to deny himselfe that God may be glorified, himselfe comforted, and others instructed by his example.

Prou. 28. 13.
Psal. 51. 3. 4.
Iob. 31. 33.

Psalm. 51. 13.

4 An earnest and feruent desire to be released of the burthen of sinne: this was apparant in the Prophet *Dauid* after his murther and adultery, which appeareth by the often gemination of the petition for Mercy: this the Apostle *Paul* expresseth also in his outcrie after the combat: this is called spiritual hunger and thirst by our Sauiour Christ, the Prophet *Esay* and the Apostle *Iohn* in the Reuelation, and by the Prophet *Dauid* in the Psalme, compared to the longing of a woman with child, and to the desire that the Hart hath to take the soile being chased with hounds.

Desire of deliuerance from sinne.
Psalm. 51.
Rom. 7. 24.
Mat. 5. 6.
Esay. 55. 1.
Apoc. 22. 17.
Psal. 143. 6.
Psalm. 84. 2.
Psal. 42. 1. 2.

This desire of grace as it is the greatest and best degree of humiliation, so it is a step to iustification, which followeth.

In the second place after humiliation, followeth iustification, which containeth these specialties. *Iustification.*

1 The matter of iustification, which is Christ, and his merits of all sorts, both in doing and suffering; in satisfying for sinne, and his abstinence and freedome from sinne; in his obedience passiue, abolishing the curse by his crosse; and actiue, in purchasing grace and glory by performing the commaundement: and habituall in the sanctification and heauenly qualification of his humane nature, with the graces of Gods Spirit out of measure. *Matter of iustification.*

2 The forme of iustification, which is the translation of our sinnes from vs to Christ, and Christs righteousnesse from himselfe to vs; *For the chastisement of our peace was vpon him, and by his stripes wee are healed:* for, that our punishment might iustly fall vpon him, first our sinnes must of necessitie be imputed to him, and then that we might be deliuered from the punishment which we had deserued, his sufferings must needs be applied vnto vs. Againe, although by the sufferings of Christ imputed vnto vs, we are freed from sinne and the curse: yet except Christ had fulfilled all righteousnesse for vs in obeying the commaundement, we had neuer been sanctified by grace, and blessed with glory, for his passion procureth our deliuerance, and his obedience purchaseth our saluation. Iustification therefore containeth: *Forme of iustification. 2. Cor. 5. 21. Esay. 53. 5. Rom. 10. 3. 4. Mat. 3. 15.*

1 The translation of our sinnes vpon Christ.
2 The imputation of Christs obedience to vs.

This imputation is performed partly by the holy Ghost, who bestoweth Christ and his merits vpon vs, partly by faith in our selues, which applieth Christs righteousnesse vnto vs. Here is the proper place of *Faith*.

3 The specialty of iustification is ye efficient cause, which is the Mercie of God, the Grace of God, the Loue of God, who of his meere mercie, grace, and loue, sent his Sonne to doe and suffer for vs *Efficient cause of iustification.*

whatsoeuer his iustice required, and doth daily applie vnto vs the vertue of both.

In the fourth and last place followeth Charitie or Loue to our brethren and enemies, which is the fulfilling of the second table of the Commaundements, and which is the finall cause of iustification in respect of men: and this is directly signified vnto vs in the condition or argument annexed to this petition: *as we forgiue our debtors*. But because all these particulars, though to another end, and after another manner, haue been already discoursed in this treatise, here of purpose I omit their further handling.

<small>Charitie, or the finall cause of iustification.</small>

4 And this may suffice for the supplication, comprehending the things we pray for in this petition: now followeth the fourth thing, which is the deprecation, containing those things which we pray against, and they are these sixe following.

<small>The deprecation of this petition.</small>

1 Blindnes of minde, which is when men continue in sinne without any consideration thereof, either banishing the thought of it out of their mind, or slubbering the matter ouer with a negligent conceit, as that we are all sinners, and the best man hath his infirmities. Againe, vnto blindnes of minde, as neere of kinne, may be added a reprobate minde, when men are bereft of all difference of good and euill, neuer making bones (as we say) of sinne against nature, which the Apostle calleth things not conuenient, or not agreeing with the light of nature.

<small>Blindnes of minde.
2. Cor. 4. 4.</small>

<small>Rom. 1. 28.</small>

2 Hardnes of heart, which is a fruit of the former, when men are neuer troubled in their consciences for most fearefull sinnes: this was that fearefull iudgement which befell *Pharaoh*, who had a heart more hard that the Adamant, neuer trembling at all that fearefull wrath which God executed vpon Egypt. Contrarie to this is a soft and fleshie heart, as the Prophet calleth it a heart prickt with the feeling of sinne, a heart that doth tremble at Gods word.

<small>Hardnes of heart.</small>

<small>Exod. 5. & 6. &c.</small>

<small>Ezech. 11. 19.
Act. 2. 37.</small>

Both these sinnes may bee intitled with one generall name, the spirit of slumber or securitie, eyes that doe not see, eares that doe not heare, a

<small>Securitie.</small>

heart that doth not vnderstand, as the Prophets prophecie.

3 Opinion of our owne righteousnesse, a matter very common with the naturall man and the ignorant multitude, who therein iumpe with the Iewes in *Pauls* time, who were taught by the Pharisies the patrons of that heresie, and with the Papists in our time ; whereas the Lord Iesus Christ reproueth the Angell of the Church of Laodicea for that very fault, who said he was rich, being indeede poore, and ignorant of his pouertie. These are proud iusticiaries, who as they are blind, so are they bolde in their blindnes ; saying they can see, and therefore their sinne remaineth, whereas if they would confesse themselues to be blind, they should haue no sinne, for Christ would take it away. <small>Opinion of our owne iustice. Rom. 10. 3. Luk. 18. 21. 11. Mark. 10. Apoc. 3. 17. Ioh. 9. 41.</small>

4 Vpon this conceit of our owne righteousnesse, followeth necessarilie either a contempt, or light estimation, or no regard at all of Christs righteousnesse and his merits. Christ saith, *the whole haue no need of the Physitian :* that is to say, they that iudge themselues to be in good health, that thinke they are righteous, will neuer regard Christ, who is the Physitian of the soule, and the physick also. <small>Neglect or contempt of Christ. Rom. 10. 3.</small>

After this followeth vnbeleefe or infidelitie, with the opposite pride and presumption, which when they haue a long time wrought vpon the heart of a carnall man, if the Lord at length open the eyes of that wretch to see his sinnes, then despaire rusheth vpon him, which is the next neighbour to vnbeleefe. <small>Vnbeleef, infidelitie presumption, despaire. Genes. 4. 13. Mat. 27. 4.</small>

6 Hatred, not forgiuing others that iniurie or wrong vs: hereto apperταineth malice, and a desire of reuenge, things too common in the world: some say, I may forgiue, but I will neuer forget: others, I will pray for him, but I will neuer trust him: some malefactors when the rope is about their necke proclaime their eternall hatred to all the executioners of iustice. Hitherto also apperταineth the discouering of our neighbours infirmities, whereas *Loue couereth a multitude of sinnes*, that is, of priuate infirmities which thou knowest in thy neighbour. <small>Hatred, Malice, Reuenge. 1. Pet. 4. 8. Prou. 10. 12.</small>

5 This may suffice for the deprecation: the thankes-giuing now followeth, which may easily be collected out of the former by induction of particulars before mentioned.

<small>The thanks-giuing of this petition.</small>

Thus the petition for grace is handled.

Now followeth the last petition, which is for perseuerance.

And leade vs not into temptation, but deliuer vs from euill.

1 The order of this petition after the former is very due and iust, for perseuerance followeth grace, and is a necessarie consequent thereof: here the doctrines mentioned in the order of the former petition are to be handled.

<small>Order of the last petition.</small>

First, that grace and perseuerance are inseparable: for no temptation, no sinne, no affliction shall be able to ouerthrow the grace of God in the man that is indued therewith, for hee hath built his house vpon the Rocke like a wise man, and therefore though the raine fall, and the floods come, and the windes blow and beate vpon the house, yet the house shall not fall, for it is builded vpon the Rocke Christ. And Christ telleth *Peter* that the gates of hell shall not preuaile against the Church that is built vpon this Rocke: and certainely if God should once giue grace to a man, and after should take it away, then this absurditie would follow that God should repent, that he should alter and change, for God truely loueth him that hath grace, and he truely hateth him that falleth away finally and totally from all grace: and so God should be as man, mutable and changeable; which is blasphemous to Gods infinite perfection, *with whom there is no variablenesse nor shadow of changing, for the strength of Israell will not lie nor repent, for hee is not a man that hee should repent.*

<small>Grace and perseuerance inseparable.</small>

<small>Mat. 7. 24. 25.</small>

<small>Mat. 16. 18.</small>

<small>Iam. 1. 17.</small>

<small>1. Sam. 15. 29.</small>

Againe, this would follow as absurd as the former, that it might be said, God hath from eternity Elected and Reprobated the same man: Christ hath both redeemed, and not redeemed the same man: the same man is flesh of Christs flesh, and bone of his bone, and a limme of the diuell: the same man is a member of the

Catholike Church, and no member of the Catholike Church: which things because they haue no congruitie with themselues, and with the course of the Scriptures, are therefore to bee reiected as grosse absurdities, and the trueth remaineth firme: That grace hath perseuerance as necessarily annexed to it, as the Sunne hath light, or the fire heate.

Secondly, this doctrine ariseth from the former, that he which hath grace can in some measure resist temptation, and if so be that sometime through the violent whirlewinde of a temptation, he take the foyle by the temptor, yet after hee recouereth himselfe and gathereth more strength and courage to the next encounter, and at the length giueth his enemie the ouerthrow, and triumpheth ouer him; and this power and grace is communicated vnto vs from Christ our head, who was therfore tempted, and ouercame the temptor, that when we are tempted we might resist and preuaile being succoured by him. Hence it is that the Apostle willeth to resist the diuell, and he will flie from vs: and Christ promiseth vs a place in his throne if we ouercome: all which doe import thus much, that as it is a thing possible to resist the diuell, to put him to flight, to ouercome him; so the children of God haue this facultie communicated vnto them from Christ that broke the serpents head.

He that hath grace resisteth the temptation.

Mat. 4.
Heb. 2. 18.
Iam. 4. 7.
Apoc. 3. 21.

1. Cor. 10. 13.

Now followe two other doctrines collected by contrarie: *viz.* that if perseuerance follow grace, then no grace no perseuerance.

First therefore, hee that wanteth grace cannot resist a temptation, for although peraduenture a wicked man may be solicited to commit some sinne whereto he hath an indisposition, yet he cannot properlie be said to resist the temptation, but only to refraine the sinne: for in resisting a temptation there is the spirituall combat betwixt the flesh and the spirit, each of them lusting against other, which is not in a man destitute of grace, who is all flesh and no spirit: and so the will of a wicked man and his affections may resist the motion of

A wicked man cannot resist temptation: though he may refraine from sinne.
Gal. 5. 17.
Rom. 7.

his vnderstanding, or his conscience may terrifie his will and affection; but there is not an opposition of grace and sinne in one and the same facultie or affection, for the strong man hath the possession of the castle, and he ruleth there as it pleaseth him without contradiction.

Luk. 11. 12.

Secondly, the wicked man wanting grace and perseuerance, must of necessitie fall into euill, according to the prouerbe of the wise man: A iust man falleth seuen times and riseth againe, but the wicked fall into mischiefe: but this doctrine shall more euidently appeare afterward in the whole discourse of the meaning of this petition, which is the second generall now following.

The wicked fall into euill.
Prou. 24. 16.

2 We are to vnderstand that there are two great enemies of grace, which continually lay siege against vs.

The meaning of this last petition.

1 The first is Temptation. 2. The second is Euill.

Against both these our Sauiour Christ teacheth vs to pray in this petition. The first enemie of grace, and impediment of preseruation is Temptation, in these words.

Leade vs not into Temptation.

Here we are to consider two things.
1 What Temptation signifieth.
2 What it is to leade into Temptation.

First, temptation in the Scripture hath diuers significations: sometime it signifieth affliction: so the Apostle *Iames* saith, that wee should account it all ioy to fall into manifold temptations, meaning afflictions: this is not the signification of the word in this place, for that is included in the next clause.

What it is to tempt, and what is temptation. Affliction is temptation.
Iam. 1. 2.

Secondly, temptation signifieth that triall which man taketh of God; so the word signifieth in the Psalme, whereas the Prophet v[p]braideth the Israelites for tempting God in the wildernes. Thus the diuell perswaded Christ to cast himselfe vpon the immediate prouidence of God, in casting himselfe down from the temple, which was to tempt God: and this is not the meaning of the word in this place.

To tempt God.
Psal. 95. 9.

Mat. 4. 7.

A paterne of true Prayer

Thirdly, temptation signifieth that triall which man taketh of man to intrap him and bring him into daunger of law: so the Pharisies and Herodians tempted Christ, and thus was Christ tempted diuers times in the Gospell: and this is not the meaning of the word in this place neither.

<small>To tempt or intrap a man. *Matth*. 22. 18.</small>

Fourthly, temptation signifieth that triall which God taketh of man to manifest to himselfe and others what is in him. So God tried *Adam* in the estate of innocencie: so God tried *Abraham* in commanding him to sacrifice his sonne: and thus God daily trieth his children for diuers ends. Neither is this the meaning of the place.

<small>To trie what is in man. *Genes*. 3. *Genes*. 22. 1.</small>

Lastly, temptation signifieth that triall which the diuell taketh of man to cause him to commit sinne by his entisements, who in this respect is called the tempter: and thus the diuell tempteth man: 1. by prosperitie, 2. by aduersitie, 3. by example, 4. by suggestion; though for the most part suggestion is the generall affection of all the other three: for that in time of prosperitie, and aduersitie, and by euill examples the diuell infuseth his temptations into our mindes, though sometime he inspireth his temptations suddenly by occasion of no obiect at all: as we may sometime haue experience by some fearfull blasphemies, which suddenly without any dependance of former cogitations or obiects rush into our mindes: and according to this latter signification temptation is taken in this place.

<small>To solicite man to sinne. *Mat*. 4. How man is prouoked to sinne by Satan.</small>

<small>What it is to lead into tentation.</small> Further, we are to consider what it is to leade into temptation: for which point we must know it containeth these foure particulars.

1 The leauing of the creature or forsaking the creature, not as though God ceased to support and sustaine the nature or naturall powers of the creature, but for that he ceaseth to supplie a second grace to the first, he withdraweth his second grace: this the Prophet *Dauid* feared, and therfore prayeth God not to forsake him ouerlong or ouermuch: and to this sense the Prophet intreateth the Lord to confirme him with a strong spirit after his lapse

<small>Desertion or the forsaking of the creature.</small>

<small>*Psal*. 119. 8. *Psal*. 51. 11.</small>

into sinne, for preuenting of future lapses. This first part is called Desertion.

2 Deliuering ouer the creature to his owne lusts: when God hath withdrawne his second grace, the first grace is not of abilitie to encounter the lusts of the flesh, but the lusts of the flesh doe fight against the spirit, and ouermaster it for the present. This phrase of deliuering vp, the Apostle applieth to the Romanes in regard of the repressing or refraining grace: saying, *God gaue them ouer to vile affections, to a reprobate minde, &c.* And after this,

Deliuering the creature to his owne lusts.

Rom. 1. 24. 26. 28.

3 The creature is in the power and hands of the diuell in a certaine measure: so as he may tempt him and preuaile ouer him to the committing of most fearefull sinnes, as he did preuaile with *Dauid,* and *Peter,* and others.

The efficacie of Satan. 1. *Chro.* 21. 1.

4 Vpon this followeth a kinde of excecation and induration, when the seruant of God maketh little conscience of sinne: and doth not sensiblie feele and perceiue Gods displeasure against sinne. This was in *Dauid,* who continued in his murder and adulterie three quarters of a yeere, in which time there was a spirituall mist of carnall securitie which couered his minde and heart, which afterward was dispersed: and thus the Lord is said actually to blinde and harden men: as we see in the kingdome of Antichrist, and in the old Iewes, and in *Pharaoh* the King of Egypt; whose eyes the Lord blinded, and whose heart the Lord hardened.

Excecation, induration: blindnes of mind, hardnes of heart. 2. *Sam.* 10. 5. & 12. 16.

2. *Thes.* 2. 11. *Esay.* 6. 10. *Exod.* 4. 21.

Here a scruple may arise, *viz.* that seeing God blindeth men, and hardeneth their hearts, he therefore may be said both to be the author of sinne, and to tempt to sinne: both which neuerthelesse the Scripture peremptorily denieth to be in God; as being contrarie to his infinite goodnes. For answere whereof, wee must remember that God may bee said to harden and blinde, and tempt, and yet neither is the author of sinne, nor a tempter to sinne.

Psal. 5. 4. *Iam.* 1. 13.

God is not the author of sin.

First, God tempteth man especially foure waies.

1 By afflictions, which are therfore called temptations, Iam. 1.

2 By a commandement speciall: as that of *Abraham*, Genes. 22. 1.

3 By prosperitie and abundance of outward things, Prou. 30. 9.

4 By occasioning obiects: as Genes. 3. God obiected the apple to *Adams* and *Eues* eye: and 2. Thess. 2. God sent vpon them strong delusions: which is to be vnderstood in regard of the obiect entising and deluding. True it is therefore that God doth tempt, but he doth not tempt to sinne: the Lords temptation may more properly be called a probation than temptation: hee rather doth trie what euill is in vs, than moue vs to euill: rather he proueth what we wil doe, than stirreth vs vp to doe any thing: wherefore wee are to distinguish betwixt these two words; *temptation* and *probation*: howsoeuer they may perhaps sometime admit one and the same signification. _{Dokimazein. Peirazein.}

Secondly, and more fully to the purpose: God hardeneth, Man hardeneth, and Satan hardeneth in diuers considerations.

1 Man hardeneth his owne heart by refusing the grace offered in the meanes of saluation: and thus Christ complaineth that when hee would haue gathered the Iewes together, they would not. And thus in the Psalme the Prophet exhorteth the people not to harden their hearts, as their fathers did at Massah and Meribah: but to heare the voyce of the Lord to day. _{How man hardeneth his owne hart. Psal. 95. 7. 8.}

2 Againe, Satan hardeneth mans heart by perswading and tempting to refuse grace, to continue in the practise of sinne, in impenitencie, and so by consequent there is such a callion or hardnes brought vpon a man, through the daily custome of sinne, by the subtiltie of Satan, that all the meanes of grace rebound backe againe, as a ball cast against a stone wall. _{How Satan hardeneth mans hart. Heb. 3. 13.}

3 Lastly, when a man is come to this passe God hath his worke also; for he withholdeth his grace, which he is not bound to giue except it please him, he being the absolute Lord of his owne: _{How God hardeneth mans heart. Mat. 20. 15.}

and hauing left vs to the swinge of our owne corruption, hee notwithstanding euery day, or very often, smiteth our hard harts with his word, with his iudgments, with his blessings, with the motions of the spirit, or of our owne conscience ; the which not breaking our stony hearts to contrition (as the stone is broken by the hammer of the workman) which is the proper effect of Gods word ; by accident the heart is hardened, as the stiddie the more strokes lighteth vpon it, the more it is beaten together, the faster is the substance, and so the harder : and so in his iustice and iudgement punisheth one sinne with another, casting occasions and obiects whereupon the corruption that is in man worketh to the committing of most vile abominations : as the Gentiles fell from idolatrie to sins against nature, they in the seate of Antichrist neglecting the loue of the truth, were strongly deluded by the occasion of entising obiects to beleeue lies : as namely, all those lying signes and fables mentioned in their Legends. And thus God hardeneth : and in the same sense he blindeth.

Ierem. 23. 29.

Rom. 1.
2. *Thes.* 2.

Summarily therefore God doth thus harden the heart, and blinde the minde, and tempt the creature, and so leade into temptation ; but is not the author of sinne, or tempter to sinne.

Thus much for temptation, which is the first enemie of grace and impediment of perseuerance : now followeth the second, which is euill.

But deliuer vs from euill.

Here also we are to consider two things.   **What is good**
1   What is euill.   **and euill.**
2   What is to deliuer from euill, or how God deliuereth from euill.

First therfore to know what euill is, we must know what good is, that by the opposition of contraries the matter may be more euident. Good is of three sorts : for there is a naturall good, a morall good, and a good instrument : and so by contrarietie : there is a naturall euill, a morall euill, and an euill instrument.

A natural good is whatsoeuer God hath at the first

created: so the Lord saith that all his works were good: which must needes be vnderstood of that naturall goodnes, that is, of the good essence and qualities wherewith God indued his creatures: for the beasts, and the plants, the foules and fishes, the heauens and meteors, the earth and metals are onely good in respect of their essence and qualities, for they are not capable of vertue or vice, seeing that God neuer gaue the law morall vnto them. *A naturall good. Genes. 1. 21.*

A morall good is whatsoeuer qualitie is in the reasonab[l]e creature agreeable to the law morall, commonly called the tenne commandements: as also whatsoeuer qualitie is in man agreeable to the Gospell, the summe whereof is repentance and faith, which are qualities supernaturall infused into man. *A morall good. Genes. 1. 21. Micah. 6. 8.*

A good instrument is whatsoeuer God in his mercie and loue to his children vseth as a meanes to procure the good of his Church, though it be the diuell, though it bee sinne, than which there is not a greater euill; yet it is not *summum malum*: for that God vseth sinne as an instrument of good, and therefore sinne is not absolutely euill, for it hath a respect of good. It is euery way euill in it selfe: but God which is infinitely good turneth euill to good, and bringeth light out of darknes: yea further whatsoeuer God vseth as an instrument of his glorie in his mercie and iustice is instrumentally good: and so there is no *summum malum*, though there be *summum bonum*. *A good instrument. Rom. 8. 28. 2. Cor. 4. 6.*

We see the kindes of good: let vs see also the kindes of euill.

A naturall euill is whatsoeuer is opposed to a naturall good: and that is commonly called *malum pœnæ*, the euill of punishment: namely, whatsoeuer serueth for the ouerthrow and destruction of Gods creature, that which God created secondarily after the fall: thus the Prophet saith directly that God created euill as well as good, that is, punishments and afflictions of all sorts, as pouertie, deformitie, sicknes, famine, death, damnation: and *A naturall euill. Esay. 45. 7.*

whatsoeuer other euill serueth for the execution of Gods iustice vpon those that violate the iustice of God.

A morall euill is whatsoeuer is opposed to a morall good, namely sinnes of all sorts, whether against the decalogue or the Gospell, commonly called *malum culpæ*: and this is the fountaine of the former euill of punishment: for if there had been no sinne, there had been no iudgements, no punishments prepared for sinne.

<small>A morall euill.</small>

An euill instrument is, whatsoeuer God in iustice and wrath against sinne and sinners turneth to the hurt of the sinner: thus the diuell, the world, riches, honour, pleasure, the word and meanes of grace, are turned to bee instruments of Gods wrath, and so of euill to the wicked: for as God doth turne euill to good to them that feare him, so he doth turne good to euil to them that hate him: for among things created by God, or deuised by the creature, there is nothing absolutely good, or absolutely euill, but euery good may haue some relation of euill, and euery euill may haue some respect of good. Thus wee see what euill is in generall, but more specially wee must know that there is furthermore *the euill of euill:* which although it bee generally suggested in the former distinction of good and euill, yet neuerthelesse here must more distinctly bee noted. Wherefore we must obserue also that there are foure combinations of good and euill, which are these following.

<small>An euill instrument.
Prou. 1. 32.</small>

1. The good of good. 2. The euill of good.
3. The good of euill. 4. The euill of euill.

The good of good is that fruite or commoditie which Gods children reape by all the gifts of God; as the benefit of health and wealth, peace and libertie, the word and all the meanes of grace, whereby the godly man is not only comforted and refreshed in his bodie, but furthermore fed and nourished and strengthened in his soule to conuersion and saluation.

<small>The good of good.</small>

The euill of good is that hurt and detriment which the wicked reape by all the gifts of God aforesaid, as that not onely their life, health, peace, libertie, wealth and prosperitie in the world, but also all

<small>The euill of good.</small>

the meanes of grace and saluation becommeth the bane and poyson both of soule and bodie to their euerlasting damnation another day: that although the wicked are nourished by their meate, and cured by their physicke, and instructed and reprooued by the word, &c. yet there is a secret poyson therewithall infused into their soules, which shall another day in Gods appointed time burst out to their vtter ouerthrow.

The good of euill is that good which the Lord as a skilfull Physition gathereth from the afflictions and sinnes of his children, as it were a purgation out of poison: for God can and doth expell one sinne with another, and many sins with afflictions: as a father, correcting, and amending the faults of his children by correction. The good of euill.

The euill of euill is that damage which the wicked sustaine by falling into sinne, and the punishment thereby deserued, which is that thereby their damnation is increased, for a great measure of wrath is heaped vp by their sins, and a greater number of sinnes are committed by their afflictions. Thus we see what euill is: and by contrary what good is. The euill of euill.

Now followeth the second thing, which is how God deliuereth from euill: which in part may be conceiued by the former distinctions. Yet thus much for the present purpose God deliuereth vs from euill four waies. How God deliuereth from euill.

First, by preseruing vs from committing of sinne.

Secondly, by freeing vs from iudgements due to sinne.

Thirdly, by freeing vs from the hurt of sinne and affliction.

Fourthly, by turning all those sinnes which we commit, and the afflictions which we sustaine, to our good.

This may suffice for the second generall poynt to bee considered in this petition, *viz.* the meaning of the words.

Now followeth the third generall, which should be the supplication: but because the petition is propounded negatiuely and by way of deprecation, as none of the rest are, therefore it shall be conuenient to alter the order formerly propounded, and to speake in the third place of the deprecation, annexing in the fourth place the supplication.

3 The things that wee pray against are these following.

1 Temptation, but not absolutely against temptation, but so far forth as it is a means to draw vs away from God to commit sinne: and so the Apostle *Paul* prayeth, that the pricke of the flesh might be remoued from him, which he tearmeth the Angell of Sathan, because that the diuell sent it for a diuelish end, howsoeuer God sent it for his humiliation and humilitie: by temptation in this place, vnderstand solicitation to sinne.

<small>The deprecation of this last petition. Against tentation. 2. *Cor.* 12. 7. 8.</small>

2 Affliction, but not absolutely against it neither: only so farre forth is it lawfull to pray against afflictions, as they are the punishments of sinne, the curse of God, meanes to driue vs to impatiencie, or to take Gods name in vaine: so *Agur* prayeth against pouertie, which is one kinde of affliction.

<small>Against affliction.</small>

<small>*Prou.* 30. 9.</small>

Here before we proceede any further, two questions or doubts must be discussed and resolued and that ioyntly, each depending of other.

1 Whether it be lawfull to pray for a temptation or a crosse.

2 How farre forth it is lawfull to pray for or against temptations and afflictions.

It may seeme at the first sight, that seeing the ende of temptation is to prouoke vs to sinne, and the end of afflictions are to destroy the creature, that therefore it is vnlawfull to pray for them. Againe, it may in like manner bee thought, that seeing through temptations God worketh much good vnto vs, and that through afflictions God teacheth vs and nurtereth vs in his law; therefore it is very lawfull to pray for a temptation and afflictions. There is a triple solution of this doubt: some say thus.

<small>Whether it be lawfull, and how far foorth to pray for or against tentation and affliction.</small>

1 That seeing temptation and affliction are in their owne nature the meanes and punishments of sinne, therefore in no case we are to pray for them, but against them: for God forbiddeth vs to practise any thing that is a means of sinne, and therefore consequently he willeth vs to pray

against all the meanes of sinne, as temptation is: and seeing afflictions in their owne nature and first institution are Gods plagues vpon sinners, we are to auoide them by all meanes possible (as we doe) and so to pray against them.

2 Others distinguish and answere thus, that we are neither to pray for them nor against them, but to commit our selues to Gods prouidence and will, to bee ordered as hee thinketh best, and if afflictions befall vs with temptations, to sanctifie them by prayer for our sanctification.

3 Lastly, others are directly of opinion, that it is lawfull, yea needfull sometime to pray for temptations and afflictions, for that they are both a part of our daily bread, though not of the body, yet of the soule. In this diuersitie of opinions it is very hard to finde out the trueth, by keeping a meane betwixt them, which must bee done, otherwise the doubts cannot be dissolued: we must know therefore for euidence sake, that we reade in the Scriptures that Gods seruants haue alwaies prayed against temptation and affliction; so the Apostle prayed against the pricke of the flesh, so the wise man prayed against pouertie: wee reade also on the other side, that the Prophet *Dauid* reckeneth affliction good for himselfe, and the man blessed whom the Lord correcteth: and the Apostle *Iames* willeth vs to account it a matter of all ioy to bee tempted and afflicted (and it is probable if that *Adam* had neuer fallen from grace, he might haue been assaulted with temptation; and why may not the diuels sometime tempt the good Angels, as well as they tempted Christ? Especially if temptation be onely the propounding of an euill obiect to the vnderstanding with a reason to enforce it.) There being then a kind of repugnancie in these two practises of the holy men in Scripture, some praying against temptation and affliction, others accounting affliction good for them, and exhorting to reioyce in temptation; they must be reconciled by the change of the respect, for howsoeuer in the Scripture there may be a shew of repugnancie, yet indeed there is none. Therefore in one respect Gods children prayed against temptation and affliction, in another respect they accounted it a blessed and ioyfull thing to bee tempted and afflicted.

*2.Cor.*12.7.8.
Prou. 30. 9.
Psal. 119. 71. & 94. 12.
Iam. 1. 2.

Temptation is to be considered according to Gods purpose, and according to the diuels intendment: God purposeth temptation to our good, Sathan intendeth our hurt. Againe, temptation must be considered with the effect that the diuell produceth through the temptation, and with the effect which God worketh thereby: Sathan by the temptation produceth sinne, the Lord he effecteth grace vpon sinne: therefore we must, and the seruants of God did pray against temptation according to the diuels intent and worke: and intreate the Lord to turne the diuels effect produced, to our good as God intendeth and worketh.

<small>Gods purpose in temptation. Sathans intent in temptation.</small>

Againe, affliction is to be considered as God first inflicted it, and as he afterward corrected it; he inflicted it as a punishment for the destruction of the creature, but he hath since in mercy to his children, altered it for the correcting and bettering of them: in the former consideration the seruants of God prayed against it, in the latter they reioyced in it, and accounted themselues blessed by it. To make answere therefore directly, wee may in some sense pray against affliction and temptation, but in no respect pray for them: yet when we are exercised by them, finding in our selues the markes of election, we may reioyce vnder them: pray God to worke his worke in vs by them, and so labour to become blessed by meanes of them; for it will not follow by good consequence, that because good redoundeth to vs by them, that therefore wee must pray for them; for by like proportion it should bee concluded, that seeing through sinne God worketh out our good, we should pray that we might fall into sinne, which is a thing most absurd and irreligious. In briefe, whatsoeuer is properly the meanes of our good, wee are bound to pray for, but that which is the meanes of our good by accident we are not to pray for, but hauing reaped good by it through Gods mercy, to blesse him for it: and when we are exercised by it to intreate his blessing by meanes of it. And thus in some measure these doubts are cleered, whether it be lawfull, and how farre forth to pray for, or against affliction and temptation. Now we are to proceede in the deprecation.

<small>Affliction is a punishment. Affliction is a correction.</small>

3 Desertion, Gods forsaking the creature, is a thing that wee especially pray against in this place : that God would not withdraw second grace from vs. *Against desertion.*

4 Lapse into sinne, which followeth vpon Gods forsaking of vs, for then we being in the hands of the diuell, and our owne lusts, they will tyrannise ouer vs. *Against lapse into sinne.*

5 Gods hardening the heart, and blinding the minde, which is a spirituall iudgement inflicted by God vpon them that customably liue in sinne. *Against Gods blinding the minde and hardning the heart.*

6 Apostasie or backsliding, which is when a man reuolteth from a former measure of knowledge or grace, or profession : Apostasie is either partiall, or totall. *Against apostasie. Heb. 3. 12. Esay. 1. 5.*

Partiall Apostasie is when a man in some poynt of doctrine erreth, whereas before he held the trueth, or when a man leeseth some grace, or measure of the same grace wherewith before he was indued : or when a man falleth away from the profession of the trueth to Gentilisme, &c. *Hymeneus*, and *Philetus*, & *Alexander*, were Apostataes in part, erring concerning the resurrection : *Dauid* fell from some measure of grace receiued, and therefore he prayeth *1. Tim. 1. 20. 2. Tim. 2. 17. 18.*
Psal. 51. 8. 12. that God would restore to him ioy and gladnes which he had lost. *Demas* he imbraced the present world, and fell from his profession to be a Gentile
2. Tim. 4. 10. againe ; thus did diuers in the Primitiue Church.

Totall Apostasie is, when a man falleth away from all the trueth, and grace, and profession of the trueth, as *Iulian* the Apostata did : hitherto appertaineth the sinne against the holy Ghost.

Against punishment of all sorts. 7 Punishments of sinne of all sorts, whether temporall and bodily, or spirituall and eternall, euill conscience, Hell, and so forth.

Against hurt of all sorts. 8 Hurt through iudgements.
9 Hurt through lapse into sinne.

10 Hurt through the meanes of saluation, and prosperitie.

11 Diuell, that God would tread Sathan vnder our feete, that hee would restraine and limit his power and malice.

Against Satan.

12 World, which is the euill examples of the world: the flattering intisements, and fearefull threates thereof.

Against the world.

13 Flesh, which is the lust and concupiscence of our heart, which continually stirreth it selfe vp, and fighteth against the spirit, that God would represse it, mortifie it, and so subdue it, that it preuaile not against vs.

Against the flesh.

Here a question is to be handled, whether it be lawfull to pray against death? The Apostle answereth, *It is appointed to all men to die once:* and therfore to pray against death absolutely is vnlawfull: yet there are certaine circumstances in death, against which it is lawfull to pray. As for example: Death is of it selfe a curse of God seruing to destroy the creature; so farre forth we pray against it: death is the entrance to hell; so farre forth we pray against death. Againe, death sometime befalleth a man suddenly, that he can haue no time to set his house in order, to admonish his wife and children and seruants to feare God: if hee bee a Minister, can haue no time to call for the brethren to exhort them: or if he be a King, can haue no time to take order for weightier matters of ye Church or Commonwealth: in these respects it is lawfull to pray against sudden death; but not simply against death, nor against sudden death, nor in all respects against sudden death: for if any person vpon presumption of time to repent at the last houre, still continuing in his sinnes al his life long, do pray against sudden death, his prayer is sinfull: for euery man should so leade his life, as if God should call for him at a moments warning, he were in some measure prepared for the Lord.

Whether it be lawfull to pray against death.
Heb. 9. 27.
It is lawfull to pray against a cursed death.
How it is lawfull to pray against sodain death.

4 These are the things that wee pray against in this petition. The things that we pray for follow.

The supplication of this petition.

1 Strength to resist temptation, and to perseuere and continue. Now because our enemies are many, and

mightie, and subtill, and euery way furnished for the assault, therfore wee had neede also be furnished with all that spirituall armour which the Apostle prescribeth: the parts whereof are these following. Some seruing for our defence: as namely, *Perseueraĉe, or strength to resist the temptation. Ephes. 6.*

1 Sound doĉtrine, which is the girdle of Veritie.
2 Vpright life, which is called the breast-plate of righteousnes.
3 Patience in affliĉtion, called the shooes of the preparation of the Gospell of peace.
4 Faith in Christ Iesus, compared to a shield, whose vertue is to quench all the firie temptations to despaire of Gods mercie.
5 Hope of life euerlasting, called a Helmet for the head. Others seruing for offence of the enemie: as namely, 1. The word of God, that is, sentences of holy Scripture, which direĉtly cut the throte of sin and temptation, like a sword. 2. Prayer of all sorts, with the properties thereof: watchfulnes and perseuerance, which are so many spirituall darts and speares to put the enemie to flight, and to abandon the temptation.

2 That God would turne our affliĉtions to our good: now that good which wee desire to bee wrought in vs through affliĉtion is manifold. *Good through affliĉtion.*

1 Humiliation: which is to cast downe our selues vnder the mightie hand of God, correĉting vs for our defaults.
2 The deniall of the world and the pleasures of sinne.
3 The sighing for the inheritance laid vp in store for vs.
4 Wisedome to preuent the malitious persecutions of the wicked, which through want of circumspeĉtion haue befallen vs.
5 Triall, purging, and refining our faith.
6 Patience and constancie.
7 Instruĉtion to the obedience of Gods commaundements.
8 Preseruation from condemnation with the world.

All these fruites, and diuers other particulars the word teacheth to be wrought in vs through affliĉtion.

Good through sinne.

3 That God would turne our sins to our good: which the Lord performeth diuersly, *viz.*

1 By reuealing vnto vs our wicked and corrupt disposition, that we are readie to fall into most grosse sinnes, if he doe not support vs euery moment with his grace.

2 By discouering our owne infirmitie and disabilitie that we are not able to resist the least, much lesse the great assaults of our spirituall enemies: and so we taking notice by lapse into sinne of our owne wickednes and weakenes, we may learne,

3 To detest our selues for our sinning nature.

4 To renounce all confidence in our selues, and our strength.

5 To relie our selues wholly vpon Gods power and his might in the time of temptation.

All these particulars are most apparant in the examples of *Dauids* and *Peters* falles, compared with their writings.

6 The Lord doth discouer vnto vs by lapse into sinne the subtilties and sleights of our spirituall enemie; the Apostle hee calleth them the methods, and many waies which he hath to circumuent and deceiue vs: for the diuell can vpon a very slender occasion procure a lapse into some grosse sinne: as *Peter* vpon the speech of a maide denied Christ.

Ephes. 6. 11.

7 The Lord doth affoord vnto vs much experience, both of his mercie and goodnes in pardoning our sinnes, as also to recouer our brethren fallen by like occasion into sinne, and to comfort them.

8 The Lord teacheth vs the spirit of meeknes and mildnes toward others that are through infirmitie ouertaken with sinne, that wee bee not too seuere censurers of them, considering our selues and our manifold lapses into the same sinnes.

This and much more good God worketh out for vs by our sins: all which must teach vs euerlasting thankfulnes.

5 This may serue for the supplication: the thanksgiuing now followeth, which may easily bee gathered from the former parts. Thus also the petitions which respect our good are

The thanksgiuing of this petition.

handled : and so the second part of this prayer is ended, *viz.* the matter.

Now followeth the third part of the Lords prayer, which is the conclusion or shutting vp of the prayer, in these words :

For thine is the kingdome, the power, and the glorie for euer : Amen.

Although this conclusion be not extant in the Latin copie of the old translator, yet it is in the Greeke : and the Greeke being more ancient than the Latin, as being the originall, the Latin being onely a translation and not canonicall, in reason the Greeke is to be preferred before the Latin : and so this clause being in the Greeke, we will take it as part of Canonicall Scripture, and so handle it, notwithstanding that the Iesuite auoucheth the contrarie : for his coniecture is, that it might bee added in the text of the Euangelist, because that the Greekes vsed to adde it in their Liturgie to the end of the Lords prayer. But this is a very simple conceit for so learned a man, to auouch that a whole sentence might creepe into the text of Canonicall Scripture, who durst bee so bold to adde it ? or who would be content to receiue it for Canonicall, if any man durst be bold to insert it into the text ? But let his dreame goe : and let vs consider of it as a part of the Lords Prayer.

The conclusion of the Lords prayer.
Whether the conclusion be canonicall.

This conclusion containeth generally the manner of making our prayers to God, as also the manner of ending our prayers which wee make : for euery seuerall petition must haue the matters expressed in this conclusion : or else it is not made in due and right manner as it ought to bee : wherefore this conclusion must bee vnderstood in euery petition ; as must also the preface.

Feruency is the summe of the conclusion.
Iam. 5. 16.
Energouméne.
What feruencie is.

The manner of making and ending our prayers, expressed in this conclusion, may bee vttered in one word, *Feruencie,* as S. *Iames* saith: *The feruent prayer of the righteous auaileth:* the word which the Apostle vseth signifieth such a prayer as is effectuall, *operatiue,* working : for the inner man must not be idle in time of prayer. Feruencie therefore is the inward operation of the soule in the time of prayer : euen as a pot boyleth and seetheth by reason of the fire put vnder ; so the soule of a man, moued through the spirit of God, as it were a hot fire within his bowels, must conceiue inwardly such sighes and groanes which cannot be expressed, which maketh a feruent and effectual prayer. This feruencie then is, when all the faculties of the minde and reasonable soule are occupied about the matter of the prayer : the vnderstanding conceiueth matter and inditeth, the memorie remembreth things needfull, the will hartilie wisheth things necessary, the affections stirring themselues according to the seuerall matters conceiued in the prayer, sometime reioycing, sometime mourning, sometime fearing, sometime hoping, sometime hating, sometime louing, and so foorth as the matter varieth : this in generall is feruencie, which hath two parts here expressed. The first is faith and assurance and confidence, *Fiducia*. The second is earnest and vehement, and ardent desire, *Votum*.

Rom. 8. 26.

Parts of feruencie: faith, desire.

The first is the principall worke of the vnderstanding : the second is the principall worke of the will : the other two parts of the soule being the handmaides of these ; for the memorie ministreth to the vnderstanding, and the affections are seruiceable to the will : the conscience is compounded of them all.

Faith, the first part of feruencie, is expressed in the conclusion by certaine arguments which shall be handled afterward : something first in generall of faith.

Of faith in prayer.

Faith is necessarily required to make a feruent prayer : the Apostle therefore calleth it the prayer of faith ; and further auoucheth that the man that doubteth, shall obtaine nothing at Gods hands : not as though any man could pray without some doubting and vnbeleefe ; but the Apostles meaning is of such doubting which raigneth in the heart, as may appeare by the text : also our Sauiour Christ requireth faith plainly if wee will obtaine ; and wee shall obtaine if wee haue faith. Now wee must alwaies remember that faith is grounded vpon Gods

Faith is necessarie in prayer. *Iam* 1. 6. 7.

Mark. 11. 24.

word, and Gods word is his will, and so our faith must be grounded vpon his will: wherefore if wee aske any thing in faith, according to his reuealed will, we shall obtaine. Now Gods will is in generall this, to grant vs euery thing that is good: if it bee euill, it is not his will nor promise to giue it: and many things are good for vs which seeme euill vnto vs; and many things are euill for vs which seeme good vnto vs: wherefore we must not define good and euill after our owne fancies, but as the truth is: God knoweth best what is good for vs, and what is euill for vs: herein therefore we must submit our wils to Gods will; alwaies being faithfully perswaded that God will graunt at our prayers euery thing good for vs. And although the new supporters of Poperie (the Iesuites I meane) auouch that such a faith is not needfull: yet the word of God, which is the ground of euery sound doctrine, teacheth vs thus much, and therefore wee ought to build our house thereupon, as on a sure and stedfast rocke, rather than vpon the sandie conceits of popish teachers. For whereas it is alleaged by them that *Dauid* when hee prayed for the life of his childe, doubted whether God would giue him life yea or nay: it may bee answered two waies: First, *Dauid* did not well to pray for the life of the childe, seeing it was expressely signified to him before of *Nathan* that the childe should die: for so doing his prayer was against Gods will reuealed. Secondly, it being a temporall blessing, *Dauid* ought to aske it conditionally if it were good; and so his assurance might be certaine to obtaine it: but *Dauid* seeing it not good for him, presently after the death of the childe is comforted, as hauing obtained all that he askt. It appeareth therefore that faith is requisite in prayer, namely such a faith as doth assure a man certainly to obtaine euery good thing hee asketh. This faith ariseth from iustifying faith, and is a necessarie consequent thereof: for a man beleeuing in Christ Iesus for the pardon of his sinne, is also assured that God will giue him all other good things: so the Apostle

Sidenotes: Faith is grounded vpon Gods will. 1. *Ioh.* 5. 14. *Psalm.* 34. 10. — A distinction of good & euill. — 1. *Tim.* 2. 8. — *Mat.* 7. — 2. *Sam.* 12. 22. — *Vers.* 14. — Faith to obtaine our prayers ariseth from iustifying faith.

reasoneth; *If God giue vs Christ, how shall he not giue vs with Christ all other things that shall be good for vs?* so Christ promiseth, that the kingdome of God and his righteousnes shal bring all other things with it as appurtenances. This may suffice for the generall view of faith.

Rom. 8. 32.

Now more specially, faith is supported by one argument principally, [*thine is kingdome,*] which may be framed after this forme.

Gods kingdome.

Euery good king will prouide, not onely for the aduauncement of his kingdome, for the obedience of his lawes, and for his honour and glorie; but also for the good and welfare of his subiects, in soule and body.

But thou Lord, art a good King, for the kingdome is thine.

Thou therefore wilt prouide, &c.

This argument doth either directly or indirectly confirme our faith for the obtaining of all the sixe petitions, as may easily be perceiued: directly it confirmeth our faith in the second, but indirectly and by consequent in all the rest.

This kingdome of God, which is the ground of the argument, is amplified by three arguments:

1 It is a powerfull kingdome. [*thine is power.*]
2 It is a glorious kingdome. [*thine is glorie.*]
3 It is an euerlasting kingdome. [*for euer.*]

And so there are three other arguments whereby our faith is supported for obtaining the petitions.

The second argument therefore which is taken from the power of God is added necessarily as an answere to an obiection, which might be opposed thus: though God be a king, yet except he haue power to subdue his enemies, the aduauncement of his kingdome shall be hindered: the answere whereof is, that as God is a king, so he is omnipotent, able to conquer all his enemies that shall rebell against him: and so this argument taken from Gods power may thus be concluded. A king that is of abilitie will aduance his kingdome, cause himselfe to be honoured, cause his subiects to obey his will, and prouide for the outward prosperitie and inward felicitie of his subiects:

Power of Gods kingdome.

God he is of abilitie being a powerfull king:
Therefore he will prouide for his honour, &c.

The third argument is taken from the glory of Gods kingdome: *Glory of Gods kingdome.*

Where first, consider the meaning of the words: *Thine is glorie:* that is, 1. Thou hast made al things for thy glory. 2. The things we aske are meanes of thy glory. 3. The things we aske shall by vs be referred to thy glory: and so the conclusion followeth: *Ergo,* graunt vs these things which we aske in these petitions.

Secondly, let vs also consider the argument framed thus, directly confirming our faith for the first petition.

That which is most deere to thy selfe thou wilt procure:

But thy glory is most deere to thy selfe:

Therefore glorifie thy selfe by vs or in vs, or giue vs grace to glorifie thy name.

Indirectly it confirmeth our faith in all the other petitions after this manner.

Thou Lord wilt further all the meanes of thy glorie:

But the enlarging of thy kingdome, the obedience of thy will, our daily bread, remission of sinne, and perseuerance in grace are meanes of thy glory:

Therefore Lord we are perswaded thou wilt cause, &c.

The fourth argument wherby our faith is strengthened, is taken from the eternitie or euerlasting continuance of this kingdome, and of the two other properties thereof, mentioned in the second and third arguments: for the kingdome, power and glory of God is euerlasting, or Gods powerfull and glorious kingdome is eternall, and that in a double respect: *The eternitie of Gods kingdome.*

1 In themselues, for that they neuer haue end:

2 In the faithfull, who doe and will euerlastingly remember and magnifie the Lord, the most mighty and glorious king.

This fourth argument is framed after this manner:

If thy kingdome, power, and glory shall euerlastingly be remembred and magnified by vs, as it is euerlasting in it selfe: then grant these our praiers which are means thereof.

But by granting these our petitions, we shall be

prouoked to procure the euerlasting remembrance of thy kingdome, power and glory, by our selues as long as we liue, by our holy seede after vs, and for euermore in thy heauenly kingdome.

Therefore we are perswaded thou wilt graunt vs these our petitions.

<small>Faith is supported: God is not perswaded by arguments.</small> Thus our faith is supported and strengthened by arguments, which are vsed not to perswade God, who is vnchangeable and immoueable in his purposes; but to perswade vs, who are of little faith, and scarse beleeue God himselfe, and therefore haue need to find out in our selues strong arguments, as it were maine pillars to support our faith, as it were a crasie house ready to fall to decay continuallie.

<small>Desire, a part of feruency.</small> The second part of feruencie is desire, which is expressed in the word, *Amen*.

As faith is the principall worke of the vnderstanding, so desire is the principall worke of the will in regard of that which we want: and as faith may well be compared to the hand or arme, laying hold vpon blessings, so desire may be compared to the brawne or sinewes of the arme or hand, the instruments of strength, whereby wee holde fast that which we apprehend. This is expressed by *Matthew* in very significant and <small>*Mat.* 7. 7.</small> forcible metaphors: *Aske*, as a begger doth to get an almes: *Seeke*, as one with a candle looketh for a iewell lost vpon the ground: *Knocke*, with strength and force to get open the gate of Mercie. The word whereby desire is expressed in an Hebrue word, and it signi- <small>What Amen</small> fieth, *verely, truely, certainely, so be it, let it bee* <small>doth signifie.</small> *so: O Lord I desire it might be so as I aske*. And this may afford an argument for the confirmation of our faith to obtaine, taken from the trueth of God framed in this forme.

Thou Lord art a God of trueth, thou art true in all thy promises; thy promises are yea and <small>Amen con-</small> Amen: thou art Amen, the faithfull and true <small>taineth an argument to</small> witnesse: thou keepest fidelitie for euer: <small>support our</small>

But thou hast promised to grant the peti- <small>faith.</small> tions of thy seruants made in feruencie of desire and faith:

Therefore grant these our petitions so qualified.

Thus the manner of making our prayers is taught vs in the conclusion of this prayer, which is feruencie in the two parts thereof, faith and desire. Now contrary to feruencie is coldnes in prayer, whereof something briefely must be spoken, that contraries may be more perspicuous by their opposition. A cold prayer is either when a man vnderstandeth not that which he bableth with his lips, or hath no assurance to obtaine that hee asketh, or regardeth it not in comparison; or prayeth liuing in sinne vnrepented of: for all these conditions are as it were colde water cast into a boyling caldron, which boyling before through heate, now ceaseth. The Apostle *Iames* compareth such prayers to waues of the sea, tost to and fro with the wind, and at length are consumed into froth, or beaten in peeces vpon the rocke: for although perhaps a cold prayer may swell in great and eloquent words, and roare with pitifull complaints and outcries, and be tumbled vp and downe in the mouth by repetitions, or in the mind by imagination; yet at the length the winds of wandring thoughts, faint affections, or grosse ignorance driueth them vpon the rockes of presumption, doubting, despaire and impenitencie, and so suddainely they are dissolued into froth, and consumed into nothing.

<small>Coldnes in prayer.</small>

<small>*Iam.* 1. 6.</small>

<small>A cold prayer obtaineth nothing.</small>

In briefe therefore to conclude this conclusion: wee must striue and wrastle with the Lord in time of prayer, as *Iacob* did with the Angell, holding him fast, not letting him goe till he blesse vs, till he change our names, and call vs Israel, men preuailing with God: that so after our prayers we may find spirituall ioy and comfort, and incouragement in all our waies, which is the fruite of feruent prayer.

<small>*Genes.* 32. 24. *Hosea.* 12. 4.</small>

Here should bee the end of this treatise, but that there are certaine extrauagant questions to bee discussed, which could not be referred to any one proper place of the former method, and yet containe matter very profitable, though onely probable and consisting of vncertainties and coniectures for the most part. The questions, with their answeres, are briefly these following.

1 Whether Christ euer prayed the Lords prayer?

The answere: It is probable that Christ did pray the
Whether Christ prayed the Lords prayer. Lords prayer himselfe, for himselfe and for vs: for although the expositors say that the word *Father* is *Naturæ nomen, non personæ*: that is to say, common to all the three persons, not proper to the first person: and therefore it would follow, that if Christ prayed this prayer, he should pray to himselfe: yet if it be said that the word *Father* may be either proper to the father, or common to all the three persons, or both; there will no absurditie follow, and the obiection is answered. Againe, if it be obiected further that Christ should pray for the pardon of sinnes, he hauing committed no sinne, thereby giuing occasion to thinke that he had sinne: the answere will be very indifferent, that Christ might vse that petition as an instrument of intercession for vs, and not as a petition for pardon of his sinne, prescribing it neuerthelesse vnto vs for a prayer of remission who had sinned: or else it might be answered, that Christ being the suretie might intreate God to pardon his sinnes, not the sinnes which he had committed, but the sinnes which were to him imputed: or the petition being deliuered plurally, (*forgiue vs*) it may bee Christ prayed for both: and there was no doubt of misconceit in his Disciples, to whom hee priuately expounded doubtfull matters: and if the matter bred any misconceit in the other auditors, it was through their own corruption and ignorance, and therein the Lords iustice might appeare in blinding their mindes and hardening their hearts, as himself teacheth, who oft times spake obscurely and ambiguously.

2 How oft Christ vsed the Lords prayer? and how?

The answere of this question is partly cer- **How oft Christ vsed the Lords prayer, and how.** taine, partly probable. It is certaine that Christ vsed the Lords prayer twice: first, he vsed it when he taught the doctrine of prayer: and so *Matthew* hath propounded it as a part of the sermon in the mount. Secondly, he vsed it when he taught his Disciples a forme of prayer, according to the example of *Iohn*, who taught his Disciples a paterne of prayer, and this was presently after Christ had ended his prayers in a certaine place, as *Luke* reporteth: whence in all probabilitie it may be collected, that *Matthew* prescribeth this prayer one way, and *Luke* another: for in *Matthew* Christ taught the doctrine of prayer, and so it is dogmaticall in *Matthew*: *Luke* saith Christ taught a prayer: for his words are, *When ye pray, say:* and so it is practical: so that Christ taught it both for a prayer which his Disciples might vse, and for the doctrine of prayer, which his Disciples might teach. Againe, it is probable that Christ neuer vsed this prayer but twice, although it cannot be demonstratiuely proued; onely this coniecture we haue, that whereas Christ maketh diuers prayers to his Father in the Euangelists, this is not mentioned, nor any petition of it in so many words, and the Euangelists neuer name it elsewhere by any speciall name, and the Apostles in their writings neuer make mention of it: but when they pray in their writings vse other formes, though still they keep themselues within the compasse of the matter and affections of this prayer (which we call the Lords prayer, both for that it was composed by Christ and vsed by him:) hence therefore it followeth probablie, that the Apostles neuer tied themselues to the words of this prayer, but varied vpon occasion. Briefly then, Christ vsed this prayer twice: but it cannot certainly be determined whether he vsed it oftner: neither can it be proued that the Apostles vsed it often.

3 Whether Christ spake all and onely the words of the Lords prayer?

<small>Whether Christ spake all and onely the words of the Lords prayer.</small> The answere is onely coniecturall: for it cannot be proued that he vsed the very words set downe by the Euangelists: the reason is, for that the Euangelists vse to set down, not all and onely the words which Christ spake, but the summe and substance of them: and if it be graunted that the Euangelists haue done it in other places, why may they not doe it in this place? especially seeing the Euangelists doe differ in words in reciting many of Christs speeches, as namely <small>Mat. 5. 3. Luk. 6. 20.</small> of the Beatitudes: *Matthew* maketh eight, *Luke* reciteth but foure: and *Luke* expresseth the contrary woes, and *Matthew* doth omit them: whence this may in al likelihood be collected, that Christ vsed diuers other words by way of exposition to the Beatitudes,

and so by consequent to the petitions of the Lords prayer: and wee see directly that Christ expoundeth one petition, *viz.* the fifth: and why might he not also expound others? seeing that other petitions are as hard to bee vnderstood as that: and this doth not any whit call into question the truth of Canonicall Scripture, but doth rather commend vnto vs the spirit of wisedome and truth wherewith they spake, in that diuers writers differing in words, still agree in matter and substance of doctrine. Vpon this question and answere dependeth another like vnto it, *viz.*

4 How the Euangelists *Matthew* and *Luke* differ in rehearsing the Lords prayer? Matth. 6. Luk. 11.

The difference betwixt Matthew and Luke in repeating the Lords prayer.

For answere whereof wee are to consider what the Papists say. They make a very great difference: for in the vulgar Latin translation there are these three clauses in *Matthew*, which are wanting in *Luke*.

First in the preface (*which art in heauen*) is wanting.

Secondly, the third petition is wholie wanting.

Thirdly, the last petition wanteth one halfe (*Deliuer vs from euill.*) Yet they say all these things are included in the other petitions, or else may necessarily bee deduced from them: but let the Popish dreames goe: and let vs see the true differences which are three in words, but the substance is all one.

The first difference in words is of the fourth petition: for *Matthew* saith, *sémeron;* Luke, *cath' eméran.*

The second difference in words is in the fifth petition: for all the words in the originall differ, except two or three.

The third difference is in the conclusion, which *Matthew* hath, and *Luke* wanteth.

Now by this difference betwixt *Matthew* and *Luke*, which is verbal not material, this cōsequence ariseth, either that the Euangelists did not precisely bind themselues to the words that Christ vttered, or else that Christ vttered the Lords prayer in diuers words at the two seuerall times when he vttered it.

5 Who prayeth best, he that saieth the Lords prayer, or he that saieth not the Lords prayer?

Who maketh the best prayer.

For answere of this question thus much:

The Lords prayer is the best forme of prayer that euer was deuised.

The Lords prayer is the best prayer that euer was deuised.

He that prayeth the Lords prayer in words and matter, prayeth well.

Hee that prayeth the Lords prayer in matter onely, prayeth well, though he vse other words, as Christ vsed other words, Iohn 17.

It is one thing to say the Lords prayer, another thing to pray it.

It is one thing to vse the Lords prayer aright, another thing to abuse it: for a good thing may be absurdly abused.

He that vseth a deuised forme of prayer aright, prayeth more acceptably to God, than he that abuseth the Lords prayer.

It is likely that he which can say nothing but the Lords prayer when he prayeth, cannot pray, but abuseth the Lords prayer.

It seemeth that that man doth not sinne which neuer vseth the words of the Lords prayer for a prayer, for that Christ did neuer intend to bind vs to the forme of words, but of matter.

He that in particular hath conceiued his wants, and accordingly made his petitions to the Lord in a conceiued prayer, may neuer the lesse end and conclude his prayer with the Lords prayer.

Diuers other doubtes concerning the vse of the Lords prayer may bee propounded; but it is not profitable to make doubts, except that they could well be dissolued: only thus much for a conclusion of this treatise of prayer: I had rather speake fiue words to God in prayer, from vnderstanding, faith and feeling, than say the Lords prayer ouer a thousand times ignorantly, negligently, or superstitiously.

FINIS.

[ornament]

PRINCIPLES
and inferences
concerning
The visible Church

Mat. 22. 29. Ye are deceived, not knowing the scriptures.

1 Cor. 14. 38. If any man be ignorant, let him be ignorant.

Iob 19. vers. 4. Though I had indeed erred myne errour remayneth with me.

vers. 19. All my secret friends abhorred mee, and they whō I loved are turned against mee.

1607

The Author to the Reader

Lo heer gentle Reader a short description of the new Testament which was once established by the blood of Christ: after that the old testament by the blood of that his crosse was disannulled: Remember that there be alwaies a difference put betwixt the covenant of grace; and the manner of dispensing it, which is twofold: the forme of administring the covenant before the death of Christ, which is called the old testament; and the forme of administring the covenant since the death of Christ which is called the new Testament or the kingdome of heaven. In this litle treatise the ordinances of Christ for the dispensing of the covenant since his death are described: read, consider, compare the truth here expressed with the frame ministerie and government of the assemblies of the land: and accordingly give sentence, iudge righteous iudgement, and let practise answerable to the truth follow therevpon: fear not the face of man, love not the world, be not deceaved with the shapes of Angels of light, cast away all preiudice against the truth, remember that Antechristianisme is a misterie of iniquity and that it beganne to work early during the Apostles life, and so grew by litle and litle to this strength & exaltation, from which it shall decline by degrees even til the man of synne be destroyed, whom the L. shall consume with the brightnes of his comming, for God which condemneth the whore of Babilon is a strong Lord. Farewell.

[ornament]

PRINCIPLES AND INFERENCES CONCERNING THE VISIBLE CHURCH

A Man may be a member of the visible church & no member of the Catholique Church. Iohn 17. 12, Gen, 4, 11. 13, Heb. 12, 17, 2 Sam. 7, 15.

A man may be a member of the Catholique church & no member of the visible church. 1 King, 14, 13. Rev. 18. 4. Rom. 11. 4. 1 King 19, 18.

The Catholique church is the company of the Elect. Iohn 17. 20. & it is invisible, Col. 1. 20.

The visible church is a visible communion of saints. Mat. 18, 12. Act. 2, 1, 41, 42. 46, & 1. 15. & 19. 7. 1 Cor, 1, 2. Phil. 1, 1. al which are to be accounted faithful and elect: Eph. 1, 1, 4. 5, 7, 11, 13 14. til they by obstinacy in syn and apostacy declare the contrary. 1 Iohn 2, 19. 2 Tim, 4. 10. & 1. 1, 19. 20. 2 Thes, 3, 14, 15. 2 Tim. 2, 17. 18–21.

It is one thing to be a Sainct, another thing to be of the visible communion of Saincts. 1 King. 14, 13. compared with 2 Chron. 13, 8–12.

The communion of Saints is eyther Invisible or visible Eph. 3, 17, Mat. 18. 10. Heb, 1. 14. 1 Cor, 13, 9–13.

The invisible cō cōmunio is with { Christ / Elect } 1 Cor 15, 28 Eph. 3, 17. 1 Cor, 13. 13

Invisible communion with Christ is by the spirit and faith. Eph. 3. 17, & 4, 4. and 2, 22

Invisible cōmunio with the Elect { Men / Angels } Heb. 1, 14. 1 Cor, 13. 13

Men Elect are { Dead / Living } Colos. 1, 20. Elect living are { vncalled / called }

Communion with the Elect living is prayer proceeding from love. Iohn 17. 20 for them that are vncalled that they may be called Rom 10, 1 for them that are called that they may be confirmed. Col. 1, 9–12.

Communion with the Elect Angels is the help of their ministery. Mat. 18, 10. Heb. 1, 14. Gen 28, 12. & 32. 1, 2. Psal 34. 7 reverence of them 1 Cor. 11. 10, & love vnto them. 1 Cor, 13, 13.

A visible communion of Sainčts is of two, three, or moe Sainčts joyned together by covenant with God & themselves, freely to vse al the holy things of God, according to the word, for their mutual edification, & Gods glory. Mat. 18 20 Deut. 29, 12. &c Psal 147, 19 & 149, 6–9. Rev. 1. 6.

This visible communion of Saincts is a visible Church. Mat. 18. 20, Act. 1, 15. & 2. 1 41, 42, 46.

The visible church is the only religious societie that God hath ordeyned for men on earth. Iohn 14. 6, Mat. 18, 20 & 7, 13. 14. 2 Chron. 13. 8–12. Act 4. 12. Rev. 18. 4. 2 Cor 6. 16–18.

All religious societies except that of a visible church are vnlawful: as Abbayes, monasteries, Nunries, Cathedralls, Collegiats, parishes.

The visible church is Gods ordināce & a means to worship god in. Eph. 4. 6–6, Marc. 13. 34. 2 Chron. 13. 10. 11. Heb. 3. 6. compared with Heb. 8. 5. & 3. 2–6

No relig[i]ous communion to be had but with members of a visible church Mat 18. 17. 20. 1 Cor, 5, 12. Act. 4. 11. 12. 2 Cor. 6. 16–18. Rev. 18. 4.

Whatsoever companie or communion of men, do worship God, being not of the communion of a visible church, Synne 2 Chron 13. 9. 10. Mat. 15. 9, 1 Cor 5 12 13

The true visible church is the narrow way that leadeth to life which few find Ioh. 14, 6, Mat. 7. 14.

Other religious communions are the broad way that leadeth to destruction which many find. Mat. 7. 13. Acts 4. 12[.]

Gods word doth absolutely describe vnto vs the only true shape of a true visible church Marc. 13, 34 1 Cor. 12. 5. Heb. 8, 5, & 3, 2–6. Rev. 22. 18. 19. 2 Tim. 3. 16. 17. Rom 14. 23. Heb. 11. 6[.]

There is one only true shape or portrayture of a true visible church for there is onely one faith and truth in

concerning the visible Church

everie thing. Ioh. 14, 6, Eph. 4. 4, 5. 1 Cor. 1. 10. 13 Ioh. 17 17

Formes, or shapes, of visible churches or religious communions, to worship God in or by, devised by men ar intellectuall Idols, or mental Idolatry. Exod. 20. 4. 5. Mat. 15, 9. 2 Chron. 13, 8–12. 1 Kin. 12, 33[.]

Visible Churches or religious cōmunions constituted according to the forged devise of men are reall Idols, and to joyne to them and to worship God in them is to joyne to Idols, or to worship God in or by Idols. by consequēt from the former

Visible churches or religious communions are either true or false. Ioh. 14. 6. Psal. 119. 128. 2 Chro. 13. 8–12. Eph. 4, 4, 5, 6.

True visible churches are such as have the true essentiall causses and properties, which Gods word ascribeth to the true visible Church. from the definition. False churches are the contrary to the true, by proportion.

To a true visible Church are requisite three things. 1. True matter. 2. true forme. 3. true properties.

The true matter of a true visible Church are Saints. Exod. 28. 9. 10. 15–21 cōpared with Rev. 21 14–21. & 1 King. 5. 17. cōpared with 1 Pet. 2, 5, Levit. 11. toto 13. 43. 44 compared with Rev. 18. 2. 1 Pet. 2. 9. Deut. 14, 2, Rom. 1. 7. 1 Cor. 1. 2. Eph 1, 1. Phil. 1. 1. 1 Pet. 1. 2. Heb. 3. 1.

Sainᶜts are men separated from all knowne syn, practising the whol will of God knowne vnto thē, Col. 1. 2. & 2, 11–13. Rom. 1, 7, and 6. 2. 12. 22. growing in grace and knowledg. 2 Pet. 3. 18. continuing to the end 1 Ioh. 2. 19.

The true form of a true visible Church is partly inward, partly outward.

The inward part of the forme cōsisteth in 3. things 1. the Spirit 2. Faith. 3. love.

The Spirit is the soule animating the whol body. Ephe. 4. 4. 1 Cor. 12. 4. 11–13 7–10. 1 Cor. 6. 17.

Faith vniteth the mēbers of the body to the head Christ: Eph. 3. 17 & 4. 13. 15. & 5. 30. 23. 1 Cor. 6. 17

Love vniteth the members of the body each to other. Eph. 2. 20. 21 et 4. 16 3. Col. 3. 14. 15.

The outward part of the true forme of the true visible church is a vowe, promise, oath, or covenant betwixt God and the Saints: by proportion from the inward forme: see also Gen. 17. 1. 2. and 15. 18. Deut. 29. 1. 9–13. 2 Chron. 29. 10 & 34. 30–32. Psal. 119. 106. Nehem. 9. 38. & 10. 29. 1 Cor. 12. 25, 26. Rom. 12. 5. 15. 16. Mat 18. 15. 17.

This covenant hath 2 parts. 1. respecting God and the faithful. 2. respecting the faithful mutually. Mat. 18. 20.

The first part of the covenant respecting God is either frō God to the faithful, or frō the faithful to God 2 Cor. 6. 16.

From God to the faithfull. Mat. 22. 32. the sum whereof is expressed 2 Cor. 6. 16 I wilbe their God.

To be God to the faithful is 1. to give Christ. 2. with Christ al things els. Esay. 9. 6. 1 Tim. 4. 8. 2 Pet. 1. 3. Rom. 8. 32. 1 Cor. 3. 21–23.

From the faithful to God 2 Cor. 6. 16. the sūme whereof is to be Gods people, that is to obey al the commandements of God. Deut 29. 9.

The second part of the covenant respecting the faithful mutually conteyneth all the duties of love whatsoever. Levit. 19, 17, Mat. 18. 15, 16. 1 Thes. 5. 14. Mat. 22. 39. 2 Thes. 3. 14. 15. Heb. 3. 13. & 10. 24. 25.

The true properties of a true Church visible are two. 1. communion in al the holy things of God: 2, the power of our Lord Iesus Christ. 1 Ioh. 1. 3 1 Cor. 10. 16. & 5. 4 5. Mat. 18. 20. Esay 55. 3. Act 13. 34.

The holy things of God are 1. Christ. 2. benefits by Christ. Rom. 8. 32.

The true church hath title, possession, and vse of Christ. Esa. 9. 6. Song 2. 16. Mat. 18. 20. 1 Cor. 3. 21–23. Eph. 5, 30[.]

The benefits which the true Church hath by Christ are the meanes of salvation and almes. 1 Tim. 14. 8. 2 Pet. 1. 3.

The meanes of salvation are: the word, Sacraments, prayers, Censures, and the ordinances of Christ for the dispensing of them all. Rom 3. 2. & 4. 11. Luk. 19. 46. Mat. 18. 15–17. Act. 2. 42. 1 Cor. 11. 23–26. Mat. 28. 19. Psal. 149. 6–9.

concerning the visible Church 255

Almes are the works of mercy yeelded to the Saintes in distresse. Aċt 2. 44. 45. & 5. 4. Mat. 25. 34–40. Heb. 13. 1–3. 1 Tim. 3. 2. & 5. 10.

The power of the L. Iesus Christ givē to the church hath three parts.

viz powre to
1. receave in Ioh. 10 3. Aċts 9. 26. 27. & 18. 27. & 6. 5
2. preserve & keep within 1 Ioh. 2. 19. 1 Pet. 1. 5
3. to cast out 1 Cor. 5. 13

The true visible church hath powre to receive in 1. Members into communion. Aċt 2, 41. and 18. 27. and 9. 26. 27. & 2. officers into office Aċt. 6. 5. and 14. 23.

The way or dore wherby both members and officers enter in is Christ, that is the way taught by Christ in his word, Ioh. 14. 6 & 10. 3. 7, 9. and 17. 17 Marc. 13. 34–37.

The way of receaving in of members is fayth testified by obedience, Aċt. 8. 36, 37, Mat. 3. 6. Luk. 7. 29. 30

Fayth is the knowledg of the doċtrine of salvatiō by Christ 1 Cor. 12. 9. Gal. 3. 2[.]

Obedience is a godly, righteous and sober life. Tit. 2. 11. 12. Rom 1, 5[.]

Members thus receaved into communion are of two sorts. 1. Prophets 2. private persons 1 Cor. 14, 24, 1 Sam. 19. 20–23

Prophets are men endued with gifts apt to vtter matter fit to edification, exhortation, and consolation. 1 Cor. 14, 3, Act. 13, 1, Rom. 12. 6.

These persons must first be appointed to this exercise by the church. 1 Cor. 14, 40, Act, 13. 1

The Prophets care must be to prophecy according to the proportiō of faith. Rō. 12, 6, 1 Cor. 14, 26.

Let the Prophets speak two or three and let the rest judge 1 Cor. 14, 29[.]

If any thing be revealed to him that sitteth by let the first hold his peace 1 Cor. 14, 30, 40

All that have gifts may be admitted to prophecy 1 Cor. 14. 31,

Private persons are 1 men 2. weomen

Private men present at the exercise of prophecy may modestly propound their doubts which are to be resolved by the prophets: Luk. 2, 46, 47, 1 Sam. 19, 20–23. 1 Cor. 14, 30[.]

Weomen are not permitted to speak in the church in tyme of prophecy. 1 Cor. 14. 34. 1 Tim. 2. 12. Revel. 2, 20.

If women doubt of any thing delivered in tyme of prophecy and are willing to learn, they must ask them that can teach them in private, as their husbands at home if they be faithful, or some other of the church. 1 Cor. 14, 35. 1 Tim 2, 12.

To this exercise of prophecy may be admitted vnbeleevers or they that are without. 1 Cor. 14, 24. Act[s], 2, 6, 13.

The exercise of prophecy, and the preaching of the word by them that are sent, is that ordinary meanes God hath appointed to convert men. 1 Cor. 14, 24. 25, Rom. 10, 14, 15.

They are sent by God to preach whō the church sendeth Act. 13, 2–4. & 8, 14. 15.

If any man be converted by other meanes it is not ordinarie. Rom, 10. 14, 15. Iohn 4, 39. 41. Act, 9, 5, 6.

Therfore they that are converted in false churches are not converted by ordinary meanes. 1 Kin. 14, 13. & 19, 18. Rom. 11, 3. 4. Rev. 18. 4.

The way of receiving officers into office is, 1 Election, 2 Approbation, 3 Ordination: which must be performed with fasting & prayer. Act, 6, 5. & 14. 23. 1 Tim. 3, 10. & 5, 22. & 4, 14. Tit, 1, 5, Act. 13. 3.

The person to be admitted into office must first be a mēber of that visible church whence he hath his calling. Act. 1, 21, 22. & 6, 3–5. & 18, 27, 28. 1 Cor. 1, 12. & 3, 6. 1 Tim. 3, 2, 3. 10.

Electiō is by most voyces of the members of the Church in ful communion. Act. 6, 5. & 14, 23.

Quære: whether weomen, servants, & children admitted into ful communion, yet vnder age may not give voyce in Elections, excommunications, and other publique affaires of the church. 1 Pet. 3, 7 Ephes. 4, 4. 1 Tim. 5, 9, 10. Num. 30. 5–10–16. 1 Cor. 14, 34. Gen. 3, 16. 1 Cor. 11, 3, 10. Gen. 18, 19. Iosh. 24. 15.

Approbation is the examining & finding the officer

elect to be according to the rules of his office. 1 Tim 3. 10. & 5. 9, 10. Act 6, 3.

In approbation every member is bound to object what he can especially they that denyed theyr voyces. Act. 15, 37, 38. 1 Tim. 3, 2. 3, 10. Act. 6, 3.

Approbation must be after election, least without cause the infirmities of the brethren be discovered: for there are faults disabling men to offices which do not disable them to be members of the church. Ezec. 44, 9–15. Act. 15, 37, 38. Mat. 18. 21. 22. *compared with* Prov. 10, 12. 1 Pet. 4, 8.

If the things objected bear weight against the officer elect, the election is voyd & they must proceed to the choice of another. 1 Tim. 3, 4, 5. & 5. 11. Act. 15, 37. 38. Ezec. 44. 10. 2 King. 23. 9.

Defects or faults that cast men out of office, are sufficient to hinder men from entring into office: by proportion.

If the things objected be frivolous the election is approved. 1 Tim. 3, 10 and they that dissented ar to consent to the rest that so the whol church may agree in one person. 1 Cor. 1, 10. Eph. 4, 3. *compared with* Act. 1, 26.

If the parties objecting stil dissent without an approved reason, they are to be reformed by censure. 1 Cor. 11. 17, 18. Mat. 18, 15–17.

Ordination is the dedication of the officer thus approved to his office. Exod. 29, 44 & 40, 12, 16. Nomb. 8, 6, 15. Heb. 5, 4, 5. Mat. 3, 13–17. Act. 13. 3. 4 1 Tim. 4, 14. Heb. 6, 2.

Ordination hath 3 parts.

The first is the powre which the church cōmitteth to the officer approved: to administer according to his office. Ioh. 20 21–23. Mat. 18, 15–20, cōpared with Exod. 29 1, 38, Nomb. 8 10. 11 Act. 6, 3, 5, & 14. 23, & 20. 28, 1 Tim. 4. 14. 2 Tim 1, 6 14.

The 2. is prayer made by the whole church for the officer invested with this powre that he may faythfully administer; Act. 6, 6, and 13, 3, & 14, 23 1 Cor. 4, 2[.]

The 3. is a charge given to the officer thus admitted to look vnto his office in all the parts thereof, Mat. 28

18. 19, 1 Tim, 5, 21, 1 Pet. 5, 1, 2. 1 Tim. 6. 13, 14, *compared with* Deut. 1, 16.

The ceremonie vsed by the Apostles in ordination is imposition of hands: which ceremony first of all was vsed in the old testament Nomb. 8, 10 thē in the new: by Christ in praying for children Mar. 10. 16 by God the Father in ordeyning Christ to his office of Mediatour, Luk. 3. 21. 22 by Christ in ordeyning the Apostles. Act. 2, 3, 4, & 1, 4. 8 by the Apostles in giving the holy Ghost, Act 8. 15–17 in ordeyning Evangelists 2 Tim, 1. 6, and in ordeyning ordinarie Ministers: Act. 6, 6, and 14, 23 by the Eldership or chur[c]h in ordeyning officers Act. 13. 3, 1 Tim. 4, 4, by the Evangelists in ordeyning officers 1 Tim 5. 22. Tit. 1. 5 & so may lawfully be reteyned and vsed in the church stil. Heb. 6. 2.

The vse of imposition of hands is twofold.

First to poynt out the officer in tyme of prayer made for him, as if it should be sayd; this is the mā. by proportion from 1 Sam 10, 24, Mat. 3. 17.

Secondly to signifie and to assure the officer to be ordeyned that the Lord by the church giveth him power to administer. Act. 13, 3, 4. & 20, 28. Ioh 20, 21.

Ordination and so imposition of hands apperteyneth to the whole church as doth election and approbation. Act. 13., 3 Num. 8, 9, 10 yet for order sake the fittest members lay on hands and perform al other the particulars of ordination for & in the name of the whole church. 1 Cor. 14, 40 *compared with* Num. 8, 9, 10. & Act. 13, 3. & 1 Tim. 4, 14, *and by proportion from* Lev. 4, 15.

The fittest persons are Elders when the Church hath them. 1 Tim 4. 14 when the church wanteth Elders men of best gifts appointed by the church. Num. 8, 9. 10.

Thus after the apostacy of Antichrist ariseth a true Ministerie in the church. Revel. 15. 4

The officers of the true visible church thus admitted are then to administer faithfully. 1 Tim. 3, 10, 1 Cor. 4, 2.

The officers of the true visible church are al absolutely described in the word of God. Heb. 3, 2. 5. & 8. 5. Rom. 12, 7, 8. Marc, 13, 34.

These officers ar of two sorts: 1 Bishops, 2 Deacons Phil. 1, 1.

The Bishops are also called Elders or Presbyters Act. 20, 17. 28. 1 Pet. 5, 1.

The Bishops or Elders joyntly together are called the Eldership or Presbyterie, 1 Tim. 4, 14 and 5, 17. *compared*

The Eldership consisteth of 3 sorts of persons or officers: viz. the Pastor, Teacher, Governours. 1 Tim 4. 14. & 5. 17.

Al the Elders or Bbs. must be apt to teach. 1 Tim. 3. 2. Tit. 1. 9.

The Pastor is a Bishop excelling in the word of wisdom or exhortation: Rom. 12, 8. 1 Cor 12, 8. he is called the Angel of the church Rev. 2. & 3.

The Teacher is a Bishop excelling in the word of knowledge or doctrine. Rom. 12, 7. 1 Cor. 12. 8

The Governour is a Bishop excelling in the quality of wise government. 1 Tim. 5, 17. Rom. 12, 8.

The Pastor and Teacher have also power to administer the Sacraments. Mat. 28, 19. Ephes. 4, 12, 2 Cor. 11, 23.

Al the Bishops deal by office in the government of the church, 1 Tim 5, 17 & are conversant about the soule and spiritual parte. Ioh. 18. 36. 2 Cor. 10, 3

The Deacons are officers occupied about the works of mercy respecting the body or outward man. Act. 6, 2.

The Deacons ar 1. men 2. or weomen deacons or widowes. Act. 6, 2. Rom. 16, 1.

Men Deacons collect and distribute with simplicity the churches treasury according to the churches necessities, and the Saincts occasions. Rom. 12, 8. 2 Cor. 8, 2–8. 1 Cor. 16, 2. 3.

The churches treasurie is silver gold or money worth, freely given by the members of the visible church for the common good[.] Lev. 27. *toto.* 2 King. 12. 4–16. Luke 21, 4. Act. 4, 34, 35. 2 Cor. 8, 2–8. & 9. 7.

The churches treasurie is holy. Mat. 27. 6. Luke 21. 4 Quaere.

None of those that are without may cast of their goods into the treasurie lest the treasury be polluted. 2 Cor. 8. 4. Iosh. 6, 17–19. Quaere

Nothing that is gotten by fraud, violence, or any wicked meanes, may be cast into the churches treasury. Deut. 23, 18. Micah 1, 7. Esa. 66. 3.

The vse of the churches treasurie is peculiar to the Saints: and it consisteth in provision for holy things, or holy persons. Deut. 14, 2, 3, 21. Exod. 30. 12–16. Quaere.

Holy things: as bread and wine for the Lords Supper, places and instruments serviceable to holy vses Exod. 25, 2, 8. Mat. 27. 7 *per contrarium.*

Holy persons: as the maintenance of church officers and the poor brethren eyther of that particular visible church or of any other true church. 1 Cor 26, 2, 3. 2 Cor. 8, 7. 1 Cor. 9, 6–14[.] 1 Tim. 5, 17, 18.

In the necessitie of the church if they that are without bestow any thing vpō the Saints they may receive and vse it with thanksgiving. 1 Cor. 10, 25, 26.

If it be manifested by evidence that the goods of them that are without offered to the Saints be the treasures of wickednes, the Saints ar not to receive and vse them to avoyd offence. 1 Cor. 10, 28. 29.

Weomen deacons or widowes are of 60 yeeres of age, qualified according to the Apostles rule. 1 Tim. 5. 9. releeving the bodily infirmities of the Saincts with cheerfulnes. Rom. 12. 8. and 16, 1

Hitherto of the churches power of receiving in: now followeth the churches powre of preserving & keeping within.

The powre of preserving within is manifested by the heedful vse of al the holy things of God by the whole church joyntly, and by every member perticularly, Marc. 13, 33–37. Heb. 10, 24. 1 Thes. 5, 14 Mat, 18, 15–17. Act. 6, 1

The Pastors cheef endeavour must be to make the church zealous holy and obedient. Rom 12, 8. 1 Cor. 12, 8. Apoc. 3. 19 *by proportion.*

The Teachers cheef care must be to preserve the church from ignorance and error 1 Cor. 12, 8. Rom. 12, 7. 1 Cor 3, 10. 12 *compared with* Tit. 1. 9.

The cheef office of the governours consisteth in preserving peace and order in the church. 1 Cor. 14 40– Rom. 12, 8. 1 Tim, 5. 17.

The Deacons cheef care must be that none of the Saincts want bodily necessaries, and that due provision be made for holy things & persons. Rom 12. 8. Iohn 13, 29. and that with simplicity Iohn 12. 6.

The widowes cheef office is to visite and relieve the widow, fatherless, sick lame, blind, impotent, weomen with child, and diseased members of the church. 1 Tim. 5. 9 Rom. 12. 8. Mat 25. 35–40.

The care of the Eldership must be to order, direct, & moderate the publique actiōs of the church. 1 Cor 14, 40. 1 Tim. 5. 17.

The prophets cheef care must be to resolve doubts, difficulties, and dark places, & to give true expositions, translations, & reconciliations of scripture. 1 Cor. 14. 26. 30. Luk. 2, 46. 47.

The office of the pastor and teacher in the exercise of prophecie is to moderate and determine all matters out of the word. 1 Cor. 14. 32. 1 Sam. 19. 20.

The care of the whole church joyntly must be to keep her powre given her by Christ, and not to suffer any open known synne, or any tyranny or vsurpation over them. Mat. 18, 15–17. Marc. 13. 37. Col. 4, 17. 3 Iohn 9. 10 Rev. 2. 2. Gal. 1, 8. 9.

The cheef care of every mēber must be to watch over his brother Marc. 13. 37. Heb. 10. 24. in bearing one anothers burden Gal. 6. 2. 1 Cor. 10, 24. 28. 29 admonishing the vnruly, comforting the feeble mynded. 1 Thes. 5. 14. admonishing the excommunicate 2 Thes. 3, 15 restoring them that are fallen. Gal. 6. 1.

Here special care must be had of admonition. Mat. 18. 15–17

Admonition must be administred with prayer & in love. 1 Tim. 4 5. Gal. 6. 1. Lev. 19. 17. 1 Tim. 1. 5 Rom 13. 8

Prayer is needful that it may please God to give his blessing to the admonition administered. Mat. 7, 7, 8. Iam. 1, 5, & 4, 2. 3.

Love must be manifested to the offender that he may be the better wonne. Eph. 4, 2. Col. 3, 14. Lev. 19. 17. 1 Pet. 4, 8.

Admonition is either private or publique. Mat. 18, 15–17.

Private admonitiō is either solitarie or before witnesses, ibidem.

Private admonition is performed by one particular brother offended, to another brother offending, and that in secret. Mat. 18. 15.

The admonisher must not tel the fault of the offender to another, but himself must admonish the offender. Psal. 15. 3. 1 Pet. 4. 8. Prov. 25. 9

If the offender repent vpon admonition, the fault must be covered Pro. 10. 12. if not: the admonisher must proceed to the secōd degree of admonition: viz. to admonish the offender before witnesse. Mat. 18. 16,

The fittest witnesses must be chosen. 1 King. 21, 10. 13. Mat. 26. 59–61. & 28. 12–15. the fittest witnesses for the most part ar the Elders, who for their wisdō & authority cā best sway with the delinquēt.

If the offender repent vpon admonition before witnesse the fault must yet be covered also. Prov. 10. 12. 1 Pet, 4, 8. Iam 5, 20.

If the offender admonished before witnesse deny the fact, then protestatiō or an oth of God must end the matter. Exod. 22. 11.

Though the admonisher know the fact to be so, and the offender deny the fact before witnesse, yet the admonisher is not to forsake the offenders cōmunion. Iohn 3, 31. & 13. 26. notwithstanding he must stil seek to bring him to repētāce Levit. 19. 17

If the offender acknowledg the fact and repent not, the admonisher and witnesses must bring the matter to the church. Mat. 18, 17.

In bringing the matter to the church if the Elders be not already interessed in the cause, it is meet to vse the advise and help of the Eldership who are fittest to deal in al pub[l]ique busynesses. 1 Cor. 14, 33, 40, 1 Tim. 5. 17

The matter being before the Church the offender is to be dealt with by al possible means, that he may come to repentance, as by admonition, by threat, by intreatie, by prayer for him &c. Gal. 6, 1, 2 Cor. 2. 6.

If the offender repent vpon the Churches admonition he is stil to be continued, and accounted a brother. 2 Cor. 2, 6. Mat. 18, 17.

Thus the church & al the members thereof shal be

preserved & kept pure within, & their cōmuniō shalbe holy: L[e]vit. 19. 17. 1 Tim. 5, 22. 1 Cor. 6, 20. & 5. 6, and so shal increase with the encreasing of God. 1 Cor. 11. 17. 2 Pet. 3. 18

All the degrees of admonition must be administred vpon the offender before the Church have any communion with him: Mat. 18, 15–17, 1 Cor. 11, 17. 1 Tim 5, 22. Levit. 19. 17 Mat. 22 39.

If a mā see his brother synne, and admonish him not, but suffer his synne vnreproved he is defiled therewith, Levit. 19, 17. Mat. 18. 15 & 22, 39. 1 Tim. 5. 22.

In solitarie admonition, if the admonisher stay in the first degree of admonition, the offender not repenting he is defiled with the synne:

In admonitiō before witnesse if the admonishers cease & stay in the second degree of admon[i]tion the offender not repenting, they are defiled with the syn.

In admonition before the church if the church bear with the partie offending and bring him not to repent: but leave him in syn and impenitency, and yet hold him stil in communion, thē the whole church is defiled: & so that is verified, a little leaven leaveneth the whol lump. 1 Cor. 5, 6. & 11, 17, Mat. 13, 33.

If a sinne be publiquely knowne in a church, or if more synnes be openly known and suffred: the whole church is defiled and leavened. ibidem.

No communion can be had with, nor no joyning cā be to, a church thus leavened without manifest cōsenting to synne. ibidem.

Therefore if the church will not reforme open knowne corruptions after due proceeding seperation must be made from it til reformation come.

Therfore separation may be made from true churches for incorrigible corruptions, and to seperate from a defiled church that is incorrigible, is not to forsake the communion of holy things, but the pollution and prophanation of holy things.

Thus much for the second part of the churches powre of preserving and keeping within.

The churches powre of casting out followeth, which is twofold.

First of officers out of office. Act. 14, 23. *compared with* Colos. 4. 17. Rev. 2. 2. Gal. 1, 8. 9.

Second of members out of communion. Mat. 18, 17. 1 Cor. 5, 4, 5. 2 Thes. 3, 6, 14. 1 Tim. 1, 20.

The cause of casting officers out of office are apostacy or disability. Ezec. 44, 10. Nom. 8, 23–26.

Apostacy is when the officers shal fall to open Idolatrie, Atheisme, heresy, or other sins equipollent of the first or second table: Ezech. 44, 10 *& by proportion drawne from* 2 King. 23, 9. 1 Tim. 3, 2. Lev. 22, 1–5. & 21. 16–24. Ezra. 2. 61, 62.

The officer vpon repentance after apostacy or syn equipollent therto may be reteyned as a member of the church, but not as an officer. Ezek, 44, 13 14. Mat. 26, 69–75 *compared with* Iohn 21, 15–18. Act. 13. 38. Quære.

Disabilitie is eyther of age, or sicknes, or mayming &c.

Disabilitie of age is when the officer can no longer by reason of old age dischardg the works of his office: then he may reteyn his dignity & ought to be honoured of al. Num. 8, 23–26. Philemon. 9.

Disability by sicknes as frenzie, Madnes, Melancholie, or by mayming as losse of the tong in the pastor or teacher &c. or by any other infirmitie disabling him to the actions of his office. Lev. 21. 16–24. *compared with* 1 Tim. 3, 2. Tit. 1, 6–9.

Quære, whither an officer may refuse an office imposed vpon him by a lawful calling. Exod. 4, 14. Ier. 1, 6, 7. 17.

Quære whether the church may suffer her officers to be translated frō her self to other churches vpon any ground. Act. 20, 28. 1 Pet. 5, 2. Act. 13 4. yea though it be granted that she have members so fit for offices as her officers are in present: yea though the life of the officer be endaungered. Act. 9, 25. Mat. 10, 23. 1 King. 18, 4.

The cause of casting members out of communion is only one: viz. syn obstinately stood in without repentance and confession after due convictiō Mat, 18, 17. Iob 31, 33. Prov. 28, 13.

Due conviction is the discovery of the synne by manifest evidence Iob 19, 4 & 32, 12, 13. & 39. 37.

Manifest evidence is eyther of the fact, or synfulnes of the fact.

The fact is evident eyther by confession of the partie that committed the fact: or by sufficient witnesse. Mat. 26, 65. Deut. 19, 15. Iohn 5. 31.

Quære, whether the testimony of them that are without is sufficient or no.

The sinfulnes of the fact is evident eyther by direct scripture, or by necessarie consequence from the scripture. Mat 22, 31, 32. & 4. 4.

Due conviction is perceyved two wayes. first by the delinquents shiftings, cavils, excursions, tergiversations &c. 1 Tim. 1, 6. Tit. 3, 11. Secondly by the conscience of them that have powre to censure the fact. Psal. 36, 1. Prov. 27, 19. Tit. 3, 10. 1 Cor. 2, 15 & 12 10.

Obstinacy in syn is the refusing of confessing and forsaking the cryme Prov. 28. 13. Mat. 18, 17. Iosh. 7. 19

If the matter be not evident, but doubtful and controversal, communion stil must be preserved peaceablie, notwithstanding diversitie of judgmēt til the truth be discovered. Phil. 3, 15, 16. 1 Cor. 13, 49–7 9.

Persons that differ in judgment are eyther strōg or weak. Rom. 15, 1.

The strōg must not maynteyn cōtroversies with the weak, nor despise them, but bear their infirmity and burden. Rom. 15, 1. & 14. 1, 3. Gal. 6, 2. 1 Cor. 13, 5, 7. & 9. 22, & 10, 23, 34.

The weak must not censure or judg the strong as delinquents, but meekly desire instruction and satisfaction. Rom. 14, 3. Mat. 7, 1–3.

Thus must men walk in diversity of opinion during which time, all men must carefully search out the trueth, and labor for information. 1 Cor. 1. 20. 2 Peter 3. 18. Phil 3. 15. Iam. 1. 5.

The powre givē the Church for casting out obstinate cōvicted offenders is the powre of excommunication. 2 Cor. 10. 3. 6. & 1. 5, 4, 5. 1 Tim. 1. 20. Gal. 5. 12. 2 Thess. 3. 6. 14. Mat. 18. 17

Quære, Whether delivering to Satan be not or conteyn not some bodily punishment inflicted vpon the offender see Act. 5, 5, 10. 1 Cor. 12, 10.

Excommunication is the depriving of the offender of the visible communion of Saints, and the benefit of all the holy things of God given to the Church. 1 Cor. 5, 4. 5. 11. 13. 2 Thess. 3, 6, 14, Mat. 18. 17.

Quære, Whether seperating withdrawing turning away from false teachers and wicked livers be the same with excommunication. 2 Thes. 3. 6 1 Tim. 6. 5, *and* 2. 3, 5, Mat. 18. 17. 1 Cor. 5. 4. 5.

Excommunication duely administred is ratified and confirmed in heaven. Mat. 18. 18. Ioh. 20. 23.

Therefore the partie excommunicate is in the hands of Sathan, and out of the Lords protection and blessing, being deprived of all the publique meanes of salvation. Mat. 18. 17. 1 Cor. 5. 5. Esay 4. 5. 6.

In excommunication consider two things: first the decreing of it which must be done by the whol church. 1. Cor. 5. 4. wherein the church must proceed as in approving her officers. Secondly the pronouncing of excommunication which must be performed by the fittest person deputed therto by the Church. 1 Cor. 14. 40.

The end of excommunicatiō is not the destruction of the offender, but the mortification of his synne, and the salvation of his soule. 1 Cor. 5. 5. 2 Thes. 3 14. 15. 1 Tim. 1. 20.

The partie excommunicate is not to be counted as an enemy, but to be admonished as a brother. 2 Thess. 3. 15. quære.

The members of the church are to avoid all religious and civil communion with him that is excōmunicate, Mat. 18. 17. 1 Cor. 5, 11, except that subjects, servants, childeren parents, wife or husband &c. that are bound to him may performe civil and naturall offices to him. 1 Cor. 7. 5. 12. 13. and by proportion.

The partie excommunicate vpon repentance is to be admitted againe into the communion of the visible Church. 2 Cor. 2. 6–8. yet so as that the Church alwayes have an especiall eye to him, as being a suspitious person that durst despise the Church, Mat. 18. 17. Ezech. 44. 10. 2 Pet. 2. 22, Heb. 10. 26. by proportion.

Quære, Whether an officer excōmunicate, vpon repentance may be agayn admitted into office; and whether must he have new vocation by election approbation, ordination yea or nay?

The visible Church walking in this holy order hath in it the presence & protection of Christ. Esa. 4, 5. 6. Mat. 28. 20. & 18. 20.

To this visible Church must al sorts of persons resort that desire to be saved. Act. 4, 12. Mat. 7, 13. 14. Ioh. 14 6.

True visible Churches are of two sorts: first pure wher no open knowne synne is suffred. Rev. 2. 7–13. & 3. 8–11. second corrupt, wherin some one or more open knowne syn is tolerated. Rev. 3. 1–6. 1 Cor. 11. 17. 21. 22.

True visible churches are so far forth good as they agree to the paterne of the word: Heb. 8. 5. Rev. cap. 2. & 3. 1 Cor 11, 2, 17, 22.

Every true visible Church hath title to whole Christ and al the holy things of God. Esa. 9. 6. 7 Song 2. 16. Ephe. 1. 22. 23

Every true visible Church is of equal powre with all other visible Churches. Apoc. cap. 2. & 3. 1 Cor. 5 and hath powre to reforme al abuses within it self 1. Cor. 11. 2. 17. which powre is spir[i]tuall as is Christs kingdome not worldly, bodily, nor carnal. Ioh. 18. 36. 2 Cor. 10. 3.–5.

The erecting of visible Churches apperteyneth to princes and private persons.

Princes must erect them in their dominions & command all their subjects to enter into them, being first prepared and fitted therto. 2 Chron. 29. & 34. and 17.

Private persons separating from al synne, and joyning together to obey Christ their king, priest and prophet, as they are bound, are a true visible Church, and haue a Charter given them of Christ therto, being but two or three. Mat. 18, 20. Act 14. 19, 20. Heb. 11. 38. and further powre then to reforme themselves they have none.

Every man is bound in conscience to be a member of some visible church established into this true order. Mat 7, 13. Rev. 18, 4.

Because every man is bound to obey Christ in his kingdome and spirituall regiment and no other Luk 19, 14, 27. and the true visib[l]e church is Christs kingdome and house Marc. 13, 34. *with* Luk 19. 14. 27. Act, 1 3. Heb, 12. 28 & 3. 6.

Therfore they that are not members of this visible

church are no subjects of Christs kingdome. Luk. 19, 27. 1 Cor. 5, 12.

This true visible church is called Christ. 1 Cor. 12. 12.

Thus much concerning the true church: the false church or the church of Antichrist followeth to be considered.

Whatsoever thing is contrarie to this order of the visible church is Antichristian by notation of the word compared with 1 Cor. 12, 12.

Whosoever taketh vpō him to erect new forms or shapes of visible churches and to appoint new officers, lawes, ministerie, worship or communion in the church is Antichrist. 1 Iohn 4, 3. 2 Thes. 2. 4. Revel. 13. 16, 17.

Whosoever yeeldeth or submitteth to any other constitution, lawes, officers ministery or worship then that of Christs appoyntment is the subject or servant of Antichrist, by necessary cōsequēce from the former. & Rom. 6, 16.

A man cannot be both the servant of Christ and of Antichrist. Mat. 6, 24.

The Author entreateth the gentle Reader not to cavil or wrangle at the contents of this present Treatise, nor to traduce or calumniate his person in secret but by writing to discover the errors thereof, which he desireth may be manifested to him, remembring that therein he shal perform a charitable work: for he that converteth a sinner from going astray out of his way shal save a soule from death, & shal hide a multitude of synnes. Iam. 5. 20.

[ornament]

THE DIFFERENCES OF THE Churches of the seperation:

CONTAYNING,

A DESCRIPTION OF THE LEITOVRGIE AND Ministerie of the visible Church.

Annexed:
AS A CORRECTION AND SVPPLEMENT TO A LITLE treatise lately published, bearing title:

Principles and Inferences, concerning the visible Church.

Published,

1. For the satisfaction of every true lover of the truth especially the Brethren of the Seperation that are doubtfull.

2. As also for the removing of an Vnjust calumnie cast vppon the Brethren of the Seperation of the second English Church at Amsterdam.

3. Finally for the cleering of the truth: & the discovering of the mysterie of iniquitie yet further in the worship & offices of the Church.

Divided into two parts
1. Concerning the Leitourgie of the Church
2. Concerning the Ministerie of the Church:

which hath two sections
One of the Eldership: Another of the Deacons office, wherto aperteineth the Treasury

BY IOHN SMYTH

Search the Scriptures: Ioh. 5. 39
Try all things keep the good thing   1 Thes. 5. 21.
Beloved: Beleeve not every Spirit.   1. Ioh. 4. 1.
The Spirits of the Prophetts are subordinate to the Prophets.   1. Cor. 14. 21.

1608.

To every true lover of the truth especially to the Brethren of the seperation: Salutations.

Not long since I published a litle methode intituled principles & inferences concerning the visible Church: Wherin chiefly I purposed to manifest the true constitution of the Church, a matter of absolute necessitie & now so cleered by the writings of the late witnesses of Iesus Christ the auncient brethren of the seperation as that it seemeth nothing can further be added. The absolute necessitie of the true constitution appeareth, becaue if the Church be truly constituted & framed, ther is a true Church: the true spowse of Christ: if the Church be falsely constituted, ther is a false Church: & she is not the true spowse of Christ: Herein therfore especially are those auncient brethren to be honoured, that they have reduced the Church to the true Primitive & Apostolique constitution which consisteth in these three things. 1. The true matter which are sayntes only. 2. The true forme which is the vniting of them together in the covenant. 3. The true propertie which is communion in all the holy things, & the powre of the L. Iesus Christ, for the maintayning of that communion. To this blessed work of the L. wherin those auncient brethren have labored I know not what may more be added: I thincke rather ther can nothing be added: but now Antichrist is perfectly both discovered & consumed in respect of the constitution by the evidence of the truth, which is the brightnes of Christs comming. Now al though they have also verie worthelie employed themselves in the Leitourgie, Ministerie, & Treasurie of the Church, both in discovering the forgeries & corruptions which the man of synne had intermingled, & also in some good degree reducing them to ther primitive puritie wherin they weere by the Apostles left vnto the Churches: Yet wee are persuaded that herein Antichrist is not vtterlie eyther revealed or abolished, but that in a verie high degree he is exalted even in the true constituted Churches:

In regard wherof, as also being enforced vppon some occasion well knowne wee thought it necessary to publish this description of the Leitourgie & ministrie of the Church: The Ministerie I say consisting of the Presbytery & Deacons office, wherto apertyneth the Treasurie, & that for these ends: partly that the truth wee walk in may be manifested to the world, among whome our opinion and practise is so straungely & falsely traduced: partly that the differences betwixt vs & the auncienter brethren of the seperation may appeare, & therby men may be occasioned to trye the truth from error & to hold it fast. And although in this writing somthing ther is which overtwharteth my former judgmēt in some treatises by mee formerly published: Yet I would intreat the reader not to impute that as a fault vnto mee: rather it should be accounted a vertue to retract erroers: Know therfor that latter though[t]s oft tymes are better then the former: & I do professe this (that no man account it straunge), that I will every day as my erroers shalbe discovered confesse them & renounce them: For it is our covenant made with our God to forsake every evill way whither in opinion or practise that shalbe manifested vnto vs at any tyme: & therefor lett no man plead now, as some have formerly done, these men are inconstant: they would have they know not what: They will never be satisfied & the like: For wee professe even so much as they object: That wee are inconstant in erroer: that wee wou'd have the truth, though in many particulars wee are ignorant of it: Wee will never be satisfied in endevoring to reduce the worship and ministery of the Church, to the primitive Apostolique institution from which as yet it is so farr distant: VVherfor my earnest desire is, that my last writing may be taken as my present judgment & so farre forth as it overthwarteth any former writing of myne let it be accounted a voluntary retractation & vnfeyned repētance of my former errors or evil wayes before the whole earth. And lett no man bee offended at vs for that wee differ from the auncient brethren of the seperation in the Leitourgie Presbyterie & Treasurie of the Church: for wee hold not our fayth at any mans pleasure or in respect of persons, neyther doe wee bynd our selves to walk according to other mens lynes further then they walk in the truth: neyther lett the world think that wee approve them in all their practises: let them justifie their proceedinges or repēt of them. wee have (wee willingly & thankfully acknowledge) receaved much light of truth from their writinges, for which mercy we alwayes blesse our God: & for which help wee alwayes shall honour them in the Lord and in the truth. But as Paull withstood Peter to his face & seperated from Barnabas that good man that was full of the holy ghost & of fayth, for just caussses: So must they give vs leave to love the truth & honour the Lord more then any man or Church vppon earth. Now if any of the adversaries of vs both shall heerby take occasion of offence, thereby to speake evill, or to withold or revolt from the truth: let these men consider with themselves: First: that they even in that theyr Ægyptian darknesse wherein they walk have their most violent oppositions & deadly contentions: Agayne, the Apostle hath foretold that it is necessary their should bee dissentions even in the true Churches that they which are approved may bee knowne: besides the truth shall by our differences bee further cleered, & theyr Antichristian worship & Ministery more & more detected, & cast into the bottomlesse pitt from whence it issued. Finally the Apostle saith that Christ is a stone to stumble at & a rock of offence to the disobedient aswell as a cheef corner stone elect & pretious to them that beleeve: & blessed are they that are not offended at Christ or his truth. So desyring the reader to weygh well what I plead & not to bee offended at the manifold quotations which are of necessity that by places compared together the truth which is a mystery may appeare & Antichristianisme which is the mysterie of iniquity may bee discovered, I cease, commending him to the grace of God in Iesus Christ, who in due tyme will bring his people out of Ægypt & Babylon spiritually so called, though for a season they are there kept in Antichristian captivity & greevous spirituall slavery; which the Lord in his due tyme effect, Amen, Amen.

Iohn Smyth.

The principall contents of this treatise & our
differences from the auncyent brethren
of the Seperation.

1 Wee hould that the worship of the new testament properly so called is spirituall proceeding originally from the hart: & that reading out of a booke (though a lawful ecclesiastical action) is no part of spirituall worship, but rather the invention of the man of synne it beeing substituted for a part of spirituall worship.

2 Wee hould that seeing prophesiing is a parte of spiritual worship: therefore in time of prophesijng it is vnlawfull to have the booke as a helpe before the eye

3 wee hould that seeing singing a psalme is a part of spirituall worship therefore it is vnlawfull to have the booke before the eye in time of singinge a psalme

4 wee hould that the Presbytery of the church is vniforme; & that the triformed Presbyterie consisting of three kinds of Elders viz. Pastors Teachers Rulers is none of Gods Ordinance but mans devise.

5 wee hould that all the Elders of the Church are Pastors: & that lay Elders (so called) are Antichristian.

6 wee hould that in contributing to the Church Treasurie their ought to bee both a seperation from them that are without & a sanctification of the whole action by Prayer & Thanksgiving.

The Differences of the Chvrches of the Seperation, Conteyning a description of the Leitourgie & Ministerie of the visible Church Annexed as a correction & supplement to a litle treatise lately published bearing title principles, & inferences concerning the visible Church.

THE FIRST PART. concerning the Leitourgie of the Church

Cap. 1. of the Kingdom of the Saynts.

The visible Church by the Apostle is called a Kingly preisthood. 1. pet. 2. 9. and the Saynts are Kings & Preists vnto God Revel. 1. 6.

The Saynts as Kings rule the visible Church. 1. Cor. 5. 12. psal. 149. 9. Mat. 18. 15–17. 1. Cor. 6. 1–9.

The visible Church is Christs Kingdom. Mat. 8. 12. Ioh. 18. 33–37. Act. 1. 3, 1. Cor. 15. 24. 25. Hebr. 12. 28.

The members of the visible Church are called the children of the Kingdom. Mat. 8. 12. And are vnder the government of the Church: Marc. 13. 34, 1. Cor. 6. 1–9. & vnder the governmēt of Christ. Luk. 19. 27.

The actions of the Church in administring the Kingdom are actions of opposition, difference, plea, & strif: as in admonition, examination, excommunication, pacification, absolution, &c. 1. Cor. 5. 3–5. & 6. 1–9. & 2. Ep. 2. 6. 7. Mat. 18. 15–17. Revel. 2. 2, 2 Chron. 19. 10–11.

Hetherto aperteyneth conference & disputation. Luc. 2. 46. 47. Act. 6. 9. & 17¦: 2, compared with psal: 122. 5. 1. King. 3. 16–27.

In examination of opinions & facts also in conference & disputation evidences of all sorts may be produced for finding out of the truth. Revel. 2. 2. 1. King 3. 25–27.

Evidences are of divers natures: as confessions & lotts: Iosh. 7. 16–21. Oathes: Exod. 22. 10. 11. bookes of all sortes. Dan. 9. 2, 1, King. 14. 19. Act 7. 22. & 17. 28. 1. Cor. 15. 33. Tit. 1. 12. Iude. vers. 14. compared with 1. Timoth. 1. 4. & Luk. 3. 25–27. namly translations, dictionaries, histories, chronicles, commentaries, &c, all which may for evidence of the truth be brought into the Church, by necessary consequence.

Actions of administring the Church or Kingdom are not actions of spirituall worship properly so called, for as the Kingdome and Preisthood of the old Testament were distinct as also their actions severall: Heb. 7. 14. Gen. 49. 10. Deut 33. 8–11. 2. Chron. 26. 18. psal. 122. 4. 5: So are the Kingdom & Preisthood of the new Testament & their actions also: which were typed by the other. Heb. 5. 4. 5. Act. 15. 7–29. with 13. 2, 3.

Chap. 2. of the Preisthood of the saynts.

Thus much of the Kingdom: now followeth the Preisthood of the Church.

The saynts as Preists offer vp spirituall sacrifices acceptable to God by Iesus Christ. 1. pet. 2. 5.

Spirituall sacrifices are such as originally proceed from the spirit: & they are called spirituall in opposition to the carnall or literall sacrifices performed by the sacrificing Preists of the old Testament: which originally proceeded from the lettre: by proportion also see. Ioh. 1. 17, 2. Cor. 3. 6. Gal. 3. 5. Ioh. 4. 20–24.

The actions of the Church in dispencing the preisthood are actions of concord or vnion: Act. 4. 24–32. philip. 3. 16. Ephes. 4. 3–6.

Actions of the Preisthood of the saynts are actions of spirituall worship properly so called. Deut. 33. 10 1. pet. 2. 5. compared with Revel. 8. 3. Heb. 13. 10. philip. 2. 17. Act. 13. 2, 1. Cor. 11. 4. & 14. 15. 22. 26–31.

In the worship of God properly so called the saynts are not to oppose, contradict, examine, or censure: to propound doubtfull & controversall points of doctryne: but in vnion spirituall to offer vp one & the same spirituall sacryfice to the Lord. Act. 4. 24–32. 1. Cor. 11. 18–20. & 10. 16. 17.

If any thing doubtfull or false be delivered in tyme of spirituall worship it is to be examyned & censured afterward. 1. Cor. 14. 31–33. 40. compared with Revel. 2. 2. Act. 17. 11.

Chap. 3. of Spirituall worship & of the Spirit.

Concerning spirituall worship consider these things following.
1. The Fountayne from whence it proceedeth.
2. The helpes wherby it is supported or furthered,
3. The essence or nature wherin properly it consisteth.

The Fountayne from whence spirituall worship proceedeth is the spirit. Act. 1. 4. 5. & 2. 4. 17. 18, 1. Cor. 12. 4, 7. 11. Eph 5. 18. 19.

The spirit signifieth 2. things. 1. the spirit of God. 2. the spirit of man: that is the regenerate part of the soule. Act. 2. 17. 18, 1. Cor. 12. 4. Rom. 7. 6. Galath. 3. 2. 3.

The Regenerate part of the soule is eyther the sanctified memory, the sanctified judgment, the sanctified hart & affections, the sanctified conscience: from all these must spirituall worship proceed. Psal. 103. 1. 2. Mat. 22. 37, 1. Timoth. 1. 5.

The work of the holy spirit is to suggest matter & to move the regenerate part of the soule, 1. Cor. 12. 8–11. Ioh. 14. 26, Luk. 24. 32–45.

The work of the memory is to have in a readynesse sufficiency of fit matter for the spirituall worship, psal. 103. 2, & 119. 16. 93.

The work of the judgment or vnderstanding is to discerne & judge truth from falsehood, right from wrong, good from bad, fit from vnfit, 1. Cor. 14. 29–32, & 11. 29. Colos. 1. 9. & 3. 16. Philip. 1. 9. 10.

The work of the hart & affections is to be moved according to the qualitie of the matter & kind of the worship. Iam. 5. 13, Ezra. 3. 10–13, 1. Cor. 14. 24. 25.

The work of the conscience is a sorowfull or consortable testimony answerable to the matter handled, 1. Timoth. 1. 5. Act. 23. 1.

Finally the work of the Regeñerat part of the soule is an Eccho correspondent to the work of the holy spirit & the condition of the word of God which in tyme of spirituall worship is administred. psal. 27. 8. Esay. 66. 5. Mat. 13. 9. Heb. 10. 5–7. Cant. 5. 4.

of the Seperation

Chap. 4. of quenching the Spirit.

In performing spirituall worship wee must take heed of quenching the spirit. 1. Thes. 5. 19. 1. Cor. 14. 30. Iob 32. 18–20.

The Spirit is quenched two wayes: By silence. By set formes of worship. Psal. 40. 1–3. 1. Cor. 14. 29–32. compared with 1. Thes. 5. 19. 20.

The Spirit is quenched by silence when fit matter is revealed to one that sitteth by & he wthholdeth it in tyme of prophecying:

The Spirit is quenched by sett formes of worship, for therein the spirit is not at liberty to vtter it self, but is bounded in: contrary to. Act. 2. 4. & 2. Cor. 3. 17. compared with Ioh. 4. 24. & Gal. 4. 31. & 5. 1.

Sett formes of worship are eyther in the memory, or in the book.

Saying set formes, of worship by rote is quenching the Spirit: & Reading sett formes of worship out of a book is quenching the Spirit: for in the one the Spirit is not manifested but the strength of the memory, in the other the matter is not brought out of the hart, but out of the book: & so in neyther of them the Spirit is at liberty.

Chap. 5. of the helps of Spiritual worship.

Thus much concerning the Fountayne from whence Spiritual worship commeth: now follow the helps wherby Spiritual worship is furthered or supported.

The helps are eyther inward or outward.

The inward helps are only the word & the spirit. Eph. 5. 18. 19. Col. 3. 16. Rom. 8. 26.

The outward helps are the manifestation of the Spirit: & the seales of the covenant: 1. Cor. 12. 7. & 2. 4. & Act. 2. 4. 42. with the instruments creatures & actions apperteyning therto.

Instruments: as the tong & eare, to speake, heare & tast withal: Act. 2. 4. 8. 1. cor. 11. 24

Creatures as bread, wine, water: Act. 8. 36–39. 1 Cor. 11. 23. Mat. 26. 27–29.

Actions as speaking, hearing, breaking bread, powring

out wine, eating, drincking, washing with water, by consequent from the former places.

The publishing of the covenant of grace & the putting to of the seales is only one concrete action or part of worship, for the publishing of the covenant giveth being to the seales, otherwise breaking bread & baptising are but putting of seales to a blanck.

Chap. 6. concerning bookes & writing.

Here a question is to be discussed: wither a book be a lawful help to further vs in tyme of spiritual worship. Revel. 10. 10. 11. Ezech. 3. 3. 4.

Bookes or writings are signes or pictures of things signified therby.

Writings are to be considered in the concrete or in the abstract.

In the concrete writings import both the signe & the thing signified therby, that is both the characters & the matter.

In the abstract writings import the signe in relation to the thing signified therby: viz. lettres, sillables, wordes, syntaxe.

Every writing is compounded of wordes.

Every worde is made of lettres & sillables except that some lettres & sillables are wordes.

Lettres or characters are significative. Revel. 1. 8. & 13. 18. Alpha, Omega, Chi, Xi, st. signify, first, last, 600, 60, 6.

Wordes are significative in the first or second intention: as Amen in the first intention signifieth truth or truly, Mat. 5. 18. Amen in the second intention signifieth Christ Revel. 3. 14. So doth Logos signify also and many other wordes of Scripture.

Syntaxe or joyning of wordes in order signifieth discourse,

As single wordes signify Logicall relations or arguments: So Syntaxe or wordes compounded in sentence signifieth Axiomes, Syllogismes, Methode.

Therefore wordes and syntaxe are signes of thinges, and of the relations and reason of thinges

of the Seperation

Hence it followeth that bookes or writinges are in the nature of pictures or Images & therefore in the nature of ceremonies: & so by consequent reading a booke is ceremoniall. For as the Beast in the Sacrifices of the ould Testament was ceremoniall so was the killing of the Beast ceremoniall.

Chap. 7. Of the kindes of bookes or writinges.

Thus much of the nature of bookes or writinges: Now follow the kindes of bookes or the distribution of writinges.

writinges may bee distinguished according to the subject or efficient

The subject of writinges are paper, parchment, wood, stone, metall. &c

If writinges bee in paper or parchment they bee called bookes, as may bee gathered from. Deut. 31. 24–26. Ierem. 36. 4.

If writinges be ingraven in stone wood or metal it is caled graving or carving: Exo. 28. 11. 2. Cor. 3. 7. Iosh. 8. 32.

The efficient of writinges are two: God, or Man.

God himselfe first engraved the law in tables of stone. Exod. 31. 18.

Men are of two sortes: Inspired, or ordinary men.

Men Inspired by the Holy Ghost are the Holy Prophets & Apostles who wrote the holy scriptures by inspiration. 2. Pet. 1. 21. 2. Tim. 3. 16. Rom. 1. 2. namely the Hebrue of the ould testament & the greeke of the new Testament.

The holy Scriptures viz. the Originalls Hebrew & Greek are given by Divine Inspiration & in their first donation were without error most perfect & therefore Canonicall.

Ordinary men write bookes of divers kindes among the rest such as have the word of God or Holy Scriptures for their object are called Theological writinges: among them Translations of the Holy Scriptures into the mother tong are cheifly to be esteemed, as beeing the most principall, yet only as the streame issuing from the fountayne, or as the greatest river of the mayne sea.

No writinges of ordinary men how holy or good soever are given by inspiration, & therefore are subject to error & imperfect & so Apocrypha.

Chap. 8. Of the Originalls of Holy Scripture, & of the partes of Holy Scripture

Holy Scriptures (as all other writinges whatsoever,) consist of two partes: of the tong & character & of the substance or matter signified by the character.

The tong or character hath apertaining to it the grammar & the Rhethorick wherof the tong or character is the subiect.

The matter or substance of the scripture hath in it, Logick, History, Cronology, Cosmography, Genealogy, Philosophy, Theologie & other like matter.

The principall parte of the matter is the Theologie

A Translation of the holy originalls may expresse very much of the matter contayned in or signified by the originall characters: it can expresse also much of the Rhethorick as Tropes & Figures of sentence.

No Translation can possibly expresse all the matter of the holy originalls, nor a thousand thinges in the Grammar, Rhethorick, & character of the tong.

A Translation so far forth as it doth truly & fully expresse any thing of the originals may be saide inspired of God & no further.

Hence it followeth that a translation be it never so good is mixt with mans devises, imperfect, not equipollent to the originalles in a thousand particulars.

The holy originalle signifie and represent to our eyes heavenly things therfor the book of the law is called a similitude of an heavenly thing Heb. 9. 19–23.

Holy Scriptures or writing beganne with Moses. Exod. 24. 4 & 31. 18. Ioh. 1. 17. 2. Cor. 3. 7.

Before Moses holy men prophesyed out of their harts & receaved & kept the truth of doctryne by tradition from hand to hand: 2. Pet. 2. 5. Iude vers. 14. 15. Deut 31. 24.

When Moses had written the lawe, he caused it to be put by the arke in the most holy place, as a witnesse against the people. deut. 31. 26. therfor the Apostle calleth it the handwriting in ordinances which was contrary to vs, which Christ nayled to his crosse. Col. 2. 14. Eph. 2. 15.

Hence it followeth that the holy originals the Hebrue scriptures of the old testament are ceremonyes. 2. Cor. 3. 3. 7. Nomb. 5. 23. 24. & by necessary consequent.

The book or tables of stone typed vnto the Iewes their hard hart voyde of the true vnderstanding of the lawe. 2. Cor. 3. 3. Heb. 8. 10. Ezech. 36. 26. 27. 2 Cor. 3. 14. 15

The Inck wherewith the lettres were written signified the Spirit of God. 2. Cor, 3. 3. Heb. 8. 10. compared with Exod. 31. 18.

The lettres written or charaĉters engraven signifieth the work of the Spirit, who alone doth write the law in our harts, by proportion: also Deut. 9. 10. compared with Heb. 8. 10.

Reading the words of the law out of the book signifieth the vttering of the word of God out of the hart: by proportion see also. 2. Cor. 3. 2. 3. 6. 1. Cor. 12. 7.

The writings of the old Testament being ceremonial are therfor abolished by Christ only so far forth as they are ceremonial: Col. 2. 14. 26. Gal. 4. 9

The thing signified by the book viz: the law of God & the new testament remayneth 2. Cor. 3. 11. 7. Heb. 8. 6. 7. 13.

Chap. 9, How the Originalls, or Holy Scriptures are to be vsed.

The Scriptures of the old Testament are commaunded to the Church—2. Pet. 1. 19. 20 & 2. Timoth. 3. 16. as also the Scriptures of the new Testament: 1. Thes. 5. 27. Col. 4. 16. & by proportion.

Heer consider these things,

1. How the Scriptures are to be vsed. 2. How they are not to be vsed.

The Holy Scriptures are the Fountayne of all truth, Ioh. 17. 17. compared with 2. Timoth. 3. 16. 17.

They are the ground & foundacion of our fayth, Ephes. 2. 20. compared with Ioh. 5. 39 & 17. 3.

By them all doctrynes & every Spiritt is to be judged: Esay 8. 20. 1. Ioh. 4. 1. Act. 17. 11.

They are to be read in the Church & to be interp[r]eted: Col. 4. 16. compared with Luk. 24. 27. & 1. Cor. 14. 27. & 12. 10. by proportion 2. Pet. 3. 16.

Neverthelesse the Holy Scriptures are not reteyned as helps before the eye in tyme of Spirituall worship: Reasons are these.

Chap. 10. Reasons proving the Originals not to be given as helps before the eye in worship.

1. Bicause Christ vsed the book to fulfill all righteousnes Mat. 3. 15 & having by the vse of the book fulfilled the law of reading he shut the book in the Synagogue, to signifie that that ceremony of bookworship, or the ministerie of the lettre was now exspired, & finished. Luk. 4. 20. Ioh. 19 30

2. Bicause reading wordes out of a book is the ministration of the lettre, 2. Cor. 3. 6. namely a part of the ministerie of the old Testament which is abolished: Heb. 8. 13: 2. Cor. 3: 11. 13. & the ministery of the new testament is the ministerie of the spirit 2. Cor. 3. 6.

3. Bicause vppon the day of Pentecost & many yeeres after the churches of the new testament did vse no bookes in tyme of spiritual worship but prayed, prophesyed, & sang Psalmes meerely out of their harts. Act 2. 4. 42. & 10. 44–48. & 19. 6. 1. cor. 14. 15–17. 26. 37.

4. Bicause no example of the Scripture can be shewed of any man ordinary or extraordinary that at or after the day of Pentecost vsed a book in praying, prophesying & singing Psalmes: if yea: let it bee done & wee yeeld.

5. Bicause none of the books of the new Testament were written many yeeres after the day of Pentecost, at the least seaven yeeres: & the Churches all that tyme could not vse the books of the new Testament which they had not.

of the Seperation 283

6. Bicause the Churches of the Greekes had no bookes to vse that they might vse lawfully: for they vnderstood not Hebru: & the Septuagints translation ought not to be vsed or made, & the Apostles made no Greek translation: And if the Apostles read the Hebrue an vnknowne tong in the Greek Churches it could not be a lawfull worship, bicause it edified not: if they had the Hebrue before their eyes & interp[r]eted Greek, let it be shewed when & where & wee yeeld vnto it.

7. Bicause as in prayer the spirit only is our help & ther is no outward help given of God for that kind of worship. So also in prophesying & singing. 1. Cor. 11. 4. & 14. 16,

8. Bicause it is against the nature of spiritual worship: for when we read wee receave matter from the book into the hart, when we pray prophesy or sing we utter matter out of the hart vnto the eare of the Church; Ezech, 2. 8–19, & 3. 1–4. Revel. 10. 8–11.

9 Bicause vpon the day of Pentecost fyerie cloven tongs did appeare, not fiery cloven bookes. Act. 2. 3. & alwaies ther must be a proportion betwixt the type and the thing typed: vpon the day of Pentecost the fiery law was given in bookes Deut: 33. 2. Exo: 24. 4. 12 vpon the day of Pentecost the fiery gospel was given in tonges Act: 2. 3. Mat: 3. 11. Act: 1. 5. the booke therefore was proper for them, the tonge for vs

10 Bicause as all the worship which Moses taught began in the letter outwardly, & so proceeded inwardly to the spirit of the faithfull: so contrariwise all the worship of the new testament signified by that typicall worship of Moses must beginne at the Spirit, & not at the letter originally. 2. Cor: 3. 6. 8. 1. Cor: 12. 7. or els the heavenly thinge is not answerable to the similitude thereof:

Therfor as in prayer the book is laid aside, & that by the confession of the aunciente brethren of the seperation: so must it be also in prophesying & singing of Psalmes as we are perswaded. 1. Cor. 11. 4. & 14. 15. 16. 26.

Quere, whither the Prophets of the Church may not in tyme of Spiritual worship, take the originals, &

interpret out of them a text, & then shut the book & prophesy from that ground of holy Scripture so interpreted. Luk. 4. 16–20

Chap. 11. objections for book worship answered.

The first objection.

Reading in the old Testament was commaunded by Moses. Deut 31. 8–13. was amplified by David. 1 Chron. 16. & 25. was practised by Iosiah 2. Chron. 34. 30. by Ezra & Nehemiah: Nehem. 8. 8. & 9. 3. allowed by our Savior Christ Luk. 4. 16. & by the Apostles, Act. 13. 14. 15. & reported as a thing of aunciente approved continuance. Act. 15. 21.

Answer to the first objection.

First the reading commaunded by Moses was only once every seaven yeere. Deut. 31. 10. 11. & therfor it was no part of ordinary worship, & ther is no commaundement in Moses given eyther to the Preists or Levites for ordinary reading of the law in the Tabernacle.

Secondly: Hence it followeth that reading in the Old Testament was no part of the worship of the tabernacle or temple, or of the service performed by the Preists therein, for all the worship that was appointed by Moses for the Preists was limited to the holy place, whither the people were not admitted.

Thirdly: therfor reading was of another nature performed in the vtter court or Synagogue or els where, eyther by the levites or any other learned men of what tribe soever: Mat: 23. 2. Luk. 4. 16. Act. 13. 15. compared with, Act. 15. 21. Deut 31. 9–11. 1. Chron. 16. 4. 7. 37. 39. & 15. 1–8. & 28. 13. 2 Chron. 34. 14. 30. 31. Nehem. 8. & 9. & so no part of worship properly so called, but only a ceremoniall ground or foundation, of inward or outward spiritual worship common to the Churches of all ages.

Lastly: it is not denyed but that reading now is to be vsed in the Church: only we say it is not a part of spiritual worship, or a lawful meanes in tyme of spiritual worship.

The second objection

Reading is comaunded in the new testament Colos: 4. 16. 1 Thes: 5. 27. and a blessing promised thereto Revel: 1. 3. and the commaundement is that it be practised in the church: therefore it is a part or meanes of the worship of the new testament.

Answer to the second objection.

Not euerie thinge performed in the chnrch is a parte of spirituall worship, for all the partes of publique administratiō of the Kingdome are done in the church, and yet cannot be sayd to be partes of spirituall worship properly so called. Chap: 1. and 2.

Moreover when he commaundeth his Epistles to be read in the Churches, his meaning is not strictly literall: that is, that the very wordes which he wrote should be repeated verbatim out of the booke: but his meaning is that the sense of the wordes or the meaning of the Apostle should be related to the brethrē, whither by reading the very wordes, by expounding the meaning by interpreting or translating. For if his meaning be that the very wordes he wrote be literaly read: thē the Greek wordes must be repeated out of the booke to all nations: which is contrary to .1. Cor. 14. 26. If his meaning be, that the sense should be given any way, by translating, by reading the translation, by interpreting his meaning in a paraphrase, commentary &c. then how will it follow that reading the Greek tong which is not vnderstood in the English Churches is a lawfull part of spirituall worship according to the literall signification of readings?

Further the Apostle wrote his Epistles to the Collossians, & Thessalonians & the other Churches vppon particular occasions for particular endes, and the commaundement of reading then was speciall in those respects to them: and the intent of the Apostle is not to enioyne the reading of them every day & in tyme of Spiritual worship to al Churches: yet wee do acknowledg the absolute necessity of reading & searching the Scriptures, Ioh. 5. 39.

Againe that reading is a lawful yea necessary meanes or help to further vs to Spiritual worship is not denyed, but this is denyed that it is a lawful help in tyme of worship, or a lawful part of Spiritual worship. For it is confessed & defended by the aunciēt brethrē of the seperation, that the originals are no lawful help in tyme of prayer: So say we they are no lawful help in tyme of prophesying & singing Psalmes, & that by equal proportion for ther is the same reason of helps in all the parts of Spiritual worship, during the tyme of performing the worship.

The third objection.

The Apostle 1. Tim. 4. 13–16 commaundeth Timothie & so all Elders to attend to reading: wher reading is joyned with exhortation & doctryne & so importeth that it is to be vnderstood of the joyning of reading in tyme of Spiritual worship

Answer to the third objection.

The circūstances of the place being wel considered wil afoard that Paul speaketh not of the execution of his office, but of preparing himself to the execution of his office; which is attayned by reading the Scriptures whereby men are fitted with matter fitt to teach & exhort: for by this meanes the gift of prophecy was preserved in Timothie vs 14. & by this meanes his proficiency should be manifested. vs 15. by this meanes he should the better save mens soules, vs 16.

The fourth objection.

Let it be graunted that the Apostles & Evangelists vsed no bookes being extraordinary men & having the extraordinary direction of the spirit, for they needed no such helps of bookes as wee doe: Yet wee being men ordinary have need of bookes, therefor they by the direction of the Spirit both have written bookes for our vse, & have commaunded vs to vse them.

Answer to the fourth objection.

This objection may as well fit bringing of bookes into the tyme of prayer, frō whēce they are justly banished: for it may be sayd that the Apostles were extraordinary men, & needed no bookes for prayer, but wee need books to help our infirmity & why may not a man as wel say the Apostle commaundeth the reading of prayers, & promiseth a blessing to reading of prayers in time of prayer as otherwise.

Again, though the holy Spirit be not given to vs in the same manner & measure as to the Apostles, yet we have the same Spirit to help vs as they had, & to the same ordinary purposes is he sent to vs by Christ as to them: namely to help our infirmityes: Rom 8. 26. for the work of the ministery: Eph. 4. 12. to be our annoynting, 1. Ioh. 2. 27. to lead into all truth: Ioh 16. 13. to be our paraclete: Ioh. 14. 16. & so by consequent to help vs to pray, prophesy, & prayse God.

Againe this objection seemeth to establish two formes of prophesying, one without bookes by the Apostles for many yeeres in the Church: another with bookes afterward taught by the Apostles: & then it followeth that the Apostles gospell was yea & nay, who first taught & practised one way, & afterward taught & commaunded to practise another way.

Lastly: The Apostles had the bookes of the Old Testament in the Hebr[e]we tong, & so might have vsed them before their eye in tyme of prophesying, eyther to read out of them to the Hebrues, or to translate and interprett out of them to the Greecians: but they did neyther of these, but only prophesyed out of their harts, as the Holy Ghost gave them vtterance. Act. 2. 4. Yea & taught the primitive Churches so to doe: 1. Cor. 14. 26. If it can be shewed that they did vse the bookes of the Old Testament in tyme of worship to read or interprete from them, lett it be shewed, & wee yeeld: if not thus wee hold & practise for the present.

Herevppon it followeth that neyther reading the originals, nor interpreting or translating out of the originals the book being before the eye, is eyther a lawfull part or meanes of Spirituall worship.

Chap. 12. Of the writings of men.

Writings of men are of divers kinds: among them are translations of the holy scriptures a most principal.

To translate the originals into any mother tong is aswell, & asmuch the work of a mans witt & learning, as to analyse the Scriptures Rhetorically or Logically, to Collect doctrines & vses Theologically, to give expositions & interpretations of places doubtfull.

The translator cannot conceave nor expresse in writing the whole mynd of the holy Spirit conteyned in the originals, but only some good part of it: the expositor, paraphrast commētator may expresse asmuch as the translator, yea & in respect of some particulars, as Hebraismes, Grecismes & the like considerations, much more.

Ther is as good warrant to translate the Scripture as to expound analyse, & draw doctryne & vses from the Scriptures. Marc. 5. 41, Mat. 1. 23, & by proportiō from 1. Cor. 12. 10 & 14. 13. 27. 39.

Ther is no better warrant to bring translations of Scripture written into the church, & to reade them as partes or helps of worship, then to bring in expositions, resolutions, paraphrasts & sermons vppon the Scripture seing al these are equally humane in respect of the work, equally divine in respect of the matter they handle.

Chap. 13. Of reading translations: & of the translation of the .72. interpreters.

Hitherto apperteyneth this question. whether reading a translation be a lawful help or meanes in tyme of Spiritual worship or a lawful part of Spiritual worship.

If originals must be laid aside as in tyme of prayer, so also in tyme of prophesying & singing, then much more must translations be laid aside at that tyme: as may further be manifested thus.

Bicause the Septuagints translation was a greevous sinne for many reasons.

1. For that the covenant of grace ought not to have been preached vnto the gentile til the fullnes of tyme. Mat. 10. 5. 6. 1. Timoth 3 16. Rom. 16. 25. 26. compared

of the Seperation

with Mat. 10. 5. 6. & 28. 19. And therfor that the Septuagints by their translation did communicate it to the Grecians, before the fulnes of tyme was their greevous sinne.

2. Bicause all the Gentills ought to have been proselytes of the Iewes Church, & to have come to Ierusalem to worship Exod 12. 43–49. Mat. 23. 15. Act. 2 10 & ought to have learned their tong & worship, which was prevented by the Septuagints translation.

3. Bicause the Hebrue characters & writings were Ceremonyes & so ought not to have been profaned among the Grecians by their writings: & as the Philistines were justly plagued for the presence of the Arke, Sam. So might the Lord justly have plagued the Grecians for that the Oracles of God were among them, & fearfully abused by them.

4. If it were vnlawful to sing one of Davids Psalmes in a strang nation as Babylon. psal. 137. 4. then much more vnlawfull was it to translate the Scriptures into a straunge tong for all the Ceremoniall law was bounded within the holy land.

5. The translation of the Septuagints out of Hebrue into Greeke, is contradictory to the Lords mercy to the Iewes church & ther special Priviledges, see psal. 147. 19. 20. Rom. 3. 1. 2. Act. 10. 28. & 22. 1–18. Eph. 2. 11–15. Act 13. 46–48. contrary also to Rom. 16. 25. 26

6. Bicause that seing the Hebrew writings were Ceremonyes it was vnlawful for the Septuagints to chandg them from their proper kind, & to picture them out by the Greek writings for the Greeks vse.

7. Bicause the Septuagints did of purpose conceale many things as judging the gentils vnworthy to know them fearing also least they should profane such holy mysteries wherein their consciences told them playnly that their translation was their synne: also they did pervert many things of purpose, ad somthing & infinitely corrupt their translation which was their greevous sinne.

Hence it followeth that seing the Septuagints translation was so greevous a sinne, therfor the Apostles would never account it holy scripture comming frō the holy ghost & so never approve the vse of it in the Greek Churches.

Againe wee never heard of any other translation before Christ, besides the Septuagints: or if ther were any, it were vnlawful by the same reasons before vsed against the Septuagints.

Further: ther could be no vse of the Septuagints translation for reading in the Latine Church of the Romanes.

Moreover the new Testament being not written, none of it till 7. 10. or 20. yeeres after Christs death, not all of it till Iohn had written who was the surviver of the Apostles, how could ther bee a translation of the new Testament written during the Apostles lives?

Besides it is never mentioned that ever any Apostle or Apostolique man or Church eyther had from the Apostles or vsed by their direction or approbation a translation of any sort, whatsoever before the eye in tyme of Spirituall worship: if yea: let it be shewed.

Lastly translations therfor beganne in the Church after the Apostles dayes in tyme of worship, & so were not from the beginning, in respect whereof they are a part of th. mystery of iniquity in worship.

Chap. 14. Of other arguments against reading translations in tyme of worship.

1. 1, Thes. 5. 21. Try all things, keep that good thing. But no man ignorant of the tongs can try whether the translation be fit or good: & therfor no man ignorant of the tongs can strictly keep or read a translation in tyme of worship.

2. Rom. 14. 23. 1 Timoth. 1. 4–7. Heb. 11. 6. whatsoever commeth not from fayth is sinne. But no man ignorant of the tongs can of faith vse the translation seing he cannot examyne it whether it be good or bad, & so beleeve or refuse it. Therfore it is not of fayth in him & so it is synne for him to vse it before the eye in tyme of worship.

3. A translation made verbatim from the originalls is absurd by reason of the difference of the dialects: & therefore vnlawfull seing it edifieth not. 1. Cor. 14. 26.

A translation paraphrastical or a paraphrast if it be lawful in time of worship to be read then why not a written sermon.

4. A paraphrast, commētarie or exposition vpon a chapter which contayneth more of the contentes of the originalles & the holy ghostes meaning is vnlawfull to be read in time of worship: therefore a translation of a chapter which contayneth lesse is vnlawfull also to be read in time of worship.

5. Levit. 22. 22. Malach. 1. 8. 13. 14. Mat. 22. 37. Rom. 12. 1. 2. Psal. 119. 45. & 103 1. God wil be served with the best we have. But ther is no one translation the best we have: seing the Lord may in tyme of worship minister better to him that administereth, if hee vnderstand the originalls: if he vnderstand not the originalls he hath it not at all: for it is another mans worke: & therefore no one translation written may be read in tyme of worship.

6. Deut. 16 16. 1 Chron. 21. 24. Eph. 4. 8. Rom. 12 3. we must worship God with our own not with another mans: with that which cost vs somthing not with that which cost vs nothing. But for one ignorant of the tongs to read the translation & offer it to God is to offer to God another mans labor not his owne: that which cost him nothing but is another mans cost: therfore it is vnlawfull.

7. Reading a translation is not commaunded nor was ever practised by Christ, the Apostles, or the primitive Churches in tyme of worship: & so being devised by man is in the account of vayne worship. Mat. 15. 9 & will-worship. Col. 2. 23. & so a kynd of Idolatry & therefore the translation it selfe before the eye in tyme of worship an Idoll & so hath a curse denounced against the vse of it in tyme of worship. Revel. 22. 18. Exod. 20. 4. 5.

8. A translation being the worke of a mans witt & learning is asmuch & as truly an humane writing as the Apocrypha (so commonly called) writings are: & seing it hath not the allowance of holy men inspired, but is of an hidden authority: it may be justly called Apocryphon, for the signification of the word importeth

so much & therefore not to be brought into the worship of God to be read.

9. All the arguments vsed agaynst the reading of homilies & prayers may be applyed agaynst the reading of translations in tyme of worship As:

1. They do stint or quench the spirit which is contrary to .1. Thes. 5. 19. 20. 2 Cor 3. 17.

2. They are not the pure word of God & so contrary to Eccles. 12. 10. Mat. 15. 9.

3. They are the private workes of men: contrary to .1. Cor 12. 7. 8. 2. Pet. 1. 20,

4. They are the private openings or interpretations of the prophesies of Scripture: contrary to ..2 pet 1. 20.

5. They contradiĉt the giftes bestowed by Christ vppon the Church for the work of the ministery: contrary to. Eph. 4. 8. 11. 12. Aĉt. 2. 4. Ioh. 16. 7.

6. They derogate from the vertue of Christs Ascētion & dignitie of his Kingdome: contrary to Eph: 4. 8.

7. They blemish Christs bounty to & care of his church. contrary to. Ioh. 14. 16. 18. 26

8. They disgrace the Spirit of God setting him to schoole. contrary to. 1: Ioh. 2. 27.

9. They bring into the Church a straunge ministratiō contrary to. 1. Cor. 12: 5. & so a new part of the gospel or covenant contrary to, Gal. 3. 15.

10. They do not manifest the spirit which commeth from within, but manifesteth the lettre which commeth from without. 2. Cor. 3. 6.

11. Therefore they are not spiritual worship Ioh 4. 24. compared with. 2. Cor. 3. 17. Gal. 5. 1. & 4. 31.

12. Children mai read a translation perfeĉtly wel: But children cannot perform any part of Spiritual worship: therfor reading a translation is no part of Spiritual worship.

Quere: whither between the parts of Spiritual worship, that is between prayer, prophesying & singing Psalmes, a man may not interpose the reading of a scripture or chapter not intending it as worship, but as a further preparation to worship.

Chap. 15. Objections for translations answered
The first Objection.

Rom. 4. 3. What sayth the Scripture & then followeth the Septuagints translation. Heb. 3. 7. The holy ghost saith: & then follow the wordes of the Septuagints translation: & it is observed that the Apostles quote the wordes of the Septuagints translation, not only wher they expound the meaning of the holy ghost: as Heb. 10. 5. & Rom. 4. 3. Wher the Apostles follow the Septuagints not the Hebrue, but also in their devises besides the original: as in the second Caynan Luk. 3. 36. 37. & in the 75. persons of Iacobs family, Act. 7. 14. where as ther is, but one caynan & 70. persons in the Hebrue.

Answer to the first Objection

If the originals themselves are not to be vsed as helps in tyme of Spiritual worship, as hath been proved then this objection is of no force for translations.

Secondly: if it were of force to bring translations to be read in the tyme of worship it were avayleable thus far even to bring in to the tyme of worship the errors of the translations: for so this objection importeth that the Apostles quote the Septuagints errors, & wheras it is said by some that in the Apostles intention it is no error, sith writing to Theophilus & the Grecians, rather then he would hazard their fayth by chaundging the Septuagints errors & correcting such an approved Translation, he thought it meet to follow that receaved devise of theirs contrary to the truth the Holy Ghost therin yeelding to mans infirmity as in the cases of Polygamy, & Divorce, and Vsury in the Old Testament: It is thus answered that the Holy Ghost needeth not the lyes of men, to work his work, nor the Septuagints errors to support the fayth of Theophilus & the Grecians: And this mischeef followeth herevppon that, rather then the fayth of Theophilus & the Grecians, should be endaungered the credit of the Holy Scriptures should be hazarded their being found in them such devises errors and contradictions. And further it is one thing by connivency to passe by sinne as was the toleration of

Polygamy Divorce & Vsury: See Act. 17. 30: Another thing to translate errors from a translation into the original, which is to approve them, & this whosoever affirmeth, speaketh litle lesse then blasphemy.

Thirdly: therfor as Antichrist hath polluted all Gods ordinances so hath he violated the original scriptures: And therfor one Caynan must be put out: For some auncient copies have it not: & for 75. Ther must be read seaventy all: Pente for Pantes: as Rom. 12. 11. Kairo, Kurio, & it is possible easily to mistake so small a matter in copying out any thing as experience teacheth.

Lastly fully to answer the objection whatsoever is good in the Septuagints translation was taken out of the New Testament, & auncient Fathers of the Greek Church: For it is manifest by historyes that the Septuagints translation is lost, & this that goeth vnder the name of the Septuagint is a patchery made out of auncient writings: and therfor the Holy Ghost doth not ayme at the Septuagints translation at all as is imported in the Objection.

The second Objection.

Ther were Greekes & Grecians: Hellenes: Kai Hellenistai. As may appeare Act. 6. 1. Rom. 1. 16. The Greekes were of the Progeny of the Greekes aswel as of the country: The Grecians were Iewes by Progeny, & borne in Grecia: Therfor Paull calleth himself an Hebrew of the Hebrewes: Philip. 3. 5. Now these Grecians had forgotten their Language & spake Greek only: And having Synagogues in the Cities where they dwelt, had the Septuagints translation read vnto them, & the Apostles comming into their Synagogues did approve that act of theirs of reading the translation & so it followeth that reading translations is lawfull in worship.

Answer to the second Objection.

The disti[n]ction of Greekes & Grecians is vayne as appeereth by these places compared together: Act. 21. 39. & 18. 2. 24. with Act. 6. 1. Philip. 3. 5. For Paul was borne at Tarsus in Cilicia, & Aquila at Pontus, &

Apollos at Alexandria, And yet are all called Iewes not Hellenists or Grecians: & Act. 6. 1. The Helenists murmured against the Hebrues, the Helenists did vnderstand the Hebrue tong, & had not forgotten their owne Language.

Secondly: it cannot be proved by Scriptures that the Helenists had the Greek translation read vnto them in the Synagogues, it is manifestly otherwise by the reasons vsed before against the translation of the Septuagints.

Thirdly, the worship of God properly so called of the whole Church of the Iewes, was performed in the Holy place at Ieruselem, & so that which was performed in the Synagogue was not properly the worship of the whole Church of the Iewes: but was of that nature that passed between Christ & the Doctors in the temple: Luk. 2. 46. compared with Act. 17. 2.

Fourthly if the Helenists did read the Septuagints translation as a part of ther proper worship hauing forgotten their owne Language, therein were committed these synnes.

1. Forgetting their tong one part of the ceremonial law. Nehem, 13. 24

2. Instituting worship in a common tong which was as vnlawfull as sacrificing a dog.

3. Therefore it was a false worship, as it was a false worship to sacrifice an vncleane beaste vnder the law

Lastly if they did reade the Septuagintes translation & the Apostles came in & heard, it doth not follow they did allow it as a parte of the worship of the new testament, no more then they did allow circumcision to be: neither did they in deede giue any allowance vnto it at all, seing they came to the synagogues where was the greatest concourse of people not to worship, but to draw them to Christ, not to approue their doings but to disproue them.

The third obiection.

Deut: 31. 12. the reasons that are alledged for readinge the law are perpetuall, and therfore the law of reading is perpetuall: the moral reasons are, hearing, learning, fearing god, & keeping his lawes.

Answer to the third objection.

First the law of reading is not moral in the particular act, but in the equity: for it was commaunded to be done but once in seaven yeare at the feast of tabernacles Deut. 31. 10. & if it had been moral in the particular act it should have been from the beginning, (which was not so, seing it beganne with Moses,) & it should continue after the end of the world: for moralities endure for ever: But bookes & so reading of bookes shal perish.

Secondly it is morall in the equity, that is, that all meanes must be vsed to attayne the knowledg of the truth wherof reading is a principall, & yet hence it followeth not that reading is eyther a part or meanes of Spiritual worship: For bookes are things meerely artificiall as are pictures & ymages, Genes. 4. 22.

Finally let it be granted that reading is morall it doth not herevppon follow that it is lawfull in tyme of Spiritual worship as a part or help thereto. Seing that reading is searching the Scripture, or preparing to the worship, & not worship it self, & seing that whē a man doth worship, he is not to prepare to worship as he doth that readeth: though I deny not but that one part of worship is a preparation to another.

The fourth objection.

Reading the law was performed in the Synagogue, & it was not tyed to the temple or the holy place, which is an argument that reading is not ceremoniall but morall, for no part of ceremonial worship was performed from the tabernacle or Temple.

Answer to the fourth objection.

The argumēt foloweth not: for although all ceremonial worship was to be performed at Ierusalem Ioh. 4. 20, Yet it is so to be construed as intended by the woman according to the lawes direction: namely, of the worship which the Preists performed as sacrificers: as may be seen: Deut. 12. 5–7, & vs. 11–19. For otherwise some ceremoniall worship, as namely circumcizion was performed any where in the land of Israel, for the males must needes be circumcized at 8. dayes old, & it was impossible to bring the males some of thē 100. miles within eight dayes space. see Chap. 20.

Againe suppose reading the law to be a morall action (which yet is not so) hence it followeth not that reading the law is a part of Spirituall worship or a lawful help therto in tyme therof: for by the same reason every morall duty may be made a part or meanes of Spirituall worship, which is absurd, for that is to confound the second table of the lawe, & the dutyes thereof with the first table & the dutyes thereof & the gospel with the law.

The fifth objection.

Luk. 4. 16. Christ stood vp to read, & read his text, & then preached out of it: Now his actions are our instructions: & therfor wee are to read wordes out of a book in tyme of preaching or prophesying.

Answer to the fifth objection.

To this objection many things may be answered.

First in that it was done in the Synagogue by Christ which was neither Preist nor Levite, it is an argument that it was no proper part of the worship of the old testament, but of that nature as was that exercise performed by Christ & the Doctors in the temple: so that reading most properly is searching the scriptures, which is not worship.

Secondly: Christ had the Originales the Hebrue text of Esay the Prophet, & read or interpreted out of it, for it is doubtfull whither he vttered the Hebrue words or speake the sense of the Hebrue in the Syriack dialect: & therfor from hence reading a translation cannot be concluded: but eyther reading or interpreting the originals.

Thirdly: Hence cannot be concluded that manner of preaching now vsed that a man shall take his text, & then devide it into parts analysing it Rhetorically, & Logically, collecting doctrynes & vses from every member or argument or word of his text. al this while he having his book before his eyes to help him at all assayes: a thing wherof I am assured the holy Scriptures yeeldeth no warrant that it may be accounted a part of Spiritual worship: For although the Scriptures may be so handled,

& that for very profitable vse, yet that is rather a Scholasticall lecture, then an Ecclesiasticall worship: it is rather an inquisition & searching of the holy Spirits intent and purpose, then prophesying.

Lastly: If wee must needes be tyed to this example of Christ (which I see no reason for seing reading was of the Old Testament) then the example of Christ shal bind also thus far, as that the book shal be layde aside, so soone as the text is read, & the book that is vsed shalbe the Originals: which is nothing for vocall but for mental reading, or for interpreting, & which I never have thought to contradict, but wherein I am ready to be overruled: For this particular see the Quere in the Chap. 10.

See also the quere Chap. 14. For interposing the reading of the translation between the parts of worship as a further preparation & help to worship succeeding.

Thus much concerning the answer to Objections made for the lawfull vse of translations in tyme of worship.

Chap. 16. Of the lawfullnes of translating the Scriptures. & the vse of translations in our account.

Although before Christs comming it was vnlawful to translate the Holy Originals from their ceremonial tong into any vulgar mother tong: yet the partition wall being now broken downe, translations are lawful & that for these reasons.

Math. 28. Christ commaundeth to goe teach all nations, & therfor all nations may have the Holy Scriptures translated into their owne vernacular tong, that therby they may learne the truth.

The Scriptures are a Creature or ordinance of God: & therfor as it is lawful to picture a man, a byrd a fish, a fowle, an angel vertue or vice, so is it lawful to picture out or resemble the Hebrue & Greek original Scriptures by any vulgar translation of any tong or Language whatsoever.

Againe as God sent the confusion of tongs as a curse. Genes. 11. 6. 7. so hath he sent the knowledg of the tongs as a blessing. Act. 2. 6. 8. & bicause the extraordinary knowledg of the tong is ceased, the ordinary knowledg of them is left for our vse, which can never be attayned *of the Seperation* 299

vnto, but by grammars & dictionaryes wherein the Hebrue words of the old Testament & Greek of the new Testament are interpreted, & if it be lawfull to expresse in our owne tong al the Hebrue & Greek words singly as in Grammars & Dictionaryes, then it is lawful so to doe with thē al joyntly in syntaxe, & that is a translation whēce it foloweth that translations of the holy scriptures are lawful & necessary.

Further: All the members of the Church cannot possiblie attayne the knowledg of the tongs, which notwithstanding they must endevour to their vtmost. 1. Cor. 14. 1. 5. & seing the Holy Ghost hath commaunded al to try & search & read: 1. Thes. 5. 21. Ioh. 5. 39. Colos. 4. 16, & all cannot trye, search, or read the originals, they must needes have translations & other Theological writings, for their better help to the true vnderstanding of the original Scriptures.

Lastly: these places of scripture compared together are sufficient warrant for the lawfulnes of translations: Mat. 1. 23. Marc, 5. 41. 1. Cor. 14. 27.

Now further wee have the translations of Holy Scripture in this account: viz:

The translation agreable to the originals.

1. Is a secondary Scripture, yet much inferior to the originals.
2. It may be read in the Church & sung in times.
3. It may be expounded in the Church.
4. It may be so vsed as a meanes to prepare vs to spiritual worship.
5. That the matter of the translation agreable to the originals is inspired: but not the writing or character.
6. That it may be made the ground of our fayth.
7. That it may be made an instrument to trye doctryne by.

This wee hold affirmatively: Negatively wee hold thus.

1. That reading the English translation is no part of the spiritual worship of the new Testament properly so called: viz: of prayer, prophecy, singing of Psalmes.
2. That reading the English translation is no lawful meanes or help in tyme of Spiritual worship.
3. That the worship of the New Testament must

not beginne in the book or lettre outwardly: but must proceed originally from the hart & Spirit.

Al other publique & private vses of translations wee allow.

Chap. 17. Concerning the vse of the translations for the hearers.

Hitherto aperteyneth another question: whither the hearers may have their translations or the originals to read or search in tyme of prophecy.

The answer is Negative that it is not lawful for these reasons.

First: the Prophets & Apostles wrote bookes, but did never devide their bookes into chapters or verses: Henry Stephen first made the verses of the New Testament: Seing therfor that chapter & verse were of mans invention, hence it followeth before chapter & verse came in the hearers could not turne to search their bookes in tyme of hearing.

Secondly: the Apostles in quoting testimonyes of the Prophets doe not quote chapter & verse, but only say: it is written: by Zachary, by Ieremy. The Scripture saith. The Holy Ghost saith, &c. Therby teaching vs that there is no vse of Chapter and verse for searching in tyme of hearing: For no doubt they preached as they wrote.

Thirdly: never was ther any mention made of any hearer that ever had his booke to search in tyme of hearing.

Fourthly: Searching quotations hindereth attention: for the mynd & affections are distracted from hearing by seeking the places: seing the mynd & hart should follow the voyce of the speaker, as in prayer, so also in Prophesying. Nehem. 8. 3.

Lastly manuscripts being few & very deere & large (ther being yet no printing found out) all could not have or bring their bookes, but there is only one kind of true or profitable hearing, eyther all to have bookes and search, or none to have them.

Seing therfor bringing bookes & searching them in tyme of hearing was not from the beginning: Therfor that also is a part of the mystery of iniquity in hearing the word.

Chap. 18. Of the nature or essence of Spiritual worship & the essenciall causses & kinds thereof.

Thus much concerning the helps of Spirituall worship: Now followeth to be considered the nature or essence thereof, which may appeare in two particulars: viz:

First in the essentiall causses of Spiritual worship.

Secondly in the proper kinds or parts of the worship of the new Testament.

The essentiall causses of Spiritual worship are the matter and the forme.

The matter of Gods worship is the holy Scriptures which conteyneth the word of God, or the Gospel, the subject whereof is Christ Iesus:

The forme or soule that quickeneth it is the Spirit. Colos. 3. 16. compared with Eph. 5. 18. 19. 20.

This may be illustrated by the ceremoniall worship of the Old Testament & the essentiall causses thereof.

The matter of the ceremonial worship of the Old Testament was the beasts, incense, Oyle, fatt, corne, wine, & the like Creatures whereof the sacrifices, offerings, perfumes, lampes, & bread were made, with al the actions therto aperteyning.

Proportionable hereto is the matter of our spiritual worship Christ Iesus & his merits: the word of God conteyned in the Scriptures which offereth Christ Iesus vnto vs: the seales of the covenant with all the actions therto aperteyning.

The form of the ceremonial worship of the Old Testament consisting in Sacrifices, (besides the manner of doing) appeared in 4. things: two wherof must be absent for the most part viz: honey & leaven: two must alwayes be present: fire & salt: Marc. 9. 49. compared with Leuit. 2. 11. 13, & 9. 24. 1. Cor. 5. 6–8.

Proportionable herevnto the forme of our Spiritual worship consisteth in the fire of the Spirit working with the word: Act. 2. 3. 4. Mat. 3. 11. Luk. 12. 49. 50. & 24. 32. 2. Tim. 1. 6. 7. Ierem. 23. 29.

In the salt of sound doctryne & grace. Mat. 5. 13. Colos. 4. 6.

In the vnleavened bread of syncerity & truth. 1. Cor.

5: 8. which was also signified by absence of honey which hath a faculty to leaven.

As the fire came downe from heaven, wherwith the sacrifices were offered: Levit. 9. 24. So the holy Ghost like fire came downe vppon the primitive Church, to make their Spiritual sacrifices acceptable: So must it doe also vppon ours: Act. 2. 3. 4.

As the fire was dayly preserved to offer withall. Levit. 6. 12. 13. & straunge fire might not be offered: Levit. 10. 1. So whatsoever worship is offered vp & is not kindled with the Spirit of grace in our harts is abhominable: 1. Cor. 12. 7. 10. 1. Pet. 2. 5.

Hence it followeth that the worship that beginneth in the book or translation commeth not originally from the Spirit, but from the lettre or ceremony, & so is not properly of the new Testament, but of the Old: 2. Corinth. 3. 6. If the translation be made by one without, it commeth from a straunge fire, & cannot be accepted, but is subject to a curse.

Thus much of the essential causses: now follow the kinds of Spiritual worship, which are 3. Praying, Prophesying, & singing Psalmes: Psal. 50. 14–17. 1. Cor. 11. 4. & 14. 15–17. 26. Iam. 5. 13. Revel. 19. 10.

Therfor praying & prophesying are joyned together as parts of worship: 1. Cor. 11. 4 & men must be vncovered at both of them.

Likewise praying & singing Psalmes are put together in the same sense: 1. Cor. 14. 15. 27 Iam. 5. 13. Act. 16. 25:

Finally: Prophesying & Psalmes are coupled together for the same purpose, 1. Cor. 14. 26.

Prayer is the shewing of our requests to God by the manifestation of the spirit: Phil. 4. 6. Rom. 8. 26. 27. 1. Cor. 14. 15.

Singing Psalmes is the shewing of our thanksgiving to God by the manifestation of the Spirit. Phil. 4. 6. 1. Cor. 14. 15–17.

Prophesying is the publishing of the covenant of Grace by the manifestation of the Spirit, Act. 2. 4. 11. 17. 18. 1. Cor. 2. 4 & 12. 7. 10. Gal. 3. 5. & it serveth specially & properly for them that beleeve: 1. Cor. 14. 22. Psal. 50. 16. 17. & it pleased the Holy Ghost to choose that word to signifie vnto vs, that as the Prophetts by inspiration of the Holy Ghost prophesyed without bookes, so must wee: the difference is in this that the inspiration was extraordinary, ours is ordinary. Revel. 19. 10.

The matter of all these 3. parts of Spiritual worship is one & the same, viz: God's word or the Scriptures, yet handled diversly.

In prayer Gods word or the Scriptures are delivered by way of petition in direction to God, requesting things for vs optatively.

In thanksgiving Gods word or the Scriptures are delivered by way of recompense or retribution to God, indicatively or imperatively.

In Prophesying the word of God or the Scriptures are delivered demonstratively, by way of doctryne, exhortation, consolation, reprehension, & by such like formes.

Howsoever it be handled or delivered the matter is one & the same the manner of delivering different: for whither we pray, prophesy or sing, it must be the word or scripture, not out of the book, but out of the hart, 1. Cor. 12. 7. 11.

The demonstration of the spirit & powre, 1. Cor. 2. 4. The manifestation of the spirit 1. Cor. 12. 7. The ministration of the Spirit: 2. Cor. 3. 8. The administring of the spirit. Gal. 3. 5. The ministration of the gift. 1. Pet. 4. 10. The dispensation of grace. 1. Pet. 4. 10. Are all one in effect, & are opposed to the ministery of the lettre or the Ceremoniall worship. 2. Cor. 3. 6.

The ministration of the old Testament is called the ministery of the lettre, seing it dispenced the ceremonial & literal ordinances & beganne in the lettre: for the Church, Ministery, worship, Government, Temple, Tabernacle, Cittie, Country, Meate, Drinck, Apparel, Cattel, Fruites of the earth, &c. Were all literall & ceremonial.

The ministration of the New Testament is called the ministery of the Spirit: seing it dispenced the true & spiritual ordinances typed by the foresaid literal ordinances, & beginneth in the spirit originally, though prepared by the lettre. 2. Cor. 3. 6–8. 24. 17. compared with Revel. 10. 10. 11.

Hence it followeth that all bookworship is Iudaisme, & so Antichristian, & therfore by consequent Idolatry, now vnder the new Testament.

Thus much of the kinds of Spiritual worship of the new Testament.

Chap. 19. How the worship of the Old Testament did type the Spiritual worship of the new Testament.

The lyteral or typical worship of the Old Testament was performed in two places. viz: eyther in the holy place, or in the court.

The ceremoniall worship performed in the holy place did type most properly the worship of the Church of the new Testament which was typed by the holy place. Revel. 11. 1. 2. 2. Cor. 6. 16. Heb. 8. 2. & 9. 11. 1. Pet. 2. 5.

The worship of the tabernacle or holy place consisted of 3. parts. 1. that which perteyned to the brasen altar. 2. that which was performed at the golden altar. 3. that which concerned the table of shewbread: Exod, 37. & 38. compared with Exod. 29. 38. Exod. 30. 7, 8 & Levit. 24. 1–9. Exod. 30. 34–38.

At the brasen altar were offered Sacrifices propitiatory & Eucharistical. Levit. 1. 3. & 7. 1–11 which signified prayer for pardon of syn through Christs sacrifice. Heb. 10. 4–14. 22. & thanksgiving. Heb. 13. 15. compared with Hose. 14. 3. & prophesying or publishing the gospel: Gall. 3. 1. For in Preaching Christ is as it were anatomized.

At the golden altar was offered the sweet perfume which signified prayer & thanksgiving. psal. 141. 2. Revel. 8. 3. 4. & by proportion. Nomb. 16. 46–48 Apoc. 5. 8–14. & preaching the gospel, 2. Cor. 2. 14–16.

Vppō the table of shewbread, was the candlestick, & twelve loaves of vnlevened bread with incense: vppon every one of them, which had this signification.

The Candlestick with his 7. lamps burning with oile olive continually drest evening & morning by Aaron & his sonnes, Levit. 24. 1–9. Signified that the Church (which is the golden Candlestick. Apoc. 1. 20. Zach. 4.) by his seaven lamps, that is the manifold gifts of the

Spirit, Revel. 4. 5. Zach. 4. 6. drest by Aaron & his sonnes, that is the dĉtyne of rothe Church, being kept pure, & caused to shine bright by the Prophets of the church Mat. 5. 14. 15. nourished & fed continually with oile olive, that is taught dayly by the spirit, Zach. 4. 14. Revel. 11. 4. doth continually give light, instruction & direction to all her members. Psal. 119. 105. Mat. 5. 16. 2. Pet. 1. 19.

The shewbread with incense therevppon afterward burnt vppon the golden altar, Levit. 24. 7. 9. Signified that the twelve tribes that is the Church continually present before the Lord are accepted through Christs perfume, Revel. 8. 3. 4. are fed with Christ Iesus the true bread of life, Ioh. 6. 35. are enlightened by his word & Spiritt, which are the true lamps of knowledg. Revel. 4. 5.

Chap. 20. Of that which was performed in the court.

As the holy place with the altar & Preists did properly Signify the Church, worship, & Saynts, Revel. 11. 1. 1. Pet. 2. 5. vnder the new Testament: So the court without the holy place whither al the people came & the typical service performed ther, did signify the confused assemblies of Antichristian persecuters & their ceremonial worship, Revel. 11. 8. which the Spirit in that place caleth gentils or heathen in those respeĉts.

The parts of typical service performed in the court were reading & Musick, wherein the Levites were cheef agents, Deut. 31. 9. 1. Chron. 16. 4. compared with vs. 7. 37. 39–42. & Chap. 25. 1–6–31. Nehem. 8. 7–9. 18. & 9. 3–6. Though the Preists also & any of the people might read & sing, Mat. 23. 2. 3. Luk. 2. 46. & 4. 16. 17. Aĉt. 13. 14. 15. Nehem. 8. 8. Marc. 14. 26.

The Scriptures read & tuned Musically were, prophecies, prayers, thanksgivings, 1. Chron. 25. 1–6. Deut 31. 10, & 2. Chron. 34. 30. Psal. 78. for prophesies with instruction. 1. Chron. 16. 7–36. Psal. 146. 147. 148. 149. 150. compared with Revel. 19. 1–8, For thanksgivings: Psal. 102. the title, & 92. title, for prayers.

As Musicall Instruments & playing vppon them was

typicall, bicause it was Artificiall: So reading of a book was typicall also bicause it is meerely Artificiall,

Hence it followeth that reading prophecies was a type of prophesying, reading prayers a type of praying, & reading thanksgivings a type of praising God or thankfulnes.

To conclude: as it followeth not that seing prayers were read in the old testament as prayers, therfor wee may read prayers now: for prayers no more doth it follow that though in the old testament they read Psalmes & prophecies, we may doe so now: namely, in the tyme of worship, or as parts, or helps of Spiritual worship, properly so called.

Therfor as the aunceint brethren of the Seperation have taken all books from before the eye in tyme of prayer, so doe wee take all bookes from the eye in tyme of prophesying & singing: & that by the same reason they being al equally excellent parts of Spiritual worship, for God is asmuch honoured in prophesying & Psalmes, as in praying & they all of them remayne in the triumphant Church in heaven: even as they were all practised by Adam in Paradise before his fal: & therfor are properly moral, & Spiritual worship.

THE SECOND PART of the Ministery of the Church

The first section   of the Eldership or Presbytery

Chap. 1. Of the names or titles of the Elders.

Thus much concerning the Leitourgie of the Church, now follow the offices of the Church, viz: the Presbytery & Deaconry, Phil. 1. 1, Esay. 66. 21. Nomb. 3. 5–10, & 16. 5. 38. & 17. Chap.

The Presbytery of the church is the company of the Elders which are for the church in the publique actions of the Church, eyther of the Kingdom or preisthood, Heb. 13. 18. 1, Thes. 5. 12. 1. Timoth. 4. 14. & 5. 17.

The presbytery is vniforme consisting of Officers of one sort, Esay. 66. 21. compared with Exod. 28. 1. & with Nomb. 11. 24. 25. 1. Timoth. 3. 1–8. Act. 14. 23. philip. 1. 1. Ierem. 23. 1–4. Ezech. 34. 1–16.

These Officers are called Elders, Overseers, or Bishops, pastors, Teachers, Governors, Leaders, prepositi, which are several names of one & the same office consisting of several works or qualifications.

For every one of these officers must be.

1. An Elder or Auncient in yeeres, 1. Timoth. 3. 6. & 5. 1.
2. Oversee the flock, 1. pet. 5. 2.   Act. 20. 28
3. Feed the flock, 1. pet. 5. 2.   Act. 20. 28.
4. Able to teach, & exhort with wholsome doctryne & convince the gainsayers, 1. Timoth. 3. 2, Tit. 1. 9. Eph. 4. 11.
5. Governe the Church. 1. Tim. 3. 4. 5. 1. Cor. 12. 28.
6. Lead the Church in al the publique affaires thereof Heb. 13. 17.
7. Are preferred to place of honor. 1. Thes. 5. 12. 1. Tim. 5. 17. & speciall labour. 1. Timoth. 3. 1.

Seing all the Elders must teach, exhort, convince, feed, oversee, rule, & lead the church therfor they may all administer the seales of the covenant: for that is a cheef work of feeding & applying the covenant & that particularly.

Chap. 2. Of reasons proving the Elders to be of one sort, viz: all Pastors.

First in the Old Testament ther was but one kind of Preists, who had al equal authority to administer al the holy things: excepting the high Preist, who typed forth Christ Iesus the high Preist of our confession: so proportionably in the New Testament ther is but one sort of Elders who succede the Preists in the dispensation of holy things. Esay. 66. 21.

As in the Old Testament ther was the sanhedrim which consisted of 70. auncients for the administration of the Kingdom, which was a type of the visible church al which Elders in their first institution Nomb. 11. 25. did prophecy & were of one kind vnder Moses: so in the new Testament vnder Christ Iesus, which is the King of the church, ther is a sunedrion or Eldership consisting of Auncients of one kind who administer for the good of the Church, Revel. 4. 4. & 5. 6.

Againe, If Pastor, Teacher, Elder had been 3. Offices formally differing the Apostle intending to teach the several offices of the Church would have mentioned them. 1. Timoth. 3. But ther he only mentioneth Bishops & Deacons according as Phil. 1. 1. [er]go: Bishops are only of one sort or kind.

Moreover, if the Apostles had ordeyned 3. Kinds of Elders, Act. 14. 23. they would have mentioned them with their several kinds of ordination: but that is not done: for in one phrase their election & ordination is mentioned: er[go] their ordination being one, their office is one & not three.

Further, if their had been 3. Kinds of Elders at Ephesus then the Apostle at Miletum would have given them several chardges as having several dutyes lying vppon them: but the Apostle Act. 20, 28. giveth them one general chardg common to them all, namely the duty of feeding the work of the Pastor: [er]go, they are all Pastors.

Besides. Eph. 4. 11. Pastors & teachers are all one office: for where as the Apostle had spoken distributively before of Apostles, Prophets, Evangelists as intending them several offices, he speaketh copulatively of pastors & teachers, exegetically teaching that they are both one office.

Lastly, if all the Elders have the pastors gifts, & the works of the pastor, & the pastors ordination, then they have all the pastors office: But all the Elders have the pastors gifts: viz: the word of wisdome or the gift of exhortation. Tit. 1. 9. & therfor the pastors worke as Act. 20. 28. 1. Pet. 5. 2. which is feeding or exhorting, and so the same ordination Acts. 14. 23. Therfor all the Elders have the same office of the pastor: & so are all of one sort.

Hence this consectary ariseth that the Eldership consisting of three sorts of Elders is the invention of man, having both an Antichristian Ministery and Government in it.

And therfor when the Popish prelacy was supprest, & the triformed presbytery substituted, one Antichrist was put down & another set vp in his place: or the beast was supprest & his image advanced.

And therfor as they that submit to the prelacy are subject to that woe of worshipping the beast, so they that submit to the triformed Presbytery are in like manner lyable to the woe denounced against then that worship the jmage of the beast.

Chap. 3. Objections for three sorts of Elders answered,

The first Objection.

1. Tim. 5. 17. In this place the Apostle maketh two sortes of Elders viz. 1. Those that Rule only: 2. Those that Teach & Rule. & Eph. 4. 11 the Apostle maketh two kindes of those that teach, Pastors, & Doctors. Therefore ther are three kindes of Elders formally differing each from other.

Answer to the first Objection.

The Apostle to Timothie teacheth that Elders are to be honoured for two workes wel ruling, & laborious or painful teaching: & the place doth not import a distribution of officers, but a commendacion of several workes of one office: & the Specialty consisteth not in the works of ruling & teaching which are common to all Elders;

but in the quality of the works viz: wel-ruling: painful-teaching as if the Apostle should say: Elders are to be had in double honour for wise Government: but much more are they to be honoured for their laborious and painful teaching: that this is so: see Tit. 1. 9. & 1. Thes. 5. 12. 13. compared with 1. Tim. 3. 1. 4.

In Timothie the Apostle saith every Bishop must be Didacticos: & Proistamenos: & therfor that some Elders are only Didacticoi, & not Proistamenoi is contrary to the Apostles intent: Further in Titus the Apostle expoundeth Didacticos to be able to exhort with wholsom doctryne & to convince the gainsayers: how then shal some of the Elders be Rulers only?

.Againe the Apostle in that place of the Ephesians speaketh copulatively of one office, & exegetically of the principal work of the pastor which is teaching: he doth not say: some pastors, some teachers, but he saith pastors & teachers: expounding the former by the latter viz: feeding by teaching which is the principal part of feeding, & for which pastors are cheefly commended, 1. Tim. 5. 17. if they labour therein painfully.

The second Objection.

1. Cor. 12. 5. 8. 28. The Apostle sayth. ther are diversityes of Ministeries: namely one that hath the word of wisdom; another the word of knowledg: another that hath Government: vs. 28. Therfor the Eldership consisteth of 3. sorts of Elders: viz: of the pastor that hath the word of wisdome of the teacher that hath the word of knowledg: of the Ruler that hath the quality of government.

Answer to the second Objection.

First it is graunted that ther are diversities of Ministeries as Eph, 4. 11, 1. Tim. 3. 1. 8. philip, 1. 1. Namely: Apostles, prophets, Evangelists, pastors, Deacons: yet it followeth not herevppon that Elders are of divers sorts as is pleaded, see vs. 28.

Againe the word Diaconia, signifieth somtyme any Spiritual work, proceeding from any member or officer of the Church, as 2. Cor. 8. 4, almes is called Diaconia: 1, Pet. 4. 10. Diaconein signifieth any work that proceedeth from any gift: So it may signifie heer: & al the workes that folow almost may be referred thether: only ther are certayne Energemata, mentioned vers 10.

The third Objection.

The Apostle Rom 12. 6–8, maketh an opposition between prophecy & an office: & maketh five kinds of officers: Pastors, Teachers, Rulers, Deacons, Widowes.

Answer to the third Objection.

That is denyed to be the true resolution of the place of the Romanes: for although ther be five several actions repeated, yet it doth not follow that ther are five several officers to perform those actions: For one person may performe then all & yet be no officer, viz: teach, exhort, rule, distribute, shew mercy, 1 Cor 14. 3. 26. 31, Roman 12. 13 1 Cor, 5. 5.

Againe the distributive particle Eite fowre tymes repeated, in prophecy, Diaconia, exhorting, & teaching, importeth thus much: That the Apostles intention is not to subordinate teaching & exhorting to Diaconia, but to oppose each of these 4. particulars to other: as thus, Prophesy is the manifestation of a gift, 1 Cor. 14. 3.

Diaconia is the office, & ther are divers kinds thereof, 1. Cor. 12. 5.

Teaching is one action or work of the prophets or officers, 1 Cor, 14. 26

Exhorting is an other action or work of them, 1 Cor. 14 3

Hence it followeth that teaching & exhorting are aswel subordinate to prophesy as to Diaconia.

Further, if Diaconia be the genus to those five species following, then I say that Diaconia signifieth not an Office, but a work: And of works there are those five kinds: That Diaconia doth somtyme signifie a work is playne: 1 Cor. 8. 4. 1. Pet. 4. 10.

Lastly: the Apostle that knew how to speake would never have made teaching & exhortation members distributive with prophesy & Diaconia, If he had intended to have made them species subordinate to Diaconia: therefor questionles that is not his intention.

The fourth Objection.

The Apostle by the commaundement of Christ writeth to the Angels of the seaven Churches of Asia: Revel. Chap. 1, & 2. & 3. That is to the Pastors which are but one in every particular Church for so the words are to the Aungel of the Church of Ephesus, &c.

Answer to the fourth Objection.

First, it can never be proved by the Scriptures that there was, but one pastor in a Church: It is plaine, Act. 20. 28. That there were many in the Church of Ephesus (that was one of those seaven Churches) that did performe the work of the pastor which is poimainein, to feed, even all the Elders of Ephesus: Act. 20. vers 17, compared with vers 28. And therfor there were many Pastors in the Church of Ephesus in Paulls tyme.

Againe, all Churches had Officers of one sort, & one kind of Presbytery, & therefor as all the Elders of Ephesus were Pastors, so were all the Elders of the six Churches of Asia & of all other Churches wheresoever in the world, if they had many Elders.

Further, the Angel of every one of those Churches doth not signify one pastor only in every Church, but eyther the College of pastors if they were many, or the company of the most sincere & holy men that most opposed the corruptions of the Church, or were most holy & zealous in life & doctryne: that an angel signifieth a cōpany of men is playne Revel. 14. 6. 8. 9. & 18. 4.

Lastly, in all likelyhood ther were some extraordinary men yet living in the churches eyther Prophets or Evangelists that had extraordinary gifts, whose Zeale & holynes might winne vnto them special estimation in the Churches: in regard whereof it might be that the Holy Ghost intending his Epistles to the whole Church, cheefly directeth them to these persons so qualified as men best able to prevayle with the Church & calleth them Aungels, whither one or more: As Iohn the Baptist is called an Aungell. Marc. 1. 2,

Chap. 4. Of the divers gifts of Elders.

Seing al the Prophets of the Church must have gifts fit for edification, exhortation & consolation: the Pastors of the Church must have gifts for the performance of the same workes kat' exochen, after an excellent manner & in a greater measure.

The Pastors excelling the prophets of the Churche in the gifts of doctryne, exhortation, consolation, may also excel one another in gifts: for al the Elders have not the same measure or degree of gifts.

In respect of the measure of gifts in the Elders, some excelling in one gift some in an other, the Holy Ghost may give several titles to the Elders or pastors.

Every Elder according as the excellency of his gift is, so must he endevour himself: edifying of the Church & in the stirring vp the gift God hath given vnto him: 1. pet. 4. 10. 11. Mat. 25. 29. 2 Tim. 1. 6. 1. Cor. 14. 12.

Although some Elder excel in one gift some in another, yet it followeth not that therefor they are several officers formally differing one from another: for not the degree measure or excellency of a gift or gifts, but the several kind & nature of gifts & works make several kinds of offices: 1. Cor. 12. 4. 5. 6.

The Elder that excelleth in government most properly may be called a ruler or Governour, although he have the gifts & powre to teach, exhort, confort, apply, & that by vertue of his office. Tit. 1. 9. Heb. 13. 17.

The Elder that excelleth in doctryne & convincing the gainsayers may most properly be called a Teacher or Doctor, though by vertue of his office he may administer al other pastoral dutyes: Act. 18. 28. & 19. 1. 1. Cor. 3. 4–6. compared with Tit. 1. 9. Eph. 4. 11. 1 Pet. 5. 2.

The Elder that exceleth in exhortation, consolatiō & application, may most properly be called a pastor or shepheard, though by vertue of his office he is to teach, convince & govern. Act. 20. 28. Tit. 1. 9. Eph. 4. 11. 1. Pet. 5. 2.

As the Apostle doth, 2. Tim. 1. 6. 1. Pet. 4. 10. So may the Church give a charg to the Elder in ordination to stir vp, attend to, & vse his proper & most pregnant

& familiar gift: which he is to mynd: & accordingly to endevour himself in his administration: & thus shal every one as his gift is excel therein to the edification of the Church. 1. Corinth. 14. 12.

Thus shall al men that have excellēcy of gifts when they shalbe added to the church be imployed in the honourable service of the Church: wheras if ther be but one pastor in a Church, men of more excellent gifts being added to the Church shall sitt still, leefe ther gifts & look on: which alone is an argument sufficient to overthrow the fancy of one pastor only in one Church.

Chap. 5. Of the works of the Presbytery or Elders in the preisthood of the Church.

Thus much concerning the presbytery: now follow the works of the Elders, or the presbytery. Which are of two sorts.
1. Workes of the preisthood of the Church.
2. Workes of the Kingdom of the Church.

For the prophecy of the Church is comprehended vnder the preisthood as a branch of it. Deut. 33. 10. Revel. 1. 6. with 1. Cor. 14. 31. Act. 2. 17. 18.

The workes of the preisthood are: prophesying, that is publishing the covenant of grace or the new Testament, wherto aperteyneth putting to the seales: praying: singing psalmes of praise & thanksgiving vnto the Lord.

The office of the Eldership or the work of the presbytery is to lead & moderate the Church in these Spiritual Sacrifices: in regard whereof they have their names: as Leaders, prepositi: &c.

Although the presbytery lead & moderate these Spiritual Sacrifices, yet the brethren are interested in vsing their gifts for the performance of al these parts of Spiritual worship, 1. Cor. 14. 31. 26. Revel. 1. 6. 1. pet. 2. 5. & that when the whole Church is come together in one: 1. Cor. 14. 23. yet things must be done in order, 1. Cor. 14. 33. 40.

Exception. The administration of the seales of the Covenant semeth to apertayne only to the Elders or presbytery, as sacrificing did only to the preists: Mat. 3. 6. & 26. 26–30 Marc. 14, 12.

Chap. 6. Of the presbytery or Elders in the Kingdom of the Church.

The workes of the Kingdom are Admonition, Conviction, Examination, Disputation, Excommunication, Absolution, & handling all matters of difference betwixt brother & brother: & if ther be any of like nature.

The Eldership is to lead & moderate the Church actions & speeches in these matters & causses of the Kingdom & government. Deut. 16. 18–20. & 1. 14–18. 2. Chron. 19. 5, 11. 1. Cor. 6. 1–8. 1. Thes. 5. 12. 13. 1. Tim 5. 17. Heb. 13. 17.

The brethren are all interested in all the parts of administration though the Elders lead & moderate them. 1. Cor. 5. 4. 5. 1. Thes. 5. 14. & 2. Ep. 3. 6. Revel. 2. 2. & 1. 4. & 1. 12. & 1. 6.

The brethren joyntly have all powre both of the Kingdom & preisthood immediately from Christ: Revel. 1. 6. 1. Pet. 2. 5. 2. Cor. 6. 6–18. Mat. 18. 20. & that by vertue of the covenant God maketh with them, Gen. 17. 7. with Act. 2. 39. Rom. 4. 11. Gal. 3. 14. 16.

Therfor when the Church wanteth an Eldership, it hath never the lesse powre to Preach, Pray, Sing Psalmes, & so by consequent to administer the seales of the covenant: also to admonish, convince, excommunicate, absolve, & al other actions eyther of the Kingdom or preisthood: by necessary consequent.

When the Church hath chosen & ordeyned her self Elders, then the Church leeseth none of her former powre, but still retayneth it entyre to herself to vse when occasion serveth: by necessary consequent.

The presbytery hath no powre, but what the Church hath & giveth vnto it: which the Church vppon just cause can take away: Colos 4. 17. Gal. 1. 9. Revel. 2. 2. 1. cor. 16. 22.

The Church hath some powre which the presbytery alone hath not, viz, powre of Elections & communication: 1. Cor. 5. 4. 5. Act. 6. 5. & 14. 23. & so by consequent of all other Sentences.

The second Section

Chap. 1. Of the Treasury of the Church, & the Deacons office.

Thus much of the office & workes of the presbytery: Now follow the office & workes of the Deacons.

The Deacons office respecteth the body & bodily necessityes of the Saints: Act. 6. 2. which is called serving tables in that place: as also bodely service of the Eldership & Church, Esay 66 21 compared with Ezech 44. 10–14 Nomb 3. 5–10.

In respect whereof the deacōs may be termed the servants of the Eldership & church as the Levites were given to serve the preists & the people in the tabernacle, nōb. 3. 5–10

The Deacons in the new testament are answerable to the Levites in the old testament: as the Elders are answerable to ther preists: Esay 66. 21. compared with. 1. Chron 26. 20

The Deacons office especially is occupyed about the treasury of the Church. 1. chron. 26. 20. compared with Act. 6. 2. Ioh. 13. 29.

Concerning the treasury consider these things,

1. Who are to contribute & what is to be given to the treasury.
2. Of what nature the treasury is, & when it is to be collected.
3. How the treasury is to be imployed & at whose appointment.

Chap. 2. VVho are to contribute.

They that have but two mites (as the poore widow in the gospell) are to contribute to the treasury, Luk. 21. 2 aswel as they that are wealthy, vs. 4. Exod. 35. 20–29.

They that have much are to give much, Luk. 21. 4. Act. 4. 39.

They that have but litle are to contribute a litle, by proportion.

All the members of the Church are to contribute somthing, bicause the almes or contribution is the manifestation of grace, even of our bowels of mercy & compassion, & a part of our holy communion, 1. Cor. 16. 2. 2. Cor. 8. 2–3, 7. Act 2. 42. Luk. 21. 4.

As al Rivers goe into the sea & flow out of the sea, so wee must all cast into the treasury, & all receave from the treasury againe as our necessityes are.

Quere: whither they that are mayntayned by the treasury are to contribute into the treasury: as the officers & poore brethren.

Chap. 3. VVhat or how much is to be given to the treasury.

So much is to be given to the treasury as may serve for supplying the present necessityes of the Church, Act. 2. 45. & 4. 34. 35.

In the necessityes of the church the rich must sel their goods & possessions for the help of the Church, Act. 2. 45. & 4. 34. 35.

In the necessityes of the Church the brethren must contribute not only according to their ability, but even beyond their ability: & their extreme poverty must abound to their rich liberality, 2. Cor. 8. 2. 3. 1. Pet. 4. 11.

A man is accepted of the Lord according to that which he hath, & not according to that he hath not, in contributing if their be a willing mynd though only two mites be given, 2. Cor. 8. 12. Luk. 21. 3.

If in the necessityes of the Church the rich brethren do not releeve the poore by contributing to the treasury & otherwise, they are vnworthy members of the Church, & vnnaturall parts of the body: & are to be censured according to the rule: Mat. 18. 15–18. 1 Timoth. 5. 20. Deut. 15. 7–11. 1. Cor. 12. 22. 25. 26.

The rich that have frends that are needy of the Church, must releeve thē themselves, & must not chardg the Church with them, 1. Tim. 5. 4. 16. vnder nephewes & widowes all poore frends are to be vnderstood by proportion.

Quere: whither: if a brother have wife & children & frends to releeve that are without: The Church is bound to releeve him so far forth as he may also releeve them.

Chap. 4. Of what nature the treasury is

The treasury is holy. Act. 2. 42. 1. Chron. 26. 20. compared with Mat. 27. 6. & 2. Cor. 8. 4. 7. Hence therfor follow these two consectaryes.

1. Every holy ordinance of God must be sanctified by prayer & thanksgiving, 1. Tim. 4. 3. 5. & therfor Almes or contribution to the treasury must be sanctified by prayer & thanksgiving: see for this point, 2. Cor. 9. 12–15, & vs. 8–11. 1. Chron. 29. 10–20.

2. Ther ought to be a seperation in almes & contributiō to the treasury aswel as in other parts of our Spiritual communion, Act. 4. 32. & 5. 13. 2. Cor. 6. 17. Act. 2. 42. Heb 13. 16. 2. Cor. 8. 7. therfor they that are without if they give any thing must lay it a part several from the treasury & it must be imployed to common vse, Mat. 27. 6. 7.

The treasury is Holy in these respects.

1. In regard of the persons that contribute who are Holy.

2. In respect of the grace manifested in contribution which must be: 1. Sympathy or compassion, 2. freenes or voluntary offering, 3. liberality or bountifullnes: Rom. 12. 13. 15. 16. 2. Cor. 9. 5–7.

3. In regard of the persons & vses wherto it is imployed which are the Saynts & their necessityes 2. Cor. 8. 4. & 9. 12. 1.

4. In regard of the Lord himself: it being a Sacrifice wherewith God is well pleased, Philip. 4. 18. Heb. 13. 16. And a memoriall of the Saynts before the Lord. Nomb. 31. 50. 54. Phil. 4. 17. & a testimony of the love of the brethren, 2. Cor. 8. 8. 24. & so confortable to the conscience.

Chap. 5. VVhen the treasury is to be collected.

The treasury is to be collected every first day of the week, when the whole Church commeth together to break bread, Act. 20. 7. compared with 1. Cor. 16. 2.

Reasons hereof are divers as followeth.

1. Bicause the Lords Supper is weekly to be administred, & so from the Treasury weekly ther must a portion

be imployed to the provision of bread & wine & other necessaryes for the more seemly administration thereof, Act. 20. 7. compared with 1. Cor. 16. 2.

2. Because the Elders are worthy of double honor, which is yeelded them by weekly mayntenance according to their labor & necessities 1. Tim. 5. 17–18. Gal. 6. 6.

3. Because the poore of the Church are weekly to be releeved, & other necessities continually supplyed Act. 6. 1. & 2. 42.

Hence it foloweth that when the greatest communion of the church is held, the communiō of this grace also of ministring to the necessities of the saynts should be exercised.

Quere: At what tyme of the Lords day, & after what manner the Treasury is to be collected.

Chap. 6. How the Treasury is to be employed.

The Church Treasury is to be employed to these Speciall vses.

1. Mayntenance of the Elders especially such among them as are most painful in the word & doctrine, 1. Tim. 5. 17. 18.

The Elders that are of hability ought not to require maintenance of the church, but ought rather to contribute to the treasury, Act. 20. 35.

The elders may sometyme vppon good grounds work with their hands for avoyding offence & helping the Church. Act. 20. 34. 35.

2. Mayntenance of the widowes & by consequent other officers that want mayntenance: 1. Timoth. 5. 3. 4. 16. Act. 6. 1.

3. Releef of the poor brethren, also orphanes, & widows of brethren deceased. Act. 2. 44. & 4. 32. 2. Cor. 8. & 9. chap. & that not only of the[ir] owne, but of other true Churches, especially of them from whom they receaved the fayth, Rom. 15. 27

4. Provision for necessary vses: as places, vessels, bread, wine, & other implements for the common necessityes of the whole body. Exod. 35. 25–29. Nomb. 7. 1. Chron. 29. 1–16.

Quere: whither if the chardg of bread & wine be very great as it falleth out in some countryes & some yeeres, & the officers & poore want mayntenance, the Lords supper may not be deferred, & not be administred every Lords day.

Chap. 13. At whose disposition the Treasury is.

Seing the Deacons are the hands of the Church as it were, & the servants of the body in the bodyly necessityes, therfor the delivering of the treasury, & so the custody of it perteyneth to them. 1. Chron. 26. 20.

The Eldership as they are to oversee the flock, & to enquire into the occasions & affaires of the whole body: & as they are officers for the whole body & in the Churches name, therfor it aperteyneth vnto them for the Church to oversee the treasury: & to take accou[n]ts of it & to appoint the disposition of it, 2. King 22. 4. Act. 11. 30. &. 4. 35.

The Church is the owner & primary possessor of the treasury, & the cheef Lord of it vnder Christ: & vnto the Church must the account be made finally.

Thus much concerning the Deacons office & workes: & concerning the treasury of the Church

FINIS

THE BAPTIST STANDARD BEARER, INC.

a non-profit, tax-exempt corporation
committed to the Publication & Preservation
of the Baptist Heritage.

CURRENT TITLES AVAILABLE IN
THE BAPTIST *DISTINCTIVES* SERIES

KIFFIN, WILLIAM   A Sober Discourse of Right to Church-Communion. Wherein is proved by Scripture, the Example of the Primitive Times, and the Practice of All that have Professed the Christian Religion: That no Unbaptized person may be Regularly admitted to the Lord's Supper. (London: George Larkin, 1681).

KINGHORN, JOSEPH   Baptism, A Term of Communion. (Norwich: Bacon, Kinnebrook, and Co., 1816)

KINGHORN, JOSEPH   A Defense of "Baptism, A Term of Communion". In Answer To Robert Hall's Reply. (Norwich: Wilkin and Youngman, 1820).

GILL, JOHN   Gospel Baptism. A Collection of Sermons, Tracts, etc., on Scriptural Authority, the Nature of the New Testament Church and the Ordinance of Baptism by John Gill. (Paris, AR: The Baptist Standard Bearer, Inc., 2006).

CARSON, ALEXANDER	Ecclesiastical Polity of the New Testament. (Dublin: William Carson, 1856).
BOOTH, ABRAHAM	A Defense of the Baptists. A Declaration and Vindication of Three Historically Distinctive Baptist Principles. Compiled and Set Forth in the Republication of Three Books. Revised edition. (Paris, AR: The Baptist Standard Bearer, Inc., 2006).
BOOTH, ABRAHAM	Paedobaptism Examined on the Principles, Concessions, and Reasonings of the Most Learned Paedobaptists. With Replies to the Arguments and Objections of Dr. Williams and Mr. Peter Edwards. 3 volumes. (London: Ebenezer Palmer, 1829).
CARROLL, B. H.	*Ecclesia* - The Church. With an Appendix. (Louisville: Baptist Book Concern, 1903).
CHRISTIAN, JOHN T.	Immersion, The Act of Christian Baptism. (Louisville: Baptist Book Concern, 1891).
FROST, J. M.	Pedobaptism: Is It From Heaven Or Of Men? (Philadelphia: American Baptist Publication Society, 1875).
FULLER, RICHARD	Baptism, and the Terms of Communion; An Argument. (Charleston, SC: Southern Baptist Publication Society, 1854).
GRAVES, J. R.	Tri-Lemma: or, Death By Three Horns. The Presbyterian General Assembly Not Able To Decide This Question: "Is Baptism In The Romish Church Valid?" 1st Edition.

	(Nashville: Southwestern Publishing House, 1861).
MELL, P.H.	Baptism In Its Mode and Subjects. (Charleston, SC: Southern Baptist Publications Society, 1853).
JETER, JEREMIAH B.	Baptist Principles Reset. Consisting of Articles on Distinctive Baptist Principles by Various Authors. With an Appendix. (Richmond: The Religious Herald Co., 1902).
PENDLETON, J.M.	Distinctive Principles of Baptists. (Philadelphia: American Baptist Publication Society, 1882).
THOMAS, JESSE B.	The Church and the Kingdom. A New Testament Study. (Louisville: Baptist Book Concern, 1914).
WALLER, JOHN L.	Open Communion Shown to be Unscriptural & Deleterious. With an introductory essay by Dr. D. R. Campbell and an Appendix. (Louisville: Baptist Book Concern, 1859).

For a complete list of current authors/titles, visit our internet site at:
www.standardbearer.org
or write us at:

he Baptist Standard Bearer, Inc.
NUMBER ONE IRON OAKS DRIVE • PARIS, ARKANSAS 72855
TEL # 479-963-3831   *FAX # 479-963-8083*
EMAIL: Baptist@centurytel.net   *http://www.standardbearer.org*

Thou hast given a standard to them that fear thee; that it may be displayed because of the truth. — Psalm 60:4

www.ingramcontent.com/pod-product-compliance
Lightning Source LLC
Chambersburg PA
CBHW050829230426
43667CB00012B/1936